D0775063

The Haynes Emissions Control Manual

by Mike Stubblefield and John H Haynes
Member of the Guild of Motoring Writers

The Haynes Automotive Repair Manual for emissions control systems

(3K7 - 10210)

ABCDE
FGHIJ
KLMNO
PQ
2

Haynes Publishing Group
Sparkford Nr Yeovil
Somerset BA22 7JJ England

Haynes North America, Inc
861 Lawrence Drive
Newbury Park
California 91320 USA

629.2528 STU
Stubblefield, Mike
The Haynes emissions
    control manual

                        $24.95
CENTRAL   31994014554676

Acknowledgements
We are grateful to the following companies for providing test equipment shown in this manual:

Rinda Technologies
P.O. Box 860
Prospect Heights, IL 60070

The John Fluke Manufacturing Company
P.O. Box 9090
Everett, WA 98206

The Actron Manufacturing Company
9999 Walford Avenue
Cleveland, OH 44102 - 4696

Equus Products Inc.
17291 Mt. Hermann
Fountain Valley, CA 92708

In addition, thanks are due to the Chrysler Corporation, Mazda Motor Corporation, Mitsubishi Motors Corporation, Nissan Motor Company, Toyota Motor Corporation and the Isuzu Motor Company for providing technical information and certain illustrations. Technical writers who contributed to this project include Larry Warren and Robert Maddox.

© **Haynes North America, Inc.** **1994, 1997, 2001, 2005**

With permission from J.H. Haynes & Co. Ltd.

A book in the Haynes Automotive Repair Manual Series

Printed in the U.S.A.

All rights reserved. No part of this book may be reproduced or transmitted in any form or by any means, electronic or mechanical, including photocopying, recording or by any information storage or retrieval system, without permission in writing from the copyright holder.

ISBN 1 56392 234 7

Library of Congress Catalog Card Number 96-78643

While every attempt is made to ensure that the information in this manual is correct, no liability can be accepted by the authors or publishers for loss, damage or injury caused by any errors in, or omissions from, the information given

"Ford" and the Ford logo are registered trademarks of Ford Motor Company. Ford Motor Company is not a sponsor or affiliate of Haynes Publishing Group or Haynes North America, Inc. and is not a contributor to the content of this manual.

Contents

Chapter 1 Introduction

Chapter 2 Troubleshooting

Chapter 3 System descriptions and servicing

Chapter 4 Vacuum diagrams and VECI labels

Chapter 5 Acronym list and glossary

Chapter 6 Computer trouble codes

Index

 Introduction

1 Introduction to emissions control and engine management systems

Automobiles and trucks are the number one cause of air pollution in this country; they contribute over *half* of the airborne pollutants - hydrocarbons, carbon monoxide, oxides of nitrogen and others - collectively referred to as "smog." The constituents of smog irritate the eyes, the nose, the throat and the lungs; some of them - such as carbon monoxide and lead - are toxic enough to cause serious illness; some are even carcinogenic. Ironically, modern vehicles (those built since about 1980) are almost 100 percent "cleaner" than '60s and '70s vehicles. So why do cars and trucks continue to produce such a disproportionate percentage of air pollution? Well, certainly, there are more vehicles on the road now than there were 10 years ago. But there's another reason. Recent studies indicate that *over one-third of the vehicles on the road right now are poorly maintained;* they're out of tune and their emissions control systems are broken, worn out, disconnected or improperly maintained. If every newer vehicle was well-tuned and its emission control systems were hooked up and well-maintained, its tailpipe emissions would be significantly less. And older vehicles? True, they will never run as efficiently as newer models, but when they're well tuned - and their first-generation smog equipment is in good working order - they pollute a lot less.

Haynes Automotive Repair Manuals already show you how to keep your vehicle well-tuned; in this manual, we're going to show you how easy it is to understand and maintain the emission control systems on your vehicle, and

we're going to show you how to troubleshoot and fix them when they malfunction.

It's time to start thinking of emission controls as an integral part of the modern vehicle. We will never clean up our skies until we take better care of our vehicles' engines and their emission control systems. Of course, not everyone is ready to accept the proposition that the vehicle owner must accept personal responsibility for the proper maintenance of his or her vehicle's emission control systems simply for the good of the environment. Fair enough. Let's put the matter in terms anyone can understand-dollars and cents. Many of you live in states such as California where regular emissions certification testing is part of owning a car or truck. These tests cost money, and repairing emission systems or replacing emission devices that malfunction costs even more money. Most states put a cap on how much money you can be forced to spend on restoring your emission control systems to their original condition, but that figure is climbing. In some states, it's already $500 or more. In many cases, these costs can be avoided, or significantly reduced, by simply maintaining your emission control systems as they age, instead of ignoring them.

Finally, there's another economic incentive for proper maintenance: A well-tuned vehicle with all its emission control systems in place and in good shape not only pollutes less, it often gets better mileage (and produces more horsepower!). Your vehicle's engine was *designed* to operate with its emission control systems intact.

2 Understanding the material in this manual

Are you one of those mechanics who's perfectly capable of understanding and fixing the most complex mechanical systems on a vehicle but intimidated when confronted by electrical or vacuum-operated devices with few or no moving parts? Is it because you like to see what it is you're dealing with?

In this manual we're going to show you a lot of information about this mysterious "invisible" world of emission control systems, information sensors, computers and actuators. It's essential that you develop a logical approach to this stuff so it doesn't overwhelm you.

First, get involved! Pop the hood and have a look at the maze of vacuum lines and the weird gadgets located all over the engine compartment. This will stimulate your thinking: "What does this do? Where does that go?"

Now have a look at the VECI label (more on the VECI later). See if you can match the actual routing of the vacuum hoses and the location of the components in the engine compartment to the schematic on the VECI.

Once you've stimulated your curiosity, open this manual and start reading. But make frequent trips back to the engine compartment. There are five things you need to learn about each emission control component or system, the computer and each information sensor or output actuator used on your vehicle:

1) What's it *called? (AIR,* EGR, EVAP, PCV, etc.)
2) *How does it* work? (electrically-actuated; vacuum - operated; both; etc.)
3) Where is it located? (engine; throttle body; intake manifold; etc.)
4) *How do 1 check or test it?* (ohmmeter; vacuum gauge; voltmeter; etc.)
5) *How do 1* replace *it?* (usually self-evident)

As you repeat this process over and over again on various vehicles, you'll discover that they often have the same names (and acronyms), work the same way, are located in the same general area, are checked/tested the same way and have similar replacement procedures! Once you understand how one EGR or PCV valve or EVAP canister works, you understand how all of them work (though their actual vacuum plumbing may vary somewhat).

When you're trying to understand how an engine management system works, visualize the computer as the "brain," the information sensors as its "nervous system" and the output actuators as its limbs. This analogy will help you ask the right questions about the role of the myriad components used in a typical management system. The computer "asks questions" about the engine through its information sensors: "What's the temperature of the intake air?" "What's the temperature of the coolant?" "What's the engine speed?" "What's the angle of the throttle valve?" etc. This stream of data never stops as long as the engine is running. Inside the computer, the data is compared to the computer's "map." The map is the computer's programmed memory of what the engine should be doing under each specific combination of circumstances - engine warming up at idle, engine warming up under load, engine accelerating, engine decelerating, engine idling with the air conditioner turned on, etc. If what the engine is actually doing (as indicated by the sensors) doesn't match what it should be doing (according to the map), the computer directs one, some or all its output actuators to alter the operating conditions of the engine until the sensors indicate that it's operating the way it should.

If you can visualize this model of the management system, you'll be able to think logically about the role of each component in the system. And thinking logically about each component enables you to ask the right questions about a part when it malfunctions and you have to troubleshoot it. In most cases, simply knowing the name of a sensor and its location tells you what it does or should be doing.

3 The Federally-mandated emissions warranty - questions and answers

Before you dive under the hood to troubleshoot or fix a problem related to emissions, there are some things you should know about the Federally-mandated extended warranty **(see illustration)** designed to protect you from the cost of repairs to any emission-related failures beyond your control.

There are actually TWO emission control warranties - the "Design and Defect Warranty" and the "Performance Warranty." We will discuss them separately.

The Design and Defect Warranty

Basically, the Design and Defect Warranty covers the repair of all emission control related parts which fail during the first five years or the first 50,000 miles of service. **Note:** *This 50,000-mile figure may increase. In fact, at the time this manual was being written, a 100,000-mile warranty was being considered. According to Federal law, the manufacturer must repair or replace the defective part free of charge if:*

1) Your car is less than five years old and has less than 50,000 miles;
2) An original equipment part or system fails because of a defect in materials or workmanship; and
3) The failure would cause your vehicle to exceed Federal emissions standards.

If these three conditions are present, the manufacturer must honor the warranty. All manufacturers have established procedures to provide owners with this coverage. The Design and Defect Warranty applies to used vehicles too. It doesn't matter whether you bought the vehicle new or used; if the vehicle hasn't exceeded the warranty time or mileage limitations, the warranty applies.

Note that the length of the warranty is five years and 50,000 miles for cars. The Design and Defect Warranty applies to all vehicles manufactured in the last five years, including cars, pick-ups, recreational vehicles, heavy-duty trucks and motorcycles. The length of the warranty varies somewhat with the type of vehicle. If you own some type of vehicle other than a car, read the description of the emissions warranty in your owner's manual or warranty booklet to determine the length of the warranty on your vehicle.

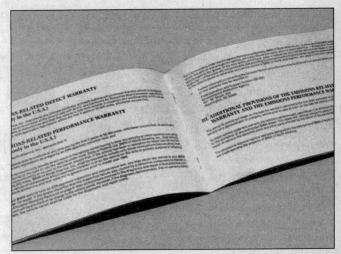

3.1 You'll find the details of your vehicle's Federally-mandated extended warranty coverage in your owner's manual or in a separate booklet like this one, in the glove box

What parts or repairs are covered by the warranty?

Coverage includes all parts whose primary purpose is to control emissions and all parts that have an effect on emissions. Let's divide these two types of parts in two categories-emissions-control parts and emissions-related parts-then divide the parts within each category into systems. Our list would look something like this:

Primary emissions control parts

Air induction system
1 Thermostatically controller air cleaner
2 Air box

Air injection system
1 Diverter, bypass or gulp valve
2 Reed valve
3 Air pump
4 Anti-backfire or deceleration valve

Early Fuel Evaporative (EFE) system
1 EFE valve
2 Heat riser valve
3 Thermal vacuum switch

The Haynes Emissions Control Manual

Primary emissions control parts (continued)

Evaporative emission control system
1 Purge valve
2 Purge solenoid
3 Fuel filler cap
4 Vapor storage canister and filter

Exhaust gas conversion systems
1 Oxygen sensor
2 Catalytic converter
3 Thermal reactor
4 Dual-walled exhaust pipe

Exhaust Gas Recirculation (EGR) system
1 EGR valve
2 EGR solenoid
3 EGR backpressure transducer
4 Thermal vacuum switch
5 EGR spacer plate
6 Sensor and switches used to control EGR flow

Fuel metering systems
1 Electronic control module or computer command module
2 Deceleration controls
3 Fuel injectors
4 Fuel injection rail
5 Fuel pressure regulator
6 Fuel pressure dampener
7 Throttle body
8 Mixture control solenoid or diaphragm
9 Air flow meter
10 Air flow module or mixture control unit
11 Electronic choke
12 Altitude compensator sensor
13 Mixture settings on sealed carburetors
14 Other feedback control sensors, switches and valves

Ignition systems
1 Electronic spark advance
2 High energy electronic ignition
3 Timing advance/retard systems

Miscellaneous parts
Hoses, gaskets, brackets, clamps and other accessories used in these systems

Positive Crankcase Ventilation (PCV) system
1 PCV valve
2 PCV filter

Emissions-related parts

The following parts have a primary purpose other than emissions control, but they still have a significant effect on your vehicle's emissions. If they break or malfunction, your vehicle's emissions may exceed Federal standards, so they're also covered by the Design and Defect Warranty. They include:

Air induction system
1 Turbocharger
2 Intake manifold

Carburetor systems
1 Carburetor
2 Choke

Exhaust system
Exhaust manifold

Fuel injection system
Fuel distributor

Ignition system
1 Distributor
2 Ignition wires and coil
3 Spark plugs

Miscellaneous parts

Hoses, gaskets, brackets, clamps and other accessories used in the above systems.

If-after reading the list above and the manufacturer's description of your warranty coverage in your owner's manual or warranty booklet - you're confused about whether certain parts are covered, contact your dealer service department or the manufacturer's zone or regional representative.

Can any part of a warranty repair be charged to you?

No! You can't be charged for any labor, parts or miscellaneous items necessary to complete the job when a manufacturer repairs or replaces any part under the emissions warranty. For example, if a manufacturer agrees to replace a catalytic converter under the emissions warranty, you shouldn't be charged for the catalyst itself or for any pipes, brackets, adjustments or labor needed to complete the replacement.

How long does the warranty apply?

Parts which don't have a replacement interval stated in the maintenance instructions are warranted for what the EPA calls the "useful life" of the vehicle, which, for cars, is, as stated before, five years or 50,000 miles. For other types of vehicles, read your warranty description in the owner's manual or the warranty booklet to determine the length of the warranty coverage.

Other parts, for example those with a stated replacement interval such as "15,000 miles or 12 months," are warranted only up to the first replacement.

Any parts that are the subject of a maintenance instruction that requires them to be "checked and replaced if necessary," or the subject of any similar requirement, are warranted for the entire period of warranty coverage.

How do you know if you're entitled to coverage?

If you or a reliable mechanic can show that a part in

one of the listed systems is defective, it's probably covered under the emissions warranty. When you believe you've identified a defective part that might be covered, you should make a warranty claim to the person identified by the manufacturer in your owner's manual or warranty booklet.

What should you do if your first attempt to obtain warranty coverage is denied?

1) Ask for the complete reason - in writing - for the denial of emissions warranty coverage;
2) Ask for the names) of the persons) who determined the denial of coverage;
3) Ask for the names) of the persons) you should contact to appeal the denial of coverage under the emissions warranty.

Once you've obtained this information, look in your owner's manual or warranty booklet for the name of the person designated by the manufacturer for warranty assistance and contact this person.

How does maintenance affect your warranty?

Performance of scheduled maintenance is YOUR responsibility. You're expected to either perform scheduled maintenance yourself, or have a qualified repair facility perform it for you. If a part failure can be directly attributed to poor maintenance of your vehicle or vehicle abuse (proper operation of the vehicle is usually spelled out in your owner's manual or maintenance booklet), the manufacturer might not be liable for replacing that part or repairing any damage caused by its failure. To assure maximum benefit from your emissions control systems in reducing air pollution, as well as assuring continued warranty coverage, you should have all scheduled maintenance performed, or do it yourself.

Do you have to show any maintenance receipts before you can make a warranty claim?

No! Proof of maintenance isn't required to obtain coverage under the emissions warranty. If a listed part is defective in materials or workmanship, the manufacturer must provide warranty coverage. Of course, not all parts fail because of defects in materials or workmanship.

Though you're not automatically required to show maintenance receipts when you make a warranty claim, there is one circumstance in which you will be asked for proof that scheduled maintenance has been performed. If it looks as if a part failed because of a lack of scheduled maintenance, you can be required to prove that the maintenance was performed.

How is your warranty affected if you use leaded gasoline in your vehicle?

When leaded gas is used in vehicles designed to run on unleaded, the emissions controls - particularly the catalytic converter - can be damaged. And lead deposits inside the engine can lead to the failure of certain engine parts. The emissions warranty does not cover ANY part failures that result from the use of leaded fuel in a vehicle that requires unleaded fuel.

Can anyone besides dealers perform scheduled maintenance recommended by the manufacturer?

Absolutely! Scheduled maintenance can be performed by anyone who is qualified to do so, *including you* (as long as the maintenance is performed in accordance with the manufacturer's instructions). If you're going to take the vehicle to a repair facility, refer to your owner's manual or maintenance booklet and make a list of all scheduled maintenance items before you go. When you get there, don't simply ask for a "tune-up" or a "15,000 mile servicing." Instead, specify exactly what you want done. Then make sure the work specified is entered on the work order or receipt that you receive. This way, you'll have a clear record that all scheduled maintenance has been done.

If you buy a used vehicle, how do you know whether it's been maintained properly?

Realistically, you don't. But it never hurts to ask the seller to give you the receipts which prove the vehicle has been properly maintained according to the schedule. These receipts are proof that the work was done properly and on time, if the question of maintenance ever arises.

And once you buy a used vehicle, you should continue to maintain it in accordance with the maintenance schedule in the owner's manual or warranty booklet (if the seller doesn't have these items anymore, buy new ones at the dealer).

What should you do if the manufacturer won't honor what you feel is a valid warranty claim?

As we said earlier, if an authorized warranty representative denies your claim, you should contact the person designated by the manufacturer for further warranty assistance. Additionally, you're free to pursue any independent legal actions you deem necessary to obtain coverage. Finally, the EPA is authorized to investigate the failure of manufacturers to comply with the terms of this warranty. If you've followed the manufacturer's procedure for making a claim and you're still not satisfied with the manufacturer's determination, contact the EPA by writing:

Warranty Complaint
Field Operations and Support Division (EN-397F)
U.S. Environmental Protection Agency
Washington, D.C. 20460

The Performance Warranty

The Performance Warranty covers those repairs required because the vehicle has failed an emission test. If you reside in an area with an Inspection/Maintenance program that meets Federal guidelines, you may be eligible for this additional Performance Warranty. For more information on the Performance Warranty, ask your local Inspection/Maintenance program official or call or write the nearest EPA office and ask for a copy of the pamphlet *"If Your Car Just Failed An Emission Test... You May Be Entitled To Free Repairs,"* which describes the Performance Warranty in detail.

You may be eligible for coverage under this warranty if:

1) Your 1981 or later car or light truck fails an approved emissions test; and

2) Your state or local government requires that you repair the vehicle; and

3) The test failure didn't result from misuse of the vehicle or a failure to follow the manufacturer's written maintenance instructions; and

4) You present the vehicle to a warranty-authorized manufacturer representative, along with evidence of the emission test failure, during the relevant warranty period; then . . .

   a) for the first two years or 24,000 miles, whichever comes first, the manufacturer must pay for all repairs necessary to pass the emissions test and . . .

   b) for the first five years or 50,000 miles, the manufacturer must pay for all repairs to primary emission control parts which are necessary to pass the emissions test.

What vehicles are covered by the Performance Warranty?

The Federally mandated Performance Warranty covers all 1981 and later cars and light duty trucks produced in the last five years. And it doesn't matter whether you bought your vehicle new or used, from a dealer or from a private party. As long as it hasn't exceeded the warranty time or mileage limitations, and has been properly maintained, the Performance Warranty applies.

What types of repairs are covered by the Performance Warranty?

Two types of repairs are covered by the Performance Warranty, depending on the age of your vehicle:

1) Any repair or adjustment which is necessary to make your vehicle pass an approved locally-required emission test is covered if your vehicle is less than two years old and has less than 24,000 miles.

2) Any repair or adjustment of a "primary emissions control" part (see "The Design and Defect Warranty") which is necessary to make your vehicle pass an approved locally required test is covered if your vehicle is less than five years old and has less than 50,000 miles.

Although coverage is limited after two years/24,000 miles to primary emission control parts, repairs must still be complete and effective. If the complete and effective repair or a primary part requires that non-primary parts be repaired or adjusted, these repairs are also covered.

What if the dealer claims your vehicle can pass the emissions test without repair?

The law doesn't require you to fail the emissions test to trigger the warranty. If any test shows that you have an emissions problem, get it fixed while your vehicle is still within the warranty period. Otherwise, you could end up failing a future test because of the same problem - and paying for the repairs yourself. If you doubt your original test results or the dealer's results, get another opinion to support your claim.

What kinds of reasons can the manufacturer use to deny a claim?

As long as your vehicle is within the age or mileage limits explained above, the manufacturer can deny coverage under the Performance Warranty only if you've failed to properly maintain and use your vehicle. Proper use and maintenance of the vehicle are *your* responsibilities. The manufacturer can deny your claim if there's evidence that your vehicle failed an emissions test as a result of:

a) Vehicle abuse, such as off-road driving, or overloading; or

b) Tampering with emission control parts, including removal or intentional damage; or

c) Improper maintenance, including failure to follow maintenance schedules and instructions, or use of replacement parts which aren't equivalent to the originally installed part; or

d) Misfueling: The use of leaded fuel in a vehicle requiring "unleaded fuel only" or use of other improper fuels.

If any of the above have taken place, and seem likely to have caused the particular problem which you seek to have repaired, then the manufacturer can deny coverage.

If your claim is denied for a valid reason, you may have to pay the costs of the diagnosis. Therefore, you should always ask for an estimate of the cost of the diagnosis before work starts.

Can anyone besides a dealer perform scheduled maintenance?

Yes! Scheduled maintenance can be done by anyone with the knowledge and ability to perform the repair. For your protection, we recommend that you refer to your owner's manual to specify the necessary items to your mechanic. And get an itemized receipt or work order for your records.

You can also maintain the vehicle yourself, as long as the maintenance is done in accordance with the manufacturer's instructions included with the vehicle. Make sure you keep receipts for parts and a maintenance log to verify your work.

Why maintenance is important to emissions control systems

Emission control has led to many changes in engine design. As a result, most vehicles don't require tune-ups and other maintenance as often. But some of the maintenance that is required enables your vehicle's emission controls to do their job properly.

Failure to do this emissions-related maintenance can cause problems. For example, failure to change your spark plugs during a 30,000-mile tune-up can lead to misfiring and eventual damage to your catalytic converter.

Vehicles that are well-maintained and tamper-free don't just pollute less - they get better gas mileage. Which saves you money. Regular maintenance also gives you better performance and catches engine problems early, *before* they get serious-and costly.

How do you make a warranty claim?

Bring your vehicle to a dealer or any facility authorized by the manufacturer to perform warranty repairs to the vehicle or its emissions control system. Notify them that you wish to obtain a repair under the Performance Warranty. You should have with you a copy of your emissions test report as proof of your vehicle's failure to pass the emissions test. And bring your vehicle's warranty statement for reference. The warranty statement should be in your owner's manual or in a separate booklet provided by the manufacturer with the vehicle.

How do you know if your claim has been accepted as valid?

After presenting your vehicle for a Performance Warranty claim, give the manufacturer 30 days to either repair the vehicle or notify you that the claim has been denied. If your inspection/ maintenance program dictates a shorter deadline, the manufacturer must meet that shorter deadline. Because of the significance of these deadlines, you should get written verification when you present your vehicle for a Performance Warranty claim.

The manufacturer can accept your claim and repair the vehicle, or deny the claim outright, or deny it after examining the vehicle. In either case, the reason for denial must be provided *in writing* with the notification.

What happens if the manufacturer misses the deadline for a written claim denial?

You can agree to extend the deadline, or it may be automatically extended if the delay is beyond the control of the manufacturer. Otherwise, a missed deadline means the manufacturer forfeits the right to deny the claim. You are then entitled to have the repair performed at the facility of your choice, at the manufacturer's expense.

If your claim is accepted, do you have to pay for either the diagnosis or the repair?

You can't be charged for any costs for diagnosis of a valid warranty claim. Additionally, when a manufacturer repairs, replaces or adjusts any part under the Performance Warranty, you may not be charged for any parts, labor or miscellaneous items necessary to complete the repair. But if your vehicle needs other repairs that aren't covered by your emissions warranty, you can have that work performed by any facility you choose.

What happens to your warranty if you use leaded gasoline?

When leaded gas is used in vehicles requiring unleaded, some emission controls (especially the catalyst) are quickly damaged. Lead deposits also form inside the engine, decreasing spark plug life and increasing maintenance costs.

If your use of leaded fuel leads to an emissions failure, your warranty won't cover the repair costs. So using leaded fuel will not only ruin some of your emission controls, it will cost you money.

Can your regular repair facility perform warranty repairs?

If you want to have the manufacturer pay for a repair under the Performance Warranty, you MUST bring the vehicle to a facility authorized by the vehicle manufacturer to repair either the vehicle or its emission control systems. If your regular facility isn't authorized by the manufacturer, tell your mechanic to get your "go ahead" before performing any repair that might be covered by the Performance Warranty.

Do you have to provide proof of maintenance when you make a warranty claim?

You're not automatically required to show maintenance receipts when you make a warranty claim. But if the manufacturer feels your failure to perform scheduled maintenance has caused your emissions failure, you can be required to present your receipts or log as proof that the work was in fact done.

If you buy a used vehicle, how do you know whether it's been properly maintained?

When you buy a used vehicle, try to get the maintenance receipts or log book from the previous owner. Also ask for the owner's manual, warranty or maintenance booklet, and any other information that came with the vehicle when it was new. If the seller doesn't have these documents, you can buy them from the manufacturer.

To guarantee future warranty protection for your vehicle, conform to the maintenance schedule provided by the manufacturer.

Does the warranty cover parts that must be replaced as a part of regularly scheduled maintenance?

Parts with a scheduled replacement interval that's less than the length of the warranty, such as "replace at 15,000 miles or 12 months," are warranted only up to the first replacement point. Parts with a maintenance instruction that requires them to be "checked and replaced if necessary," or some similar classification, receive full coverage under the warranty. However, should you fail to check a part at the specified interval, and should that part cause another part to fail, the second part will NOT be covered, because your failure to maintain the first part caused the failure.

The manufacturer may or may not require that such replacement parts be a specific brand. But if a test failure is caused by the use of a part of inferior quality to the original equipment part, the manufacturer may deny your warranty claim.

What if the manufacturer won't honor a claim you believe to be valid?

First, use the information contained above to make your case to the dealer. Then follow the appeals procedure outlined in your vehicle's warranty statement or owner's manual. Every manufacturer employs warranty representatives who handle such appeals. The manufacturer must either allow your claim or give you a *written* denial, including the specific reasons for denying your claim, within 30 days, or you are entitled to free repairs.

Also, the Environmental Protection Agency is authorized to investigate the failure of manufacturers to comply with the terms of this warranty. If you've followed the manufacturer's procedures and you're still unimpressed with the reason for denial of your claim, contact the EPA at:

Warranty Complaint
Field Operations and Support Division (EN-397-F)
U.S. Environmental Protection Agency
Washington, D. C. 20460

Finally, you're also entitled to pursue any independent legal actions which you consider appropriate to obtain coverage under the Performance Warranty.

4 Emissions-related routine maintenance

The cheapest and easiest way to keep your emissions system operating properly is simply to check it over on a regular basis. This is the best to way spot trouble because many of these systems have few (if any) symptoms as they wear out or degrade in operation. Because the emissions, fuel and ignition systems are interrelated, a minor problem in one can have a ripple effect on others. These minor malfunctions among several systems can eventually lead to a breakdown which could have been avoided by a simple check and maintenance program. When the vehicle is new, the emissions system should only be serviced by a factory authorized dealer service department to protect the factory warranty. Refer to Chapter 3 for information on the design and operation of these systems.

Note: *The following maintenance schedule is generalized. Your particular vehicle may require additional maintenance and/or different intervals. Refer to the Haynes Automotive Repair Manual for your vehicle for more specific information. Also, the following schedule only concerns equipment that affects emissions. Your vehicle will require additional maintenance for its other components.*

Every 15,000 miles or 12 months, whichever comes first

Check the operation of the heated air intake system (Chapter 3, Section 5)
Check and, if necessary, replace the air filter
Check and, if necessary, replace the PCV filter (if equipped)

Replace the ignition points and adjust the dwell (early models with point-type ignition systems only)
Check and adjust, if necessary, the ignition timing'
Check and adjust, if necessary, the engine idle speed`

Every 30,000 miles or 24 months, whichever comes first

Inspect the catalytic converter system (Chapter 3, Section 7)
Inspect the evaporative emissions control system (Chapter 3, Section 2)
Inspect the Positive Crankcase Ventilation (PCV) system (Chapter 3, Section 3)
Check the Exhaust Gas Recirculation (EGR) system (Chapter 3, Section 1)
Inspect the air injection system (Chapter 3, Section 4)
Check all emissions system hoses for cracking, disconnections and deterioration
Replace the spark plugs
Check the operation of the carburetor choke (if equipped)
Inspect the spark plug wires, and, on vehicles with distributor type ignition systems, inspect the distributor cap and rotor
Check the carburetor or fuel injection throttle body mounting nut or bolt torque

"Many modern vehicles do not require ignition timing and idle speed checks. The Haynes manual for your particular vehicle will tell you whether or not these checks are required.

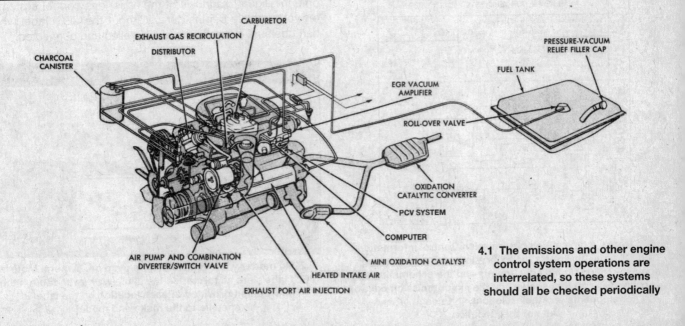

4.1 The emissions and other engine control system operations are interrelated, so these systems should all be checked periodically

5 The Vehicle Emissions Control Information (VECI) label

What is a VECI label?

The Vehicle Emissions Control Information (VECI) **label (see illustrations)** identifies the engine, the fuel system and the emission control systems used on your specific vehicle. It also provides essential tune-up specifications, such as the spark plug gap, slow-idle speed, fast-idle speed, enriched-idle speed, initial ignition timing setting (if adjustable), breaker point dwell and carburetor adjustment instructions.

Some VECI labels simply provide the specs for these adjustments; others even include brief step-by-step adjustment procedures. Most labels also provide a simplified vacuum diagram of the emissions control devices used on your vehicle and the vacuum lines connecting them to each other and to engine vacuum. You won't find everything you need to know about your emissions systems on the VECI label, but it's a very good place to start.

The information on the VECI label is specific to your vehicle. Any changes or modifications authorized by the manufacturer will be marked on the label by a technician making the modification. He may also indicate the change with a special modification decal and place it near the VECI label.

What does a VECI label look like?

The VECI label is usually a small, white, adhesive-backed, plastic-coated label about 4 X 6 inches in size, located some where in the engine compartment. It's usually affixed to the underside of the hood, the radiator support, the front upper crossmember, the firewall or one of the inner wheel wells.

What if you can't find the VECI label?

If you're not the original owner of your vehicle, and you can't find the VECI label anywhere, chances are it's been removed, or the body part to which it was affixed has been replaced. Don't worry - you can buy a new one at a dealer service department.

Be sure to give the parts department the VIN number, year, model, engine, etc. of your vehicle; be as specific as possible. For instance, if it's a high-altitude model, a 49-state model or a California model, be sure to tell them, because each of these models may have a different fuel system and a unique combination of emission control devices.

Don't just forget about the VECI label if you don't have one. Intelligent diagnosis of the emissions control systems on your vehicle begins here. Without the VECI label, you can't be sure everything is still installed and connected.

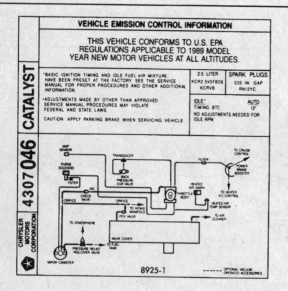

5.1 Here's a typical **Vehicle Emission Control Information (VECI) label** (this one's for a Chrysler) - note the warning against ignition timing adjustments and the schematic-style vacuum diagram that shows you the major emission control components and their relationship to each other, but not their location

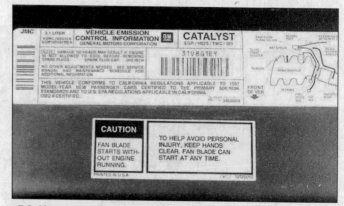

5.2 No matter what vehicle they're used on, General Motors VECI labels are all formatted the same way, even though the information provided at each location on the label is specific to the make and model

6 Diagnostic tools

Digital multimeter

Lots of interesting high-tech gadgets for testing emission control devices and systems are available. Simple visual checks will identify many problems, but there are two tools you must have to do all the tests in this manual. One of them is a digital multimeter and the other is a hand-operated vacuum pump and gauge. We'll get to the vacuum pump in a minute. First, let's look at the multimeter.

The multimeter is a small, hand-held diagnostic tool that combines an ohmmeter and voltmeter - and sometimes an ammeter (which you won't need for the tests in this book) - into one handy unit. A multimeter can measure the voltage and resistance in a circuit. Many emission devices and systems are electrically powered, so the multimeter is an essential tool.

There are two types of multimeters: Conventional units (a box with two leads) and probe types (small, hand-held units with a built-in probe and one flexible lead) **(see illustrations)**. Probes - which are about the same size as a portable soldering pen-are easier to use in tight spaces because of their compact dimensions. And you don't need three hands to hold a meter and two test leads all at the same time (you can hold the meter in one hand and the single lead in the other). But probes usually have less features than conventional units.

Why a *digital* multimeter? Partly because digital meters are easier to read, particularly when you're trying to read tenths of a volt or ohm. But mainly you need a digital meter - instead of an "analog" (needle type)-because digital multimeters are more accurate than analog meters.

Using a multimeter to read voltage is simply a matter of selecting the voltage range and hooking up the meter **IN PARALLEL (see illustration)** to the circuit being checked.

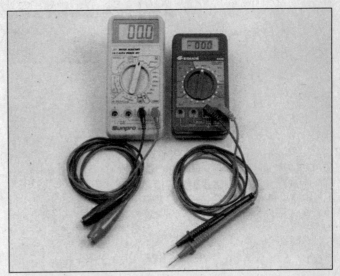

6.1 These two high-impedance digital multimeters are accurate, versatile and inexpensive, but each unit is equipped with a different type of lead: The one on the left uses insulated alligator clips which don't have to be held in place, freeing your hands for using the meter itself; the unit on the right has a pair of probes, which are handy for testing wires and terminals inside connectors (Our advice? Buy both types of leads, or make your own)

Older analog (needle-type) meters have always allowed a certain amount of voltage to "detour" through this parallel circuit, which affects the accuracy of the measurement being taken.

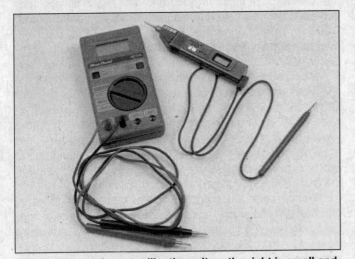

6.2 A probe-style meter like the unit on the right is small and easy to use because one of the probes is integrated into the housing, leaving your other hand free to hold the single ground lead

6.3 To make a voltage measurement, turn the mode switch or knob on your multimeter to the Volts DC position and hook up the meter in PARALLEL to the circuit being tested; if you hook it up in series, like an ammeter or ohmmeter, you won't get a reading and you could damage something (note how the positive probe is being used to make contact with a wire through the backside of the connector without actually unplugging the connector)

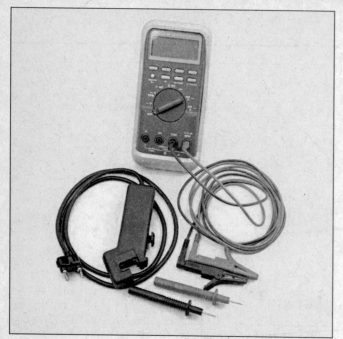

6.4 Top-of-the-line multimeters like this Fluke Model 88 can do a lot of things besides just measure volts, amps and ohms - using a wide array of adapters and cables, most of which are included in the basic kit, they can check the status of all the important information sensors, measure the duty cycle of feedback carburetors and idle air control motors, and even measure the pulse width of the fuel injectors

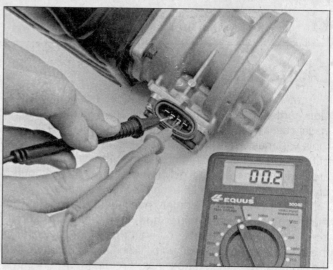

6.5 To measure resistance, select the appropriate range of resistance and touch the meter probes to the terminals you're testing; the polarity (which terminal you touch with which lead) makes no difference on an ohmmeter because it's self-powered and the circuit is turned off

This leaking voltage isn't that important when you're measuring 12-volt circuits - and you just want to know if a circuit has 12 or 13 or 14 volts present. If some of the voltage trickles through the meter itself, your judgment call about the health of the circuit is unaffected. But many emission control and engine management circuits operate at five volts or less; and some of them operate in the millivolt (thousandths of a volt) range. So voltage readings must be quite accurate-in many cases to the tenth, hundredth or even thousandth of a volt. Even if an older analog meter could measure voltage values this low (and even if you could read them!), the readings would be inaccurate because of the voltage detouring out of the circuit into the meter.

Digital meters have 10-Meg ohms (10 million ohms) resistance built into their circuitry to prevent voltage leaks through the meter. And this is the main reason we specify a digital voltmeter. When you shop around for a good meter, you may find a newer analog type meter with a high-resistance circuit design similar to that of a digital meter, but it will still be difficult to read when performing low-voltage tests, so don't buy it - get a digital model!

Some of the more sophisticated multimeters **(see illustration)** can perform many of the same functions as scanners, such as checking camshaft and crankshaft position sensors, feedback carburetors, fuel injection on-time, IAC motors, MAF sensors, MAP sensors, oxygen sensors, temperature sensors and throttle position sensors.

Ohmmeters

So why don't we just specify a digital *voltmeter*? Because you'll also need to use an ohmmeter a lot too: Some solenoids and other devices have specific resistance values under specified conditions, so you'll need an ohmmeter to test them. And sometimes the engine won't start, so there's no voltage available to test. When these situations arise, you'll need a good digital ohmmeter to measure resistance (expressed in ohms). But don't buy a separate ohmmeter; get a digital multimeter with an ohmmeter built in.

An ohmmeter has its own voltage source (a low-voltage DC power supply, usually a dry-cell battery). It measures the resistance of a circuit or component and is always connected to an open circuit or a part removed from a circuit. **Caution:** *Don't connect an ohmmeter to a "live" (hot) circuit; current from an outside source will damage an ohmmeter.*

Because an ohmmeter doesn't use system voltage, it's not affected by system polarity. You can hook up the test leads to either side of the part you want to test **(see illustration)**. When you use an ohmmeter, start your test on the lowest range, then switch to a higher range that gives you a more precise reading. Voltage and current are limited by the power supply and internal resistance, so you won't damage the meter by setting it on a low or high scale.

Temperature and the condition of the battery affect an ohmmeter's accuracy. Digital ohmmeters are self-adjusting, but if you're using an analog meter, you must adjust it every time you use it: Simply touch the two test leads together and turn the zero adjustment knob until the needle indicates zero ohms, or continuity, through the meter on the lowest scale.

6.6 Get a thermometer with a range from zero to about 220 degrees - there are automotive-specific thermometers available, but a cooking thermometer will work

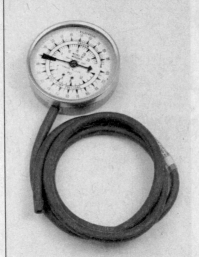

6.7 A vacuum gauge can tell you whether the engine is producing good intake vacuum, help you determine whether the catalytic converter is blocked and help you diagnose a wide variety of engine-related problems

Thermometer

If you're going to be testing coolant temperature sensors, get a good automotive thermometer **(see illustration)** capable of reading from zero to about 220-degrees F. If you can't find an automotive-specific unit, a good cooking thermometer will work.

Vacuum gauge

Measuring intake manifold vacuum is a good way to diagnose all kinds of things about the condition of an engine. Manifold vacuum is tested with a vacuum gauge **(see illustration),** which measures the difference in pressure between the intake manifold and the outside atmosphere. If the manifold pressure is lower than the atmospheric pressure, a vacuum exists. Vacuum is measured in inches of mercury (in-Hg) and in kilo Pascals (kPa) or in millimeters of mercury (mm-Hg). The Atmospheric pressure at sea level is 30 in-Hg. For every 1000 foot increase in altitude, above approximately 2000 feet, the atmospheric pressure drops one inch.

In this book, we'll show you how to diagnose a restricted exhaust system with a vacuum gauge. To hook up the gauge, connect the flexible connector hose to the intake manifold, air intake plenum, or any vacuum port below the carburetor or throttle body. On some models, you can simply remove a plug from the manifold or carburetor/throttle body; on others, you'll have to disconnect a vacuum hose or line from the manifold, carb or throttle body and hook up the gauge inline with a tee fitting (included with most vacuum gauge kits).

A good vacuum reading is about 15 to 20 in-Hg (50 to 65 kPa) at idle (engine at normal operating temperature). Low or fluctuating readings can indicate many different problems. For instance, a low and steady reading may be caused by retarded ignition or valve timing. A sharp vac-

uum drop at intervals may be caused by a burned intake valve. Refer to the instruction manual that comes with your gauge for a complete troubleshooting chart showing the possible causes of various readings.

Vacuum leak detector

Determining whether you've got a vacuum leak is one thing; finding it is another. In this Chapter, we'll show you how to find a vacuum leak using simple, inexpensive tools (see "Finding vacuum leaks").

The most technologically advanced method of detecting leaks is the ultrasonic leak detector **(see illustration).** Air rushing through a vacuum leak creates a high-frequency sound. An ultrasonic leak detector can "hear" these high frequencies. When its probe is passed over a leak, the detector responds to the high-frequency sound by emitting a warning beep. Some detectors also have a series of LEDs that light up as the frequencies are received. The closer the detector is moved to the leak, the more LEDs light up, or

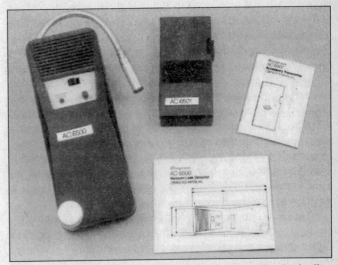

6.8 The ultrasonic leak detector is the most technologically sophisticated tool for finding vacuum leaks, but it's also expensive and not required for the tests in this manual

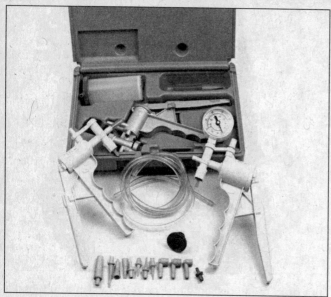

6.10 When connecting a vacuum pump/gauge to an emissions device (such as the Corvette EGR solenoid in this photo), make sure you've got airtight connections at the pump (arrow) and at the fitting or pipe of the device (arrow), or the test results won't mean much

6.9 A hand-operated vacuum pump and gauge tool is indispensable for troubleshooting emission systems - it can help you track down vacuum leaks and test all vacuum-operated devices; Mityvac pumps (shown) are available as inexpensive plastic models, like the two in the foreground (one of which can be purchased without a gauge), and sturdier metal units like the one in the box; they come with a variety of fittings and adapters, and can be used for a host of other applications besides emissions tests

the faster the beeping occurs. This allows you to zero in on the leak. An ultrasonic leak detector can sense leaks as small as 1/500th of an inch and accurately locate the leak to within 1/16-inch. These detectors are accurate, but they're also expensive and hard to find.

Vacuum pump/gauge

Two tools are indispensable for troubleshooting emission control systems. One is a digital multimeter; the other is a hand-operated vacuum pump equipped with a vacuum gauge **(see illustration)**.

Many underhood emission control system components are either operated by intake manifold vacuum, or they use it to control other system components. Devices such as check valves, dashpots, purge control valves, solenoids, vacuum control valves, vacuum delay valves, vacuum restrictors, etc. - all these devices control vacuum in some way, or are controlled by it. They amplify, block, delay, leak, reroute or transmit vacuum. Some of them must control a specified amount of vacuum for a certain period of time, or at a certain rate. A vacuum pump applies vacuum to such devices to test them for proper operation.

Suitable vacuum pump/gauges are sold by most specialty tool manufacturers. Inexpensive plastic-bodied pump/gauges-available at most auto parts stores - are perfectly adequate for diagnosing vacuum systems. Make sure the scale on the pump gauge is calibrated in "in-Hg" (inches of mercury). And buy a rebuildable pump (find out

whether replacement piston seals are available). When the seals wear, the pump won't hold its vacuum and vacuum measurements will be inaccurate. At this point, you'll have to rebuild the pump.

Using a vacuum pump is simple enough. Most pump kits include an instruction manual that describes how to use the pump in a variety of situations. They also include a variety of adapters (tee-fittings, conical fittings which allow you to connect two lines of different diameters, etc.) and some vacuum hose, to help you hook up the pump to vacuum, hoses, lines, fittings, pipes, ports, valves, etc. Manufacturers also sell replacements for these adapters and fittings in case they wear out, or you lose them. Sometimes, you may need to come up with a really specialized fitting for a more complicated hook-up. A good place to find weird fittings is the parts department of your local dealer. A well-stocked parts department has dozens of special purpose vacuum line fittings designed for various makes and models. Draw a picture of what you want for the parts man and chances are, he'll have the fitting you need.

Here are a few simple guidelines to keep in mind when using a vacuum pump:

1) When hooking up the pump **(see illustration)**, make sure the connection is airtight, or the test result will be meaningless.

2) Most factory-installed vacuum lines are rubber tubing (some are nylon). Make sure you're using the right-diameter connector hose when hooking up the pump to the device you wish to test. When you attach a connector hose with a larger inside diameter (I.D.) than the outside diameter (O. D.) of the fitting, pipe, port, etc. to which you're attaching it, the vacuum reading will be inaccurate, or you may not get a vacuum reading. If you use a hose or line with a smaller I.D. than the O.D. of the fitting, pipe, port, etc. to which you're hooking up the pump, you'll stretch your connector hose and it will be useless in future tests.

6.11 Scanners like the Actron Scantool and the AutoXray XP240 are powerful diagnostic aids - programmed with comprehensive diagnostic information for your vehicle, they can tell you just about anything you want to know about your engine management system, but they're a bit expensive

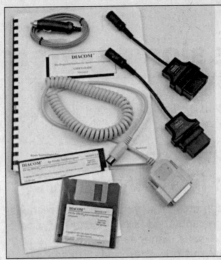

6.12 Diagnostic software, such as this kit from Diacom, turns your IBM PC, XT, AT or compatible into a scan tool, saving you the extra cost of buying a scanner but providing you with all the same information

3) In general, use as few pieces as possible to hook up the pump to the device or system being tested. The more hoses, adapters, etc. you use between the pump and the device or system being tested, the more likely the possibility of a loose connection, and a leak.

4) Don't apply more vacuum than necessary to perform a test, or you could damage something. If the pump won't build up the amount of vacuum specified for the test, or won't hold it for the specified period of time because the piston seal is leaking, discontinue the test and rebuild the pump.

5) When you're done with the test, always break the vacuum in the pump before you detach the line or hose from the system. Breaking a connection while vacuum is still applied could cause a device to suck dirt or moisture into itself when exposed to the atmosphere.

6) Always clean the fitting, pipe or port to which you've hooked up the pump and reattach the factory hose or line. Inspect the end of the factory hose or line. It's flared, frayed or torn, cut off the tip before you reattach it. Make sure the connection is clean and tight.

7) Clean your pump, adapter fittings and test hose, and put them away when you're done. Don't leave the pump laying around where it could be dropped and damaged.

Scanners, software and trouble-code tools
Scanners (computer analyzers)

Hand-held digital scanners **(see illustration)** are the most powerful and versatile tools for analyzing engine management systems used on later models vehicles. Unfortunately, they're also the most expensive. In this manual, we're going to show you how to troubleshoot sensors and actuators without resorting to analyzers.

Software

Software **(see illustration)** is available that enables your desktop or laptop computer to interface with the engine management computer on many 1981 and later General Motors and Chrysler vehicles.

Such software can output trouble codes, identify problems without even lifting the hood, solve intermittent performance problems and even help you determine the best repair solutions with on-line technical help. We tested Rinda Technology's Diacom software. It runs on any IBM PC, XT, AT or compatible. The kit includes the software, an instruction manual and the interface cables you need to plug in your computer.

Trouble-code tools

A new type of special tool - we'll call it the trouble code tool - has recently become available to the do-it-yourselfer **(see illustration)**. These tools simplify the procedure for extracting trouble codes from your vehicle's engine management computer. Of course, you can extract trouble codes without special tools. And we'll show you how to get those codes with nothing fancier than a jumper wire or (on Fords) an analog multimeter or voltmeter. But trouble code tools do make the job a little easier and they also protect the diagnostic connector terminals and the computer itself from damage.

6.13 Trouble code tools simplify the task of extracting trouble codes

7 Emissions systems and components

Note: *For information on troubleshooting and repairing these systems, see Chapter 3.*

Positive Crankcase Ventilation (PCV) system

No piston ring can provide a perfect seal between piston and cylinder; some unburned air/fuel mixture and combustion byproducts always manages to get past the rings on the compression and power strokes. These gases - mainly hydrocarbons, or HC - are known as crankcase vapors, or blow-by gases.

Once these harmful pollutants get into the crankcase, they can mix with the engine oil, reducing its viscosity and lubricating properties. Moisture from the combustion process also condenses and makes its way into the crankcase along with unburned fuel, soot, and dust to form sludge. This condensation can also combine with unburned hydrocarbons and fuel additives, and sulfur from the original crude oil, to form carbonic acid, sulfuric acid and hydrochloric acid. These acids etch, corrode and rust the internal bearing surfaces of the engine, resulting in shorter service life.

Blow-by gases also increase crankcase pressure, which eventually builds up to a point at which engine seals or gaskets can no longer contain it, resulting in oil leakage past the seals.

The Positive Crankcase Ventilation (PCV) system **(see illustration),** which was the first factory-installed emissions control system (introduced in 1961), prevents HC from escaping from the engine's crankcase into the atmosphere and allows it to "breathe" by permitting a charge of fresh air to enter the crankcase and mix with blow-by gases. Using intake-manifold vacuum to route air into and through the crankcase, the PCV system removes this mixture of vapors from the crankcase by venting it into the intake manifold, then into the combustion chambers where it's burned with the air/fuel mixture.

There are four general types of PCV systems:

1) Type 1 (open system)
2) Type 2 (restricted system)
3) Type 3 (tube-to-air cleaner system)
4) Type 4 (closed system)

The first three of these PCV systems are known as "open" types because the crankcase has some form of opening into the atmosphere through an unrestricted or partially restricted oil filler or breather cap. However, open type systems haven't been used since 1968 (since 1964 in California vehicles).

The fourth type, the closed system **(see illustration 3.1 in Chapter 3),** is used today on all domestic and imported vehicles. Like the first three systems, it ventilates the engine to prevent the buildup of harmful materials like sludge, but it allows no escape of blow-by gases into the atmosphere, even during heavy acceleration.

How do you find the PCV system?

First, look for the PCV valve. Once you find the valve, the hoses are easy to identify. The valve is normally located in one of the following places:

1) A rubber grommet in the valve or rocker arm cover **(see illustration).**

7.1 A typical Positive Crankcase Ventilation (PCV) system

7.2 A common location for PCV valves is right in the rubber grommet in the rocker arm cover (this one's on a 2.8L V6 in a Ford Aerostar)

2) At the junction of the hoses **(see illustration)**.
3) Flight in the intake manifold itself.

On some fuel-injected models, the PCV system doesn't even use a PCV valve; to find the PCV system on these models, locate the hose which connects the plenum (the chamber between the throttle body and the intake manifold) to the crankcase (usually through a camshaft, rocker arm or valve cover).

Evaporative emissions control system

The Evaporative emissions control (EVAP, EEC or ECS) system **(see illustrations)** prevents the escape of gasoline vapors from the fuel tank, carburetor vents, intake manifold, etc. into the atmosphere. At one time, these vapors constituted almost 20 percent of the hydrocarbons emitted from a typical vehicle. Because they're basically raw hydrocarbons, their release into the atmosphere promotes the formation of smog. Trapping them in an evaporative emissions system and directing them into the engine combustion chambers reduces pollution and provides a slight increase in fuel economy. All 1970 and later California vehicles are equipped with an evaporative emissions system; all 1971 and later Federal vehicles have one too.

All 1970 and 1971 Chrysler vehicles and some Ford vehicles used the crankcase as the vapor storage area. In these early systems, fuel vapors from the fuel tank and carburetor accumulated within the engine's crankcase when the vehicle wasn't in operation. When the engine was started, the PCV system moved the vapors from the crankcase into the intake manifold.

Since 1972, all vehicles sold in this country have used a "carbon (charcoal) canister" as the storage receptacle for

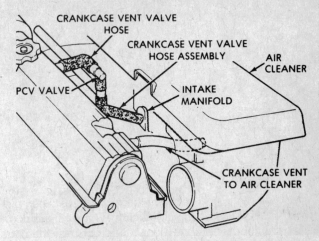

7.3 Some PCV valves are located inline with the hoses connecting the crankcase to the intake

fuel vapors. This cylindrical black plastic container is usually easy to locate. Most manufacturers put it in the left or right front corner of the engine compartment.

One important thing you should know about evaporative emissions systems is their method of purging. Older vehicles with evaporative canisters simply use engine vacuum to "purge" (empty) the canister when the engine is started (and intake vacuum is high).

There are three basic types of vacuum-operated purging methods:

1) Constant purge
2) Variable purge
3) Two-stage purge

In constant-purge systems, the rate at which purging air flows through the canister is more or less fixed, regard-

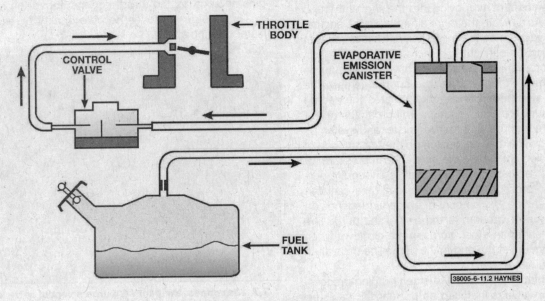

7.4 Details of a typical EVAP system

7.5 On carbureted vehicles, a likely location for the canister purge solenoid valve is right in the purge line between the EVAP canister and the carburetor, as shown on this Ford Aerostar van

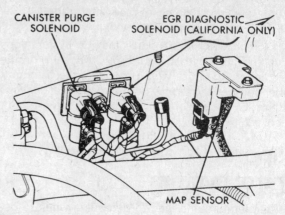

7.6 A common location for the canister purge solenoid valve on fuel-injected vehicles is the firewall or an inner fender panel, where it's often installed as part of an array of other solenoids

less of how much air the engine consumes. This is usually accomplished by simply teeing into the PCV line to the carburetor, thus using intake vacuum to draw air through the charcoal granules in the canister. Even though vacuum varies with changes in engine load, an orifice in the purge line provides the system with a relatively constant air flow rate through the canister when the engine is running.

In a variable purge system, the purge line is connected to the air cleaner. So the movement of air through the canister is a result of the intake air for the carburetor passing over a tube projecting into the air cleaner snorkel. The air flow over this tube creates a vacuum that moves the vapors out of the canister and into the airstream entering the snorkel. The purge is variable because the air flow entering the air cleaner regulates its action, i.e. the amount of purge air entering the canister from the atmosphere is in proportion to the amount of air moving into the engine through the air cleaner. As a result, the more air entering the engine, the greater the vacuum on the purge line and the amount of purge air entering the canister.

If you've got a variable purge system, you'll see a purge line entering the air cleaner near the snorkel (where the velocity of the air entering the snorkel creates the necessary low-pressure area, or vacuum, which causes atmospheric pressure to force air into the canister and system).

Or, the purge line may be located on the "clean" side of the air cleaner element, where the difference in pressure, or "pressure drop," across the air filter itself is enough to permit atmospheric pressure to force air through the canister. As in the snorkel type, the amount of purge air depends on the pressure drop or vacuum at the end of the purge line inside the air cleaner. In other words, more air flows when there's more vacuum at the end of the purge line than when only a slight vacuum exists.

Some manufacturers use a two-stage purging process. A special purge valve is installed on or near the canister. This valve is operated by a ported vacuum signal that

opens a second passage from the canister to the intake manifold.

A ported vacuum signal is taken from a passage above the throttle valve; there's no vacuum in this passage when the throttle closes at idle, but the signal increases in proportion to the amount of throttle valve opening beyond this point. When the ported vacuum signal reaches a predetermined level, it activates the purge valve. The valve opens up a second passage from the canister to the intake manifold, allowing extra purge air to enter the canister. This air assists in reactivating the granules and carrying the vapors into the engine.

Another ported-vacuum design dispenses with the purge valve and, instead, uses an extra ported vacuum connection on the carburetor to purge the canister. The port is above the upper portion of the throttle valve, so there's no purge air through the purge line at idle. Flow begins as soon as the throttle opens above the idle position. This design improves hot-idle quality by eliminating canister purging at idle.

7.7 Sometimes, the canister purge solenoid valve is right where you'd expect to find it - right above the charcoal canister (Ford Taurus/Mercury Sable)

Some purge valves are controlled by a temperature-control valve which senses engine coolant temperature. When the temperature is lower than a predetermined value, the temperature control valve closes the purge valve. This prevents canister vapors from entering the intake manifold or air cleaner, reducing HC and CO emissions during engine warm-up. When the temperature reaches a certain level, the valve allows the purge valve to open, and normal operation of the system begins.

Newer vehicles manufactured since the advent of computerized engine management systems use a computer-controlled canister purge solenoid **(see illustrations)** to control the canister purge valve. The computer monitors engine temperature and load to determine when to open and close the purge solenoid.

Air injection systems

The air injection system introduces oxygen (fresh air) into the hot exhaust gases when the engine is running. This promotes further oxidation (burning) of the unburned hydrocarbons and carbon monoxide in the exhaust, which reduces HC and CO emissions, respectively. The oxygen in the injected air combines with carbon monoxide to form carbon dioxide, a harmless gas, and it unites with hydrocarbons to produce water, in the form of vapor.

In some vehicles, the air injection system directs air into the exhaust manifold; in others, it injects air through the cylinder head, at the exhaust ports, allowing the oxidation process to begin a little further upstream.

There are two basic types of air injection systems-those with air pumps and those without. Systems which use air pumps are easy to identify: They use a mechanical vane-type pump **(see illustration)** driven by an accessory belt.

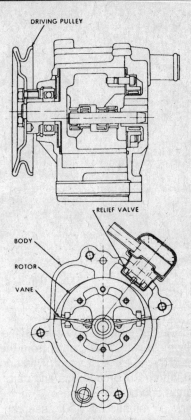

7.8 A cutaway view of typical Japanese air pump (this one's from an Isuzu Pickup)

Here's how a typical pump-type system **(see illustration)** works: The air pump receives filtered air from the air cleaner assembly and pumps it through the air switching (or control) valve and the check valve, then transmits this filtered air into an air manifold assembly mounted on the

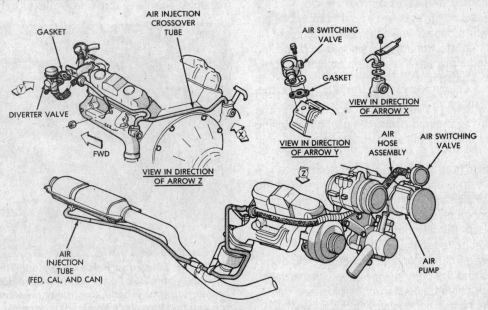

7.9 A typical pump-type air injection system

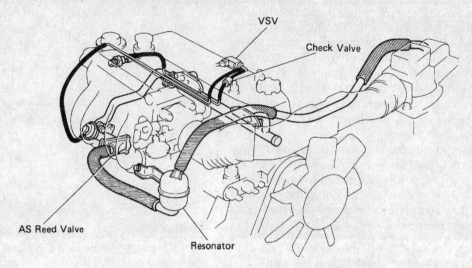

VSV

Check Valve

AS Reed Valve

Resonator

7.10 A typical air aspirator-type (passive) air injection system

cylinder head. As hot exhaust gases leave the combustion chamber, they meet with a blast of air from the air injection nozzles located in the exhaust ports. This added air helps to burn the unburned hydrocarbons and carbon monoxide that survived the combustion process.

Pump-type air injection systems use various types of valves to route air to the exhaust manifold, to the exhaust pipe between the oxidation and reduction catalysts (on newer models) or to atmosphere. These valves have a bewildering variety of names: mixture control valve, check valve, switching valve, diverter valve, relief valve, switch/relief valve, air bypass valve, etc. No matter what they're called, they all perform the same few tasks. Keep this in mind when reading the following description of our typical air injection system, and when trying to figure out how the air injection system works on your vehicle.

When it receives a high vacuum signal from the intake manifold, the mixture control valve introduces ambient air through the air filter into the intake manifold to dilute the momentarily rich fuel mixture that occurs on initial throttle closing, eliminating backfiring.

During heavy engine load conditions (near wide open throttle), the air switching valve diverts air from the air pump to the atmosphere to prevent overheating of the catalytic converter. This function occurs at a predetermined level of intake vacuum.

The check valve **(see illustration 4.7 in Chapter 3)** is a one way valve which prevents exhaust gas from entering and damaging the air pump if the pump ceases operation because of a drivebelt failure.

Once you locate the air pump - which is usually supported by a bracket bolted to the block, just like the air conditioning compressor, alternator, and power steering pump - you'll be able to find the other devices (the diverter valve, relief valve, check valves, injection manifolds and tubes, etc.) by tracing the hoses that originate at the pump.

Since 1975, some Chrysler, Ford and GM - and many import - vehicles have used a much simpler air injection system. This system is referred to as an aspirator-air, pulse-air or suction-air system **(see illustration)**. Regardless of the name, all versions of this type of air system are passive-instead of an air pump, they use exhaust pressure pulsations to draw air into the exhaust system. Every time an exhaust valve closes, there's a period when the pressure inside the manifold drops below that of the atmosphere. During these low-pressure (relative vacuum) pulses, air from the clean side of the air cleaner is drawn into the exhaust manifold(s).

The typical passive air injection system consists of a length of hose from the air cleaner to the aspirator valve, injection valve, pulse air valve, etc. **(see illustration),** and a piece of steel tubing between the valve and the exhaust manifold. The valve itself (regardless of the fancy name) is

7.11 The valves on a Pulse Air System (Thermactor II) look like this - on a 2.3L Ford Tempo, they're down by the starter motor (on your vehicle, they might be somewhere else, but you can find them by following the hoses or lines between the air pump and the exhaust system)

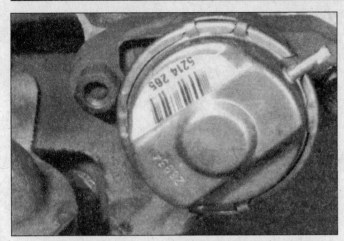

7.12 Most EGR valves are bolted directly to the intake manifold and connected to the exhaust manifold with a short section of metal tubing

7.13 Some EGR solenoids are installed on a bracket near the EGR valve, such as this one on a Nissan Maxima (left arrow). The arrow on the right points to the air injection system solenoid

simply a one-way check valve which uses metal reeds or a spring-loaded diaphragm to admit air into the exhaust manifold, but prevents hot exhaust gases from escaping.

To determine whether you've got a passive system, refer to the VECI label; to locate the system and its components, look for the valve first and trace the hoses back to the air cleaner.

Exhaust Gas Recirculation (EGR) system

High combustion temperatures produce nitrogen oxide (NOx), a constituent of ozone. There are two ways to reduce peak combustion temperatures: Spark control systems and Exhaust Gas Recirculation (EGR) systems.

Spark control systems hold down combustion temperatures by limiting ignition timing advance during acceleration from idle to cruise (the condition under which NOx emissions are highest). Before the introduction of the catalytic converter, spark control systems were widely used; today, they're still in use, but they're no longer considered the optimal means of reducing NOx emissions.

Since the introduction of the catalytic converter, EGR systems have emerged as a better way to control NOx. EGR systems reduce peak combustion temperatures by diluting the incoming air/ fuel mixture with a small amount of "inert" (won't undergo a chemical reaction) exhaust gas. A 6-to-14 percent concentration of exhaust gas, routed from the exhaust system to the intake manifold, mixes with the air/fuel mixture entering each cylinder, and reduces the mixture's ability to produce heat during combustion.

Why? Because exhaust gas contains little or no oxygen, so it dilutes the air/fuel charge with a noncombustible gas. And since this inert exhaust gas is displacing some of the oxygen in the highly combustible air/fuel mixture, it reduces the quality of the total charge reaching each of the cylinders.

Also, the injected exhaust gases are hot, so they expand the air/fuel mixture in the intake manifold. This reduces the concentration of combustible materials swept into and compressed by the piston in each of the engine's cylinders. So the mixture of air, fuel and exhaust gas entering the combustion chambers isn't as powerful when ignited. And it therefore creates less heat than an undiluted air/fuel mixture would otherwise produce.

Not all engine operating conditions produce excessive NOx emissions. At idle, for example, the engine creates little NOx, so exhaust gas recirculation is unnecessary. The engine also operates more efficiently - and the vehicle is more driveable - if the EGR system is turned off during wide-open throttle operation. In fact, the only time the EGR system should operate is at vehicle speeds between 30 and 70 mph, when NOx emissions are high.

And at low engine temperatures, exhaust gas recirculation may not be necessary. When engine temperature is low, so is the formation of NOx. Turning off the EGR system at such times improves engine warm-up and vehicle driveability.

The amount of exhaust gas admitted to the intake air is controlled by the EGR valve, which is the primary component of the system. Finding the EGR valve is easy: Most EGR valves are bolted to the intake manifold and connected to the exhaust manifold with a short section of metal tubing or passages in the intake manifold **(see illustration)**. Most EGR valves have a vacuum hose connected to them that provides the signal to open the valve. The hose is connected to the intake manifold. Often, there's a temperature valve and/or solenoid valve in the vacuum line between the EGR valve and manifold.

The EGR valves used on modern vehicles with engine management systems are turned on and off by an EGR control solenoid valve controlled by the computer. The solenoid is usually located near the EGR valve, either on its own bracket or on the firewall **(see illustrations)**. Some computer-controlled EGR valves also use a position sen-

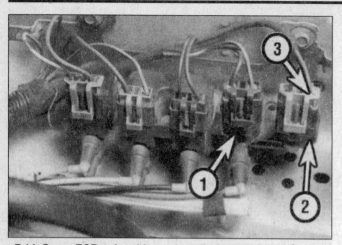

7.14 Some EGR solenoids are installed on the firewall, in an array of other solenoids, such as these units on a Ford Thunderbird - the vacuum valve (1) supplies vacuum to the electronic EGR valve when energized; when de-energized, the vent valve (2) vents the EGR valve to the atmosphere through a small vent (3)

7.15 Some EGR valves are also equipped with a position sensor like this unit on a Ford Thunderbird - the position sensor is almost always mounted right on top of the EGR valve

sor, usually atop the EGR valve itself, to fine-tune the flow of gases into the intake by incremental adjustments to the actual valve inside **(see illustration)**.

Catalytic converter

The catalytic converter is probably the most effective of the principal emissions control components we'll look at. The catalytic converter, which has been installed on all vehicles since 1975, reduces the levels of HC, CO and NOx in the exhaust by providing an additional area for the oxidation or reduction of these pollutants to occur and a catalyst to promote these changes.

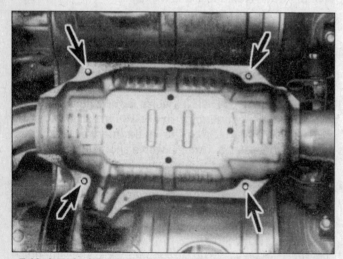

7.16 A typical catalytic converter (Nissan 300ZX) - the "cat" looks sort of like a muffler, except that it's made out of stainless steel and is surrounded by heat shields: the one above is to protect the underbody of the vehicle from the cat's high operating temperature and the one below is to prevent the cat from starting a fire or burning the home mechanic!

The catalytic converter **(see illustration),** which looks like another muffler, is located in the engine's exhaust system somewhere between the exhaust manifold and the muffler. If the vehicle has two exhaust pipes (one for each cylinder bank), you will find a catalytic converter in each exhaust pipe. And some vehicles actually have two catalytic converters in a single exhaust pipe **(see illustration)**. These earlier dual-converter setups are simply a pair of converters, different in size but identical in function; both units, which are referred to as "mini" and "main" converters, are oxidation catalysts.

Later dual converter setups-which have become the norm on modern vehicles-actually perform different functions: One converter is a reduction catalyst and the other is an oxidation catalyst. Most recent designs incorporate both the reduction and the oxidation catalyst into one unit, known as a three-way catalyst or a hybrid converter.

How do you find the catalytic converters)? Raise the vehicle, place it securely on jackstands and look for a large, stainless-steel canister in the exhaust pipe. It will have heat shields and insulating pads behind it to protect the underside of the vehicle from the heat shed by the converter when it's operating.

Heated air intake systems

The air-fuel mixture must be a fine mist or vapor to burn completely in the combustion chamber. To create this vapor, the fuel must be well-dispersed, in the form of thousands of tiny, uniform droplets in the intake air. If it isn't, driveability suffers-the engine runs roughly; more importantly, mileage suffers and large amounts of hydrocarbons and carbon monoxide are emitted out the tailpipe. In fact, automobiles pollute more during their initial warm-up phase than at any other time during their operation.

On modern vehicles with port fuel injection, this isn't a problem; even when the engine is cold, the injectors spray a fine mist right into the intake port, just above the intake

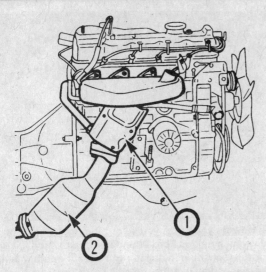

7.17 Some vehicles, such as Chryslers and Mitsubishis, use a dual converter setup: The "mini" converter (1) is up front, right at the exhaust manifold and the "main" converter (2), is further downstream in the exhaust system

valve, where it mixes instantly with the rush of incoming air each time the valve opens and the piston goes down.

But on older vehicles with carburetors - and to some extent, even on those vehicles which use "single-point" injectors (single or dual injectors at the throttle body itself) - the fuel entering the intake must be dispersed far upstream from the actual intake ports, and must maintain a uniform dispersion all the way to the combustion chamber. Once these engines are at their normal operating temperature, the ambient temperature of the carburetor/ throttle body, the runners in the intake manifold and the intake port area assures good vaporization. But when a carbureted/single point injected engine is started cold, the air-fuel mixture doesn't vaporize well, and it tends to form irregularly sized droplets, and even fall out of suspension, sticking to the walls of the intake manifold runners. So the intake area on these vehicles needs some external heat source while the engine is still warming up; that's why they're equipped with a heated air intake system of some sort.

Heated air intakes are nothing new. The earliest designs consisted of a metal cowl fastened to the exhaust manifold(s), a flexible section of metal ducting connecting it to the cold air snorkel of the air cleaner and a heat control (damper) "door" or flap inside the snorkel that mixes air heated by the manifolds) with cold ambient (outside) air in response to changes in the vacuum signal in a vacuum line connecting the vacuum motor to intake vacuum. This vacuum signal is controlled by a temperature sensing valve located inside the air cleaner housing. This design, generally referred to as a thermostatically controlled air cleaner, works so well that it's still with us today. There are many variations around, but they all work basically the same way.

The heated air intake system is pretty simple in operation: If the ambient temperature is below around 85-degrees F. when you start the engine, the temperature

sensing vacuum valve inside the air cleaner remains closed, allowing full intake vacuum to get to the vacuum motor, which closes the door to outside air and opens it to the hot air tube from the exhaust manifold cowl.

As the engine warms up, so does the temperature of the air inside the air cleaner, since it's being heated by the exhaust manifold(s). The temperature sensing valve in the air cleaner housing begins to open, bleeding off the vacuum signal to the motor, and allowing the spring-loaded door to start closing off the heated air tube and opening the cold ambient air snorkel.

By the time the engine is fully warmed up, the vacuum sensing valve is fully open, so no vacuum gets to the door motor. The door completely shuts off the heated air tube and allows nothing but outside air into the snorkel.

On some models, a cold weather modulator traps vacuum to the motor if manifold vacuum drops off as a result of the throttle opening while the air cleaner is cold. Some systems use a retard delay valve instead of a cold weather modulator. The retard delay valve traps the vacuum for a few seconds when the throttle opens.

To further improve driveability and lower emissions, many vehicles are also equipped with an additional device: a bimetallic coil or vacuum diaphragm-operated heat-control valve **(see illustration)**. This device provides more precise control of intake manifold heating, improving vaporization of the air-fuel mixture.

Heat-riser valves go by several names. General Motors calls them Early Fuel Evaporation (EFE) valves, Ford calls them Heat Control Valves (HCV), Chrysler calls them power heat control valves, etc. But they all look and work the same.

Here's how a typical valve works: A rotating valve is housed inside a cast iron body which fits between the exhaust manifold and the exhaust pipe. Linked to the shaft that extends through the cast iron body and attaches to the valve is a diaphragm inside a vacuum motor or a bimetallic coil.

The diaphragm type turns the shaft and valve by reacting to a vacuum signal from the intake manifold via a ported vacuum switch. On computer-controlled engines, the vacuum system also includes an electric solenoid-operated vacuum valve. When the diaphragm receives a full or high manifold vacuum signal, it closes the valve, sending hot exhaust gases up through a heat riser, through special passages in the intake manifold, and back into the exhaust system. When the signal to the motor is low or is cut off completely, a spring behind the diaphragm pushes the heat-riser valve open, and the gases go straight out the exhaust pipe.

The bimetallic-coil type works the same way, but it simply responds to the temperature of the housing itself, which is about the same temperature as the exhaust manifold.

Another device which improves vaporization by heating the mixture during cold starts is an electrically heated grid installed between the carburetor or throttle body and the intake manifold **(see illustration 5.4 in Chapter 3)**. This device is operated by a relay controlled by a temperature switch that shuts the relay off after a couple of minutes.

7.18 One likely place to find the air temperature sensor is the air cleaner housing, such as this Manifold Air Temperature (MAT) sensor on a Pontiac Fiero - air temperature sensors are also often located in the intake manifold or intake runners

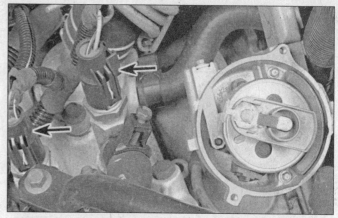

7.19 How do you know you've got the right sensor on a vehicle such as this Ford Thunderbird, on which the air temperature sensor is installed right next to another sensor, and they're identical in appearance? Try to determine whether it's installed in a coolant passage in the intake manifold (a coolant temperature sensor) or an air intake runner (an air temperature sensor)

7.20 Coolant temperature sensors, such as this Engine Coolant Temperature (ECT) sensor on a Plymouth Sundance, are usually installed in the thermostat housing

7.21 This coolant temperature sensor on a Ford Probe is installed in the intake manifold, but note that it's protruding into a coolant passage in the manifold which leads to the thermostat housing in the foreground

The engine management system

By the late 1970's, many vehicles' ignition systems were controlled by a computer. I n quick succession, most other engine systems were also placed under computer control. Since 1980, most vehicles sold in the US have been equipped with computerized engine management systems to help reduce emissions.

No matter how fancy the name, no matter how sophisticated the system, all engine management systems consist of the same three basic types of components: information sensors, a computer and actuators or controls.

1) Every engine management system has a wide variety of *information sensors* (as many as a dozen or more) which monitor various operating conditions of the engine (such as coolant temperature, intake air temperature, throttle position angle, engine speed, etc.) **(see illustrations)**.

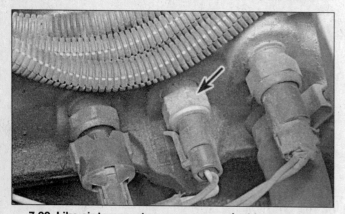

7.22 Like air temperature sensors, coolant temperature sensors, such as this one (arrow) between two other sensors on a Pontiac Grand Am, can be difficult to identify- if you're unable to identify the sensor you're looking for using the "air-intake-passage vs.-coolant-passage-installation" approach, trace the electrical leads back to the main harness or to the device to which they're attached; if that doesn't work, try counting the number and color of the electrical leads, then refer to a wiring diagram

7.23 Crankshaft position sensors are installed either in the side of the block, such as this unit on a Chevrolet Corsica/Beretta, next to the crankshaft at the front of the engine. . .

7.24 . . . or inside the distributor assembly, such as this unit on a Nissan pickup truck

7.25 Knock sensors, such as this Electronic Spark Control (ESC) sensor on a Chevrolet Corvette, are usually installed in the block, where they can detect harmful detonation in the combustion chamber

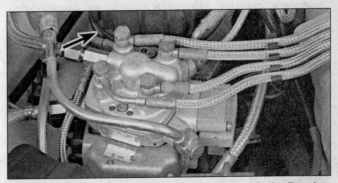

7.26 One of the earliest air flow meter designs is the Bosch plate-type unit (arrow) found on all German vehicles with continuous injection (CIS, CIS-E), such as this unit on a VW Fox with Bosch CIS-E - finding the air flow meter on one of these vehicles is easy: It's always right next to the fuel distributor, the device with all the braided-stainless-steel fuel lines attached (in fact, the air flow meter and the fuel distributor are always housed in one integral unit known as the mixture control unit)

7.27 Vane-type air flow meters, such as this unit (arrow) on a Ford Explorer, use a spring-loaded swinging door connected to a variable resistor to send a variable voltage signal to the computer - this type of air flow meter is always located downstream from the air cleaner housing and upstream from the throttle body

7.28 The latest air flow meters, such as this Mass Air Flow (MAF) unit on a Chevrolet Corsica, use a heated resistance wire to measure air flow by sending a voltage signal to the computer that varies in proportion to the mass of air passing over the wire - this type of air flow meter is also located between the air cleaner housing and the throttle body

7.29 Some air flow meters, such as this unit on a Nissan pick-up truck, are mounted right on the side of the throttle body - these units also use a hot wire to measure air flow mass, but they re-route some of the air entering the throttle body into a side passage, where the wire is located

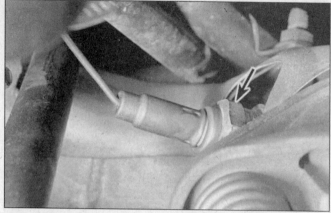

7.30 Manifold Absolute Pressure (MAP) sensors, such as this Chevrolet Corsica unit, are usually a black plastic box located on the firewall, and usually have the same parts:

1 *MAP sensor assembly*
2 *Mounting screws (some units are simply clipped onto a bracket)*
3 *MAP sensor vacuum line (goes to intake manifold vacuum)*
4 *MAP sensor electrical connector (usually goes to main engine harness)*

7.31 Oxygen sensors are easy to find (but not always easy to get to): They're always in the exhaust system, somewhere between the exhaust manifolds) and the catalytic converters) - this unit (arrow) as seen from underneath the vehicle, is in the left exhaust manifold of a Pontiac Grand Am (there's usually another one in the other manifold on V6s and V8s)

7.32 The Throttle Position Sensor (TPS) is always mounted on the carburetor or throttle body, usually right on the end of the throttle valve shaft, such as this TBI-mounted unit on a Chevrolet full-size pickup truck

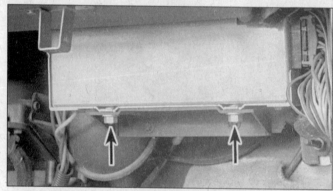

7.33 Computers can be anywhere there's room, but there are three common locations: Many are installed beneath the right side of the dash - usually right under the glove box, as on this Pontiac Grand Am

2) The sensors transmit this data, as a variable voltage signal, to a *computer* **(see illustrations)** which analyzes this information by comparing it to the "map" inside its memory. The map is simply a program which very specifically details how the engine should be operating under every conceivable operating condition (cold starts, warm-ups, acceleration, deceleration, etc.).

3) If the computer notes a discrepancy between what's happening and what the map says SHOULD be happening under a given set of circumstances, the computer transmits commands, again in the form of voltage data, to a smaller group of devices known as actuators, or controls **(see illustrations),** which alter the operating conditions of the engine (richen or lean the fuel/air mixture, advance or retard the ignition, open or close the EGR valve, open or close the EVAP canister purge valve, etc.).

And that's it! The details vary somewhat from system to system, but not much. All engine management systems use the same three types of components - a bunch of sensors, one computer and several controls. So don't make engine management systems more complicated than they really are.

7.34 Another likely location is behind the kick panel (the small triangular area just in front of the front door and beneath the extreme right end of the dash) as on this Chevrolet Corsica

7.35 A third computer location is between the seats, as on this Pontiac Fiero, or even underneath one of the front seats (arrows point to electrical connector and mounting bolt locations)

7.36 Ignition system computers, such as this GM Electronic Spark Control (ESC) module on a Chevy pickup, are usually on the firewall - but even if they're not, you can always identify them by their large multi-pin connector which connects them to a knock sensor, the ignition coil, the battery, etc. (arrows point to electrical connector and mounting bolt locations)

7.37 Look for control solenoids in arrays, such as this one on a Dodge Dakota-this computer-controlled switching solenoid (arrow) controls the vacuum signal to the switch/relief valve on the air injection system

7.38 This computer-controlled Auxiliary Air Control (AAC) valve is located on the intake manifold on a Nissan Maxima- as coolant temperature rises, the valve gradually closes, restricting auxiliary air flow

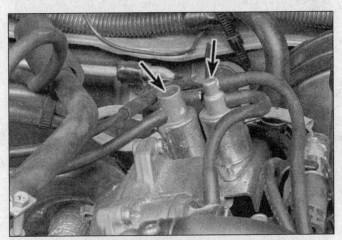

7.39 Some EGR control solenoids are located on small brackets which can be mounted anywhere in the engine compartment - the EGR control solenoid, or vacuum cut solenoid, is on the left on this Nissan Maxima (the control solenoid on the right is for the Air Injection Valve (AIV)

7.40 This EGR control solenoid on a Ford Tempo is bolted to a bracket mounted on the left strut tower, another popular mounting point for solenoids

8 Basic vacuum troubleshooting

What is vacuum?

First, let's look at what vacuum is. In science, the term "vacuum" refers to a total absence of air; in automotive mechanics, vacuum refers a pressure level that's lower than the earth's atmospheric pressure at any given altitude. The higher the altitude, the lower the atmospheric pressure.

You can measure vacuum pressure in relation to atmospheric pressure. Atmospheric pressure is the pressure exerted on every object on earth and is caused by the weight of the surrounding air. At sea level, the pressure exerted by the atmosphere is 14.7 "pounds per square inch" (psi). We call this measurement system "pounds per square inch absolute" (psia).

The gauge on a hand-operated vacuum pump ignores atmospheric pressure at sea level and reads zero instead. In other words, on a gauge, atmospheric pressure, or zero psi, is the starting point of our measurements. We call this measurement system "pounds per square inch gauge" (psig).

But vacuum gauges don't measure vacuum in psia or psig; instead, they measure it in "inches of Mercury" (in-Hg). Once in a while, you'll see another unit of measurement on some gauges; it's expressed in "kilopascals" (kPa). Another unit of measurement, used on manometers, is expressed in "inches of water" (in H20).

How is vacuum created in an internal combustion engine?

Positive pressure always flows to an area with a "less positive," i.e. relatively negative, pressure. This is a basic law of physics. Viewed from this perspective, an engine is really nothing more than an air pump. As the crankshaft rotates through two full revolutions, the engine cycles through its intake, compression, power and exhaust strokes. The first and last of these strokes-the intake and exhaust strokes-are identical to the action of the intake and exhaust strokes of any air pump: The intake "pulls" in air; the exhaust expels it.

During the intake stroke, the piston moves downward from its top dead center position. At the same time the exhaust valve closes and the intake valve opens. This downward movement of the piston in the cylinder creates a relative vacuum, drawing the air-fuel mixture into the cylinder through the open intake valve.

After the engine compression and power strokes are completed, the intake valve is still closed but the exhaust valve opens as the piston begins moving upward on its exhaust stroke. The rising piston forces the spent exhaust gases out through the open port.

The partial vacuum created by the engine's intake stroke is relatively continuous, because one cylinder is always at some stage of its intake stroke in a four, six or eight-cylinder engine. On carbureted engines, this intake vacuum is regulated, to some extent, by the position of the choke plate and the throttle valve; on fuel-injected engines, it's regulated strictly by throttle valve position, since there is no choke plate. When the choke plate or throttle valve is in its closed position, air flow is reduced and intake vacuum is higher; as the plate or valve opens, air flow increases and vacuum decreases.

How is vacuum used in automotive emission control systems?

Today, vacuum applications go way beyond fuel metering. Intake vacuum is now used to operate all sorts of devices and systems on automobiles. Vacuum-operated devices are used in the air intake system to control air temperature to improve fuel vaporization and combustion. Vacuum is used to control some automatic chokes and most throttle kickers to ease engine startups, warm-ups and cold drive-aways. Spark advance on many Seventies and Eighties vehicles is controlled by a vacuum-operated diaphragm at the distributor. Engine vacuum controls operation of accessories such as power brake boosters, automatic transmission vacuum modulators, cruise control systems, air distribution system doors and heater/air conditioner systems.

Most emission control systems also depend on vacuum for proper operation. These systems use numerous vacuum-operated devices that respond to vacuum, electronic, temperature or electronic-temperature inputs to activate and deactivate output actuators which control emissions by altering engine operation in accordance with

changing loads and operating temperatures.

There are three basic types of vacuum controls. They are:

1) **Vacuum delay valves** - Also known as restrictors, these valves are used to delay vacuum flow. They're usually located in the vacuum line between the vacuum source and some vacuum-controlled device.

2) **Vacuum diaphragms**-These controls, usually referred to in this book as actuators, are used to operate various vehicle mechanical parts, such as throttle linkages on carburetors and throttle bodies, or EGR valves.

3) **Vacuum switches and valves**-These devices, also known as solenoids, control vacuum flow and are usually operated electrically or thermostatically.

Where can you find vacuum diagrams?

The factory service manual for your vehicle normally contains vacuum diagrams. Even your owner's manual may contain a diagram or two. But the quickest way to determine what vacuum devices are used in the emission control systems on your vehicle is to refer to the vacuum diagram located in the engine compartment. Most vehicles have a vacuum diagram (or "schematic") located somewhere in the engine compartment. It's usually affixed to the underside of the hood for convenient reference when working on your vehicle.

Raise the hood and find your VECI label. Most manufacturers place the vacuum diagram right on the VECI label. Some put it on a separate label, near the VECI label.
Note: *The diagrams in this manual are typical examples of the type you'll find on your vehicle's VECI label, in your owner's manual, in a Haynes Automotive Repair Manual (ARM) or in a factory service manual. But they're instructional-they DON'T necessarily apply to your vehicle. When you're working on emission control systems, if you notice differences between the vacuum diagram affixed to your vehicle and those in the owner's manual, a Haynes ARM or a factory manual, always go with the one on the vehicle. It's always the most accurate diagram.*

Where can you buy replacement vacuum diagrams?

Like VECI labels, vacuum diagrams are available at your authorized dealer service department. (Of course, as mentioned above, sometimes they're part of the VECI label). You can also find vacuum diagrams in the factory service manual for your vehicle.

Typical vacuum schematics

There are two types of vacuum schematics. The currently favored style shows how various vacuum devices are interconnected, but it doesn't always tell you where these devices are actually located in the engine compartment. The newer style, which is just beginning to see widespread use, not only shows you what the devices look like, it also tells you where they are.

Finding vacuum leaks

Vacuum system problems can produce, or contribute to, numerous driveability problems, including:

1 Deceleration backfiring
2 Detonation
3 Hard to start
4 Knocking or pinging
5 Overheating
6 Poor acceleration
7 Poor fuel economy
8 Rich or lean stumbling
9 Rough idling
10 Stalling
11 Won't start when cold

The major cause of vacuum-related problems is damaged or disconnected vacuum hoses, lines or tubing. Vacuum leaks can cause problems such as erratic running and rough idling.

For instance, a rough idle often indicates a leaking vacuum hose. A broken vacuum line allows a vacuum leak, which allows more air into the intake manifold than the engine is calibrated for. Then the engine runs roughly due to the leaner air/fuel mixture.

Another example: Spark knock or pinging sometimes indicates a kinked vacuum hose to the EGR valve. If this hose is kinked, the EGR valve won't open when it should. The engine, which requires a certain amount of exhaust gas in the combustion chamber to cool it down, pings or knocks.

Here's another: A misfire at idle may indicate a torn or ruptured diaphragm in some vacuum-activated unit (a dashpot or EGR valve, for instance). The torn diaphragm permits air movement into the intake manifold below the carburetor or throttle body. This air thins out the already lean air/fuel mixture at idle and causes a misfire. A misfire may also indicate a leaking intake manifold gasket or a leaking carburetor or throttle body base gasket. If a leak develops between the mating surfaces of the intake manifold and the cylinder head, or between the carburetor or throttle body base gasket and the intake manifold, the extra air getting into the engine below the gasket causes a misfire.

If you suspect a vacuum problem because one or more of the above symptoms occurs, the following visual inspection may get you to the source of the problem with no further testing.

1) Make sure everything is routed correctly - kinked lines block vacuum flow at first, then cause a vacuum leak when they crack and break.

2) Make sure all connections are tight. Look for loose connections and disconnected lines. Vacuum hoses and lines are sometimes accidentally knocked loose by an errant elbow during an oil change or some other maintenance.

3) Inspect the entire length of every hose, line and tube for breaks, cracks, cuts, hardening, kinks and tears **(see illustration)**. Replace all damaged lines and hoses.

4) When subjected to the high underhood temperatures of a running engine, hoses become brittle (hardened). Once they're brittle, they crack more easily when subjected to engine vibrations. When you inspect the vacuum hoses and lines, pay particularly close attention to those that are routed near hot areas such as exhaust manifolds, EGR systems, reduction catalysts (often right below the exhaust manifold on modern FWD vehicles with transverse engines), etc.

5) Inspect all vacuum devices for visible damage (dents, broken pipes or ports, broken tees in vacuum lines, etc.

6) Make sure none of the lines are coated with coolant, fuel, oil or transmission fluid. Many vacuum devices will malfunction if any of these fluids get inside them.

7) What if none of the above steps eliminates the leak? Grab your vacuum pump and apply vacuum to each suspect area, then watch the gauge for any loss of vacuum.

8) And if you still can't find the leak? Well, maybe it's not in the emissions system; maybe it's right at the source, at the intake manifold or the base gasket between the carburetor or throttle body. To test for leaks in this area, squirt a noncombustible cleaning solvent such as carburetor cleaner or point cleaner (or WD-40, but it's messier) along the gasket joints with the engine running at idle. If the idle speed smooths out momentarily, you've located your leak. Tighten the intake manifold or the carb/throttle body fasteners to the specified torque and recheck. If the leak persists, you may have to replace the gasket.

An alternative to spraying solvent is to use a short length of vacuum hose as a sort of "stethoscope," listening for the high pitched hissing noise that characterizes vacuum leaks. Hold one end of the hose to your ear and probe close to possible sources of vacuum leakage with the other end. **Warning:** *Stay clear of rotating engine components when probing with the hose.*

Repairing and replacing vacuum hose

Replace defective sections one at a time to avoid confusion or misrouting. If you discover more than one disconnected line during an inspection of the lines, refer to the vehicle vacuum schematic to make sure you reattach the lines correctly. Route rubber hoses and nylon lines away from hot components, such as EGR tubes and exhaust

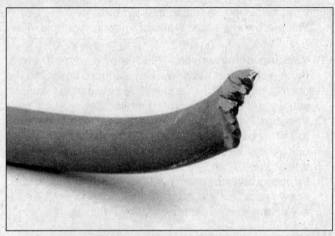

8.1 **This vacuum hose was routed too close to an exhaust manifold - after being overheated repeatedly, it finally cracked and broke**

manifolds, and away from rough surfaces which may wear holes in them.

Most factory-installed vacuum lines are rubber, but some are nylon. Connectors can be bonded nylon or rubber. Nylon connectors usually have rubber inserts to provide a seal between the connector and the component connection.

Replacing nylon vacuum lines can be expensive and tricky. Using rubber hose may not be as aesthetically pleasing as the OEM nylon tubing, but it's perfectly acceptable, as long as the hoses and fittings are tightly connected and correctly routed (away from rough surfaces and hot EGR tubes, exhaust manifolds, etc.).

Here are some tips for repairing nylon vacuum hoses and lines:

1) If a nylon hose is broken or kinked, and the damaged area is 1/2-inch or more from a connector, cut out the damaged section (don't remove more than 1/2-inch) and install a rubber union.

2) If the remaining hose is too short, or the damage exceeds 1/2-inch in length, replace the entire hose and the original connector with rubber vacuum hoses and a tee fitting.

3) If only part of a nylon connector is damaged or broken, cut it **apart** and discard the damaged half of the harness. Then replace it with rubber vacuum hoses and a tee.

Note: *The identification numbers on the accompanying illustrations refer to the old fittings and hoses - and their corresponding replacements - so you don't get mixed up.*

9 Checking electrical connections

Check the electrical connections to the computer, all sensors and actuators and all other emissions devices. Make sure they're properly mated and tightly coupled. Wiggle and shake the connectors to ensure they're tight. Loose connectors should be unplugged and inspected for corrosion **(see illustrations)**. Look closely at the connector pins and tabs. If corrosion is present, clean it off with a small wire brush and electrical contact cleaner (available in aerosol form). Some connectors might require the use of a special conductive grease to prevent corrosion.

9.1 Most connectors have one or more tabs like this (arrow) that must be lifted before the halves can be separated

9.2 Some connectors, such as this one on a Toyota throttle position sensor, have a spring clip that must be pried up before the connector can be unplugged

9.3 This Ford SPOUT connector is a bit unusual - a plastic plug must be pulled out of the connector housing before it can be disconnected - don't lose the plug!

9.4 Many modern engine-management system connectors have flexible seals (arrow) to keep moisture off the terminals and prevent corrosion - make sure the seal isn't damaged in any way

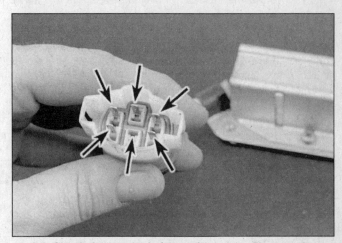

9.5 Check the terminals (arrows) in each connector for corrosion that will cause excessive resistance in the circuit, or even an open circuit

10 Preparing for emissions certification testing

Over half of all states now require regular (annual or biannual) emission certification tests. Many also require smog inspections when vehicle ownership changes hands. Obviously, if you've "modified" (tampered with) your vehicle's smog equipment, this periodic ritual of having your vehicle "smogged" can give you an anxiety attack. And even if you're the type of owner who would never dream of disconnecting a single vacuum line - but you're also the type who neglects scheduled vehicle maintenance, including emission-related components - the prospect of a smog test can be disconcerting. If you fall into either of these two general groups, you're not alone. Recent statistics from some states indicate that nearly one-third of all vehicles fail to meet emissions standards their first time through.

It doesn't have to be that way. With regular engine maintenance and a straight-forward check of emissions-related components, you can catch nearly all the potential failures which might turn up in a state inspection. And you might as well get used to it, because state-certified smog testing is going to become stricter and more frequent as time goes on. Specific testing procedures and standards for various emissions levels vary from state to state, but the idea - lowering the HC, CO and NOx levels - is the same everywhere. So the following information should save you time and money. Time because you won't have to go back several times to pass the test; money because you won't have to shell out extra dollars for the repairs needed to enable your vehicle to pass the test.

Generally, a stock (untampered with) engine will pass the state smog test as long as it's been recently tuned and all the emissions related hardware is intact, hooked up and working properly. If your vehicle hasn't had a tune-up recently, now is the time to do it.

The following items should be checked carefully before a smog.

1) Make a quick visual check of all emissions control systems to be sure all components are in place and hooked up correctly. If you have reason to suspect a system is not functioning correctly, check it, as described in Chapter 3.
2) Inspect all underhood vacuum hoses for cracks, loose connections and disconnected hoses.
3) Inspect all underhood electrical wiring for cracks, torn wires, loose or corroded connections and unplugged connectors.
4) Check the air filter carefully, since a dirty, restricted air filter will cause a rich fuel/air mixture, increasing emissions. Also check the PCV filter, if equipped (see Chapter 3).
5) On carbureted models, check the choke to be sure it's opening all the way when the engine is warmed up (here again, the rich fuel/air mixture caused by a closed choke will increase emissions).
6) Finally, before having vehicle car tested, make sure the engine and exhaust (catalytic converter) system are up to normal temperature (10 to 15 minutes of driving time).

How do you pick a shop for an emissions test?

Where do you take your vehicle for a smog test? Well, if you already have a good working relationship with a local shop-and it's certified to do smog testing - by all means stick with that shop. But if you don't have a regular shop, there are several factors worth considering: First, look at what the shop charges. This isn't as important as you might think; the inspection fees charged by private garages are generally regulated by the state, so there may not be that much difference in fees from one shop to another. The important thing to keep in mind is that the fee charged by most shops is usually a lot lower than its normal hourly labor rate. In other words, doing emissions testing can be a marginally profitable - or even a losing proposition - for shops. So how does a shop turn a smog test into a money maker? Basically, by charging you their normal labor rate for fixing problems if your vehicle fails its smog test.

Of course, you're certainly not obligated to have your vehicle repaired by the same shop that inspects it for compliance with state smog laws. But the shop owner hopes you will do just that, to avoid the inconvenience of moving the vehicle to another shop. Whether you decide to have the vehicle repaired by the same shop that inspects it, or take it somewhere else, depends on how much you trust the shop's ethics.

Also, try to find a shop that does not charge for re-testing your vehicle if it should fail the test. Re-testing fees-particularly if your vehicle must be re-tested more than once - can really add up.

The emissions test

Most state smog certification inspections consist of two parts:

1) An under-hood visual inspection - to make sure everything is installed and connected.
2) An analysis of the composition of the exhaust gases coming out the tailpipe, both at idle and at median on-the-road engine speeds.

You might survive the first part of the test even if something is missing or everything isn't hooked up, because the mechanic may or may not be familiar with the emissions devices and systems that are supposed to be fitted to your engine. But don't bet on it. The software programs employed by most state-approved emissions-testing analyzers display this information - component identification and location of all emission components for your specific model - on the video screen of the analyzer.

But even if your vehicle passes the visual inspection phase in spite of a missing or disconnected device or system, the engine will probably fail the second part of the test, which is performed with an infrared gas analyzer.

A probe, which is shoved up the tailpipe, detects the amount of hydrocarbons (HC), carbon monoxide (CO) and oxides of nitrogen (NOx) in the exhaust stream, and transmits this information to a computer which measures these levels to a high degree of accuracy (expressed in "parts per million," or ppm). This analysis of the exhaust gases is usually conducted both at idle speed and at about 2500 to 2800 rpm. If the engine fails either part, the vehicle fails the test.

The analyzer computer prints out two hard copies of the HC and CO readings, one for you and one for the shop's inspection records. How do you know whether the analyzer's conclusions are accurate? Most analyzers are self-calibrating: Every time they're turned on to perform a test, they verify the validity of their calibration against reference gases contained inside their own apparatus.

If your vehicle passes its emissions test, you're allowed to drive it for another year or two. If it fails, you have a "grace period," usually a month, to bring the vehicle up to specification so that it can pass (unless, of course, you have waited until the last minute to submit your vehicle to the test and your registration is about to expire, in which case you have considerably less time to fix it!).

What if your vehicle fails the emissions test?

If your vehicle fails its emissions test, see the information on the Performance Warranty in Section 3 of this Chapter.

11 Resetting emissions maintenance reminder timers

Until recently, the oxygen sensors and EGR systems on most vehicles required periodic inspection or replacement, so they were equipped with emissions maintenance reminder lights which came on periodically to remind you to perform the specified maintenance. After you've completed the service, the timer for the emissions maintenance reminder light must be reset. The following information will help you locate the timer on your vehicle.

You'll note that later models aren't included here. That's because the oxygen sensor and EGR valve on these models don't need to be regularly inspected or replaced; they've been designed to last a lot longer to comply with the Federally mandated extended warranty. If the oxygen sensor or EGR valve fail on a newer vehicle, you'll usually get a trouble code (see Chapter 2).

Also be aware that the following information does not apply to service interval reminder lights that come on periodically to remind you that it's time to perform routine non-emissions service, such as oil and filter changes.

Alfa Romeo

1   Every 30,000 miles on the Spider 2.0L, Graduate and Quadrifoglio, and every 60,000 miles on the GTV-6 2.5L, a light on the dash will come on as a reminder to check the system and replace the oxygen sensor.
2   To reset the mileage counter after replacing the sensor on the Spider 2.0L, Graduate and Quadrifoglio, locate the counter on the left side of the engine compartment. Remove the plastic cover by drilling through the shank of the attaching screws. Remove the cover, then rotate and press the button. Using new screws, reinstall the cover.
3   On the GTV-6 2.5L, remove the ECU cover panel and the lower right side parcel shelf. Locate the mileage counter under the right side of the dash. Push the white reset button. Make sure the emission reminder light is out.

American Motors

1980 and 1981 models

An emissions maintenance reminder light on the instrument panel, which indicates that the oxygen sensor needs to be serviced, comes on every 30,000 miles. If the sensor is faulty, it must be replaced. After servicing the sensor, reset the light activating switch.

You'll find the switch in the engine compartment,

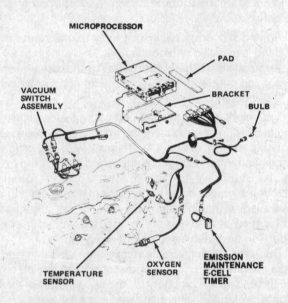

11.1 On American Motors vehicles, you'll find the emissions maintenance E-cell timer under the dash, in the wire harness for the computer; don't try to reset the timer (you can't) - replace it

between the upper and lower speedometer cables, next to the firewall. Slide up the rubber boot. With a small screwdriver, turn the reset screw clockwise 1/4-turn until the detent resets in the switch.

1982 through 1984 models (except Alliance and Encore)

The emission maintenance light comes on every 1000 hours of engine operation to let you know that the oxygen sensor must be serviced. After you've serviced the sensor, replace the emission maintenance E-cell timer. You'll find the E-cell timer under the dash, in the wire harness leading to the computer (see illustration). Remove the timer from its enclosure and insert a replacement unit.

1987 Eagle wagon

An emission light timer will start flashing the Oxygen Sensor Service light at 82,500 miles. At this time, both the sensor and timer should be replaced. You'll find the timer under the dash panel (to the right of steering column). Remove the mounting screws and disconnect the wiring. Installation is the reverse of removal.

Audi

The mileage counter is located on the firewall, under the seat, under the dash or behind the instrument cluster, depending on the model. On models which require regular service for both the EGR system and the oxygen sensor, the counter has separate reset buttons for each system. The EGR light comes on at 15,000 mile intervals. Check the system for defects, then reset the counter (see below). The oxygen sensor light comes on at 30,000 mile intervals (60,000 mile intervals on 100/200 models). Replace the sensor, then reset the counter (see below).

Pre-1984 Audi 4000 and 5000S

The inline mileage counter is mounted under the dash, to the left of the steering column near the pedal assembly. Remove the lower dash cover on the driver's side. Once you know where the counter is and you've developed the right "touch," you can dispense with this step and reach the reset button with a bent rod. The reset button for the reminder light is white.

1984 and later Audi 4000 and non-turbo 5000 and 5000S

When the light comes on, replace the oxygen sensor. To reset the mileage counter, you must remove the instrument cluster, disconnect the speedometer cable at the transaxle end and remove the steering wheel to give yourself room to work. Remove the instrument cluster cover screws. Pull the instrument cluster out of the dash as far as the attached wiring and speedometer cable allow.

Find the small plastic cover at the top of the cluster, near the imprinted OXS and break it off. Press the switch to reset the counter. Once you know where the switch is located, you can reach it next time without totally removing the cluster. Installation is the reverse of removal.

1984 through 1988 Audi 5000 Turbo and 100/200 Turbo

The mileage counter is located under the rear seat. Push the seat cushion toward the rear of the vehicle, then lift the front of the cushion to release the cushion retainers. Move the cushion out of the way. The counter is located on the left side of the vehicle. Push the button marked OXS on the reset box. Cycle the ignition to the On position and make sure the reminder light goes off. Installation is the reverse of removal. Replace the oxygen sensor.

All other Audi models

To turn off the reminder light on all other models, trace the speedometer cable to the reset box, which is installed inline with the cable (see illustration 13.19). To reset the counter, press the white button on the box and make sure the reminder light goes out.

BMW

Pre-1983 models

The OXYGEN light in the dash will light up every 30,000 miles (every 25,000 miles on 528I models) as a reminder to replace the sensor. The inline mileage counter is located above the left frame rail, near the transmission. Make sure the white reset button makes an audible "click" when you press it (If it doesn't, the reminder light will remain on). Replace the mileage counter if the button won't click. 528e and 1983 633CSi models have no reset switch. On these models, remove the instrument cluster, then remove and discard the bulb for the OXYGEN light.

1983 and later models

On models through January 1985, when the oxygen sensor light comes on, service the sensor and remove the bulb from the indicator. No reset switch is provided. On February 1985 and later models, there's a reset button on the rear of the light control assembly that's located near the pedal assembly. Press this button to reset the light after you have serviced the oxygen sensor.

Chrysler Motors

1980 passenger cars and 1980 through 1987 light-duty trucks and vans

A mileage counter activates the emissions reminder light. Two types are used. If your vehicle is equipped with the mechanical type, see the reset procedure above for 1980 and 1981 American Motors models.

The electronic type uses a 9-volt battery which supplies power to the electronic counter, preventing memory loss when the vehicle battery is disconnected. On 1987 Dakota models, the mileage counter in the odometer will illuminate the reminder light at 52,500, 82,500 and 105,000 miles.

On all other models, the reminder light will illuminate between 12,000 and 30,000-mile intervals. **Caution:** *During the resetting procedure, the vehicle battery MUST be connected to prevent power loss to the computer memory.*

To reset the electronic type, locate the Green, Red, White or Tan plastic case behind the instrument panel in the lower left instrument cluster area. Slide the case from the bracket and open the cover. Remove the 9-volt battery and insert a small rod or screwdriver into the hole in the switch to close the contacts. Replace the battery with a new 9-volt alkaline type. Close the case switch back into bracket.

1988 and some 1989 light-duty trucks and vans

The Emission Maintenance Reminder (EMR) module's purpose it to remind you to service the vehicle emissions control system. It's not an emissions warning system. The EGR system, PCV valve, oxygen sensor, delay valves and

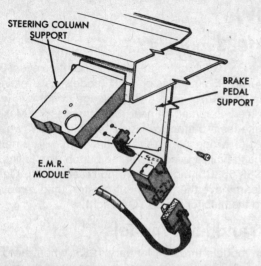

11.2 An exploded view of a typical Emission Maintenance Reminder (EMR) module on the steering column behind the instrument panel (1988 Dodge Ram van shown)

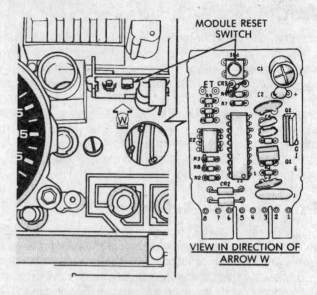

11.3 A typical module reset switch on the back of the instrument cluster (1988 Dodge/Plymouth mini-van)

purge valve should all be checked and, if necessary, replaced.

The EMR module will illuminate the "MAINT REQD" dash light at a predetermined time. Mileage alone won't cause the light to come on. The light will stay on until the EMR module is reset by inserting a small screwdriver into the hole in the module (RWD models only) and depressing the reset switch (FWD and RWD models).

The EMR module is located on the steering column behind the instrument panel on RWD vans and in the instrument cluster on FWD vans (see illustrations). On trucks, it's located behind the far right side of the dash panel next to the glove box (see illustration). On Dakota models, the module is located on a bracket below the headlight switch on the back of the instrument panel (see illustration).

Other 1989 light-duty trucks and vans

Resetting the Emissions Maintenance Reminder (EMR) light timer requires a special tool (a Chrysler DRB-II tester). Take the vehicle to a dealer service department to have the timer reset.

Eagle Premier (1988 and 1989)

Every 7500 miles, a Vehicle Maintenance Monitor (VMM) will illuminate a SERVICE interval reminder light to indicate regular maintenance is due. After the required service is performed, press the RESET button on the dash below the VMM display. Hold the button until you hear a beep. The VMM display is cleared.

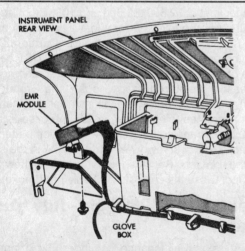

11.4 A typical EMR module installation on a full-size Dodge Pick-up truck, located behind the far right end of the dash (1988 model shown)

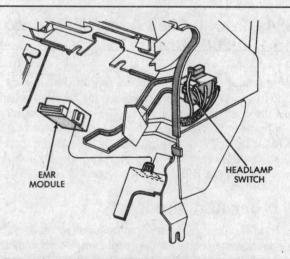

11.5 A typical EMR module installation on a Dodge Dakota Pick-up truck, located on a bracket below the headlight switch on the back of the instrument panel (1988 model shown)

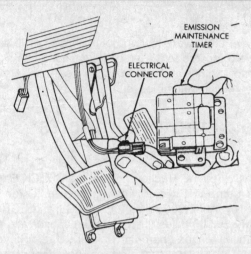

11.6 A typical emissions indicator light timer on a Jeep Wrangler, located near the accelerator pedal

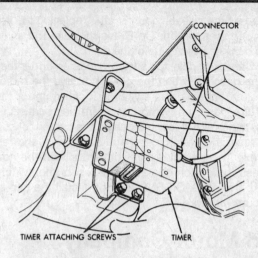

11.7 A typical emissions indicator light timer on a Jeep Cherokee, located to the right of the steering column

1988 and 1989 Jeep

Canadian and 49-State models are equipped with an emission maintenance indicator light on the instrument cluster. This light will come on one time at 82,500 miles to alert you that emission service is required. At this time, the oxygen sensor and PCV valve must be replaced and all other emission components should be inspected and serviced or replaced as necessary.

The indicator timer is located under the dash, near the accelerator pedal or to the right of the steering column (see illustrations). The timer can't be reset. To turn off the light, the timer must be replaced or disconnected. Since the timer and the sensor are interdependent, if the timer prematurely fails, the oxygen sensor should be replaced at the same time to preserve the correct replacement interval. Some models are equipped with a computer malfunction indicator light. If it comes on and remains on while you're driving, the vehicle requires service.

After you've repaired the fault(s) and cleared the fault code(s), the malfunction indicator light should go out. Some

models may use a dual-function indicator light, which is also used to indicate that emission component service is due. After performing the required service, reset the indicator light.

Chrysler imports
Arrow, Colt, Colt Vista, Champ, Challenger, Conquest and Sapporo cars and D 50/Ram 50 and Arrow Pick-ups and Raider

1   On some carbureted models, an EGR or MAINTENANCE REQUIRED warning light in the dash will come on as a reminder to have the EGR system serviced every 50,000 miles and/or the oxygen sensor replaced every 80,000 miles.

2   After servicing or replacing the components, reset the mileage counter. On some models, the reset switch is located on the back of the instrument cluster, near the speedometer cable junction. Slide the switch to the other side to reset the indicator light. On other models, the reset switch is on the lower right-hand corner of the instrument cluster, behind the instrument cluster face trim (see illustration).

Datsun
(See Nissan)

Fiat

1   Fuel-injected models are equipped with an oxygen sensor. After 30,000 miles of operation, a warning light in the dash will come on to indicate that the oxygen sensor must be replaced.

11.8 On some carbureted Mitsubishi models (including those sold by Chrysler under the Dodge or Plymouth name), the mileage counter is at the lower right corner of the instrument cluster

2   To reset the mileage counter after replacing the sensor, locate the reset switch. On Brava models, the switch is located behind the left side of the dash.

3   On Strada models, the switch is located under the center of the dash (between the glove box and the radio). On Spider 2000 models, the switch is located under the left side of the dash, above the accelerator pedal. On X1/9 models, the switch is located behind the center console.

4   To reset the switch, cut the retaining wire and remove the screw. Insert a small screwdriver through the housing and press the switch contact. This resets the switch and turns out the EX GAS SENSOR light. Install the cap screw and secure with wire.

Ford Motor Company

1985 through 1987 light-duty trucks, 1988 non-EEC light-duty trucks and 1989 heavy-duty trucks

These vehicles use a maintenance reminder light to indicate emission system maintenance is required. The control unit (timer) for the maintenance light is located under the dash near the steering column or behind the glove box. The control unit may be hidden behind a bracket on some models. The maintenance light is triggered after 2000 key starts (about 60,000 miles). After servicing the emission system, reset the light on models with a resettable timer.

1   Turn off the ignition. Remove the tape from the reset hole in the timer. Lightly push a small Phillips screwdriver into the hole in the timer marked RESET and turn the ignition switch to the RUN position.

2   The light should stay on while the screwdriver is pressed down. Hold down the screwdriver for about five seconds. Remove the screwdriver. The light should go out within two to five seconds. If it doesn't, repeat Steps 1 and 2.

3   Cycle the ignition from the OFF to the RUN position. The light should glow for two to five seconds. This verifies that the maintenance reminder light is reset. **Note:** *Some non-EEC models, such as the 1988 2.0L Ranger and 6.1L and 7.0L gasoline trucks use a non-resettable control unit. Replace it with a resettable type.*

General motors

Every 30,000 miles (15,000 for Cadillac), a reminder flag appears in the speedometer face to remind you to service the oxygen sensor.

1980 models (except Cadillac)

Remove the instrument panel trim plate. Remove the instrument cluster lens. Using a pointed tool, apply a light downward pressure on the notches of the flag until it's reset. An alignment mark will appear in the left center of the odometer window when the flag is fully reset.

1980 Cadillac

Remove the lower steering column cover. The sensor reset cable is located to the left of the speedometer cluster. Pull the cable lightly (no more than two lbs. force). Reinstall the lower steering column cover.

General Motors imports

GEO

On 1989 Federal Tracker models, the CHECK ENGINE light (the computer system malfunction indicator light) comes on every 50,000 miles for the PCV and EGR systems, every 80,000 miles for the oxygen sensor and every 100,000 miles for the charcoal canister, to remind you to service and/or replace these system components. After servicing and/or replacing components, reset the CHECK ENGINE light by sliding the cancel switch to its opposite position. The three-wire cancel switch is located on the main wiring harness, behind the instrument panel.

1984 through 1986 Sprint

The SENSOR light will start flashing on the dash at 30,000 mile intervals. This indicates the ECM is in good condition and the oxygen sensor needs to be replaced. To reset the SENSOR light, locate the SENSOR light cancel switch on the right side of the fuse box. Return the cancel switch to the OFF position. Start the engine to verify that the light is now off.

Isuzu

On Isuzu Pick-up and Trooper II models, the oxygen sensor must be replaced every 90,000 miles. When this mileage has elapsed, an O2 indicator light on the dash will come on. To turn off the indicator light on the Trooper II, slide the reset switch (see illustration) on the rear of the instrument cluster. To reset on Pick-up models, you'll need to remove the instrument cluster. Remove the masking tape

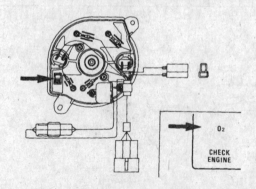

11.9 To turn off the O2 indicator light on an Isuzu Trooper, remove the instrument cluster, locate the reset switch (arrow) on the rear of the instrument cluster and slide the switch to its opposite position

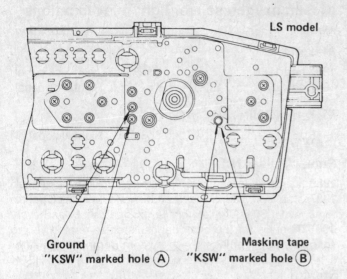

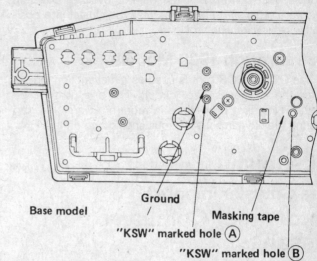

LS model

Ground
"KSW" marked hole (A)

"KSW" marked hole (B)

Masking tape

Base model

Ground

"KSW" marked hole (A)

"KSW" marked hole (B)

Masking tape

11.10 To turnoff the O2 indicator light on an Isuzu Pick-up, remove the instrument cluster, remove the masking tape from hole "B", remove the screw from hole "A" and screw it into hole "B"

from hole "B" **(see illustration)**. Remove the screw from hole "A" and insert it into hole "B".

Jaguar

1   Fuel-injected Jaguars are equipped with an oxygen sensor. When the oxygen sensor warning light comes on at 30,000-mile intervals, replace the sensor.

2   To reset the counter after replacing the sensor, locate the interval counter - it's installed inline with the speedometer cable. Reset the counter using Key (BLT-5007) supplied in the kit with the new sensor.

3   Models with electronic speedometers have a mileage counter in the trunk. The counter is behind the left side trim, next to the wheel well, behind the panel at the rear of the seat. To reset the counter, push the white button.

Mazda

All Federal 1988 and 1989 Pick-ups

1   Besides displaying computer system malfunction codes on California models, the CHECK engine warning light on Federal B2200 and B2600 Pick-ups does double duty as an emission maintenance reminder light. It comes on at 60,000-mile intervals for the EGR system and 80,000-mile intervals for the oxygen sensor.

2   To reset the warning light after servicing the indicated component, locate the brown and white, black and green wires under left side of the dash - they are taped to the wiring harness above the fuse/relay block.

3   At 60,000-mile intervals, unplug the black wire connector from the brown and white wire connector and plug it into the green wire connector. At 80,000-mile intervals, return the black wire connector to the brown and white wire connector.

All Federal 1989 MPVs

1   Besides displaying computer system malfunction codes on California models, the CHECK engine warning light comes on every 80,000 miles to indicate oxygen sensor service is needed.

2   To reset the warning light after servicing the oxygen sensor, remove the instrument cluster. Locate the reset holes labeled "NC and "NO" on the rear of the instrument cluster. Remove the screw from the lettered reset hole and install it in the other hole. After another 80,000 miles, return the screw to the original hole.

Federal B2000 Pick-up

The warning light comes on every 60,000 miles to indicate that it's time to service the EGR system. To reset the warning light after service, locate the black wire and green wire connector under the dash (it's above, and to left of, the fuse box). Unplug the connector and leave it disconnected. The light won't come on again.

Mercedes Benz
1980 through 1985 Models

1   When the OX-SENSOR light comes on at 30,000 miles, you must replace the oxygen sensor and reset the mileage counter.

2   To reset the counter on 280 series vehicles, locate the mileage counter - it's inline with the speedometer cable, under the dash. Unplug the wiring plug from the counter and leave it disconnected. No reset switch is provided.

3   To reset the counter on all other models, you'll have to partially remove the instrument cluster. Insert a hooked steel wire between the right side of the cluster and the dash. Turn the hook to engage the cluster and pull the clus-

ter out of the spring retaining clips. Remove the bulb from the lower corner of the cluster. Press the cluster into position. No reset switch is provided.

1986 through 1989 Models

The O2 SENSOR light is used as a malfunction indicator for the oxygen sensor circuit. There is no mileage counter. No reset procedure is required. Servicing and repairing the oxygen sensor circuit should turn off the light.

Mitsubishi

(See Chrysler imports)

Nissan

CHECK engine light

Some 1988 and 1989 models are equipped with a CHECK engine light. The light comes on when the computer control unit senses a system malfunction. It will reset itself only when the system is repaired.

Oxygen sensor warning light

1   After 30,000 miles of operation, the oxygen sensor light in the dash will come on to indicate that oxygen sensor should be inspected. If the sensor is faulty, it must be replaced.

2   After the sensor has been inspected and/or replaced, turn off the warning light. Most models use a wire harness connector which, when disconnected, turns off the light.

3   Some 1985 through 1987 Nissan models use a reset relay located behind the left or right kick panel or the glove box, under the center console or a seat. To reset the relay, go to Step 6.

4   On 1985 and 1986 Federal Pick-ups, disconnect the yellow and white harness at 50,000 miles, and the yellow and black harness at 100,000 miles. On 1985 and 1986 California Pick-ups, disconnect the yellow wire harness at 90,000 miles. The harnesses are located above the hood release cable, under the dash.

5   To locate the single warning light harness connector on models without sensor light relays, seethe accompanying chart showing the location of oxygen sensor light connectors on various models. Unplug connector and leave it unplugged. The reminder light will no longer illuminate.

6   On models with sensor light relays, locate the relay. See the accompanying chart showing the location of the oxygen sensor light relay on various models. To reset the relay, push the reset button on the relay or remove the tape over the reset hole and insert a small screwdriver into the reset hole. Push lightly to reset. Reset the relay at 30,000 and 60,000 miles. At 90,000 miles, locate and disconnect the warning light wire connector. See the accompanying chart showing the location of the oxygen sensor light connector on various models.

Nissan oxygen sensor light relay locations

Model	Location
Maxima	
1985 and 1986	Left kick panel
1987	Right kick panel
Pick-up (California)	
1986	Right kick panel
Pulsar/Pulsar NX	
1986	Right kick panel
1987	Left kick panel
Sentra	
1986 and 1987	Right kick panel
Stanza	
1986 and 1987	Right kick panel
Stanza Wagon	
1986 and 1987	Under right seat
200SX	
1985 1/2 through 1987	Behind grille, left of console
300 ZX	
1986 and 1987	Near glove box

Note: *The 1987 digital dash uses a relay. On the 1987 analog dash, unplug one of three connectors located near glove box at 30,000 mile intervals.*

Nissan oxygen sensor light connector locations

Model	Location
Maxima and Maxima/810	
1980 through 1984	
Yellow and blue wire	Near the hood release
1985 through 1987	
Green-and-red and green-and-white wires	Near the hood release
Pick-up	
1980 through 1984	
Yellow-and-white wire	Near the hood release
Pulsar/Pulsar NX	
1983 through 1986	
Light green-and-black and light green wires or	
Two black-and-white wires	Near the fuse box
1987	
Red-and-black and red-and-blue wires	Above the fuse box

Model	Location

Sentra

1982 and 1983
Green-and-yellow or
green-and-black wire ....Above the fuse box
1984
Light green-and-black and
light green wires ....Near the hood release
1985 and 1986
Light green-and-black wire ....Above the fuse box
1987
Red-and-blue and
red-and-black wires ....Above the fuse box

Stanza

1984 through 1986
Yellow-and-red wire or yellow
and yellow-and-green wires....Behind the left kick panel
1987
Green and brown wires ....Above the fuse box

Stanza Wagon

1986 and 1987
Red-and-yellow or
red-and-blue wire ....Behind the instrument panel

200SX

1980 through 1984
Green-and-white wire ....Under far right side of dash
1985 through 1987
Pink and purple wires ....Behind the fuse box

280ZX

1982 and 1983
Green-and-yellow wire..................Under right side dash

300ZX

1984
White connector......................Behind the left kick panel
1985 and 1986
White connector ....Above the hood release
1987"
Gray-and-red and gray-and-blue
wires or yellow wire ....Above the hood release

* *Digital dash only. On analog dash, at 30,000-mile intervals, unplug one of the three connectors located behind the glove box*

Peugeot

EGR warning light

1   All 1980 604 models are equipped with an EGR warning light which comes on at 12,500-mile intervals. When the light comes on, service the EGR system, then reset the mileage counter.

2   To reset the mileage counter, unbolt the maintenance switch from the inside of the left front wheelwell. Pull down the switch without disconnecting the speedometer cables.
3   Remove the outer and inner covers from the counter and turn the reset button counterclockwise until it reaches the stop point. This resets the counter to zero. Make sure the warning light is out. Replace the covers and reinstall the counter.

Oxygen sensor warning light

1   All 505 models with gasoline engines are equipped with an oxygen sensor warning light which comes on at 30,000-mile intervals. When the warning light comes on, replace the oxygen sensor and reset the mileage counter.
2   To reset the mileage counter, locate the switch below the brake master cylinder and remove the plastic cover and plug. Use a small punch or rod to press the reset button. Replace the plug and cover.

Porsche

All 1980 and later models are equipped with an oxygen sensor. On all models except the 928S with LH-Jetronic fuel injection and the 944, an OXS light comes on at 30,000-mile intervals as a reminder to replace the sensor. (On 928S models with LH-Jetronic and on 944 models, there is no warning light - replace the oxygen sensor every 60,000 miles.) After replacing the sensor, reset the warning light as follows:
1   On 911 models, disconnect the battery negative cable and remove the speedometer. The counter will be visible through the speedometer mounting hole.
2   Use a thick piece of wire or a thin rod to press the white reset button. Push the reset button all the way in against its stop. Make sure the warning light is out.
3   On 924 models, after replacing the oxygen sensor, and with the vehicle still raised, locate the mileage counter on the left engine mount and use a thick wire or thin metal rod to push in the reset button. Be sure to push the button in all the way to the stop. Make sure the OXS light is out.
4   On 928 and 928S models with CIS fuel injection, the counter is located at the right of the passenger's seat floor. Remove the counter cover retaining screw and cover. Press the reset button all the way in against the stop. Make sure the warning light is out.

Renault

1   On models equipped with an oxygen sensor, a dash-mounted warning light comes on at 30,000-mile intervals as a reminder to replace the sensor.
2   To reset the mileage counter after replacing the sensor, locate the counter inline with the speedometer cable. Cut the retaining wires and remove the cover by disengaging the clips.
3   Turn the reset button 1/4-turn counterclockwise towards the "O" mark to reset the counter. Make sure the OXYGEN SENSOR light is out. Replace the cover and secure it with new wires.

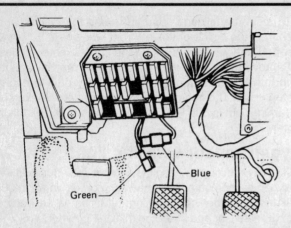

11.11 To reset the EGR warning light on 1985 through 1987 Subaru models with the 1.8L engine, remove the cover from underneath the left side of the dash, pull down the connectors from behind the fuse panel, unplug the blue connector and plug it into the green connector (1985 Subaru shown)

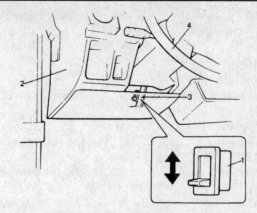

11.12 To reset the cancel switch on a Suzuki Samurai, locate the switch under the dash near the steering column, and flip the switch to its opposite position

1   *Cancel switch*   3   *Steering column mounting bracket*
2   *Dash*   4   *Steering wheel*

Saab

1   All 1980 and later models use an oxygen sensor. On all models except 1985 through 1987 Turbo models, the EXH maintenance light on the dash comes on every 30,000 miles. The oxygen sensor should be replaced at this time. The above-mentioned turbo models don't use an EXH maintenance light. On these models, replace the oxygen sensor every 60,000 miles.

2   To reset the mileage counter for the EXH light, press the reset button on the mileage counter. The counter is located under the instrument cluster, next to the flasher relay. Reach under the knee panel, find the counter and press the reset button.

Subaru

On 1985 through 1987 models with a 1.8L engine, an EGR warning light will turn on. To reset the light after servicing the EGR system, remove the left cover under the instrument panel. Pull down the connectors behind the fuse panel **(see illustration)**. Unplug the connector from the blue connector and plug it into the green connector.

Suzuki

1   On Samurai models, a SENSOR light will start flashing every 60,000 miles. The light will only flash with a warm engine at 1500 to 2000 RPM, indicating the ECM is in good condition and the oxygen sensor needs replacement.

2   When all emission system service procedures have been completed, locate the SENSOR light cancel switch under the dash, near the steering column **(see illustration)** and flip the switch to its opposite position. Start the engine and drive the vehicle to verify that the light doesn't flash.

Toyota

1   All 1980 Celica (six-cylinder), Supra and Cressida models and all 1981 models with gasoline engines (except Starlet models) are equipped with an oxygen sensor. At 30,000-mile intervals, a mileage counter activates a warning light on the dash. The oxygen sensor must be serviced at this time. After servicing the sensor, reset the warning light.

2   To reset the warning light, remove the white cancel switch **(see illustration)** from the top of the left kick panel,

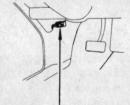

Oxygen Sensor Maintenance Warning Light
Cancel Switch

11.13 The cancel switch for the oxygen sensor warning light is located behind the left kick panel on most 1980 and 1981 Toyota models (on Cressida models, it's behind the small panel next to the steering column; on Celica Supra models, it's on the bracket above the brake pedal)

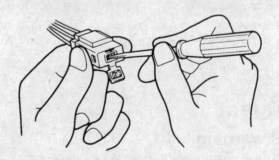

11.14 To reset the cancel switch on 1980 and 1981 Toyotas, open the switch cover and move the switch to its opposite position with a small screwdriver

except on Cressida and 1980 Celica Supra models. On Cressida models, remove the small panel next to the steering column. On the 1980 Celica Supra, the black cancel switch is located on the bracket above the brake pedal.

3　On all models, open the switch cover and move the switch to the opposite position **(see illustration)**.

Triumph

1　All fuel-injected models are equipped with an oxygen sensor. When the light on the dash comes on at 30,000-mile intervals, replace the oxygen sensor.

2　After replacing the sensor, locate the interval counter inline with the speedometer cable. Reset the counter with the key (BLT-5007) supplied in the kit with the new sensor.

Volkswagen

EGR maintenance light

Check EGR system operation when the EGR light comes on every 15,000 miles. After checking the system, reset the mileage counter (see below).

Oxygen sensor warning light

Replace the oxygen sensor when the OXS light comes on at 30,000 miles. After the new sensor is installed, reset the mileage counter (see below).

Resetting the mileage counter

1　On some Rabbit and Pick-up models, remove the instrument cluster cover plate. Using a hooked rod, reach into the opening at the upper left corner by the speedometer and pull the release arm to reset the counter. The left arm resets the EGR, the right arm resets the oxygen sensor.

2　On Vanagon models, locate the mileage counter under the spare tire or under the driver's floorboard inline with the speedometer cable. Using a pointed instrument, depress the reset button. Make sure the light is out.

3　On all other models, locate the mileage counter on the

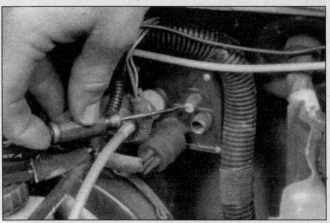

11.15 On most 1980 through 1984 VW models (except Vanagons), you'll find the mileage counter on the firewall, inline with the speedometer cable - to reset it, simply push in the oxygen sensor reset button (1980 VW Pick-up shown)

firewall, inline with the speedometer cable, and push the white reset button **(see illustration)**. Make sure the light is out.

Volvo

1　On 1980 through 1985 models (and 1986 760 GLE models) equipped with an oxygen sensor system, a warning light in the dash will come on every 30,000 miles as a reminder to replace the sensor.

2　To reset the warning light after replacing sensor on 1980 through 1984 models, locate the mileage counter inline with the speedometer cable. Press the reset button. Make sure the reminder light is out.

3　On 1985 models and 1986 760 GLE models, locate the unit under the dash (follow the wires or the small cable from the back of the speedometer to the unit). Remove the retaining screw and switch cover. Press the reset button. Make sure the reminder light is out. Install the switch cover.

4　On 1986 models (except 760 GLE) and 1987 and 1989 models, there's no warning light for oxygen sensor service intervals.

12 Can you modify an emissions-controlled vehicle?

Basically, yes!, so long as you leave all emissions systems intact and the EPA (or, if you live in California, the California Air Resources Board [CARB]) has certified all the components you're planning to install. **Note:** *The components must be certified for use* on your particular *vehicle. Also, nothing you do on the vehicle* can *be considered "tampering. "*

What is tampering?

EPA regulations and many state laws prohibit tampering with the emissions components originally installed on the vehicle. They also prohibit replacing an emissions-related component with a non-original component, unless that component has been specifically certified for use on the vehicle. "Emissions-related" components are any components that have an effect on emissions. Although their primary function is not emissions control, authorities consider many engine, fuel and exhaust system components to be emissions related. These include camshafts, intake and exhaust manifolds, air cleaners and carburetors or fuel-injection systems. Even aftermarket replacement computer chips must be certified for use in the vehicle.

Tampering with emissions system components (for example, removing an air pump, disconnecting an EGR vacuum hose or even replacing an air cleaner with an aftermarket unit that doesn't have the original emissions provisions) is not only illegal, it can decrease your engine's performance. Vehicles designed for operation with emissions control devices often run better when the systems are hooked up and working properly. This is particularly true of newer, computer-controlled vehicles in which the computer uses information from the emissions systems to control the engine's operation.

Since most smog inspections involve a visual inspection as well as exhaust gas analysis, you'll be caught if you tamper with your emissions systems or emissions-related components. And there's usually no limit on how much you have to spend to correct components that have been tampered with; you'll have to put everything back the way it was, regardless of cost, or you won't get registered.

And don't figure you can fool the inspectors. They have on-line information or books that tell what equipment must be installed on the vehicle, and inspectors are usually pretty good at spotting non-original equipment, such as a non-certified high-performance carburetor.

Don't fall into the trap of figuring you can change a camshaft without worry, since it's inside the engine and won't be found on a visual inspection. Many long-duration camshafts cause the engine to emit excessive pollutants at idle. You may pass the visual inspection, but you might fail the exhaust analysis. Considering the amount of work and expense involved in replacing a camshaft, it pays to make sure it is certified for use in your vehicle.

What modifications can you make?

Aftermarket equipment

Many aftermarket manufacturers offer equipment that is designed for use on emission-controlled vehicles. These components include carburetors, intake manifolds, exhaust headers and camshafts **(see illustrations)**. Avoid components that are for racing use only. These often say "for off-highway use only" or "not for use in pollution-controlled vehicles" in their product literature. If you doubt any piece of equipment, check with the manufacturer to see if the component is EPA or CARB certified.

12.1 This Holley high-performance carburetor is certified for use on many Chevrolets through the mid 1970's - certified replacement carburetors like this are available for many earlier models that don't have a computer

12.2 If your vehicle is equipped with EGR, make sure the certified aftermarket intake manifold you select has a mounting point for the EGR valve (arrow)

12.3 Computer-controlled ignition systems like this one can give a slight increase in performance and fuel economy to vehicles that don't already have a computer - check to be sure they're certified for use on your vehicle

Engine swaps

Most states permit swapping similar engines. However, If you are planning to swap an engine into your vehicle from a different year vehicle, check the laws in your state to determine whether the emissions requirements apply to the vehicle or the engine. For example, if you have an older vehicle and are swapping in a newer engine, you may only be required to meet the emissions standards the vehicle has always had to meet. But, in some states, you may be required to meet new, possibly tougher, standards based on the emissions controls the vehicle from which the engine is coming originally had installed on it.

Conversely, installing an older engine in a newer vehicle does not necessarily mean your emissions requirements will be lenient. In fact, you'll often be required to update the older engine with the same level of emissions equipment originally installed on the newer vehicle.

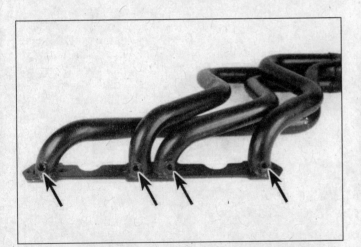

12.4 If you have an air injection system on your vehicle and the injection tubes are threaded into the exhaust manifold, make sure the certified exhaust headers you select have provisions for mounting the tubes in the same place (arrows), and . . .

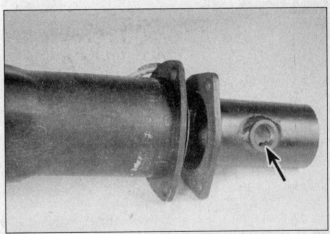

12.5 . . . if your vehicle is equipped with an oxygen sensor, be sure to use a collector on the end of the header that has a mounting hole for the sensor (arrow)

2 Troubleshooting

A malfunctioning emissions control component or system can cause a variety of problems, ranging from obvious symptoms like excessive noise, engine overheating, backfiring and visible exhaust smoke to problems that are harder to track down, such as an occasional fuel smell, poor driveability or decreased fuel mileage. On the other hand, sometimes the only symptom will be a failed emissions test.

This Chapter provides a reference guide to the more common problems which may occur during the operation of your vehicle. The first part of this Chapter deals with symptom-based diagnosis, which applies to vehicles equipped with computer-controlled fuel and emissions control systems as well as older, pre-computer vehicles. Under each symptom is a list of possible causes, with references to the appropriate Chapter and Section which will cover the system or component more thoroughly.

The second part of this Chapter deals exclusively with vehicles having computer-controlled fuel and emissions control systems.

Most vehicles falling into this category have the ability to store "trouble codes" within the memory of their computers when a problem with the fuel or emissions control system occurs. On most vehicles these codes can be retrieved and, while they can't indicate the exact problem, they can direct you to the malfunctioning circuit or system, which will reduce your diagnosis time. If the vehicle you are working on is equipped with a computer-controlled fuel and emissions system, consult this part first to see if any trouble codes are stored. If so, refer to the indicated Chapter and Section that covers that particular system or component for a more complete diagnosis procedure. If there aren't any stored trouble codes, then refer to the symptom-based diagnosis.

Take note that in certain instances when a problem arises in the fuel or emissions control system of a computer-controlled vehicle, no code will be stored. And, under some circumstances, a code may set with no noticeable driveability symptom.

1 Symptom-based troubleshooting

Note: *The causes listed here are primarily related to the emissions and engine management systems. For other possible causes of the listed symptoms, refer to the Haynes Automotive Repair Manual for your specific vehicle.*

1 Engine noise

Grinding or rumbling - Air injection pump defective (see Chapter 3, Section 4)

Groaning - leak in Air injection system (see Chapter 3, Section 4)

Clatter - heat control valve defective (see Chapter 3, Section 5)

Hiss - vacuum leaks (see Chapter 1, Section 8)

2 Engine cranks but won't start

Carbon (charcoal) canister full of fuel (see Chapter 3, Section 2)

Faulty MAP, MAF or coolant sensor or circuit (see Chapter 3, Section 8)

EGR valve stuck open (see Chapter 3, Section 1)

Faulty canister vent valve (see Chapter 3, Section 2)

Incorrect fuel pressure

3 Engine cranks but is hard to start

Dirty air filter

PCV valve stuck open (see Chapter 3, Section 3)

Vacuum leak (see Chapter 1, Section 8)

Faulty carburetor bowl vent valve causing flooding (see Chapter 3, Section 2)

Defective coolant sensor or circuit (see Chapter 3, Section 8)

Defective air temperature sensor or circuit (see Chapter 3, Section 8)

Defective MAF sensor or circuit (see Chapter 3, Section 8)

Defective MAP sensor or circuit (see Chapter 3, Section 8)

Faulty TPS or circuit (see Chapter 3, Section 8)

Cold engine: Malfunctioning choke (carbureted models) or fuel injection system

4 Engine starts but won't run

Faulty canister vent valve (see Chapter 3, Section 2)

EGR valve stuck open (see Chapter 3, Section 1)

5 High oil consumption

PCV valve clogged or stuck open (see Chapter 3, Section 3)

6 Rough idle

Clogged air filter

Incorrect ignition timing

Dirty throttle plate or throttle bore (fuel-injected vehicles)

Minimum idle speed adjustment out of specification (fuel-injected vehicles) (refer to the VECI label under the hood)

EGR valve stuck open or leaking (see Chapter 3, Section 1)

Vacuum leak (see Chapter 1, Section 8)

PCV valve stuck open or closed (see Chapter 3, Section 3)

Cold engine:

Heat control valve stuck open (see Chapter 3, Section 5)

EFE heater inoperative (see Chapter 3, Section 5)

Warm engine:

Heat control valve stuck closed (see Chapter 3, Section 5)

Power to EFE heater after engine has warmed up (see Chapter 3, Section 5)

TPS or circuit malfunctioning or out of adjustment (see Chapter 3, Section 8)

MAF sensor or circuit out of adjustment or malfunctioning (see Chapter 3, Section 8)

7 Hesitation or stumble on acceleration

Accelerator pump in carburetor defective

Faulty TPS or circuit (see Chapter 3, Section 8)

Malfunctioning air temperature sensor or circuit (see Chapter 3, Section 8)

MAP sensor or circuit faulty (see Chapter 3, Section 8)

Leak in air intake duct or faulty MAF sensor or circuit (see Chapter 3, Section 8)

Ignition timing incorrect

Dirty throttle plate or throttle bore (fuel-injected vehicles)

8 Sluggish performance

Restricted exhaust system (most likely the catalytic converter) (see Chapter 3, Section 7)

Vacuum leak (see Chapter 1, Section 8)

EGR valve stuck open (see Chapter 3, Section 1)

EFE heater inoperative (cold engine) or restricted (see Chapter3, Section 5)

Heat control valve stuck open (during cold engine operation) (see Chapter 3, Section 5)

Heat control valve stuck shut (during warm engine operation) (see Chapter 3, Section 5)

Incorrect ignition timing

Low or uneven cylinder compression pressures

Choke plate not opening fully

MAP sensor or circuit malfunctioning (see Chapter 3, Section 8)

9 Stalls on deceleration or when coming to a quick stop

EGR valve stuck open (see Chapter 3, Section 1)
Leak at base of EGR valve (see Chapter 3, Section 1)
Idle speed too low
TPS misadjusted or defective (see Chapter 3, Section 8)
Idle Speed Control or Electronic Air Control Valve
    misadjusted or malfunctioning (see Chapter 3, Section 8)

10 Surging at steady speed

Dirty air filter
Vacuum leak (see Chapter 1, Section 8)
Carburetor bowl vent valve stuck open (see Chapter 3,
    Section 2)
EGR valve stuck or leakage around base (see Chapter 3,
    Section 1)
Problem with oxygen sensor or circuit (see Chapter 3,
    Section 8)
Misadjusted or defective TPS or circuit (see Chapter 3,
    Section 8)
Defective Mass Air Flow (MAF) sensor or circuit (see
    Chapter 3, Section 8)
Defective MAP sensor or circuit (see Chapter 3, Section 8)
Misadjusted or malfunctioning mixture control solenoid in
    carburetor (General Motors carbureted models with
    computer control [see Chapter 3, Section 6])
Fuel pressure incorrect (fuel-injected vehicles)
Defective Vehicle speed sensor or circuit (see Chapter 3,
    Section 8)
Torque Converter Clutch (TCC) engaging/disengaging (see
    Chapter 3, Section 8)

11 Engine diesels (runs on) when shut-off or idles too fast

Vacuum leak (see Chapter 1, Section 8)
EGR valve stuck closed, causing overheating (see
    Chapter 3, Section 1)
Heat control valve stuck closed (see Chapter 3, Section 5)
Idle speed too high - check for correct minimum idle speed
    (fuel-injected vehicles [refer to the VECI label under the
    hood]),
Idle Speed Control (ISC) motor or solenoid (see
    Chapter 3, Section 8) or fuel cutoff solenoid (carbureted
    models [see Chapter 3, Section 6])
Excessive engine operating temperature

12 Backfiring (through the intake or exhaust)

Vacuum leak in the PCV or canister purge line
    (see Chapter 1, Section 8 and Chapter 3, Sections 2 or 3)

Faulty air injection valve (see Chapter 3, Section 4)
Incorrect ignition timing

13 Poor fuel economy

Dirty air filter
EFE heater inoperative (see Chapter 3, Section 5)
Heat control valve stuck open or closed (see Chapter 3,
    Section 5)
PCV problem - valve stuck open or closed, or dirty PCV
    filter (see Chapter 3, Section 3)
Carburetor bowl vent valve stuck open, or faulty canister
    purge valve (see Chapter 3, Section 2)
Heated air intake flap stuck shut (see Chapter 3, Section 5)
Defective oxygen sensor (see Chapter 3, Section 8)

14 Pinging (spark knock)

Ignition timing incorrect
Heated air intake flap stuck closed (engine warm)
    (see Chapter 3, Section 5)
Bi-metal sensor in air cleaner housing malfunctioning
    (engine warm) (see Chapter 3, Section 5)
Power to EFE heater when the engine is warm (see
    Chapter 3, Section 5)
EGR valve inoperative (see Chapter 3, Section 1)

15 Engine runs hot

Heated air intake flap stuck closed (see Chapter 3,
    Section 5)
Bi-metal sensor in air cleaner housing malfunctioning
    (engine warm) (see Chapter 3, Section 5)
Power to EFE heater when the engine is warm (see
    Chapter 3, Section 5)
EGR valve inoperative or restricted EGR passage (see
    Chapter 3, Section 1)

16 Exhaust smoke

Black (overly rich fuel mixture) - Dirty air filter or restricted
    intake duct
Blue (burning oil) - PCV valve stuck open or PCV filter dirty
    (see Chapter 3, Section 3)

17 Fuel smell

Fuel tank overfilled
Leaking canister (see Chapter 3, Section 2)
Fuel vapor line or return line leaking or disconnected (see
    Chapter 3, Section 2)
Fuel feed line leaking

2 General information

When diagnosing problems on engines controlled by computer systems, remember that many driveability symptoms and/or problems may not necessarily be caused by the computer. The computer is only responding to the input (or change of input information) of the many sensors controlled by the fundamental systems previously discussed in this Book. Unless all of the basic engine systems are properly functioning, the electronic controls have inaccurate information to manage the engine fuel and emissions systems properly.

Condemning a computer, input sensor or output actuator, before verifying that the fundamental systems are operating correctly usually leads to an incorrect diagnosis. Besides wasting your time, you'll find that the electronic components of engine management systems are generally expensive and usually not returnable, even if a mistake has been made in diagnosis.

Before proceeding to the electronic control system tests make the following general checks:

1   The engine is in good overall mechanical condition, as indicated by compression and vacuum tests.
2   The battery is clean and free of connection corrosion, in good condition and fully charged.
3   The starting and charging systems operate properly.
4   All fuses and fusible links are intact.
5   All electrical connectors are free of corrosion and connected securely.
6   All vacuum lines are in good condition, correctly routed, and attached securely.
7   The air and fuel supply systems are free of restrictions and working properly.
8   The PCV, EGR and EVAP and other emissions systems are working properly and maintained as required.
9   The coolant level and condition is good, and the thermostat is in place and is of the correct operating temperature.
10   The engine oil level and condition are good.
11   The ignition system is in good condition with no signs of cross-firing, mis-firing, carbon tracks, corrosion, or wear.
12   The base timing and idle speed are set to specifications found on the VECI label.
13   The computer is going into closed loop operation.

Note: *If in doubt about the condition of any of these items, refer to the appropriate Sections of Chapter 8 and recheck the component(s) or systems in question.*

On-board computer systems not only control the engine fuel, ignition and emission functions in an attempt to achieve optimum efficiency, but on most systems they also have a built-in diagnostic feature. When the computer detects a fault, it stores a **trouble code** in its memory. The code can usually be retrieved from the computer's memory by following a certain procedure. A trouble code doesn't necessarily indicate the exact cause of a problem, but it will direct you to a particular component, circuit or system, which may simplify diagnosis.

While it may not be possible for the home mechanic to repair all of these faults, the codes can allow you to be better informed when explaining a problem to a mechanic, if the need arises.

Operating modes

If, after all the basic troubleshooting procedures have been performed, the tune-up meets specifications, and the driveability problem still exists, it is time to look more closely at the computer/engine management systems.

Computer controlled engine management takes place in two modes, "open-loop" and "closed-loop". The computer must be able to get from "open-loop" to "closed-loop" operation, in order to properly monitor and control the engine management systems.

Open-loop is the operating mode of the system when the vehicle is first started and the engine and the oxygen sensor are warming up. Until all the required criteria are met, such as time and temperature, the computer will remain in "open-loop". This means that all computer controlled functions will stay "fixed" at the manufacturers predetermined default settings. **Note:** *These default settings may also be used in the event of a component failure. They allow the vehicle to run, although poorly, in the "limp-in" mode until repairs can be made.*

Although previously discussed, closed-loop is the normal operating mode of a warmed-up engine and an oxygen sensor warm enough to generate a working signal to the computer (the system also waits a predetermined amount of time before going into closed-loop even if the engine and oxygen sensor are already at operating temperature).

On some vehicles, a few minutes at idle can cause the oxygen sensor to cool enough to allow the system to return to open-loop; on these vehicles, the system may even switch back and forth as the oxygen sensor temperature rises and falls.

Retrieving codes

There are a variety of methods of trouble code retrieval, depending on the manufacturer. Most systems work in conjunction with a light on the dash which illuminates when a fault is detected and a code is stored. The light is marked - "CHECK ENGINE", "POWER LOSS", "SERVICE ENGINE SOON" - or something similar, and is used to blink the codes stored in the computer when manually triggered through the diagnostic connector, if the vehicles computer allows access to trouble codes in this manner.

On other models, the code can be accessed by connecting a voltmeter to the diagnostic connector and counting the needle sweeps or in an LED readout on the computer itself.

Each manufacturer's procedure for retrieving and clearing trouble codes is described at the beginning of the following tables.

Once the codes are retrieved, check them against the chart for your vehicle. **Caution:** *Because engine management* systems may differ by year and model, certain trouble codes indicate different problems, depending on the vehicle being repaired. Since this is the case, it would be a good idea to consult your dealer or other qualified repair shop before replacing any electrical component, as they are usually expensive and can't be returned once they are purchased.

Some models require a special diagnostic scanner or tool to retrieve the codes. These scanners are easy to use to gather information, and are relatively inexpensive (see Chapter 5).

Note 1: *When the battery is disconnected, vehicle computer and memory systems may lose memory data. Driveability problems may exist until the computer systems have completed a relearn cycle.*

Note 2: *If the stereo in your vehicle is equipped with an anti-theft system, make sure you have the correct activation code before disconnecting the battery.*

OBD II systems

For some years there has been a gradual process of making and enforcing a "universal" set of computer codes that would be applied by all auto manufacturers to their self-diagnostics. One of the first automotive applications of computers was self-diagnosis of system and component failures. While early on-board diagnostic computers simply lit a "CHECK ENGINE" light on the dash, present systems must monitor complex interactive emission control systems, and provide enough data to the technician to successfully isolate a malfunction.

The computer's role in self-diagnosing emission control problems has become so important that such computers are now required by Federal law. The requirements of the "first generation" system, nicknamed OBD I for On-Board Diagnostics, have been incorporated into 1993 through 1995 models. The purpose of On Board Diagnostics (OBD) is to ensure that emission related components and systems are functioning properly to reduce emission levels of several pollutants emitted by auto and truck engines. The first step is to detect that a malfunction has occurred which may cause increased emissions. The next step is for the system to notify the driver so that the vehicle can be serviced. The final step is to store enough information about the malfunction so that it can be identified and repaired.

The latest step has been the establishment of the OBD II system, which further defines emissions performance, and also regulates the code numbers and definitions.

The basic OBD II code is a letter followed by a four-digit number. Most manufacturers also have many additional codes that are *specific* to their vehicles. Although many of the self-diagnostic tests performed by early OBD systems are retained in OBD II systems, they are now more sensitive in detecting malfunctions. Where there may have been only one code for an oxygen sensor malfunction, there are now six codes that narrow down where the performance discrepancy is. OBD II systems perform many additional tests in areas not required under the earlier OBD. These include monitoring for engine misfires and detecting deterioration of the catalytic converter.

OBD II systems started appearing on a few models in 1994, a few more in 1995 and almost all models in 1996. At first, a very expensive scan tool was required to read the codes. Now, however, the aftermarket has come up with inexpensive scan tools for the home mechanic to use (see Chapter 5). For most OBD II vehicles, the scan tool is the only way to extract and clear trouble codes. For some OBD II vehicles, however, the manufacturer has kept the "count-the-blinks" method of using the Malfunction Indicator Light (MIL) or Check Engine Light, in addition to the mandated five-character scanner codes, so these vehicles can still be diagnosed by the do-it-yourself mechanic. However, the blinking light codes will not give the detailed information now available from the mandated Federal OBD II codes. **Note:** *To determine if your vehicle is OBD II or not, look at the VECI (Vehicle Emission Control Information) decal on the top of the radiator fan shroud. If it's OBD II, the decal will indicate "OBD II certified".*

Retrieving codes on OBD-II systems

Besides a standardized set of diagnostic trouble codes, the Federal government's OBD-II program mandates a standard 16-pin diagnostic link connector (DLC) for all vehicles. The DLC is also referred to as a J1962 connector (a designation taken from the physical and electrical specification number assigned by the SAE). Besides its standard pin configuration, the J1962 must also provide power and ground circuits for scan tool hook-up. The SAE has also recommended locating the DLC or J1962 connector under the driver's end of the dash. At the time of publication, this is a recommendation, not a requirement. Most - but not all - manufacturers are complying with this recommendation. If you can't find the DLC on your vehicle, refer to your owner's manual.

Now that all new vehicles have a standardized connector and a universal set of diagnostic trouble codes, the same scan tool can be used on any vehicle, and any home mechanic can access these codes with a relatively affordable generic scan tool.

All aftermarket generic scan tools include good documentation, so refer to the manufacturer's hook-up instructions in your scan tool manual. Before plugging a scan tool into the DLC, inspect the condition of the DLC housing; make sure that all the wires are connected and that the contacts are fully seated in the housing. Inside the connector, make sure that there's no corrosion on the pins and that no pins are bent or damaged.

Trouble codes by manufacturer

Beginning on the next page are procedures for extracting trouble codes from specific vehicle types. Refer to Chapter 6 for lists of the actual trouble codes.

Refer to Chapter 6 for a list of trouble codes

3 Trouble code retrieval

Acura

Retrieving codes

The Engine Control Unit (ECU) stores the codes which are accessed by reading the flashing Light Emitting Diode (LED) on the unit (early models) or the CHECK ENGINE light on the dash (later models). (If the ECU has two LED's, the red one is for codes.) On OBD-II models, the Check Engine light is referred to as a Malfunction Indicator Light (MIL). The ECU on 1990 and earlier Legend sedans and Integra models through 1989 is located under the front passenger seat (see illustration). On Legend coupes, 1991 and later Legend sedans, 1990 through 1994 Integras and all Vigor models, the ECU is found under the dashboard on the passenger's side behind the carpet; 1990 Legends incorporate a flip-out mirror so the LED can be seen. On 1995 through 1999 Integra models, the ECM is located behind the right kick panel. On 1997 2.2CL models, 1998 and 1999 2.3CL models, 1995 through 1999 2.5TL models, 1997 through 1999 3.0CL models, 1996 through 1998 3.2TL models and 1996 through 1999 3.5RL models, the ECM (models with a manual transaxle) or PCM (models with an automatic transaxle) is located below the right (passenger side) front footrest. On 1996 through 1999 SLX models and on 1999 3.2TL models, the PCM is located behind the center of the dash, below the radio.

3.1 The ECU on 1990 and earlier Legend sedans and 1989 and earlier Integra models is located under the passenger front seat.

pause between each code. **Note:** *The self-diagnostic system switched to OBD II on some models in 1994, others in 1995, and all are OBD II in 1996, but DTC codes can still be accessed through the malfunction indicator light on the dash.*

1990 and earlier Legend, 1991 and earlier Integra

When the ECU sets a code, the Check Engine light on the dashboard will illuminate. To access the codes, turn the ignition switch On, then count and record the number of times the LED flashes. On 1986 through 1989 models, the light will blink a sequence the sum total representing the code number (for example, 14 short blinks is code 14). On 1990 Legends and 1990 and 1991 Integras, the light will hold a longer blink to represent the first digit of a two-digit number and then will blink short for the second digit (1 long and 8 short blinks is 18). If the system has more than one problem, the codes will be displayed in sequence, pause, then repeat.

1991 and later Legend and all 1992 and later models

To access the codes on these models, locate the two-terminal diagnostic connector. On Legend and Integra models it's located under the right side of the dash, behind the glove box. On Vigor models it's located behind the right side of the center console, under the dash. On all other models, it's located under the left end of the dash. With the ignition On (engine not running), bridge the two terminals of the diagnostic connector with a jumper wire. Any stored codes will be displayed on the CHECK ENGINE light on the dash, in a series of flashes. For example, a code 14 would be indicated by one long flash, a pause, then four short flashes. If more than one code is present, the codes will be displayed in numerical order, with a

Clearing codes

1990 and earlier Legend, 1991 and earlier Integra

To erase the codes after making repairs, remove the Hazard fuse at the battery positive terminal (Integra) or Alternator Sense fuse in the under hood relay box (Legend) for at least ten seconds.

1991 and later Legend and all 1992 and later models

To erase codes after making repair to these models, remove the BACK-UP fuse from the relay box under the hood (Integra, Vigor) or the ACG (fuse no. 15) from the fuse box under the left side of the dash (Legend) for at least 10 seconds. On all other models, erase the codes by removing the ECM fuse from the under-dash fuse/relay panel. On 1995 through 1999 Integra models the fuse/relay panel is located under the left end of the dash. On 1995 through 1999 2.5TL models, the fuse panel is located behind the left end of the dash. On 1997 2.2CL models, 1998 and 1999 2.3CL models and 1997 through 1999 3.0CL models, the fuse/relay panel is located in the left kick panel. On 1996 3.2TL models, the fuse/relay panel is located above the right kick panel. On 1996 through 1999 SLX models, 1997 through 1999 3.2TL models and 1997 through 1999 3.5RL models, the fuse/relay panel is located behind the left kick panel. **Caution:** *If the stereo in your vehicle is equipped with an anti-theft system, make sure you have the correct activation code before removing the fuse.*

Audi

Retrieving codes on pre-OBD-II models

Drive the vehicle for five or more minutes (on turbocharged models, the engine must exceed 3000 rpm and 17psi of boost), and then let it idle. If the vehicle won't start, crank the engine over for at least six seconds and then leave the ignition switch turned to ON. Now, proceed to the instructions below for your specific model. **Note:** *Some models are not included because special (and very expensive) diagnostic tools are needed to access the trouble codes.*

1988 through 1990 models with 1984 cc engine

Note: On these models, you'll need the special Audi tester (part no. US1115) or a suitable equivalent tool, to access the diagnostic trouble codes.

1   On models with a diagnostic connector in the engine compartment (next to the fuel distributor), hook up the special Audi tester (part no. US1115) between the diagnostic connector and the positive battery terminal. (On some models, the diagnostic connector is in the fuse panel, on the fuel pump relay).

2   To display a stored trouble code, install the spare fuse in the top of the fuel pump relay for four seconds. The tester will display the code.

3   Repeat this procedure to access each stored code.

4   To erase the stored code(s), install the spare fuse and leave it in for at least 10 seconds.

1987 and 1988 models with turbocharged 2226 cc engine or 2309 cc engine

Note: On these models, the codes are displayed by a flashing Malfunction Indicator Lamp (MIL).

1   Bridge the test contacts of the diagnostic trigger on the pump relay for four seconds. The MIL will flash the code.

2   Repeat this procedure to access each stored code.

1989 through 1991 models with 2226 cc SOHC turbocharged engine (one knock sensor) or with 2309 cc engine

Note: On non-California versions of these models, you'll need the special Audi tester (part no. US1115) or a suitable equivalent tool, to access the diagnostic trouble codes. On
California models, the codes are also displayed by a flashing Malfunction Indicator Lamp (MIL).

1   Hook up the special Audi tester (part no. US1115) between the positive terminals of the dark-colored and the light-colored diagnostic connectors.

2   Using a jumper wire, bridge the negative terminals of the dark-colored and light-colored connectors for four seconds. The tester will display the code or, on California models, the MIL will flash the code.

3   Repeat this procedure to access each stored code.

1990 and 1991 models with 2226 cc SOHC turbocharged engine (two knock sensors)

Note: On non-California versions of these models, you'll need the special Audi tester (part no. US1115) or a suitable equivalent tool, to access the diagnostic trouble codes. On California models, the codes are also displayed by a flashing Malfunction Indicator Lamp (MIL).

1   Hook up the special Audi tester (part no. US1115) between positive diagnostic terminals 1 and 3.

2   Using a jumper wire, bridge negative terminals 1 and 2. The tester will display the code or, on California models, the MIL will flash the code.

3   Repeat this procedure to access each stored code.

1990 and 1991 models with 3562 cc V8 engine

1   Bridge the upper terminals of diagnostic connectors 1 and 4 with the special Audi tester (part no. US1115).

2   Crank the engine for five seconds, and then leave the ignition switch turned to ON.

3   Using a jumper wire, bridge the lower terminals of diagnostic connectors 1 and 2. The test light or, on California models, the ENGINE light, will flash the code.

4   Repeat the above procedure to access each stored code.

5   After code 0000 has flashed, all stored codes have been displayed.

Refer to Chapter 6 for a list of trouble codes

BMW

The EFI system control unit (computer) has a built-in self-diagnosis system which detects malfunctions in the system sensors and alerts the driver by illuminating a Check Engine warning light in the instrument panel. The computer stores the failure code until the diagnostic system is cleared by removing the negative battery cable for a period of five seconds or longer. The warning light goes out automatically (after five engine starts) when the malfunction is repaired.

Retrieving codes

There are two types of codes accessible on a BMW. The flash codes (listed here) and trouble codes that can be retrieved only with a BMW tester. This manual only addresses codes accessible without using a special BMW tool.

The Check Engine warning light should come on when the ignition switch is placed in the On position. When the engine is started, the warning light should go out. The light will remain on (with the engine running) once the diagnostic system has detected a malfunction or abnormality in the system. In order to read the codes, it is necessary to turn the key to the On position (engine not running), depress the accelerator pedal 5 times (6 times on 12-cylinder models) within 5 seconds (make sure the pedal reaches wide open throttle each time) and wait for any stored codes to be displayed.

The diagnostic code is the number of flashes indicated on the Check Engine light. If any malfunction has been detected, the light will blink the digit(s) of the code. For example on 1988 3-Series models, code 3 (coolant temperature sensor malfunction) will blink three flashes. There will be a pause (3 seconds) and then any other codes that are stored will be flashed. On 1989 and later 3, 5 and 7-Series models, code 1223 (coolant temperature sensor malfunction) will flash the first digit and then pause, flash the second digit (2 flashes) pause, flash the third digit (2 flashes) pause and finally flash the fourth digit (3 flashes). There will be another pause and the computer will start the next stored trouble code (if any) or it will repeat the code 1223. Once all the codes have been displayed, the Check Engine light will remain on. In order to re-check the codes, simply turn the ignition key Off and then back On (repeat procedure) and the codes will be repeated.

The trouble code tables in Chapter 6 indicate the diagnostic code along with the system or component that is affected **Note:** *Diagnostic codes that are not emissions or engine control related (electronic transmission, ABS, etc.) will not be accessed by this system.*

Clearing codes

Caution: *If the stereo in your vehicle is equipped with an anti-theft system, make sure you have the correct activation code before disconnecting the battery.*

After repairs have been made, the diagnostic code can be canceled by disconnecting the negative battery cable for 5 seconds or longer. After cancellation, perform a road test and make sure the warning light does not come on. If desired, the check can be repeated.

Chrysler, Dodge and Plymouth - domestic cars and light trucks

Note: *On the models covered by this manual, the CHECK ENGINE light, located in the instrument panel, flashes on for three seconds as a bulb test when the engine is started. The light comes on and stays on when there's a problem in the EFI system.*

Retrieving codes

Note: *Later models are all equipped with OBD II engine management systems, but Chrysler has continued the use of blinking light codes in addition to the mandated five-character codes accessible only with a scan tool.*

The self diagnosis information contained in the SBEC or SMEC (computer) can be accessed either by the ignition key or by using a special tool called the Diagnostic Readout Box (DRB II). This tool is attached to the diagnostic connector in the engine compartment and reads the codes and parameters on the digital display screen. The tool is expensive and most home mechanics prefer to use the alternate method. The drawback with the ignition method is that it does not access all the available codes for display. Most problems can be solved or diagnosed quite easily and if the information cannot be obtained readily, have the vehicle's self diagnosis system analyzed by a dealer service department or other properly-equipped repair shop.

To obtain the codes using the ignition key method, first set the parking brake and put the transaxle in Park (automatic) or Neutral (manual).

Raise the engine speed to approximately 2500 rpm and slowly let the speed down to idle.

Cycle the air conditioning system, if equipped (on briefly, then off).

If the vehicle is equipped with an automatic transmission, with your foot on the brake, select each position on the transmission (Reverse, Drive, Low etc.) and bring the shifter back to Park. This will allow the computer to obtain any fault codes that might be linked to any of the sensors controlled by the transmission, engine speed or air conditioning system.

To display the codes on the dashboard (POWER LOSS or CHECK ENGINE light), turn the ignition key On, Off, On, Off and finally On (engine not running). The codes will begin to flash. The light will blink the number of the first digit then pause and blink the number of the second digit. For example: Code 23, throttle body temperature sensor circuit, would be indicated by two flashes, then a pause followed by three flashes.

Certain criteria must be met for a fault code to be entered into the engine controller memory. The criteria may be a specific range of engine rpm, engine temperature or input voltage to the engine controller. It is possible that a fault code for a particular monitored circuit may not be entered into the memory despite a malfunction. This may happen because one of the fault code criteria has not been met. For example; The engine must be operating between 750 and 2000 rpm in order to monitor the Map sensor circuit correctly. If the engine speed is raised above 2400 rpm, the MAP sensor output circuit shorts to ground and will not allow a fault code to be entered into the memory. Then again, the exact opposite could occur: A code is entered into the memory that suggests a malfunction within another component that is not monitored by the computer. For example; A fuel pressure problem cannot register a fault directly but instead, it will cause a rich/lean fuel mixture problem. Consequently, this will cause an oxygen sensor malfunction resulting in a stored code in the computer for the oxygen sensor. Be aware of the interrelationship of the sensors and circuits and the overall relationship of the emissions control and fuel injection systems.

The trouble code table in Chapter 6 is a list of the typical trouble codes which may be encountered while diagnosing the system. If the problem persists after these checks have been made, more detailed service procedures will have to be performed by a dealer service department or other qualified repair shop.

Clearing codes

Caution: *If the stereo in your vehicle is equipped with an anti-theft system, make sure you have the correct activation code before disconnecting the battery.*

Trouble codes may be cleared by disconnecting negative battery cable for at least 15 seconds. However, on OBD II models the codes can only be cleared with the use of a scan tool.

Refer to Chapter 6 for a list of trouble codes

Eagle

Summit and Talon (1988 on)
Retrieving codes

Locate the diagnostic connector in or under the glove compartment. On some late-model Summit models, it may be next to the fuse box **(see illustration)**. Connect an analog voltmeter to the upper right (+) and lower left (-) connector terminals. On 1994 and later Summit models, connect the voltmeter (+) to the upper left terminal of the male, 12-pin connector and (-) to either of the upper-middle two of the female connector (on station wagon models, grounding the upper left terminal of the 16-pin connector is all that's necessary). Turn on the ignition On (engine Off) and watch the voltmeter needle. It will display the codes as long or short sweeps of the needle. For example, two long sweeps followed by three short sweeps is code 23. Count the number of long and short needle sweeps and write the codes down for reference. Continuous short pulses indicate that all is normal and there are no codes.

In 1995, some models appeared with OBD II systems, while others still had OBD I systems. Some of these models may not display codes on a voltmeter, but grounding the diagnostic connector should still provide codes through the MIL light on the dash. On all OBD II models from 1995 on, the OBD II codes can only be retrieved using a scan tool.

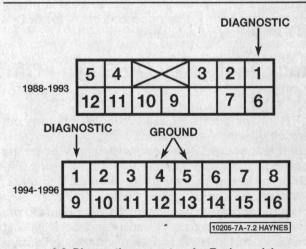

3.2 Diagnostic connectors for Eagle models

Clearing codes

Caution: *If the stereo in your vehicle is equipped with an anti-theft system, make sure you have the correct activation code before disconnecting the battery.*

After making repairs, disconnect the cable from the negative terminal of the battery to erase codes from the computer memory. **Caution:** *If you disconnect the battery from the vehicle to clear the codes, this will erase stored operating parameters from the computer and may cause the engine to run rough for a period of time while the computer relearns the information.*

Premier (1991 and 1992) and Vision (1993 through 1997)

Retrieving codes

Turn the ignition switch On, Off, On, Off, On and watch the flashes of the Power Loss or Check Engine light on the dash. The codes will blink the number of the first digit, then pause and blink the number of the second digit. For example, Code 23 would be 2 blinks, pause, 3 blinks.

Clearing codes

Caution: *If the stereo in your vehicle is equipped with an anti-theft system, make sure you have the correct activation code before disconnecting the battery.*

After making repairs, disconnect the cable from the negative terminal of the battery to erase codes from the computer memory. **Caution:** *If you disconnect the battery from the vehicle to clear the codes, this will erase stored operating parameters from the computer and may cause the engine to run rough for a period of time while the computer relearns the information.*

Refer to Chapter 6 for a list of trouble codes

Ford, Lincoln and Mercury

Retrieving codes

Note: *Trouble codes are not retrievable on models with an EEC-V engine management system (a special scan tool must be used).*

The diagnostic codes for the EEC-IV systems are arranged in such a way that a series of tests must be completed in order to extract ALL the codes from the system. If one portion of the test is performed without the others, there may be a chance the trouble code that will pinpoint a problem in your particular vehicle will remain stored in the PCM without detection. The tests start first with a Key On, Engine Off (KOEO) test followed by a computed timing test then finally a Engine Running (ER) test. Here is a brief overview of the code extracting procedures of the EEC-IV system followed by the actual test:

Quick Test - Key On Engine Off (KOEO)

The following tests are all included with the key on, engine off:

Self test codes - These codes are accessed on the test connector by using a jumper wire and an analog voltmeter or the factory diagnostic tool called the Star tester. These codes are also called Hard Codes.

Separator pulse codes - After the initial Hard Codes, the system will flash a code 11 (separator pulse) (1990 and earlier) or code 111 (1991 and later) and then will flash a series of Soft Codes.

Continuous Memory Codes - These codes indicate a fault that may or may not be present at the time of testing. These codes usually indicate an intermittent failure. Continuous Memory codes are stored in the system and they will flash after the normal Hard Codes. These codes are either two digit (1988 through 1991) or three digit codes (1992 through 1995). These codes can indicate chronic or intermittent problems. Also called Soft Codes.

Engine running codes (ER)

Running tests - These tests make it possible for the PCM to pick-up a diagnostic trouble code that cannot be set while the engine is in KOEO mode. These problems usually occur during driving conditions. Some codes are detected by cold or warm running conditions, some are detected at low rpms or high rpms and some are detected at closed throttle or wide open throttle.

I.D. Pulse codes - These codes indicate the type of engine (4, 6 or 8 cylinder) or the correct module and Self Test mode access.

Computed engine timing test - This engine running test determines base timing for the engine and starts the process of allowing the engine to store running codes.

Wiggle test - This engine running test checks the wiring system to the sensors and output actuators

Cylinder balance test - This engine running test determines injector balance as well as cylinder compression balance. **Note:** *This test should be performed by a dealer service department.*

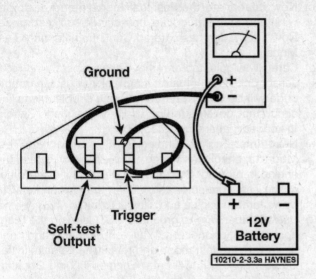

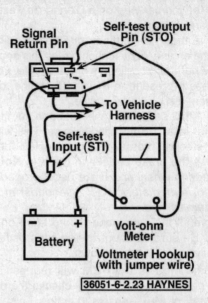

3.3a On 1984 and earlier Ford systems, hook up the volt/ohm meter as shown to read the trouble codes

3.3b To output codes on a Ford with the EEC-IV system, connect a voltmeter as shown and, using a jumper wire, bridge the self-test input connector to the signal return pin (terminal 2)

Position the parking brake ON, Shift lever in PARK (NEUTRAL in manual transmission vehicles), block the drive wheels and turn off all electrical loads (air conditioning, radio, heater fan blower etc.). Make sure the engine is warmed to operating temperatures (if possible).

Perform the **KOEO tests:**

a) Turn the ignition key off for at least 10 seconds.

b) Locate the diagnostic Test connector inside the engine compartment **(see illustrations)**. Install the voltmeter leads onto the battery and pin number 4 (STO) of the test connector. Install a jumper wire from the test terminal to pin number 2 of the Diagnostic Test terminal (STI) **(see illustration)**.

c) Turn the ignition key On (engine not running) and observe the needle sweeps on the voltmeter. For example code 23, the voltmeter will sweep once, pause 1/2 second and sweep again. There will be a two second pause between digits and then there will be three distinct sweeps of the needle to indicate the second digit of the code number. On three digit codes, the sequence is the same except there will be an additional sequence of numbers (sweeps) to indicate the third digit in the code. Additional codes will be separated by a four second pause and then the indicated sweeps on the voltmeter. Be aware that the code sequence may continue into the continuous memory codes (read further). **Note:** *Later models will flash the Check Engine light on the dash in place of the voltmeter.*

Interpreting the continuous memory codes:

After the KOEO codes are reported, there will be a short pause and any stored Continuous Memory codes will appear in order. Remember that the "Separator" code is 11, or 111 on 1992 and later models. The computer will not enter the Continuous Memory mode without flashing the

separator pulse code. The Continuous Memory codes are read the same as the initial codes or "Hard Codes". Record these codes onto a piece of paper and continue the test.

Perform the **Engine Running (ER) tests:**

a) Remove the jumper wires from the Diagnostic Test connector to start the test

b) Run engine until it reaches normal operating temperature

c) Turn the engine OFF for at least 10 seconds

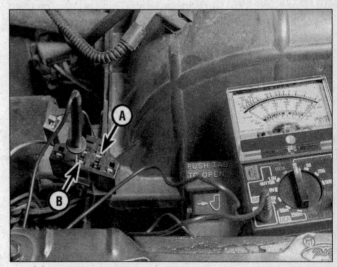

3.3c This is how it looks on a real vehicle - insert a jumper wire from terminal number 2 (A) to self- test input connector, then install the negative probe of the voltmeter into terminal number 4 (B) and position the positive probe to the battery positive terminal

d) Install the jumper wire onto Diagnostic Test connector and start the engine.

e) Observe that the voltmeter or Check Engine light will flash the engine identification code. This code indicates 1/2 the number of cylinders of the engine. For example, 4 flashes represent an 8 cylinder engine, or 3 flashes represent a six cylinder engine.

f) Within 1 to 2 seconds of the I.D. code, turn the steering wheel at least 1/2 turn and release. This will store any power steering pressure switch trouble codes.

g) Depress the brake pedal and release. **Note:** *Perform the steering wheel and brake pedal procedure in succession immediately (1 to 2 seconds) after the I.D. codes are flashed.*

h) Observe all the codes and record them on a piece of paper. Be sure to count the sweeps or flashes very carefully as you jot them down.

On some models the PCM will request a Dynamic Response check. This test quickly checks the operation of the TPS, MAF or MAP sensors in action. This will be indicated by a code 1 or a single sweep of the voltmeter needle (one flash on CHECK ENGINE light). This test will require the operator to simply full throttle ("goose") the accelerator pedal for one second. DO NOT throttle the accelerator pedal unless it is requested.

The next part of this test makes sure the system can advance the timing. This is called the Computed Timing test. After the last ER code has been displayed, the PCM will advance the ignition timing a fixed amount and hold it there for approximately 2 minutes. Use a timing light to check the amount of advance. The computed timing should equal the base timing plus 20 BTDC. The total advance should equal 27 to 33 degrees advance. If the timing is out of specification, have the system checked at a dealer service department.

Finally perform the **Wiggle Test:** (This test can be used to recreate a possible intermittent fault in the harness wiring system.)

a) Use a jumper wire to ground the STI lead on the Diagnostic Test connector.

b) Turn the ignition key On (engine not running).

c) Now deactivate the self test mode (remove jumper wire) and then immediately reactivate self test mode. Now the system has entered Continuous Monitor Test Mode.

d) Carefully wiggle, tap or remove any suspect wiring to a sensor or output actuator. If a problem exists, a trouble code will be stored that indicates a problem with the circuit that governs the particular component. Record the codes that are indicated.

e) Next, enter Engine Running Continuous Monitor Test Mode to check for wiring problems only when the engine is running. Start first by deactivating the Diagnostic Test connector and turning the ignition key Off. Now start the engine and allow it to idle.

f) Use a jumper wire to ground the STI lead on the Diagnostic Test connector. Wait ten seconds and then deactivate the test mode and reactivate it again (install jumper wire). This will enter Engine Running Continuous Monitor Test Mode.

g) Carefully wiggle, tap or remove any suspect wiring to a sensor or output actuator. If a problem exists, a trouble code will be stored that indicates a problem with the circuit that governs the particular component. Record the codes that are indicated.

If necessary, perform the Cylinder Balance Test. This test should be performed by a qualified automotive service department.

Clearing codes

To clear the codes from the PCM memory, start the KOEO self test diagnostic procedure and install the jumper wire into the Diagnostic Test connector. When the codes start to display themselves on the voltmeter or Check Engine light, remove the jumper wire from the Diagnostic Test connector. This will erase any stored codes within the system.

Caution: *Do not disconnect the battery from the vehicle to clear the codes. This will erase stored operating parameters from the KAM (Keep Alive Memory) and cause the engine to run rough for a period of time while the computer relearns the information.*

Refer to Chapter 6 for a list of trouble codes

Ford imports

Aspire (1.3L), Escort/Tracer (1.8L), Probe (2.5L V6) and Villager (3.0L V6)

These models are equipped with a unique Electronic Engine Control (EEC) system, which differs from Ford EEC-IV and EEC-V systems with respect to the diagnostic connectors and the trouble codes.

Aspire (1.3L)
Retrieving codes

Connect a jumper wire from terminal STI to GND (see illustration). Also, connect a voltmeter from the STO terminal and engine ground. With the ignition key ON (engine not running), watch the sweeps of the voltmeter needle. The voltmeter must be analog to see the movement of the needle as it sweeps across the face of the meter. **Note:** *It is also possible to read the trouble codes from the CHECK ENGINE light on the dash. Simply ground the STI and GND terminals with a jumper wire and watch the light on the dash as it flashes the stored trouble code(s).*

Clearing codes

Remove the jumper wire and close the cover on the DIAGNOSTIC electrical connector. Check the indicated system or component or take the vehicle to a dealer service department or other qualified repair shop to have the malfunction repaired. After repairs have been made, the diagnostic code must be canceled by detaching the cable from the negative terminal of the battery, then depressing the brake pedal for more than five seconds. After cancellation, perform a road test and make sure the warning light does not come on. If the original trouble code is repeated, additional repairs are required.

Escort/Tracer (1.8L)
Retrieving codes

Locate the EEC diagnostic or self-test connector located behind the battery in the engine compartment. To read the codes with an analog voltmeter, turn the ignition key to the OFF position, connect the voltmeter positive lead to the EEC STO line and the negative lead to ground. Connect the EEC STI terminal to ground with a jumper wire. Set the voltmeter on a 20-volt scale. To read the codes with the

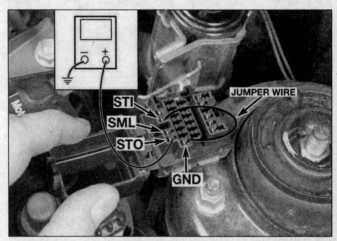

3.3d Diagnostic test connector location and code retrieving terminals (1994 and 1995 Ford Aspire models)

Check Engine light, connect the EEC STI terminal to ground with a jumper wire.

Clearing codes

Disconnect the jumper wire from the STI terminal and ground. Disconnect the negative battery cable. Depress the brake pedal for 5 to 10 seconds.

Probe (2.5L V6)
Retrieving codes

Connect a jumper wire from terminal STI to GND (see illustration). Also, connect a voltmeter from the STO terminal and engine ground. With the ignition key ON (engine not running), watch the sweeps of the voltmeter needle. The voltmeter must be an analog type to see the movement of the needle as it sweeps across the face of the meter. **Note:**

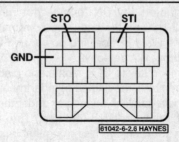

3.3e Diagnostic test connector code retrieving terminals (1993 through 1995 Ford Probe 2.5L V6 models)

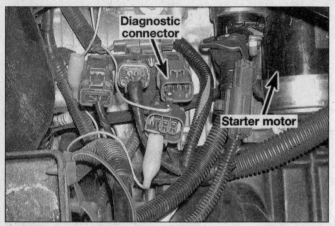

3.3f Engine compartment diagnostic connector location (1993 through 1995 Mercury Villager 3.0L V6 models) (there's another connector under the left end of the dash, but it's only for scan tool use)

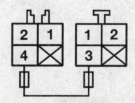

3.3g Diagnostic test connector code retrieving terminals (1993 through 1995 Mercury Villager 3.0L V6 models)

It is also possible to read the trouble codes from the CHECK ENGINE light on the dash. Simply ground the STI and GND terminals with a jumper wire and watch the light on the dash as it flashes the stored trouble code(s).

Make sure the battery voltage is greater than 11 volts, the transaxle is in Neutral, the accessories are off, the throttle valve is closed and the engine is at normal operating temperature, then turn the ignition switch to the ON position but do not start the engine. The computer will begin outputting or flashing the codes.

Clearing codes

Remove the jumper wire and close the cover on the diagnostic connector. Check the indicated system or component or take the vehicle to a dealer service department or other qualified repair shop to have the malfunction repaired. After repairs hayne been made, the diagnostic code must be canceled by detaching the cable from the negative terminal of the battery, then depressing the brake pedal for more than five seconds. After cancellation, perform a road test and make sure the warning light does not come on. If the original trouble code is repeated, additional repairs are required.

Villager (3.0L V6)

Retrieving codes

Turn the ignition key ON (engine not running). The CHECK ENGINE light on the dash should remain ON. This indicates that the PCM is receiving power and the CHECK ENGINE light bulb is not defective.

Turn the ignition key to OFF, locate and disconnect the diagnostic connector in the engine compartment **(see illustration)**. (There is a data link connector under the left end of the dash, but it's only for scan tool use.) Turn the ignition key ON (engine not running). Using a suitable jumper wire bridge the appropriate terminals **(see illustration)**. Wait two seconds and remove the jumper wire, then reconnect the engine compartment diagnostic connector. **Note:** *Failure to follow this procedure exactly as described may erase stored trouble codes from the PCM memory.*

Carefully observe the CHECK ENGINE light/MIL lamp flashes on the instrument cluster. If everything in the self-diagnosis system is functioning properly, the computer will flash a code 55 (OBD-I). The code will be represented by five long flashes on the CHECK ENGINE light/MIL lamp followed by five short flashes. If the computer has actual trouble codes stored, carefully observe the flashes and record the exact number onto paper. For example, code 43 (throttle position sensor or TPS circuit) is indicated by four long flashes followed by three short flashes.

If the ignition key is turned OFF during the code extraction process and possibly turned back ON, the self-diagnostic system will automatically invalidate the procedure. Restart the procedure to extract the codes. **Note:** *The self-diagnostic system cannot be accessed if the engine is running.*

Clearing codes

Turn the ignition key OFF for at least three seconds. Turn the ignition key back ON and disconnect the diagnostic connector. Using a suitable jumper wire bridge the same two terminals you bridged to retrieve the codes. Wait two seconds and remove the jumper wire, then reconnect the diagnostic connector and turn the ignition key OFF. **Caution:** *Do not disconnect the battery from the vehicle to clear the codes. This will erase stored operating parameters from the memory and cause the engine to run rough for a period of time while the computer relearns the information. If necessary, have the codes cleared by a dealer service department or other qualified repair facility.*

Always clear the codes from the PCM before a new electronic emission control component is installed onto the engine. The PCM will often store trouble codes during sensor malfunctions. The PCM will also record new trouble codes if a new sensor is allowed to operate before the parameters from the old sensor have been erased. Clearing the codes will allow the computer to relearn the new operating parameters relayed by the new component. During the computer relearning process, the engine may experience a rough idle or slight driveability changes. This period of time, however, should last no longer than 15 to 20 minutes.

Refer to Chapter 6 for a list of trouble codes

General Motors

Domestic cars and trucks (except Geo, Nova and Sprint)

All models except Cadillac with 4.1L, 4.5L, 4.6L, 4.9L and 6.0L engines and Buick Riviera/Oldsmobile Toronado (1986 through 1992)

Retrieving codes

The Check Engine light on the instrument panel will come on whenever a fault in the system has been detected, indicating that one or more codes pertaining to this fault are set in the Electronic Control Module (ECM). To retrieve the codes, you must use a short jumper wire to ground a diagnostic terminal. This terminal is part of an electrical connector known as the Assembly Line Diagnostic Link (ALDL) **(see illustrations)**. On most models the ALDL is located under the dashboard on the driver's side. If the ALDL has a cover, slide it toward you to remove it. Push one end of the jumper wire into the ALDL diagnostic terminal (B) and the other into the ground terminal (A), except on certain later models **(see illustration 3.4b)**. **Caution:** *Don't crank the engine with the diagnostic terminal grounded - the ECM could be damaged.*

When the diagnostic terminal is grounded with the ignition On and the engine stopped, the system will enter Diagnostic Mode and the Check Engine (or Service Engine Soon) light will display a Code 12 (one flash, pause, two flashes). The code will flash three times, display any stored codes, then flash three more times, continuing until the jumper is removed.

The new government-mandated OBD II diagnostic system was initially used on some GM models starting in 1994. Some other models switched in 1995, and all models use this system in 1996. This system uses five-character codes which can only be accessed with an expensive scan tool. To know if your model has the OBD II system, look at the VECI emission label on the radiator fan shroud. If it is OBD II, it should say "OBD II certified" somewhere on the decal.

Clearing codes

After checking the system, clear the codes from the ECM memory by interrupting battery power. Turn off the ignition switch (otherwise the expensive ECM will be damaged) disconnect the negative battery cable for at least 30 seconds, then reconnect it. **Caution:** *If you have an anti-theft radio, make sure you know the activation code before disconnecting the battery. An alternative method of clearing the codes is to disconnect the ECM's fuse from the fuse panel for 30 seconds.*

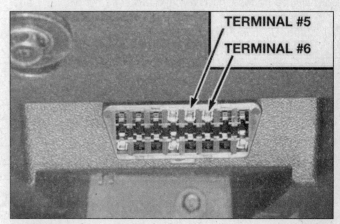

3.4a On most GM models (domestic) the ALDL connector is located under the dash, usually on the drivers side - to output trouble codes, jump terminals A and B with the ignition On

3.4b Some 1995 GM vehicles have the 16-pin connector like the OBD II system, but have accessible OBD I codes (check your emission decal for which system you have) - on this 1995 S-10 pickup with a 16-pin connector, bridge terminals 5 and 6 to extract trouble codes

Cadillac 4.1L, 4.5L, 4.6L, 4.9L and 6.0L engines and Buick Riviera/Oldsmobile Toronado (1986 through 1992)

Obtaining and clearing OBD system codes

The ECM will illuminate the CHECK ENGINE light (also known as the SERVICE ENGINE SOON light) on the dash if it recognizes a component fault for two consecutive drive cycles. It will continue to set the light until the codes are cleared or the ECM does not detect any malfunction for three or more consecutive drive cycles. **Note:** *Some diagnostic trouble codes will not set the CHECK ENGINE or SERVICE ENGINE SOON light, it is always a good idea to access the self diagnostic system and look for any trouble codes which may exist that have not set the CHECK ENGINE light.*

The Haynes Emissions Control Manual

The diagnostic codes for OBD-I systems can be extracted from the ECM using two methods. The first method requires accessing the computers self-diagnostic mode with the use of the Electronic Climate Control Panel or CRT display. To extract the diagnostic trouble codes using this method proceed as follows:

Cadillac Deville and Fleetwood models

a) Turn the ignition key ON (engine not running). **Note:** *Before you begin the code extraction process, be sure to obtain a pad of paper and a pencil to write down any stored trouble codes as they're displayed.*

b) Simultaneously press the OFF and WARMER buttons on the electronic climate control panel until "**-1.8.8**" illuminates on the climate control panel and "**8.8.8**" illuminates on the fuel data center (**see illustrations**). **Note:** *If all of the panel segments do not illuminate, it will be necessary to remove the affected display panel and have it serviced at a dealer service department or other qualified repair facility. Burnt out or broken panel segments will lead to incorrect trouble code displays, thereby leading to misdiagnosis of a particular system or component.*

c) After the segment check has been performed, "**8.8.8**" will be displayed on the fuel data center for approximately two more seconds, this indicates the beginning of the diagnostic trouble codes.

3.5a To enter the diagnostic service mode on Cadillac, Buick Riviera and Olds Toronado models, simultaneously press the OFF and WARMER buttons on the climate control panel

d) ECM trouble codes will now be displayed numerically from the lowest denomination to the highest on the fuel data center in two separate passes. The first pass will contain the ECM history codes and the second pass will contain the ECM current codes. All ECM trouble codes will begin with an "**E**" prefix.

e) The display "**. E**" designates the start of ECM history codes (first pass).

f) The display "**. E . E**" designates the start of ECM current codes (second pass).

ENTERING SERVICE MODE	Turn ignition key to the ON position. Simultaneously press the OFF and WARMER buttons on the electronic climate control panel for three seconds.
SEGMENT CHECK	Visually inspect that "**-1.8.8**" illuminates on the electronic climate control panel and that "**8.8.8**" illuminates on the fuel data center after the OFF and WARMER buttons are pressed for three seconds.
DIAGNOSTIC TROUBLE CODE DISPLAY (ECM TROUBLE CODES)	After the service mode has been entered all ECM diagnostic trouble codes will automatically be displayed. "**.. E**" designates the start of the ECM history codes. "**. E . E**" designates the start of the ECM current codes. Write down all trouble codes as they're being displayed, if any trouble codes are missed turn the ignition key OFF and restart the procedure.
DIAGNOSTIC TROUBLE CODE DISPLAY (BCM TROUBLE CODES)	After the ECM trouble codes, the BCM trouble codes will automatically be displayed. "**.. F**" designates the start of the BCM history codes. "**. F . F**" designates the start of the BCM current codes. Write down all trouble codes as they're being displayed, if any trouble codes are missed turn the ignition key OFF and restart the procedure.
SYSTEM READY MODE	After all diagnostic trouble codes have been displayed or if no codes are present , the fuel data center will display a "**.7.0**" this indicates that the system is ready for further instructions or testing.
CLEARING CODES	Enable to clear codes, the fuel data center must first display a system ready mode ("**.7.0**"). To clear ECM codes, simultaneously press the OFF and HI buttons on the electronic climate control panel until "**E.0.0**" is displayed. To clear BCM codes, simultaneously press the OFF and LO buttons on the electronic climate control panel until "**F.0.0**" is displayed.

3.5b Trouble code extraction process - quick reference chart (Cadillac Deville and Fleetwood models)

Chapter 2 Troubleshooting

g) If no ECM codes are present, the self-diagnostic system will bypass the ECM code symbols (". E" or ". E. E") and begin to display the BCM codes.

h) After the ECM trouble codes, the self diagnostic system will now begin to display the BCM trouble codes numerically from the lowest denomination to the highest on the fuel data center in two separate passes. The first pass will contain the BCM history codes and the second pass will contain the BCM current codes. All BCM trouble codes will begin with an "F" prefix.

i) The display ". F" designates the start of BCM history codes (first pass).

j) The display ". F. F" designates the start of BCM current codes (second pass).

k) When all ECM and BCM codes are finished being displayed or if no codes are present ".7.0" will be displayed. This code indicates a system ready status and the beginning of a switch test mode for various components within the self-diagnostic system. *Note:* Because of the complexity of the remaining OBD system, all further testing of the self diagnostic system is considered beyond the scope of the home mechanic and should be performed by a dealer service department or other qualified repair facility.

l) To clear ECM trouble codes, simultaneously press the OFF and HI buttons on the electronic climate control panel until "E.0.0" is displayed.

m) To clear BCM trouble codes, simultaneously press the OFF and LO buttons on the electronic climate control panel until "F.0.0" is displayed.

n) To exit the self-diagnostic system at any time, press the "AUTO" button and turn the ignition key OFF.

Cadillac Eldorado and Seville, Buick Riviera and Oldsmobile Toronado models

a) Turn the ignition key ON (engine not running). **Note:** *Before you begin the code extraction process, be sure to obtain a pad of paper and a pencil to write down any stored trouble codes as they're displayed.*

b) Simultaneously press the OFF and WARMER buttons (OFF and TEMP UP buttons on 1990 and later Buick models) on the electronic climate control panel until "-1.8.8" illuminates on the climate control panel and all the lights illuminate on the instrument panel cluster **(see illustrations). Note 1:** *If all of the panel segments do not illuminate, it will be necessary to remove the affected display panel and have it serviced at a dealer service department or other qualified repair facility. Burnt out or broken panel segments will lead to incorrect trouble code displays, thereby leading to misdiagnosis of a particular system or component.* **Note 2:** *On vehicles equipped with a CRT display, scroll the CRT menu and select the "CLIMATE CONTROL" page, press the OFF and WARMER buttons until the CRT beeps twice or the "SERVICE MODE" page is present on the CRT screen.*

c) After the segment check has been performed, ECM trouble codes will now be displayed numerically from the lowest denomination to the highest on the climate control panel or the instrument panel cluster. **Note:** *All*

ENTERING SERVICE MODE	Turn ignition key to the ON position. Simultaneously press the OFF and WARMER buttons on the electronic climate control panel or the climate control page on CRT equipped models for three seconds.
SEGMENT CHECK (NON-CRT MODELS)	Visually inspect that "-1.8.8" illuminates on the electronic climate control panel and all the lights on the instrument panel cluster illuminate after the OFF and WARMER buttons are pressed for three seconds.
DIAGNOSTIC TROUBLE CODE DISPLAY	After the service mode has been entered all diagnostic trouble codes will automatically be displayed. Write down all trouble codes as they're being displayed, if any trouble codes are missed turn the ignition key OFF and restart the procedure.
SYSTEM LEVEL MODE (ECM or BCM)	To select a system level, press the fan LO button to scroll to the desired system level, then press the fan HI button to enter your selection. A system level must be selected before the computer can proceed to the next menu. On CRT equipped models use the NO pad on the "SERVICE MODE" page to scroll and the YES pad to enter your selection.
CLEARING CODES	To clear codes, press the fan LO button to scroll to the "CLEAR CODES" menu, then press the fan HI button to enter your selection. A **"CODES CLEAR"** message should appear for approximately three seconds. On CRT equipped models use the NO pad on the "SERVICE MODE" page to scroll and the YES pad to enter your selection.

3.5c Trouble code extraction process - quick reference chart (Cadillac Eldorado and Seville, Buick Riviera and Oldsmobile Toronado models)

Cadillac models display the trouble codes on the climate control panel. All Buick and Oldsmobile models display the trouble codes on the CRT (if equipped) or the instrument panel cluster on models without a CRT.

d) All ECM trouble codes will begin with an **"EO"** prefix and will be followed by the suffix **"C "** (current) or **"H"** (history). Suffix **"C"** (current) after the trouble code indicates that the fault was still present the last time the ECM performed a self-diagnostic check. Suffix **"H"** (history) after the trouble code indicates that the fault was not present the last time the ECM performed a self-diagnostic check.

e) If no ECM codes are present, the self-diagnostic system will display a "NO ECM CODES" message or a "NO X CODE" message.

f) After the ECM trouble codes, the self diagnostic system will now begin to display the BCM trouble codes numerically from the lowest denomination to the highest. All BCM trouble codes will begin with a **"B"** prefix and again will be followed by the suffix **"C "** (current) or **"H"** (history) as described in above.

g) If no BCM codes are present, the self-diagnostic system will display a "NO BCM CODES" message or a "NO X CODE" message.

h) When all ECM and BCM codes are finished being displayed the self-diagnostic system will display codes for other subsystems such as the CRT, instrument panel cluster and the SIR system. **Note 1**: *Because of the complexity of the remaining OBD system, All further trouble code diagnosis and system testing on the CRT, instrument panel and SIR systems is considered beyond the scope of this manual and should be performed by a dealer service department or other qualified repair facility.* **Note 2**: *If a "NO X DATA" message appears on the display screen at any time during the trouble code extraction process it signifies that the BCM lost communication with that particular system and cannot retrieve any codes until the communication line or circuit is fixed.*

i) To clear trouble codes, you must first select the system level to be cleared. Press the fan LO button on the climate control panel until the system to be cleared (**"ECM"** or **"BCM"**) is displayed, then press the fan HI button to select (enter) the system.

j) Second you must select the test type. Again press the fan LO button until the **"CLEAR CODES"** menu is displayed, then press the fan HI button to select (enter) the test type. A **"CODES CLEAR"** message should appear for three seconds. **Note 1**: *This procedure must be performed for each system level to be cleared. Example: clearing both the ECM and the BCM codes requires performing this procedure twice, once for the ECM system codes and a second time for the BCM system codes.* **Note 2**: *On models equipped with a CRT display*

3.5d The Data Link Connector (DLC) (arrow) is located to the left or right of the steering column, depending on the model year of the vehicle (Cadillac, Buick Riviera and Oldsmobile Toronado models)

it will be necessary to press the NO button on the "SERVICE MODE" page to scroll through the system levels and the test types and then press the YES button to select (enter) the system levels and "CLEAR CODES" menu.

The second method uses a special SCAN tool that is programmed to interface with the OBD-I system by plugging into the DLC **(see illustration)**. When used, the SCAN tool has the ability to diagnose in-depth driveability problems and it allows data to be retrieved from the ECM stored memory. If the tool is not available and intermittent driveability problems exist, have the vehicle checked at a dealer service department or other qualified repair shop.

All models

Always clear the codes from the ECM before a new electronic emission control component is installed onto the engine. The ECM will often store trouble codes during sensor malfunctions. The ECM will also record new trouble codes if a new sensor is allowed to operate before the parameters from the old sensor have been erased. Clearing the codes will allow the computer to relearn the new operating parameters relayed by the new component. During the computer relearning process, the engine may experience a rough idle or slight driveability changes. This period of time, however, should last no longer than 15 to 20 minutes. **Caution:** *Do not disconnect the battery from the vehicle to clear the codes. This will erase stored operating parameters from the memory and cause the engine to run rough for a period of time while the computer relearns the information. If necessary, have the codes cleared by a dealer service department or other qualified repair facility.* **Note:** *If using a OBD-I SCAN tool, scroll the menu for the function that describes "CLEARING CODES" and follow the prescribed method for that particular SCAN tool.*

Refer to Chapter 6 for a list of trouble codes

General Motors imports

Geo (Metro, Prizm, Storm, Tracker)
Chevrolet (Sprint, Nova and Spectrum)

Storm

Retrieving codes

You must use a short jumper wire to ground the white diagnostic connector. This terminal is part of the Assembly Line Diagnostic Link (ALDL), located under the dash near the ECM **(see illustration)**.

Turn the ignition switch to ON (engine not running). Jumper the two outer cavities of the three-terminal connector. The Check Engine light will flash a Code 12 three times, then display the stored codes.

Clearing codes

After making repairs, clear the memory by removing the ECM fuse for at least ten seconds.

Geo Storm - Electronic Control Module (ECM) - replacement

Note: *This system is equipped with an Engine Control Module (ECM) with an Erasable Programmable Read Only Memory (EEPROM). The calibrations (parameters) are stored in the ECM within the EEPROM. If the ECM must be replaced, it is necessary to have the EEPROM programmed with a special scanning tool (TECH 1) available only at dealership service departments. The EEPROM is not replaceable on these vehicles. In the event of any malfunction with the EEPROM (Code 51), the vehicle must be taken to a dealership service department for diagnosis and repair.*

Sprint

Retrieving codes

With the engine at normal operating temperature, turn the "diagnostic" switch located under the steering column to the On position **(see illustration)**.

The codes will then be flashed by the Check Engine light on the dashboard.

Clearing codes

After checking the system, clear the codes from the ECM memory by turning the "diagnostic" switch Off.

Metro

Retrieving codes

Insert the spare fuse into the diagnostic terminal of the fuse block.

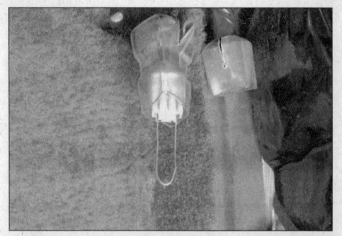

3.6 The Assembly Line Data Link (ALDL) is located under the passenger side glove box behind the kick panel - to activate the diagnostic codes, jump terminals 1 and 3 (the two outer terminals of the *white* connector)

Turn the ignition switch On (engine Off).

Read the diagnostic codes as indicated by the number of flashes of the Check Engine light on the dashboard. Normal system operation is indicated by Code 12. If there are any malfunctions, the light will flash the requisite number of times to display the codes in numerical order, lowest to highest.

Clearing codes

After testing, remove the fuse from the diagnostic terminal and clear the codes by removing the tail light fuse (otherwise the clock and radio will have to be reset).

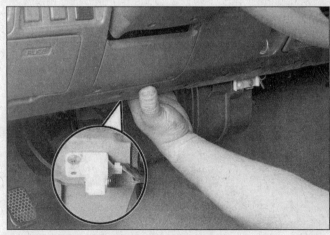

3.7 On 1987 and 1988 Sprint models, the diagnostic switch is located under the instrument panel

3.8 To display the codes on 1988 Nova (fuel injected) models, insert a jumper wire into the Check Engine connector with the ignition switch in the On position

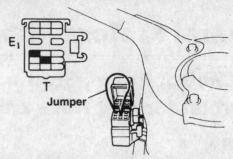

3.9 On 1989 and later Geo Prizm models, insert a jumper wire between terminals T (or TE1) and E1 of the diagnostic connector to retrieve the codes

Nova (fuel-injected models only)

Retrieving codes

With the ignition switch On, use a jumper wire to bridge both the terminals of the Check Engine connector located near the wiper motor **(see illustration)**. The Check Engine light will flash any stored codes.

Clearing codes

After checking, clear the codes by removing the ECM fuse (with the engine Off) for at least ten seconds.

Prizm

Retrieving codes

With the ignition On (engine Off), use a jumper wire to bridge terminals T and E1 of the "diagnostic" connector in the engine compartment **(see illustration).**

Start the engine; the Check Engine light will then flash any stored codes.

Clearing codes

After checking, clear the codes by removing the ECM fuse (with the engine Off) for at least ten seconds.

Tracker

Retrieving codes

On 1989 and 1990 models, insert the spare fuse into the diagnostic terminal of the fuse block.

On 1991 through 1994 (and 1995 TBI) models, use a jumper wire to bridge terminals 2 and 3 of the ECM check connector located in the engine compartment near the battery **(see illustration)**.

On 1995 models with port fuel injection, bridge the diagnostic and ground terminals of the check connector **(see illustration)**.

Turn the ignition switch On (engine Off).

Read the diagnosis codes as indicated by the number of flashes of the Check Engine light on the dashboard. Normal system operation is indicated by Code 12. Code 12 will flash three times, then if there are any malfunctions, the light will flash the requisite number of times to display the codes in numerical order, lowest to highest.

Clearing codes

After testing, remove the fuse or jumper wire and clear the codes by removing the tail light fuse (otherwise the clock and radio will have to be reset).

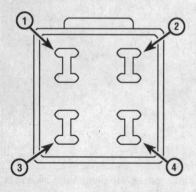

3.10 Obtain the codes on later Tracker models by using a jumper wire between the number 2 and 3 terminals of the test connector located next to the battery

1   Duty check terminal
2   Diagnostic test terminal
3   Ground terminal
4   Test switch terminal

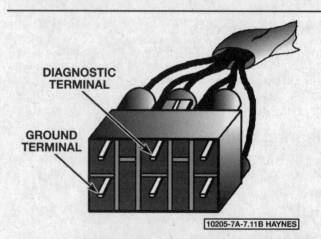

DIAGNOSTIC TERMINAL

GROUND TERMINAL

10205-7A-7.11B HAYNES

3.11 On 1995 Trackers with port fuel injection, bridge the diagnostic and ground terminals with a jumper wire

Honda

Retrieving codes

Accord (1985) and Civic (1985 through 1987)

The computer is located under the passenger's seat and displays the codes on four lights numbered, from left to right, 8-4-2-1. With the ignition On (engine Off), the lights will display the codes in ascending order.

Accord and Prelude (1986 and 1987)

The computer is located under the driver's seat. With the ignition switch On, the red light on the computer will display the codes by blinking (code 12 would be one blink, pause, two blinks) with a two second pause between codes.

Accord, Civic and Prelude (1988 and 1990)

Pull back the carpeting on the passenger's side kick panel for access to the computer.

With the ignition On, the light on the computer will display the codes by flashing.

All later models (1991 through 1995 (except 1995 Accord V6)

Note 1: *The two-digit trouble codes used on 1991 through 1995 models can be retrieved with the following procedures.*

Note 2: *The 1995 Accord V6 and all 1996 and later Honda models are equipped with OBD II diagnostics. The new, five-character codes are accessible only with an OBD II scan tool or Honda factory PGM tester.*

To view self-diagnosis information from the computer memory, install a jumper wire onto the diagnostic terminal **(see illustration)** located in the upper left corner under the dash. **Note:** *On 1991 Prelude models, the diagnostic connector is located in the engine compartment next to the fuse/relay block. On 1992 and later Prelude models, it's located behind the center console, near the accelerator pedal. On Odyssey models it's located behind the center console on the left side.* The codes are stored in the memory of the computer and when accessed, they blink a sequence on the Check Engine light to relay a number or code that represents a system component failure.

With the ignition On, the computer will display the coded flashes in a variety of combinations. The Check

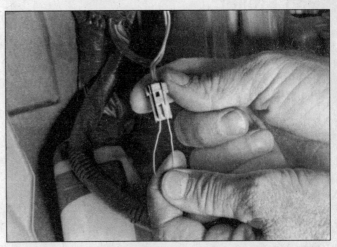

3.12 On most models, the diagnostic connector is located under the passenger side glove box behind the kick panel. To activate the diagnostic codes, bridge the terminals with a jumper wire or paper clip, then turn the ignition to the On position

Engine light will blink a longer blink to represent the first digit of a two digit number and then will blink short for the second digit (for example, 1 long blink then 6 short blinks for the code 16 [fuel injector]). **Note:** *If the system has more than one problem, the codes will be displayed in sequence then a pause and the codes will repeat.*

When the computer sets a trouble code, the Check Engine light will come on and a trouble code will be stored in the memory. The trouble code will stay in the computer until the voltage to the computer is interrupted. To clear the memory, remove the Back-Up fuse from the relay box located in the right side of the engine compartment. **Note:** *Disconnecting the Back-Up fuse also cancels the radio pre-set stations and the clock setting. Be sure to make a note of the various radio stations that are programmed into the memory before removing the fuse.*

Caution: *To prevent damage to the computer, the ignition switch must be off when disconnecting or connecting power to the computer (this includes disconnecting and connecting the battery).*

Clearing codes

The procedure for clearing codes is the same for all systems. To clear the codes after making repairs, make sure the ignition is Off, then disconnect the negative battery cable for ten seconds.

Refer to Chapter 6 for a list of trouble codes

Hyundai

1988 Stellar
Retrieving codes

With ignition off, connect an analog voltmeter to the diagnostic connector located in the engine compartment, behind the right strut tower. Turn the ignition On (engine Off) and watch the voltmeter needle.

It will display the codes as sweeps of the needle. The needle will sweep in long or short pulses over a ten-second period with each period separated by six-second intervals.

Short sweep = 0; Long sweep = 1
10000 = 1
01000 = 2
11000 = 3
00100 = 4
10100 = 5
01100 = 6
11100 = 7
00010 = 8
00000 = 9

Clearing codes

Clear the codes after repairs by disconnecting the negative battery cable for 15 seconds.

Sonata, Excel (1990 on), Scoupe 1991 and 1992) and Elantra
Retrieving codes

Locate the diagnostic connector. On 1989 Sonata models this is under the dash, to the left of the steering column. On all other models, it's under the driver's side kick panel **(see illustration)**.

Connect an analog voltmeter to the diagnostic connector ground terminal and MPI diagnostic terminal **(see illustration)**.

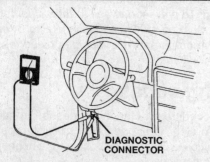

3.13a The self-diagnostic connector is located on the fuse panel (all models except 1989 Sonata)

Turn the ignition On.

Count the voltmeter needle sweeps and write them down for reference. Long sweeps indicate the first digit in two-digit codes. The short sweeps indicate the second digit. For example, two long sweeps followed by one short sweep indicates a code 21.

Clearing codes

To clear the codes, disconnect the negative battery cable for 15 seconds.

Scoupe (1993 through 1995) and Accent

The diagnostic connector is still in the driver's kick panel area, but on these models, you must ground the #10 wire for three seconds to get the codes to display on the MIL light **(see illustration 3.13b)**. Do not ground for more than 4 seconds. If 4444 is displayed, there are no stored codes. The first stored code will be displayed over and over; to go to the next code, repeat the grounding procedure. Keep going through the procedure until 3333 is displayed which indicates the end of the self-diagnosis (all stored codes have been displayed).

Clearing codes

To clear the codes, disconnect the negative battery cable for 15 seconds.

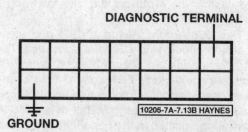

DIAGNOSTIC TERMINAL

10205-7A-7.13B HAYNES

GROUND

Excel (1990 on), Sonata (1990 on), Scoupe (1991 and 1992) and Elantra

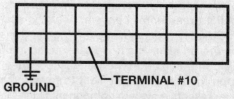

GROUND — TERMINAL #10

Scoupe (1993 on) and Accent

3.13b Diagnostic terminal positions

Refer to Chapter 6 for a list of trouble codes

Infiniti

All models are equipped with a Malfunction Indicator Light (MIL). As a bulb check, the light glows when the ignition is turned on and the engine is not running.

On **California** models, the MIL glows when a fault is detected with the engine running. A corresponding trouble code will set in the computer memory. The MIL also glows if the computer or crankshaft position sensor malfunctions.

On **Federal** models, the MIL glows only when the computer or crankshaft position sensor malfunctions with the engine running.

The self-diagnostic system can detect ECCS malfunctions and store related trouble codes. Intermittent codes are also stored. All codes are stored until cleared from memory. If an intermittent does not reoccur within 50 ignition key cycles, it will be cleared from memory.

Retrieving codes

Turn the ignition to the On position (don't start the engine).

Using a screwdriver, rotate the mode selector on the computer completely clockwise and wait approximately two seconds. After two seconds, turn the selector counterclock-wise as far as it will go. This will put the computer in the diagnostic mode, causing the red LED to flash trouble codes, if any are present. For example, two long flashes, pause, followed by four short flashes indicates a code 24. If there is more than one code stored in memory, the codes will be displayed in numerical order; each code will be separated by a two second pause. **Note 1**: *On 1990 to 1995 models, it is the red LED on the computer which will flash. On 1996 models, it is the Malfunction Indicator Light (MIL) that will flash the codes.* **Note 2**: *Be sure the selector is in the fully counterclockwise position before driving the vehicle.*

Computer Location

On G20 models, the computer is located under the dash, in the center console. On J30 and Q45 models, the computer is located behind the right kick panel.

Clearing Codes

Note: *Ensure all diagnostic codes are accessed from the computer memory before disconnecting the battery.*

Stored memory can be erased by disconnecting the negative battery cable.

Isuzu

I-Mark (RWD), California pick-up (1982 on), Amigo, Trooper, Rodeo, Pick-up (1984 on), Impulse (1983 and later non-turbo)

Retrieving codes

The above models that have a Check Engine light on the dash will have the self-diagnostic feature.

To retrieve the codes, first find the diagnostic connectors. These can be located in the engine compartment, under the dash or near the computer. The connectors are usually found behind the drivers trim panel **or** under the dash, on the passenger side, tucked or taped out of the way in the harness.

With the ignition switch On, connect the two leads of the diagnostic connectors together to ground them (**see illustration**).

Trooper and Rodeo V6 and I-Mark (FWD)

Retrieving codes

To retrieve the codes, use a short jumper wire to ground the diagnostic terminal. This terminal is part of an electrical connector known as the Assembly Line Diagnostic Link (ALDL). The ALDL is usually located under the dashboard or in the console near the computer.

Push one end of the jumper wire into the ALDL diagnostic terminal and the other into the ground terminal.

On I-mark models terminals A and C must be jumpered together (the two outer terminals on the three terminal connector).

On 1989 through 1991 V6 Trooper and Rodeo models, jumper terminals A and B. On 1992 and later models, jumper terminals 1 and 3 (on these models the connector is located to the right of the accelerator pedal).

All of the above models

With the diagnostic terminal now grounded and the ignition on with the engine stopped, the system will enter the Diagnostic Mode and the Check Engine light will display a Code 12 (one flash, pause, two flashes).

The code will flash three times, display any stored codes, then flash three more times, continuing until the jumper is removed.

Note 1: *On feedback carbureted models through 1989, after the code 12 is shown, disconnect the jumper and start the engine to display codes. On some models the codes 13,*

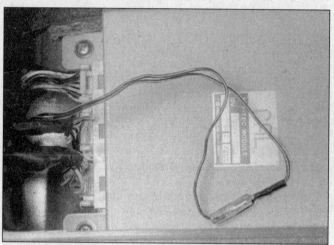

3.14 Typical diagnostic hook-up - make sure the ignition switch is On before connecting the terminals

15, 31, 44 and 45 will only show after the engine has run for five minutes at part throttle (after already reaching normal operating temperature).
Note 2: *All 1996 models use the ODB II diagnostic system, which requires an expensive scan tool to access and clear the codes.*

Clearing codes

After checking the system, remove the jumper and clear the codes from the computer memory by removing the appropriate fuse (ECM on four-cylinder models, BLM on V6) for ten seconds.

Jaguar XJS and XJ6 (1988 through 1994)

Note: *Trouble codes are not retrievable on 1995 and later models (a special scan tool must be used).*

All models are equipped with a Check Engine light. When the check engine light remains on, the self-diagnostic system has detected a system failure.

Hard Failures

Hard failures cause the check engine light to glow. Fault codes are stored in the Electronic Control Module (ECM) memory. All codes except Codes 26 and 44 will cause the check engine light to remain illuminated (with the ignition on) until the fault is corrected and the ECM memory

is cleared.

Codes 26 and 44 - the check engine light will remain on only until the next ignition on/off cycle. The codes will no longer be indicated by a check engine light, but will still be stored in ECM memory.

If the light comes on and remains on during vehicle operation, the cause of malfunction can be determined using the diagnostic trouble code table.

If a sensor fails, the control unit will use a substitute value in its calculations to continue engine operation. In this condition, the vehicle is functional but poor driveability may occur.

Retrieving codes

To access any stored trouble codes, turn the ignition to the Off position and wait five seconds. Turn the ignition key to the On position, but don't crank the engine.

Locate the Vehicle Condition Monitor (VCM)/trip computer display panel near the speedometer and press the VCM button. Any stored trouble codes will be shown on the display panel. If the engine is started the code will disappear from the display, but the CHECK ENGINE light will stay on. **Note 1:** *On V12 models, the code will display without pushing the button.* **Note 2:** *Not every code is displayed through the dash light, and only the first priority code will display, until it is fixed and cleared. If there is a second code, it will not be displayed until the first is fixed and cleared.*

Clearing codes

Turn the ignition key to the Off position, then detach the cable from the negative terminal of the battery for at least 30 seconds.

Refer to Chapter 6 for a list of trouble codes

Jeep

Retrieving codes

1984 through 1986 four-cylinder and V6 models

To extract this information from the ECM memory, you must use a short jumper wire to ground terminals 6 and 7 on the diagnostic connector **(see illustration)**. The diagnostic connector is located in the engine compartment on the left (driver's side) fenderwell. **Caution:** *Do not start the engine with the terminals grounded.*

Turn the ignition to the On position - not the Start position. The CHECK ENGINE light should flash Trouble Code 12, indicating that the diagnostic system is working. Code 12 will consist of one flash, followed by a short pause, and then two flashes in quick succession. After a longer pause, the code will repeat itself two more times.

If no other codes have been stored, Code 12 will continue to repeat itself until the jumper wire is disconnected. If additional Trouble Codes have been stored, they will follow Code 12. Again, each Trouble Code will flash three times before moving on.

Once the code(s) have been noted, use the Trouble Code chart to locate the source of the fault.

It should be noted that the self-diagnosis feature built into this system does not detect all possible faults. If you suspect a problem with the Computer Command Control System, but the CHECK ENGINE light has not come on and no trouble codes have been stored, take the vehicle to a dealer service department or other repair shop for diagnosis.

Furthermore, when diagnosing an engine performance, fuel economy or exhaust emissions problem (which is not accompanied by a CHECK ENGINE light) do not automatically assume the fault lies in this system. Perform all standard troubleshooting procedures, as indicated elsewhere in this manual, before turning to the Computer Command Control System .

Finally, since this is an electronic system, you should have a basic knowledge of automotive electronics before attempting any diagnosis. Damage to the ECM or related components can easily occur if care is not exercised.

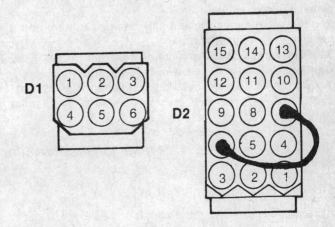

3.15 On 1984 through 1986 four-cylinder and V6 models, jump terminals 6 and 7 of the diagnostic connector to output trouble codes

The Haynes Emissions Control Manual

1987 through 1990 models

A special scan tool is required to retrieve trouble codes on these models. Take the vehicle to a dealer service department or other qualified shop.

1991 on

The self-diagnostic capabilities of this system, if properly used, can simplify testing. The Powertrain Control module (PCM) monitors several different engine control system circuits.

Hard failures cause the Malfunction Indicator Light (MIL) (may also be referred to as "CHECK ENGINE" Light) to glow and flicker until the malfunction is repaired. If the light comes on and remains on (light may flash) during vehicle operation, determine the cause of malfunction using the self-diagnostic tests. If a sensor fails, the PCM will use a substitute value in its calculations, allowing the engine to operate in a "limp-in" mode. In this condition, the vehicle will run, but driveability may be poor.

Intermittent failures may cause the MIL to flicker or stay on until the intermittent fault goes away. However, the PCM memory will retain a corresponding fault. If a related fault does not reoccur within a certain time frame, the related fault will be erased from PCM memory. Intermittent failures can be caused by a faulty sensor, bad connector or wiring related problems.

Test the circuits and repair or replace the components as required. If the problem is repaired or ceases to exist, the PCM cancels the fault after 50 ignition on/off cycles. A specific fault results from a particular system failure. A fault does not condemn a specific component; the component is not necessarily the reason for failure. Faults only suggest the probable malfunction area.

Service precautions

1   When the battery is disconnected, vehicle computer and memory systems may lose memory data. Driveability problems may exist until the computer systems have completed a relearn cycle.
2   The vehicle must have a fully charged battery and a functional charging system.
3   Probe the PCM 60-pin connector from the pin side.
Caution: *Do not back- probe PCM connector.*
4   Do not cause short circuits when performing any elec-trical tests. This will set additional faults, making diagnosis of the original problem more difficult.
5   When checking for voltage, **do not** use a test light - use a digital voltmeter.
6   When checking for spark, ensure that the coil wire is no more than 1/4-inch from a ground connection. If the coil wire is more than 1/4-inch from ground, damage to the vehicle electronics and/or PCM may result.
7   Do not prolong testing of the fuel injectors, or the engine may hydrostatically (liquid) lock.
8   Always repair the lowest fault code number first.
9   Always perform a verification test after repairs are made.

Retrieving codes

Note 1: *Although other scanners are available, the manufacturer recommends using Diagnostic Readout Box II (DRB-II).The malfunction indicator light (MIL) method can be used, without the need for the diagnostic scanner, but not all trouble codes can be accessed and has limited diagnostic capability. Due to the prohibitive cost of the Diagnostic Readout Box II, only the MIL method will be discussed here.*
Note 2: *Beginning in 1996, all models are equipped with the OBD II diagnostics system. Although a scan tool is required to retrieve and clear the new, five-character codes, the basic two-digit codes can still be retrieved from the MIL light.*

Start the engine, if possible, and shift the transmission through all of the gears. Place the shifter in the Park position, then turn the air conditioning on and off.

Stop the engine, then turn the ignition key to the On position, then Off, then On, then Off, then On again within three seconds. This will cause any stored trouble codes to be displayed by flashing the Malfunction Indicator Light (MIL or CHECK ENGINE light).

Code 55 indicates all of the trouble codes have been displayed.

Clearing codes

Caution: *If the stereo in your vehicle is equipped with an anti-theft system, make sure you have the correct activation code before disconnecting the battery.*

Trouble codes may be cleared by disconnecting the negative battery cable for at least 15 seconds.

Refer to Chapter 6 for a list of trouble codes

Lexus

Retrieving codes

When the system is placed in diagnostic mode, stored fault codes are displayed through a blinking CHECK ENGINE light on the dash. To obtain an output of diagnostic codes, verify first that the battery voltage is above 11 volts, the throttle is fully closed, the transaxle is in Neutral, the accessory switches are off and the engine is at normal operating temperature.

Turn the ignition switch to ON (engine not running). Do not start the engine. Use a jumper wire to bridge terminals TE1 and E1 of the service electrical connector **(see illustration)**. **Note:** *The self-diagnosis system can be accessed by using either test terminal no. 1 (engine compartment) or test terminal no. 2 (under the left end of the dash).*

Read the diagnosis code as indicated by the number of flashes of the "CHECK ENGINE" light on the dash. Normal system operation (no codes found) is indicated by a constant blinking (two times per second). Each code will be displayed by first blinking the first digit of the code, then pause, followed by a pause, followed by blinking the second digit of the code. For example, Code 24 (IAT sensor) will flash two times, pause, and then flash four times. Each flash, and the pause between each flash, is exactly the same length, except for the pause between the flashes for each digit. That pause is longer so that you can distinguish between the first and second digits of the code.

If there are any malfunctions in the system, their corresponding trouble codes are stored in computer memory and the light will blink the requisite number of times for the indicated trouble codes. If there's more than one trouble code in the memory, they'll be displayed in numerical order (from the lowest to the highest) with a 2-1/2 second pause interval between each one. (To ensure correct interpretation

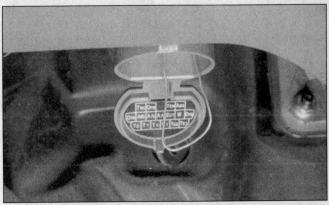

3.16 To access the Lexus self-diagnosis system, locate the diagnostic connector under the left end of the dash (shown) or in the engine compartment (not shown) and use a jumper wire or paper clip to bridge terminals TE1 and E1

of the flashing CHECK ENGINE light, watch carefully for the end of one code and the beginning of the next; otherwise you'll become confused by the apparent number of flashes and will misinterpret the display). After the code with the largest number of flashes has been displayed, there will be another pause and then the sequence begins all over again.

Clearing codes

After the malfunctioning component has been repaired/replaced, the CHECK ENGINE light will reset itself, but the trouble code(s) stored in computer memory must be canceled. To do so, simply turn the ignition to OFF and remove the 20-amp EFI fuse from junction fuse box no. 2. Wait at least ten seconds before reinstalling the fuse. Road test the vehicle and verify that no fault codes are present.

Mazda

All models

Hard Failures

Hard failures cause the Check Engine light to illuminate and remain on until the problem is repaired.

If the light comes on and remains on (light may flash) during vehicle operation, the cause of the malfunction can be determined using the diagnostic code charts.

If a sensor fails, the computer will use a substitute value in its calculations to continue engine operation. In this

condition, commonly known as "limp-in" mode, the vehicle will run but driveability will be poor.

Intermittent Failures

Intermittent failures may cause the Check Engine light to flicker or illuminate and go out after the intermittent fault goes away. However, the corresponding code will be retained in the computer memory. If a related fault does not reoccur within a certain time frame, the code will be erased from the computer memory. Intermittent failures may be caused by sensor, connector or wiring related problems.

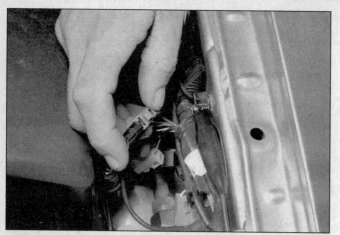

3.17a To retrieve the trouble code, use a jumper wire and ground the green 1-pin connector to a bolt on the body

Retrieving codes

1989 to 1991 models (except Miata); 1992 and 1993 MPV, 1993 and earlier pick-ups

The diagnostic connector is located in the engine compartment, back of left front strut tower (**see illustration**).

Trouble codes are accessed by using a jumper wire to ground the single-pin, green-wire connector.

1990 and 1991 Miata

On these models, a factory diagnostic tool must be used to retrieve codes.

1994 Pick-ups

Refer to the Ford trouble code retrieval procedure, and use the Ford EEC-IV three-digit code list. **Note:** *1995 and later pick-ups use the Ford EEC V engine management system; trouble codes on these models must be retrieved with a special scan tool.*

1992 to 1995 models, except pick-ups

Using a jumper wire, connect the self-diagnostic connector terminal TEN with the ground terminal (**see illustration**). The connector is located near the left shock tower.

1995 Millennia

These models are equipped with OBD II diagnostic

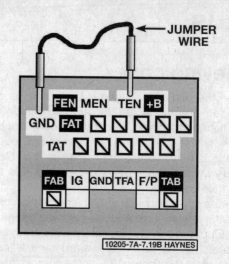

3.17b On 1992 through 1995 Mazdas (except pick-ups), bridge terminals TEN and GND to output trouble codes

systems, which require the use of an expensive scan tool to retrieve the new, five-character diagnostic codes.

All models

With the ignition On and engine Off, observe the check engine light; any stored trouble codes will be displayed by flashes of the light. For example, two long flashes, pause, followed by four short flashes indicates a code 24.

If the light glows continuously, the check engine light circuit may be grounded or the computer may be defective **Note:** *If there is more than one code stored, they will be displayed in order from the lowest number to the highest number.*

Clearing codes

Disconnect the negative battery cable. Depress the brake pedal for at least 20 seconds. Reconnect the battery cable and reconnect the jumper wire. Turn the key to the ON position for at least six seconds, then start the engine and run it at a high idle (2000 rpm) for at least three minutes. If no codes are displayed on the MIL, the codes have been cleared successfully. Shut the engine off and disconnect the jumper wire.

Refer to Chapter 6 for a list of trouble codes

Mercedes

Before retrieving codes the following pretest conditions must be met:

1   Start and run engine until engine oil temperature is 176°F (80°C).
2   Turn air conditioning **off**.
3   Make sure the shift lever is in **Park**.
4   Check all fuses and replace as necessary.
5   Verify battery voltage is 11-to-14 volts.

Retrieving codes:

HFM-SFI system (except C220, C280, 400, 190E and 500)

Turn the ignition On (engine not running).

Press the non-locking switch, located on diagnostic connector in right rear corner of the engine compartment **(see illustration)**, for 2-to-4 seconds. HFM-SFI control unit will begin output of any fault codes present by flashing the LED light on diagnostic connector.

If the LED only flashes once, this indicates no fault codes are stored. If fault codes are stored, the LED will flash indicating fault code 3.

Press the push-button again for 2-to-4 seconds. If more fault codes are stored, the LED on the diagnostic connector will display the next code.

Continue pressing the push-button for 2-to-4 seconds at a time until the LED lights steadily, indicating the end of fault code display.

Record all fault codes and refer to the trouble code identification table. **Note:** *Other 1994 and later models are equipped with OBD II diagnostic systems, which require the use of a special tool to retrieve trouble codes.*

Clearing codes

On Federal vehicles, disconnect the negative battery cable. Stored trouble codes will be erased when the battery is disconnected.

On California vehicles, disconnecting the battery will not erase the codes. Each code that is stored in the CIS-E control unit will have to be erased individually.

Press the non-locking switch located on the diagnostic connector in the right rear corner of the engine compartment for 2-to-4 seconds.

When the fault is displayed, press the non-locking switch for 6-to-8 seconds. That code is now cleared. Repeat the procedure until all stored codes have been erased.

Press the Start button on the pulse counter for 2-to-4 seconds, maximum. The pulse counter will display the fault code. Press the start button again for 6-to-8 seconds. The fault code is erased when the pulse counter no longer displays the fault code.

Repeat the procedure for other stored fault codes. When the pulse counter displays "1", no faults are stored.

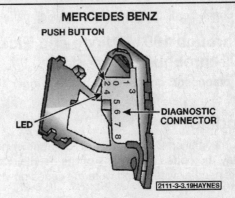

3.18 Location of the diagnostic connector is in the right rear corner of the engine compartment

Mitsubishi

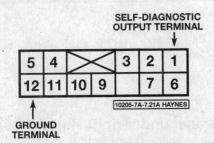

3.19a To put the ECU into code retrieval mode, connect an analog voltmeter to the indicated terminals of the connector - most models have this diagnostic connector

Retrieving codes

With the engine Off, locate the diagnostic connector. On most models, an analog voltmeter is connected to the diagnostic connector, the positive lead from the voltmeter to the test terminal, and the ground lead to the ground terminal **(see illustrations)**. **Note:** *On all 1995 models (except the Expo, Summit wagon, and pickup models) the MIL lamp must be used, by jumping the test and ground terminals of the connector with a jumper wire and observing the flashes of the MIL lamp on the dash. The location of the diagnostic connector varies with model and year:*

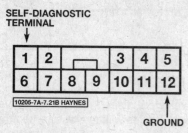

3.19b On 1990 and 1991 Monteros, the connector is slightly different in layout - this one is located in the glove compartment area

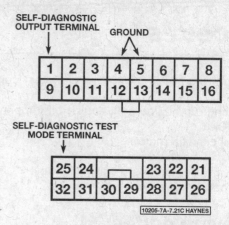

3.19c Location of the self-diagnostic terminals on 1992 and later Mitsubishi models

1983 through 1986 fuel-injected models

The diagnostic connector is located under the battery or on the right side firewall near the computer, depending on model.

1987 through 1989, except Galant and Mirage, 1990 through 1991 Montero

The diagnostic connector is in or under the glove compartment.

1987 through 1991 Galant and Mirage

The connector is behind the left side kick panel.

1990 through 1991 Eclipse and Pick-up, all 1992 through 1995 models

The diagnostic connector is located near the fuse block.

All models

Turn the ignition On and watch the voltmeter needle. It will display the codes as sweeps of the needle. Count the number of needle sweeps and write the codes down for ref-erence. Long sweeps represent the tens digit, short sweeps represent the ones digit, i.e. one long and one short would be DTC code 11. Only continuous short sweeps indicates the system has no stored codes. On 1994 and 1995 models, the following models are accessed by using a voltmeter: Precis, Mirage, Eclipse, and pickup models. The Montero can be accessed with either a voltmeter *or* a jumper wire in place of the voltmeter connections, which indicates flashes on the MIL lamp instead of voltage sweeps. The following models are accessible only through the blinking MIL: Galant, Diamante, and 3000GT. **Note:** *1995 models are equipped with OBD II diagnostic systems, which require the use of an expensive scan tool to retrieve the new, five-character diagnostic codes, however, the basic MIL/voltmeter codes can still be obtained also.*

Clearing codes

Clear the codes by disconnecting the negative battery cable for 30 seconds.

Refer to Chapter 6 for a list of trouble codes

Nissan/Datsun cars and trucks

ECU location

To access the self-diagnostic procedures and extract trouble codes, the ECU (computer) must be located. Location varies with the year and model as follows:

Under dash, behind the center console

Maxima 1986 to 1994; Sentra 1991 to 1995; 200SX and 300SX, 1990 to 1995; 1993 to 1995 Altima

Behind glove box

Maxima, Quest 1995; 1991 to 1995 300ZX

Under passenger seat

Pick-up and Pathfinder, 1987 to 1995, Pulsar, Stanza, Sentra, 1987 to 1989

Under driver's seat

Stanza wagon, 1987, Sentra 4WD 1990

At kick panel under right side of dash

300ZX, 1986 to 1989; 240SX 1987 to 1995

At kick panel under left side of dash

200SX, 1987 to 1988

3.20a On all except TBI-equipped pick-ups and 1984 through 1986 300ZX, select the diagnostic mode by turning the ECU mode selector clockwise, gently, until it stops

Retrieving codes, 1984 to 1989

Remove the computer. **Caution:** *Do not disconnect the electrical connector from the computer or you will erase any stored diagnostic codes.*

Turn the ignition switch to On. **Note:** *On 1984 to 1986 models (except pickups with TBI) start the engine and warm it to normal operating temperature.*

Turn the diagnostic mode selector on the computer fully clockwise or turn the mode selector switch (a hand-operated switch on some models) to On **(see illustrations)**.

Wait until the inspection lamps flash. **Note:** *The LED-type inspection lamps are located on the side or top of the computer* **(see illustration)**. The inspection lamps flash once for each level of diagnostics, i.e. one flash is Mode I, two flashes is Mode II. After the inspection lamps have flashed three times (Mode III is the self-diagnostic mode that will display codes), turn the diagnostic mode selector fully counterclockwise or turn the mode selector to Off.

On 1984 to 1986 300ZX models, start the procedure by turning the screw counterclockwise, turn the ignition ON, make sure the bulbs stay on, then turn the screw clockwise. Later 300ZX models are diagnosed the same as other models.

The computer is now in the self-diagnostic mode. Now, count the number of times the inspection lamps flash.

First, the red lamp flashes, then the green lamp flashes. **Note:** *The red lamp denotes units of ten, the green lamp denotes units of one. Check the trouble code chart for the particular malfunction. For example, if the red lamp flashes once and the green lamp flashes twice, the computer is displaying the number 12, which indicates the air flow meter is malfunctioning.*

If the ignition switch is turned off at any time during a diagnostic readout, the procedure must be re-started. The stored memory or memories will be lost if, for any reason, the battery terminal is disconnected.

Retrieving codes, 1990 to 1995

Beginning with 1990 models, there are two types of diagnostics systems, the dual-LED type as described above, and a new single-LED system. The dual-LED system works the same as the previous models, with a red and a green light.

The single-LED system (Pathfinder and pick-up models) has only two Modes, with Mode II being the self-diagnostic mode for trouble code retrieval. The red LED will

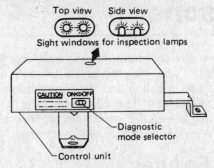

3.20b On TBI-equipped pick-ups, activate the diagnostic mode by pushing the mode switch to the left - the red and green lights should begin flashing

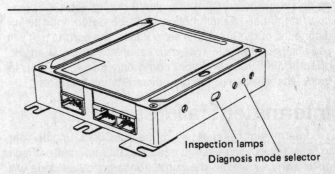

3.21 On 1984 through 1986 300ZX models, verify the diagnostic mode selector is turned fully counterclockwise using a small screwdriver

flash a long flash (.6 seconds) for the tens digit and short flashes (.3 seconds) for the single digits.

Note: *All 1995 models have a Malfunction Indicator Lamp (Check Engine light), and instead of using the LED's on the computer to read codes, the MIL flashes the codes (except Pathfinder and pick-up models, which still have the dual-LED system). Also, most 1995 models are equipped with OBD II diagnostics systems. Although an expensive scan tool is required to retrieve the new, five-character diagnostic codes, the basic codes can still be obtained using the flashing MIL.*

Clearing codes

On early TBI-equipped pick-up models, to erase the memory after self-diagnosis codes have been noted or recorded, turn the diagnostic mode selector to On. After the inspection lamps have flashed four times, turn the diagnostic mode selector to Off Turn the ignition switch to Off.

On all other early models, erase the memory by turning the diagnostic mode selector on the computer fully clockwise. After the inspection lamps have flashed four times, turn the mode selector fully counterclockwise. This will erase any signals the computer has stored concerning a particular component.

Note: *On all models, disconnecting the negative cable of the battery will clear all stored codes. On later models, unless the battery is disconnected, stored codes for problems that have been fixed will remain stored until the vehicle has made 50 restarts.*

Porsche

The vehicle computer, the Digital Motor Electronics (DME) control unit, has the ability to store fault codes related to fuel injection and ignition systems. Detected faults are stored for at least 50 engine starts. If the positive battery cable or the DME control unit connector is disconnected, the fault code memory will be cleared.

Hard Failures

Hard failures cause the Check Engine light to illuminate and remain on until problem is repaired. If the light comes on and remains on (light may flash) during vehicle operation, the cause of malfunction must be determined using diagnostic code tables. If a sensor fails, the control unit will use a substitute value in its calculations to continue engine operation. In this condition, commonly known as limp-in mode, the vehicle will run but driveability will be poor.

Intermittent failures

Intermittent failures may cause the Check Engine light to flicker or illuminate. Light goes out after intermittent fault goes away. However, the corresponding trouble code will be stored in computer memory. If the fault does not reoccur within a certain time frame, related code(s) will be erased from computer memory. Intermittent failures may be caused by sensor, connector or wiring related problems.

Check engine light

The check engine light comes on if a component related to fuel injection and/or ignition system fails.

The check engine light is installed in oil the temperature/pressure gauge cluster. The light comes on as a self-test when the ignition switch is in the On position.

After the engine starts, the throttle valve closes, and the Check Engine light goes out to indicate that there are no codes stored in the computer memory.

If the check engine light remains on, a fault is present (hard failure) in the DME engine management system. If the check engine light comes on, or flickers, while driving, a fault in the DME engine management system has been identified (intermittent failure).

If the idle speed switch is open during the starting sequence, the check engine light will come on. As soon as the idle speed switch closes while driving, the check engine light goes out after a 4-second delay.

If the full throttle switch is faulty (shorted to ground), the check engine light will remain on constantly.

Some fault codes cannot be displayed using the check engine light. In such cases, retrieve the fault code(s) through the diagnostic connector, and repair the condition(s) causing the check engine light to come on.

Retrieving codes

On models with a CHECK ENGINE light, turn the ignition key to the On position, then depress the accelerator pedal to the floor and hold it there for five seconds. The CHECK ENGINE light should go out then come on again. At this point, take your foot off the accelerator pedal; the next series of flashes on the CHECK ENGINE light will represent the first trouble code. Write down the code number, then depress the accelerator pedal again for five seconds, then release the pedal and record the second trouble code. Repeat this procedure until all of the trouble codes have been output and code 1000 is displayed, indicating the end of the sequence.

On models without a CHECK ENGINE light, you'll need a Porsche tester (No. 9288 or 9268) or a suitable aftermarket code reader to display the codes. Plug the factory tester or the code reader into the diagnostic connector, which is located in the right (passenger) footwell on 944 and 968 models, and in the right kick panel on 928 models.

Clearing codes

Ensure the fault that was causing the check engine light to come on has been corrected, then depress and hold the accelerator pedal at wide open throttle (WOT) for more than 12-seconds.

The check engine light will go out briefly after 3, 7 and 10-second intervals to indicate that fault code memory has been cleared.

To clear codes stored in memory, momentarily disconnect the electrical connector from the DME control unit The fault code memory will be cleared.

Refer to Chapter 6 for a list of trouble codes

Saab

Retrieving codes

Fault codes can be retrieved from 1988 through 1994 models equipped with LH 2.4, LH 2.4.1 and LH 2.4.2 fuel injection systems. You'll need Saab's switched jumper wire (part no. 8393886) or a suitable substitute to ground the diagnostic connector. Connect one end of the jumper wire to the no. 3 pin in the three-pin socket inside the diagnostic connector (located in the right rear corner of the engine compartment on 900 models; on the left side of the engine compartment on 9000 models). Connect the other end of the jumper wire to ground. Turn the ignition switch to ON; the CHECK ENGINE light will come on. Set the jumper switch to ON (this grounds ECU pin 16); the CHECK ENGINE LIGHT will go out. Watch the CHECK ENGINE light. After about 2-1/2 seconds, it will flash briefly, indicating that the first diagnostic code is going to be displayed. As soon as the CHECK ENGINE light flashes, turn the jumper switch to OFF.

The first fault code will now be displayed. A single flash, followed by a long pause, indicates the number 1. A single flash, followed by a short pause, another single flash, and a long pause, indicates the number 2. A flash, short pause, flash, short pause, flash, long pause sequence indicates the number 3. Each code has four digits. Each two digits are separated by a longer pause. Each four-digit code is flashed repeatedly until the jumper wire switch is again turned to ON; again, CHECK ENGINE light will flash briefly, after which you turn the jumper wire switch to OFF and the next fault code is displayed. And so on. Repeat this procedure until all fault codes have been displayed and noted. When all stored codes have been flashed, or all faults have been repaired, the CHECK ENGINE light will display an uninterrupted series of flashes. If you want to display the codes again, turn the jumper wire switch to ON. This time watch for *two* short flashes, then turn the jumper wire switch to OFF. Repeat the above procedure.

Clearing codes

Set the jumper switch to ON and watch the CHECK ENGINE light. After three short flashes, turn the jumper wire switch to OFF. The CHECK ENGINE light will either flash a continuous series of long flashes (Code 00000) or it will flash Code 12444 (fault codes stored in memory have been erased).

Saturn

The Computer Command Control (CCC) system consists of an Electronic Control Module (ECM) and information sensors which monitor various functions of the engine and send data back to the ECM.

This system is equipped with an Erasable Programmable Read Only Memory (EEPROM). The calibrations (parameters) are stored in the ECM within the EEPROM. If the ECM must be replaced, it is necessary to have the EEPROM programmed with a special scanning tool called TECH 1 available only at dealership service department. **Note:** *The EEPROM is not replaceable on these vehicles. In the event of any malfunction with the EEPROM (Code 51),* *the vehicle must be taken to a dealership service department for diagnosis and repair.*

The ECM controls the following systems:

> *Fuel control*
> *Electronic spark timing*
> *Exhaust gas recirculation*
> *Canister purge*
> *Engine cooling fan*
> *Idle Air Control (IAC)*
> *Transmission converter clutch*
> *Air conditioning clutch control*
> *Secondary air*

Retrieving codes

Note: *A special tool is required to retrieve trouble codes on 1996 and later models.*

The CCC system has a built-in diagnostic feature which indicates a problem by flashing a Check Engine light on the instrument panel. When this light comes on during normal vehicle operation, a fault in one of the information sensor circuits or the ECM itself has been detected. More importantly, a trouble code is stored in the ECM's memory.

To retrieve this information from the ECM memory, you must use a short jumper wire to ground the diagnostic terminal. This terminal is part of an electrical connector known as the Assembly Line Data Link (ALDL) **(see illustration).**

3.22 The Assembly Line Data Link (ALDL) is located under the driver's side dashboard near the kick panel. To activate the diagnostic codes, jump terminals B and A

The Haynes Emissions Control Manual

The ALDL is located underneath the dashboard, to the left of the driver's foot area.

To use the ALDL, remove the plastic cover and with the electrical connector exposed to view, push one end of the jumper wire into the diagnostic terminal (B) and the other end into the ground terminal (A). When the diagnostic terminal is grounded, with the ignition On and the engine stopped, the system will enter the Diagnostic Mode. **Caution:** *Don't start or crank the engine with the diagnostic terminal grounded.*

In this mode the ECM will display a "Code 12" by flashing the Check Engine light, indicating that the system is operating. A code 12 is simply one flash, followed by a brief pause, then two flashes in quick succession. This code will be flashed three times. If no other codes are stored, Code 12 will continue to flash until the diagnostic terminal ground is removed.

After flashing Code 12 three times, the ECM will display any stored trouble codes. Each code will be flashed three times, then Code 12 will be flashed again, indicating that the display of any stored trouble codes has been completed.

When the ECM sets a trouble code, the Check Engine light will come on and a trouble code will be stored in memory. If the problem is intermittent, the light will go out after 10 seconds, or when the fault goes away.

Clearing codes

The trouble code will stay in the ECM memory until the battery voltage to the ECM is interrupted. Removing battery voltage for 10 seconds will clear all stored trouble codes. Trouble codes should always be cleared after repairs have been completed. **Caution:** *To prevent damage to the ECM, the ignition switch must be Off when disconnecting or connecting power to the ECM.*

Subaru

Retrieving codes

There are self-diagnostic connectors on all models which, when connected together with the key ON (engine off) flash diagnostic codes through the LED light on the oxygen monitor on the ECU. The connectors are under the steering wheel, to the left of the module on most models. On carbureted and SPFI injected 1989 models, the test connectors are located on the engine side of the firewall, on the driver's side. Impreza models have the ECU and test connectors located behind the right side of the dash instead of the left. On SVX models the connectors are located behind the driver's side kick panel.

There are four test modes. With *neither* test connector connected, and the ignition key ON (not running) the light will display codes that relate to starting and driving. With *only* the "Read Memory" connector connected, historic codes will be displayed. With *only* the "Test Mode" connector connected, a dealership technician can perform dynamic tests. The last mode is for clearing codes (see text below).

The codes are displayed as pulses of the Light Emitting Diode (LED) mounted on the module. The long pulses (1.2 seconds) indicate tens and the short pulses (.2 seconds) indicate ones. Pulses are separated by .3-second pauses, and codes are separated by 1.8-second pauses. **Note:** *On 1989 MPFI models, the oxygen sensor monitor light and ECU are mounted under the rear seat package shelf, and are accessible only from the trunk.*

On 1990 models, the trouble codes on the Justy are viewed on the oxygen monitor light only, while on other models, the codes can be viewed on either the oxygen monitor or the Malfunction Indicator Lamp (Check Engine light) on the dash.

1995 Impreza and Legacy models have OBD II diagnostics systems. The OBD II codes can be extracted and cleared with either a Subaru factory tool, called the Subaru Select Monitor, or with a universal OBD II scan tool. Although an expensive scan tool is required to retrieve these new, five-character diagnostic codes, the basic codes can still be obtained using the flashing MIL.

Clearing codes

Codes will clear only when the faulty system or circuit is repaired. After making the repairs, codes can be cleared by connecting *two* pairs of connectors, the self-diagnostic connectors, and the "Read Memory" connectors that are usually located right next to the diagnostic connectors. To begin, start with a warmed-up engine, turn the engine off, connect both pairs of connectors, then start the engine. This should clear the codes.

Refer to Chapter 6 for a list of trouble codes

Toyota

The Check Engine warning light, which is located on the instrument panel, comes on when the ignition switch is turned to On and the engine is not running. When the engine is started, the warning light should go out. If the light remains on, the diagnosis system has detected a malfunction in the system.

Retrieving codes

To obtain an output of diagnostic codes, verify first that the battery voltage is above 11 volts, the throttle is fully closed, the transaxle is in Neutral, the accessory switches are off and the engine is at normal operating temperature.

Locate the diagnostic connector. The connector is located in several different places, depending on model. In most models it is near the left shock tower in the engine compartment, or near the master cylinder. In Previa models, it is under the driver's seat, In many later vehicles, it is mounted near the fuse/relay box in the engine compartment.

Turn the ignition On (engine not running), then use a jumper wire to bridge the terminals of the service electrical connector **(see illustration)**. Later models use a multi-pin connector **(see illustration)** for use with a factory scan tool, but a jumper wire between the TE1 and E1 terminals will make the MIL blink if there are codes. The connector is usually located in the engine compartment near one of the strut towers, or in the passenger compartment under the dash or near the driver's seat.

The 1989 to 1992 Cressida has a different-shaped connector **(see illustration)**, which performs both static and dynamic (vehicle running, see *Test mode* below) self-diagnostics. The 1993 to 1995 Camry and Supra have the same type connector, and the following 1993 models have the same dual-function self-diagnosis capability, but with a

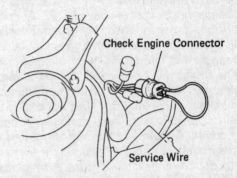

3.23a On 1984 Camrys, 1987 Corollas and 1986 and earlier pick-ups, bridge the terminals of the round Check Engine connector with a jumper wire to obtain the diagnostic codes (Corolla shown, others similar)

standard-looking connector: Corolla, Land Cruiser, MR2 and T100 (refer to the plastic cover for the positions of terminals TE1 and E1).

Read the basic diagnostic codes on all models by watching the number of flashes of the Check Engine light on the dash. Normal system operation is indicated by Code No. 1 (no malfunctions) for all models. The Check Engine light displays a Code No. 1 by blinking once every quarter-second consistently.

If there are any malfunctions in the system, their corresponding trouble codes are stored in computer memory and the light will blink the requisite number of times for the indicated trouble codes. If there's more than one trouble code in the memory, they'll be displayed in numerical order (from lowest to highest) with a pause interval between each one. The digits are simulated by half-second flashes, with 1.5-second pauses between numbers. For example, two flashes, pause, three flashes will indicate code 23. After the

3.23b To access the self diagnostic system, locate the test terminal and using a jumper wire or paper clip, bridge terminals TE1 and E1. On later models, the test terminal is a multi-pin connector, usually with a protective plastic cover over it - using a jumper wire or paper clip, bridge terminals TE1 and E1

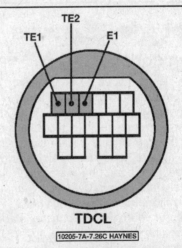

TDCL

10205-7A-7.26C HAYNES

3.23c The 1989 to 1992 Cressida have a different type connector located behind the left dash area, which offers two types of testing modes

code with the largest number of flashes has been displayed, there will be another pause and then the sequence will begin all over again.

Note: *The diagnostic trouble codes 25, 26, 27 and 71 use a special diagnostic capability called "2 trip detection logic". With this system, when a malfunction is first detected, it is temporarily stored into the ECM on the first test drive or "trip". The engine must be turned off and the vehicle taken on another test drive "trip" to allow the malfunction to be stored permanently in the ECM. This will distinguish a true problem on vehicles with these particular codes entered into the computer. Normally the self diagnosis system will detect the malfunctions but in the event the home mechanic wants to double-check the diagnosis by canceling the codes and rechecking, then it will be necessary to go on two test drives to confirm any malfunctions with these particular codes.*

To ensure correct interpretation of the blinking Check Engine light, watch carefully for the interval between the end of one code and the beginning of the next (otherwise, you will become confused by the apparent number of blinks and misinterpret the display). The length of this interval varies with the model year.

Beginning in 1994, some Toyota models are equipped with the new OBD II diagnostic system, which requires an expensive Toyota or generic OBD II scan tool to access the new, five-character diagnostic codes. There is no consumer access to the codes through the MIL lamp. 1994 OBD II models include: Camry 3.0L, supercharged Previa, T100 2.7L; 1995 models include the Avalon, Camry 3.0L, Land Cruiser, supercharged Previa, Tacoma, Tercel, and the T100.

"Test" mode diagnostics

Those 1989 through 1993 models mentioned above as having the dynamic testing capability exhibit the standard codes on the MIL with the jumper wire connecting the E1 and TE1 pins. After such a self-diagnosis, turn the key OFF and connect the E1 to the TE2 pin. Now drive the vehicle (above 10 mph) around for about five minutes, trying if you can to simulate the driving conditions under which any driveability problems have occurred in the past.

Stop the vehicle, but keep it running. Switch the jumper wire from the TE2 terminal to the TE1 terminal and read the codes on the MIL. This procedure will self-diagnose some problems which do not show up on the basic static test.

Clearing codes

After the malfunctioning component has been repaired/replaced, the trouble code(s) stored in computer memory must be canceled. To accomplish this, simply remove the 15A EFI fuse for at least 30 seconds with the ignition switch off (the lower the temperature, the longer the fuse must be left out). On Corolla models before 1993, pull the STOP fuse.

Cancellation can also be affected by removing the cable from the negative battery terminal, but other memory systems (such as the clock) will also be canceled.

If the diagnosis code is not canceled, it will be stored by the ECM and appear with any new codes in the event of future trouble.

Should it become necessary to work on engine components requiring removal of the battery terminal, first check to see if a diagnostic code has been recorded.

Volkswagen

Digifant I and II systems

Retrieving codes

Some vehicles equipped with the Digifant engine management system and sold in California have control units with a fault diagnosis capability.

This system indicates faults in the engine management system through a combination rocker switch/indicator light located to the right of the instrument cluster. **Note:** *Not all California models are equipped with a fault diagnosis system. Also, there are several variations among those so equipped. We recommend consulting with a VW dealer service department if you have any questions about the specific system used on your model.*

If it's operating properly, the light comes on briefly when you turn on the ignition. After a short period of driving, it also comes on to report any fault codes that might be stored in memory.

To display any stored fault codes, turn on the ignition - but don't start the engine - and depress the rocker switch for at least four-seconds. The indicator will display any stored fault codes in a series of flashes. For example, two flashes, followed by one flash, followed by four flashes, followed by two flashes, indicates the code 2-1-4-2, which means there's a problem with the knock sensor.

Clearing codes

To erase the fault codes from computer memory, make sure the ignition switch is turned off. Unplug the coolant temperature sensor harness connector.

Depress and hold the rocker switch and, with the switch depressed, turn on the ignition. The codes will then be erased.

Reconnect the coolant temperature sensor. Finally, test drive the vehicle for at least 10 minutes.

CIS-E Motronic systems

The CIS-E Motronic engine management system is used on vehicles equipped with the 2.0L 16-valve engine (engine code 9A). The Motronic system combines the fuel control of the CIS-E fuel injection system with the control of ignition timing, idle speed and emissions into one control unit.

The fuel injection and idle speed control functions of CIS-E Motronic are similar to those used on the CIS-E system. But the Motronic system uses "adaptive circuitry" in its oxygen sensor system. Adaptive circuitry enables the oxygen sensor system to adjust the operating range of fuel metering in accordance with subtle changes in operating conditions caused by such things as normal engine wear, vacuum leaks, changes in altitude, etc.

Retrieving codes

The CIS-E Motronic engine management system can detect faults, store these faults in coded form in its memory and, when activated, display the codes. Each code corresponds to a specific component or function of the Motronic system which should be checked, repaired and/or replaced. When a code is stored on a California vehicle, the "Check" light on the dashboard is illuminated.

You can access trouble codes by using the diagnostic connectors (located under the shifter boot) to activate the memory of the control unit, which displays any stored code(s) on an LED test light **(see illustration)**. Here's how to read the trouble codes on a CIS-E Motronic system.

Make sure the air conditioning is switched off. Verify that fuse numbers 15 (engine electronics), 18 (fuel pump, oxygen sensor) and 21 (interior lights) are good. Inspect the engine ground strap (located near the distributor). Make sure it's in good shape and making a good connection.

Test drive the car for at least five minutes. Make sure the engine speed exceeds 3000 rpm at least once, the accelerator is pressed all the way to the floor at least once and the engine reaches its normal operating temperature.

After the test drive, keep the engine running for at least two minutes before shutting it off. Switch off the ignition. Connect an LED test light to the diagnostic connectors **(see illustration)**. Switch on the ignition.

Any stored fault codes are displayed by the LED as a sequence of flashes and pauses. For example, two flashes, a pause, one flash, a pause, two flashes, a pause and one flash indicates a code 2121, which means there's a prob-

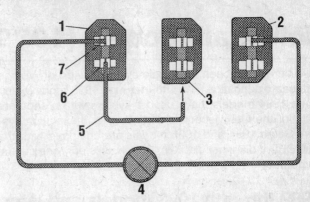

3.24 Here's how to bridge the terminals of the diagnostic connector with a jumper wire and an LED test light to output the codes on a CIS-E Motronic system (the connector is located under the shifter boot)

1	Black connector	5	Jumper wire
2	Blue connector	6	Negative terminal
3	White connector	7	Positive terminal
4	LED test light		

lem in the idle switch circuit. A complete guide to the codes, their causes, the location of the faulty component and the recommended repair are contained in the accompanying tables.

To display the first code on 1988 to 1992 models, connect a jumper wire (as shown in illustration) for at least four seconds, then disconnect it. The LED will flash, indicating a four-digit code. To display the next code, connect the jumper wire for another four seconds, then detach it, and so on. Repeat this process until all stored codes have been displayed.

On 1993 and later models, a special scan tool is required to access all of the diagnostic information. However, using a VW jumper harness, the major four-digit codes can be displayed on the MIL.

Clearing codes

To erase trouble codes from the computer memory after all individual codes have been displayed as described in the previous steps, connect the jumper wire for more than four seconds - this erases the permanent fault storage memory of the control unit.

Refer to Chapter 6 for a list of trouble codes

Volvo, all models (1989 on)

There have been two basic systems used on Volvos with self-diagnostics. The 1989 through 1993 models, and some 1994 models, have used a system with a separate ECU for the fuel injection and another for the ignition system. Some 1994 and 1995 models are equipped with the new OBD II diagnostic system, which uses only one central computer.

1989 through 1993 models and later non-turbo, non-OBD II models)

Locate the diagnostic unit behind left strut tower, and remove its cover **(see illustration)**. Connect the selector cable to socket number 2, which tests the fuel system for codes. Turn the ignition switch to the On position (engine not running). Enter the diagnostic mode by pressing the push button on the diagnostic unit for at least one second, but not more than three seconds.

Watch the red LED, and count the number of flashes in 3-flash series. Flash series are separated by 3-second intervals. Write down all codes.

If no codes are stored, the LED will flash 1-1-1, indicating the fuel system is operating properly.

To access the ignition codes, repeat the above procedure, but with the selector cable plugged into the number 6 socket on the diagnostic unit. **Note:** *Most turbocharged* *models have separate codes for the turbo system which are accessed by hooking the diagnostic cable into socket number 5.*

1994 and later models with OBD II

The 850 Turbo and 960 models have the new, five-character OBD II codes, which are accessible only with the Volvo factory scan tool or a generic (still expensive) OBD II scan tool (used only in socket number 2). There are many more specific codes in the OBD II system than the previous three-digit codes. However, the three-digit codes can still be retrieved from the factory diagnostic unit as described above for earlier models.

Clearing codes

Once all the faults have been corrected, turn the ignition switch to the On position (engine not running). Read the codes again, then depress the button for five seconds and release. After three seconds the LED should light up. While the LED is lit, depress the button again for five seconds, after releasing the button the LED should stop shining.

Verify that the memory is erased by depressing the button for more than one second, but not more than three seconds. The LED should flash 1-1-1, indicating the memory is clear.

3 System descriptions and servicing

1 Exhaust Gas Recirculation (EGR) system

What it does

The EGR system controls nitrogen oxide (NOx) emissions. The system works by allowing a specific amount of exhaust gas to pass from the exhaust manifold into the intake manifold to dilute the air/fuel mixture going to the cylinders.

EGR valves are designed specifically to recirculate the exhaust gas with the air/fuel mixture, thereby diluting the air/fuel mixture enough to keep the NOx compounds within breathable limits. It was discovered that short peak combustion temperatures create NOx. By blending the exhaust gas with the air/fuel mixture, scientists discovered that the rate of combustion slowed down, the high temperatures were reduced and the NOx compounds were kept within limits. Modern engines are equipped with oxidation/reduction catalysts and feedback carburetion or fuel-injection systems that keep the NOx compounds to a minimum. Even with these newer, more efficient systems, the EGR system is still necessary to reduce the excess emissions.

How it works

Early EGR systems are made up of a vacuum-operated valve that admits exhaust gas into the intake manifold (EGR valve), a hose that is connected to a carburetor port above the throttle plates and a Thermostatic Vacuum Switch (TVS) spliced into a pipe that is threaded into the radiator or, more typically, into the coolant passage near the thermostat. The TVS detects the operating temperature of the engine.

At idle, the throttle blocks the port so no vacuum reaches the valve and it remains closed. As the throttle uncovers the port in the carburetor, a vacuum signal goes into the EGR valve and slowly opens the valve, allowing exhaust gases to circulate in the intake manifold.

Since the exhaust gas causes a rough idle and stalling when the engine is cold, the TVS only allows vacuum to the EGR valve when the engine is at normal operating temperature.

Also, when the pedal is pushed to the floor on acceler-ation, there is very little ported vacuum available, resulting in very little mixture dilution that will interfere with power output.

The EGR valve on early carbureted engines without computer controls acts solely in response to the temperature and venturi vacuum characteristics of the operating engine. The EGR valve on engines with computerized controls acts on direct command from the computer after it (the computer) has determined exactly all the working parameters (air temperature, coolant temperature, EGR valve position, fuel/air mixture etc.) of the engine. EGR valves on computerized vehicles normally have a computer-controlled solenoid in line between the valve and vacuum source.

They also often have a position sensor on the EGR valve that informs the computer what position the EGR valve is in.

There are two common types of EGR valves; ported vacuum EGR valves and backpressure EGR valves. Besides the common ported type EGR valve described in the previous paragraphs, there are basically two types of backpressure EGR valves; The most common type is the positive backpressure valve and the other is the negative backpressure valve. It is important to know the difference between positive and negative backpressure valves because they work differently and they are tested differently. Never substitute a positive for a negative backpressure EGR valve. Always install original equipment from the manufacturer when it comes time to repair the EGR valve.

Positive backpressure EGR valve

This type of valve is used largely on domestic models. It uses exhaust pressure to regulate EGR flow by means of a vacuum control valve. The stem of the EGR valve is hollow and allows backpressure to bear onto the bottom of the diaphragm. When sufficient exhaust backpressure is present, the diaphragm moves up and closes off the control valve, allowing the full vacuum signal to be applied to the

1.1 This Isuzu P'up backpressure transducer is typical of many models - it's on the intake manifold, near the distributor

upper portion of the EGR diaphragm. This opens the valve and allows recirculation to occur during heavy loads.

Be careful not to incorrectly diagnose this type of EGR valve. Because backpressure must be present to close the bleed hole, it is not possible to operate the EGR valve with a vacuum pump at idle or when the engine is stopped. The valve is acting correctly when it refuses to move when vacuum is applied or it refuses to hold vacuum. Remember that anything that changes the pressure in the exhaust stream will mess up the calibration of the backpressure system. This includes glass-pack mufflers, headers or even a clogged catalytic converter.

To distinguish this valve, turn the valve upside down and note the pattern of the diaphragm plate. Positive backpressure valves have a slightly raised X-shaped rib. Negative backpressure EGR valves are raised considerably higher. On some GM EGR valves, the only way to distinguish each type is by a letter next to the date code and part number. N means negative while P means positive.

Negative backpressure EGR valve

In this system, the bleed hole is normally closed. When exhaust backpressure drops (reduced load), the bleed valve opens and reduces the vacuum above the diaphragm, cutting the vacuum to the EGR valve. The negative backpressure EGR valve is similar to the positive backpressure EGR valve but operates in the OPPOSITE way. This type of valve is typically used on engines that have less than natural backpressure such as high-performance vehicles with free-flowing mufflers and large-diameter exhaust tubing.

Other types of EGR valves

Dual-diaphragm EGR valve

This EGR valve receives ported vacuum to the upper portion of the vacuum diaphragm while the lower portion receives manifold vacuum. The simultaneous response characteristics control both throttle position and engine load. The dual-diaphragm system is easily recognized by the two vacuum lines attached to the EGR valve.

Ford air pressure EGR valve

Most commonly installed on 1978 and 1979 Ford EEC-I systems, this type of EGR valve is operated by the thermactor air pump pressure instead of vacuum. Pump output is routed to the underside of the diaphragm. Some models are equipped with an EGR position sensor also.

Ford electronic control EGR valve

This EGR valve resembles the air pressure type but it is dependent on the computer and the EGR position sensors to detect the correct conditions and regulate the EGR valve angle.

Chrysler/Mitsubishi dual EGR valve

Most commonly equipped on the 2.6L silent shaft engine, this type of EGR valve uses both a primary and secondary EGR valve mounted at right angles to each other. This system allows for accurate measurement of the exhaust gases.

Computer controls

On the newer type computerized EGR systems, the EGR valve is regulated by the use of different sensors, transducers or vacuum solenoids directly linked to the EGR valve. Here is a list with a brief explanation for each type:

Remote backpressure transducer

This device is not mounted inside the EGR valve, but instead it is found in the vacuum line leading to the EGR valve (see illustration). At idle or light loads, the transducer bleeds off the signal to prevent recirculation to the EGR valve.

Electronic pressure sensor

This capacitive sensor converts exhaust system backpressure into an analog voltage signal that is sent directly to the computer for analysis. This type of pressure sensor is commonly found on newer EEC-IV Ford systems.

Venturi vacuum amplifier

Venturi vacuum from the carburetor indicates engine load and air consumption, but it is inherently too weak to transfer as information to the EGR system. By amplifying the venturi vacuum, the EGR valve is regulated by strong manifold vacuum. These systems also store vacuum in a reservoir for an extra supply when the engine is idling.

Wide open throttle valve

This device is located in-line between the EGR valve and the vacuum source. Controlled by a signal from the carburetor venturi, the wide open throttle valve bleeds off the signal to the EGR valve at wide open throttle to eliminate any mixture dilution and any power loss.

Air cleaner temperature sensor

This sensor cuts off vacuum to the EGR valve until a certain temperature is reached. Instead of reading coolant temperature, the sensor detects air temperature. This is commonly used on carburetor spark port vacuum systems.

Solenoid vacuum valve

This valve works directly with the computer to control the vacuum signal. It is found most commonly on the GM systems and it is referred to as "pulse width modulation."

Electronic vacuum regulator

Instead of the on/off function of a solenoid vacuum valve, the electronic vacuum regulator adjusts vacuum to the EGR valve by way of the pressure sensor and the computer. This device is most commonly found on Ford EEC-III and EEC-IV systems.

Delay timer

This valve interrupts the vacuum to the EGR valve to prevent stalling when the engine is cold. The actual delay time can be anywhere from 30 to 90 seconds after the engine is started. The delay timer works in conjunction with a solenoid vacuum valve.

Charge temperature switch

This switch senses the temperature of the intake system also, but it acts strictly as an ON/OFF switch to prevent current from reaching the delay timer when the temperature is below 60-degrees F. This prevents any EGR mixture and consequently rough idle or stalling when cold. This system is commonly found on Chrysler emissions systems.

EGR valve position sensors

These sensors detect the exact position of the EGR valve and send the information to the computer. These sensors are discussed in detail in Section 8.

Electronic EGR valve

Some of the most recent designs (primarily from GM) employ an EGR valve that is not operated by vacuum at all - an electronic solenoid in the valve is operated electrically by the computer. Diagnosing systems with these valves is beyond the scope of the home mechanic.

Diagnosis and checking

Note: *The following procedures do not apply to vehicles equipped with electronic EGR valves. These vehicles must be taken to a dealer service department or other repair shop for diagnosis.*

Symptoms of bad EGR valves

EGR system malfunctions are recognized by common symptoms and running conditions that can be singled out with some basic testing and knowledge. The most common symptom is a rough idle or stalling when the engine is cold (and often when the engine is warmed up, too). Most problems in the EGR system are reduced to exhaust gases recirculating when they should not or not recirculating when they should. In the former case, the addition of exhaust gas to the intake air/fuel mixture when the engine is cold will make the engine run rough or even cause it to stall. On the other hand, without the exhaust gases recirculating after the engine is warm, the engine will react with detonation, increased combustion temperatures and a high output of NOx compounds.

One advantage with having your vehicle tested for emissions is that most professional mechanics will analyze the high NOx compound readings and make a quick check on the EGR valve.

The test will vary the emissions levels if in fact the EGR valve and/ or system components are faulty. Then it is just a matter of changing the faulty parts.

On the other hand, it is sometimes difficult to distinguish a fuel system problem from an EGR system problem. One typical example of this was a fellow who owned a Ford van with a 302 engine. After he had accelerated and passed a car on the interstate highway and slow downed to pull off the exit, the engine would start to misfire and sometimes even stall. Well, at this point he would pull over to the breakdown lane and turn the engine OFF and start it up again only to have the engine running smooth once more. After a multitude of tune-ups, carburetor overhauls and ignition system checks, a mechanic suggested he pull over into the breakdown lane, but instead of turning the engine OFF, simply pull the vacuum line off the EGR valve and see if the engine smooths back out. To make a long story short, the EGR valve (backpressure type) was sticking in the open position causing the exhaust gases to flow back into the intake system at low speed which in turn caused the rough engine conditions. When the fellow shut the engine OFF, the pressure causing the EGR valve to stick was removed and it closed itself. He replaced the EGR valve and the engine performed smoothly at all speeds.

Checking EGR systems

There are several basic system EGR checks that you can perform on your vehicle to pinpoint any problems. If the EGR valve stem is accessible, push it up or down (against spring pressure) to see if it can move and operate freely **(see illustration)**. If it is stuck, remove the valve and clean it thoroughly. If it still does not budge, replace it with a new unit.

If the EGR valve stem moves smoothly and the EGR system continues to malfunction, check for a pinhole vacuum leak in the diaphragm of the EGR valve. Obtain a can of spray carburetor cleaner and attach the flexible "straw" to the tip. Aim carefully into the diaphragm areas of the EGR valve and spray around the actuator shaft while the engine is running. Listen carefully for any changes in engine rpm. If there is a leak, the engine rpm will increase and surge temporarily. Then it will smooth back out to a constant idle. The only way to properly repair this problem is to replace the EGR valve with a new unit.

1.2 Use your finger to check for free movement of the diaphragm within the EGR valve

1.3 Typical coolant temperature controlled thermostatic vacuum switch - two port style

1   Vacuum present when hot   2   To vacuum source

Another method is a visual check. After the engine has been warmed up to normal operating temperature, open the throttle to approximately 2,500 rpm and observe the EGR valve stem as it moves with the rise in engine rpm. Use a mirror if necessary. If it doesn't move, remove the vacuum hose and check for vacuum with a gauge or just feel with the tip of your finger. **Note:** *On the Ford pressure-activated EGR valves, you should feel pressure instead. If there is no vacuum or pressure, check the EGR system controls.*

Test the EGR valve with the engine running and at normal operating temperature. This test will tell you if the gas flow passages are open and if the gas flow is proper. Remove the vacuum line from the EGR valve and plug it with a golf tee or other suitable device. Attach a hand vacuum pump to the EGR valve. With the engine idling, slowly apply 15 in-Hg of vacuum to the valve and watch the valve stem for movement. If the gas flow is good, the engine will begin to idle rough or it may even stall. If the stem moves but the idle does not change, there is a restriction in the valve (see Cleaning the EGR valve, below), spacer plate or passages in the intake manifold. If the valve stem does not move or the EGR valve diaphragm does not hold vacuum, replace the EGR valve with a new part.

Another common check is for the thermostatic vacuum switch (TVS). This switch is usually regulated by a bimetal core that expands or contracts according to the temperature. The valve remains closed and does not operate as long as the coolant temperature is below 115 to 129-degrees F. As the coolant temperature rises, the valve will open and the EGR system will operate. Remove the switch and place it in a pan of cool water and check the valve for vacuum **(see illustration)** - vacuum should not pass through the valve. Heat the water to the specified temperature (over 129-degrees F) and make sure the valve opens and allows the vacuum to pass. If the switch fails the test, replace it with a new part.

A vacuum gauge can be used to check for excessive exhaust backpressure by observing any vacuum variation. Disconnect a vacuum line connected to an intake manifold port. Install a vacuum gauge between the disconnected vacuum line and the intake manifold port. Block the wheels and set the parking brake. Start the engine and gradually increase speed to 2,000 rpm with the transmission in Neutral. The reading from the vacuum gauge should be above 16 in-Hg. If not, there could be excessive backpressure in the exhaust system. To verify an excessive backpressure problem or a vacuum leak, perform the following:

1   Turn the ignition key OFF.

2   Disconnect the exhaust system at the exhaust manifold.

3   Start the engine (despite the loud exhaust roar) and gradually increase the engine speed to 2,000 rpm.

4   The reading from the exhaust manifold vacuum gauge should be above 16 in-Hg.

5   If 16 in-Hg. is not attained, the exhaust manifold may be restricted (or the valve timing or ignition timing may be late, or there could be a vacuum leak).

6   If 16 in-Hg. is attained, the blockage is most likely in the muffler, exhaust pipes, or catalytic converter. Also, if the catalytic converter debris has entered the muffler, have it replaced also.

Remember, don't condemn a backpressure-type valve until you're sure the exhaust system is stock, has no leaks and it is not clogged or restricted. Also, don't try to get the positive backpressure-type to hold vacuum with the engine off or idling.

Cleaning the EGR valve

The bottoms of EGR valves often get covered with carbon deposits, causing them to restrict exhaust flow or leak exhaust. The valve must be removed so the bottom can be cleaned. There are important points that must be observed when cleaning EGR valves: Never use solvent to dissolve deposits on EGR valves unless you are extremely careful not to get any on the diaphragm. Clean the pintle and valve seat with a dull scraper and wire brush and knock out loose carbon by tapping on the assembly. Some EGR valves can be disassembled for cleaning, but be sure the parts are in alignment before assembly.

2 Evaporative emissions control (EVAP, EEC or ECS) system

What it does

Evaporating fuel accounts for up to 20% of a vehicle's potential pollution, so since 1971 Federal law has required Evaporative emissions control systems on most vehicles. The system traps fuel vapors that would normally escape into the atmosphere and re-routes them back into the engine where they are burned **(see illustration)**.

The system consists of a fuel tank with an air space for heat expansion that allows the vapors to collect and flow to the charcoal canister, the tank cap and associated hoses and tubes. The cap contains a check valve to provide pressure and vacuum relief to the system. On carbureted models, the float bowl has a vent which connects to the canister by a tube.

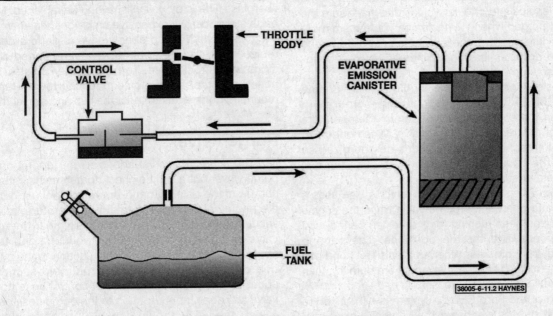

2.1a Typical EVAP system flow diagram

2.1b To remove a typical canister, label and detach the vacuum lines, then remove the canister clamp bolt (arrow) and lift the canister out

2.1c Apply vacuum to the signal hose port on the purge control valve and check that air flows through the purge hose port (the larger port below the signal hose port which is shown with the hose still connected)

How it works

With the engine off, the vapors flow from the tank (and carburetor float bowl, on models so equipped) to the canister where they are absorbed in the charcoal until the engine is started. When the engine is running, the vapors are then purged from the canister and routed to the intake manifold or air cleaner and into the combustion chambers where they are burned.

The system operates using a purge control valve which allows engine vacuum to suck the vapors from the canister at the appropriate time while outside air enters the canister by way of a tube or filter. This purge valve is usually mounted on the canister body, but can also be located remotely or in a hose. Some earlier models have an air intake and filter at the bottom of the canister.

The operation of the purge valve is controlled on some models by solenoids and/or delay valves that make sure the vapors will be purged when the engine can burn them most efficiently. On later models, the system is controlled by the computer and operates in slightly different ways, depending on manufacturer.

On Chrysler models with the Single Module Engine Controller (SMEC) system, the controller grounds a solenoid when the engine is below operating temperature so no vacuum can reach the purge valve. When operating temperature is reached, this solenoid is de-energized so vacuum can then purge the fuel vapors through the fuel injection system or carburetor.

The computer on later model GM vehicles also uses a solenoid valve to operate the purge valve when the engine is hot, after it has been running for a specified period, and at certain speeds and throttle positions. The purging increases until the computer receives a rich fuel condition signal from the oxygen sensor (the vapors are burned), then is regulated until the signal decreases.

Operation of the Ford EEC IV system is similar to the GM system. It purges whenever the engine is at normal operating temperature and off idle.

Checking and component replacement

Note: *Symptoms of problems with the evaporative emissions control system include poor idle, stalling, generally poor driveability and a strong gasoline smell.*

Canister

The canister is usually found in the engine compartment, but may also be located under the vehicle. Some models have more than one canister **(see illustration)**.

Look the canister over for cracks and damage. If the canister is cracked or the inside is soaked with gas, it will have to be replaced. Reach underneath to see if there is a filter in the bottom (later model canisters are sealed). If the fiberglass filter is dirty, it will have to be replaced. Most auto parts stores carry inexpensive emissions replacement parts such as filters. You'll probably have to go to a dealer for a replacement canister, but some well-equipped auto parts stores may stock them. To replace the canister, mark the hoses with tape before disconnecting them. Remove the mounting bolts or disconnect the clip and detach the canister.

Purge valve

There are many variations in the operations of the purge valve, but a simple check to determine if it's working can be made using a hand-operated vacuum pump. With the engine at normal operating temperature, remove the vacuum hose (the hose that's usually near the top of the valve and connected to engine vacuum) and the larger purge hose from the valve. Apply suction to the purge hose port on the valve-the valve should hold suction. Apply about 16 in-Hg of vacuum to the control hose port on the valve and again apply suction to the purge hose port on the valve - the valve should flow air (not hold suction) **(see illustration)**. If the valve does not perform as described, it is probably faulty. Never apply vacuum to the carburetor bowl vent hose outlet of the valve.

Replacing a purge valve located in a hose is a simple matter of detaching the valve (note which direction it faces) from the hoses. A faulty canister-mounted valve will probably require replacement of the canister.

Purge solenoid

Follow the hoses from the top of the canister until you locate the purge solenoid (sometimes the solenoid is located on top of the canister). These solenoids are usually controlled by the computer or other devices so about the only check that can be made is to determine that the connector is securely plugged in and the vacuum hose is not damaged or leaking. Further testing will have to be done by a mechanic or a dealer service department. To replace, unplug the hose and electrical connector and detach the solenoid.

Carburetor float bowl vent valve

Inspect the hose between the carburetor and the canister for cracks or damage. If you suspect that a solenoid-type bowl vent valve is malfunctioning, you'll have to remove it from the carburetor, then apply about ten volts to jumper wires inserted in the connector. The valve should close, preventing air from passing through. If it doesn't, replace the solenoid with a new one.

Vacuum-actuated vent valves are mounted remotely from the carburetor and the charcoal canister. Although these valves operate in different ways, depending on design, they are generally kept closed by engine vacuum. Disconnect the vacuum source hose, connect a hand vacuum pump and make sure the valve holds vacuum. If it doesn't, mark and detach the hoses and install a new valve.

Filler cap and relief valve

Remove the cap. On some models it's possible to detach the valve by unscrewing it from the cap. Look for a damaged or deformed gasket and make sure the relief valve is not stuck open. If either is not in good condition, replace the filler cap with a new one. Replacement caps are generally available at auto parts stores. Make sure you get the right cap because the wrong one may not let the system

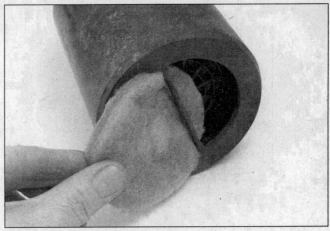

2.2 Replace the charcoal canister filter by pulling it out and inserting a new one

vent properly, causing fuel starvation and could even collapse of the fuel tank.

Vacuum delay valve

If the engine is hard to start when hot, the delay valve could be faulty. Disconnect the vacuum hose, connect a vacuum pump and see if the valve will hold vacuum. If it doesn't, replace the canister with a new one.

Canister filter

Some models are equipped with a filter at the bottom of the charcoal canister which should be replaced when it gets dirty **(see illustration)**.

Hoses

Trace the hoses leading to and from the canister to make sure they aren't disconnected or split. Your sense of smell can be a valuable diagnostic tool here because gasoline and its residue have a strong smell which can tip off the location of even a small crack in a hose.

Always mark the hoses with tape before disconnecting them because even one misrouted hose can cause major problems. Make sure to use only hoses designed for fuel system use.

3 Positive Crankcase Ventilation (PCV) system

What it does

When the engine is running, a certain amount of the fuel/air mixture escapes from the combustion chamber past the piston rings into the crankcase as blow-by gases. The Positive Crankcase Ventilation (PCV) system is designed to reduce the resulting hydrocarbon emissions (HC) by routing them from the crankcase to the intake manifold and combustion chambers, where they are burned during engine operation.

How it works

The PCV system is basically a check valve with hoses for directing crankcase blow-by back into the combustion chambers in the engine **(see illustration)**. It consists of a hose which directs fresh air from the air cleaner into the crankcase, the PCV valve (basically a one-way valve that allows the blow-by gases to pass back into the engine) and associated hoses. On some models a separate filter for the PCV system is located in the air cleaner housing. Some models have a fixed orifice (usually in a hose) instead of a PCV valve that must be kept clear or rough idling and stalling can result.

Checking

Note: *Symptoms of problems with the PCV system include rough idling or high idle speed and stalling. A clogged PCV system can cause oil leaks around the PCV valve, oil filler and dipstick.*

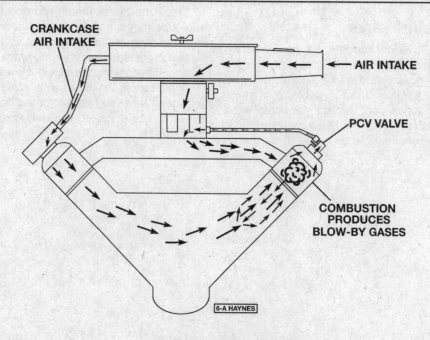

3.1a **Typical PCV system flow**

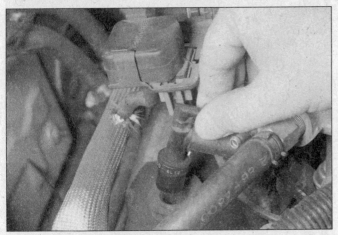

3.1b Shake the PCV valve; it should rattle

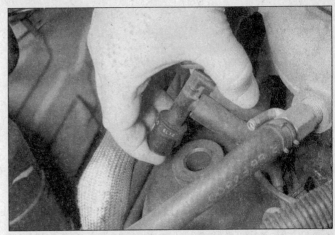

3.2 With the engine running, put your finger over the end of the PCV valve; you should feel vacuum

PCV valve

The PCV valve is usually located in the valve cover, in the intake manifold, in the oil filler cap or on the side of the engine block. Remove the valve and shake it; it should rattle freely **(see illustration)**. If it is stuck or dirty, replace it with a new one. To check the valve operation with the engine running at idle, pull the PCV valve out of the mount and place your finger over the valve inlet. A strong vacuum will be felt and a hissing noise will be heard if the valve is operating properly **(see illustration)**. Replace the valve with a new one if it is not functioning as described. Do not attempt to clean the old valve. PCV valves for most models are available inexpensively at auto parts stores.

Hoses

Trace the hoses from the valve cover to the other connections and check for cracks and leaks. Mark the hose connections with tape so you know where they go and disconnect them. Check the hoses to make sure they aren't clogged (a major PCV system problem). Clean a clogged hose by blowing compressed air through it or by using a long wire and solvent. If any hoses are soft, collapsed, cracked or deteriorated, replace them with new ones. Be sure to use oil-resistant hose of the same type. This hose is available in bulk at auto parts stores, although you may have to get replacement molded hoses at a dealer.

PCV filter

Whenever the air cleaner element is replaced, check the PCV filter **(see illustrations)**. Removable filters can be washed in solvent, squeezed out and reinstalled. If the filter is clogged, replace it with a new one. They are available at most auto parts stores. Filters made of wire mesh can simply be cleaned, re-oiled and reinstalled.

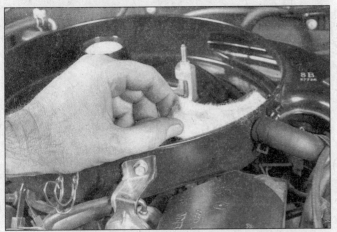

3.3 On some models, you can pull the PCV filter out with your fingers

3.4 On this type of PCV filter, the housing is held in place by a clip; it should be replaced as a unit

4 Air injection systems

What it does and how it works

This Section deals with the air injection systems that are present on earlier carbureted engines as well as some updated computerized engines. The air injection system on most vehicles is simply a specialized series of components (e.g., an air pump, pulley, drivebelt, injection tubes and several different types of air management valves) attached to the engine for the purpose of injecting air into the exhaust downstream from the exhaust ports to help complete the combustion of any unburned gases after they leave the combustion chamber.

The formal names of these systems include the "AIR" (Air Injection Reaction) by GM, "Thermactor" by Ford and "Air Injection" by Chrysler. Mechanics commonly refer to this system as the "smog pump."

Regardless of the names, their functions are the same. The air injection introduces fresh air, high in oxygen content, into the exhaust of an operating engine. This process causes further oxidation (burning) of the hydrocarbons and carbon monoxide left in the hot exhaust gases. In other words, the oxygen unites with the carbon monoxide to form carbon dioxide, a harmless gas. The oxygen also combines with the hydrocarbons to produce water, usually in vapor form. As a result, the air injection system is a very efficient process to lower both HC and CO emissions from any automotive type gasoline engine.

In some vehicles, the air injection system directs the air into the base of the exhaust manifold to assist the oxidation process in this area. Other vehicles have systems that inject the air through the cylinder head, at the exhaust ports, causing the oxidation process to begin within this area. Vehicles equipped with three-way catalytic converters often have air injected directly into the converter.

Air injection systems are less common on modern engines. Automakers have designed newer systems that meet emission standards without air injection. Some engines are equipped with a passive (often called Pulse Air) system, which does not use an air pump. In this system, positive and negative exhaust pressures pull air into the exhaust system by way of special reed or check valves **(see illustration)**.

All things considered, the different systems serve one common purpose: to inject air into the exhaust system and help burn any fuel that did not ignite while in the combustion chamber.

By today's standards, the "smog pump" is considered a performance robber or gas mileage reducer. For many years it was quite common to find many of the air injection systems completely removed from the engine and the exhaust ports capped with brass plugs! Eventually, the law required all air injection systems to be intact and ready to perform as originally intended. It became necessary to dig into the garage or even hunt wrecking yards for the pump, hoses and valves that were originally installed on the vehicle.

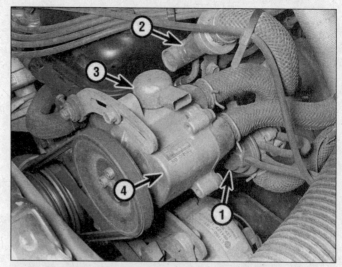

4.1 The air injection valves are usually found near the air pump-the relief valve on this pump is used to vent excessive pressure to the atmosphere

1	Air switching valve	3	Relief valve
2	Check valve	4	Air pump

4.2 This is what the air pump and injection lines look like after they have been removed from the engine

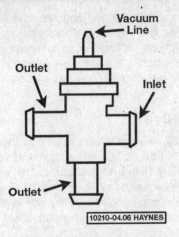

4.3 A typical diverter valve

Checking the air injection system

When the air injection system is working correctly, you should hear a slight whirring sound that rises in pitch as the engine rpm's increase. Common problems associated with an air injection system are excessively noisy pumps, screeching or whining drivebelts, backfiring (diverter valve), or failing the emissions test.

Another common problem is an exhaust leak in or around the air injection components. First check all the fittings in the exhaust manifold that attach the injection lines **(see illustration)**. Stripped threads or broken tubes (usually at the bends) cause the exhaust gases to enter the engine compartment and eventually the passenger compartment. Next check the exhaust manifold itself for cracks, warpage or burned-out gaskets. Replace any necessary component to seal the exhaust system.

Checking air injection systems usually involves checking the valves (check valve, diverter valve, bypass valve and switching valve) for proper functions and response. Each different air injection system has a different combination of these valves, so it is best to familiarize yourself with their differences.

Diverter and switching valves

There are instances where the injected air can cause problems. When the engine is decelerating, the fuel mixture in the combustion chamber is rich and air injected into the exhaust can cause backfiring.

To prevent this problem, the system requires a diverter valve. This valve reroutes the injection system air away from the exhaust system during deceleration. The diverter valve is located downstream of the air pump. On some vehicles the diverter valve is mounted on the fenderwell or on the firewall and in combination with other types of management valves.

On some GM engines, the switching valve is located downstream of the diverter valve. On computer-controlled models, this device switches air to the catalytic converter when the engine is in closed loop. In open loop, the switching valve sends air to the exhaust manifold. The main purpose is to get the engine management system into closed loop (normal) operation as soon as possible by heating the oxygen sensor.

Typically, the air must pass through the diverter valve before it goes anywhere else in the system. Most of the time the air is directed one way, except when the vehicle is decelerating. In this situation, the air gets diverted into the air cleaner or into the atmosphere.

There are different methods of controlling the diverter valve depending on the year of the vehicle. On older carbureted engines, a vacuum line running from the carburetor signals the valve to switch airflow while on computerized engines, the computer decides when the best time is depending upon the information it receives from the throttle position sensor, temperature sensor etc.

Diverter valves are commonly called "anti-backfire" valves. When the valve is not working properly, the engine will sputter and pop as the vehicle is decelerating. Also, the valve might get stuck in the divert position and cause the CO and HC levels to increase abnormally high. In either case, check carefully to make sure the diverter valve is not stuck in any one position!

Another quick check is to find out if there is an ample amount of fresh air coming from the air pump. Squeeze the main hose that sends fresh air to the diverter valve and feel for a steady pulsation that increases when the engine rpm's are increased. Also, check the outgoing hoses after the diverter valve for a steady pulsation of air as it gets channeled into the exhaust system (acceleration) or into the air cleaner (deceleration).

On older carbureted engines, remove the vacuum line **(see illustration)** to the diverter valve and check to make sure that the pressurized air does not get diverted but instead continues to flow into the exhaust system. Install the vacuum line and check that the air is diverted on deceleration.

The Haynes Emissions Control Manual

On newer computerized engines, check the electrical connections on the switching solenoids to verify complete contact and proper voltage signals. These systems might suffer from electronic problems, so we recommend they be diagnosed by a dealer service department or other repair shop.

Check valve

The check valve is a simple device that allows air to flow one direction (to the exhaust manifold) but not the other direction (exhaust backpressure toward the air pump). If a check valve fails in an air pump system, exhaust gas will escape and contaminate the pump and hoses. This can also cause backpressure loss and offset the EGR valve operation.

Check valve failure is obvious when exhaust soot is detected in and around the air pump. To test a check valve, remove it and blow through it toward the manifold end, then attempt to blow through the valve in the other direction. Normal air flow should be in one direction only.

Bypass valve

Bypass valves and combination bypass/diverter valves can cause a loss of air to the exhaust if they fail in the bypass mode. If they fail open, they can put air into the exhaust system when it is rich. This often causes backfire and can melt the catalytic converter substrate.

Check a normally closed bypass valve with the engine at a fast idle. Remove the small vacuum hose from the diaphragm upper portion of the bypass valve and feel for air to vent out the bottom (to the atmosphere).

Check a normally open bypass valve with the vacuum line attached to the bypass valve. The air should flow toward the outlet.

If the bypass valve fails the test, replace it with a new unit. If the vacuum source from the engine has been cut off, check the vacuum control system.

Air control solenoids on Fords

Many vehicles are equipped with a Thermactor air control system that uses an air control valve to channel air from the air pump to either the exhaust manifold, the catalytic converter or back into the atmosphere, depending on the operating conditions of the engine. When the engine is cold, the air control valve directs air to the exhaust manifold to reduce HC and CO VACUUM emissions. When the engine is warm, the air SUPPLY control valve directs air to the three-way catalytic converter to control NOx compounds as well as HC and CO. If the engine idles for an unusually long time, the air control valve directs the air back into the atmosphere to avoid overheating the catalytic converter.

The operation of the air control valve is regulated by the computer by way of two vacuum control solenoid valves; The Thermactor Air Bypass (TAB) and the Thermactor Air Diverter (TAD). The TAB and TAD valves are directly connected to engine vacuum and the valves are in complete control of the air control valve functions by their ability to switch the vacuum supply to certain portions of the valve. The TAB and TAD valves are normally CLOSED, and vent vacuum only when they are de-energized.

The computer controls manifold vacuum to the air control valve bypass circuit by activating the TAB valve. This allows air from the air pump to vent into the atmosphere by way of the bypass circuit. When the computer activates the TAD valve, manifold vacuum passes from the diverter valve, through the air control valve (one unit) and from there the air goes to the catalytic converter instead of the exhaust manifold.

The TAB and TAD valves can fail and prevent the catalytic converter from receiving extra oxygen. This off-balance situation can increase the emission levels of HC, CO and NOx compounds.

There are several checks you can perform if a system with these valves is suspect:

Turn the ignition key OFF and disconnect the electrical connectors from the TAB and TAD valves. Use an ohmmeter and check the resistance of the valves. It should range from 50 to 110 ohms. More or less resistance indicates that the solenoid is faulty and must be replaced with a new part.

Turn the key ON (engine not running) - the TAB and TAD valves should both be receiving battery voltage. If the reading is less, check the harness for continuity. This is a difficult procedure and requires a thorough wiring diagram.

Check the mechanical operation of the TAB and TAD valves with a vacuum pump. Connect the pump to the inlet port on the valve (manifold) and plug the outlet port (air control valve). Apply vacuum. With the key OFF, the valve should lose vacuum (bleed down). With the key ON, the TAB and TAD valves should open and hold vacuum (only if the outlet port is securely plugged). If necessary, use a jumper wire to apply battery voltage to the TAB and TAD valves. This test will indicate if the valve is directing the vacuum properly.

With the engine running, check the vacuum supply at the TAB and TAD valve. Each valve should receive approximately 10 in-Hg. of manifold vacuum at idle. If the reading is low or zero, check the vacuum lines for leaks and correct hose routing.

The TAB and TAD valves are emissions control components and they are covered under the vehicle manufacturer's emissions warranty of 5 years or 50,000 miles. Be sure to check with your dealership service department before replacing either of these valves. If you absolutely have to change the TAB and TAD valves, on some vehicles, the two valves are separate parts (as in the 2.3L four-cylinder engines) while other models, the valves are a single unit (V6 and V8 engines).

Air injection system noise check

The pump-driven air injection system is not completely noiseless. Under normal conditions, noise rises in pitch as the engine speed increases. To determine if noise is the fault of the air injection system, detach the injection pump drivebelt (after verifying that the belt tension is correct) and operate the engine. If the noise disappears, proceed with the following diagnosis. **Caution:** *The pump must accumulate 500 miles before the following check is valid.*

If the belt noise is excessive:

a) Check for a loose belt and tighten as necessary.
b) Check for a seized pump and replace it if necessary.
c) Check for a loose pulley. Tighten the mounting bolts as required.
d) Check for loose, broken or missing mounting brackets or bolts. Tighten or replace as necessary.

If there is excessive mechanical noise:

a) Check for an overtightened mounting bolt.
b) Check for an overtightened drivebelt.
c) Check for excessive flash on the air pump adjusting arm boss and remove as necessary.
d) Check for a distorted adjusting arm and, if necessary, replace the arm.

If there is excessive noise (whirring or hissing sounds):

a) Check for a leak in the hoses (use a soap and water solution to find the leaks) and replace the hose(s) as necessary.
b) Check for a loose, pinched or kinked hose and reassemble, straighten or replace the hose and/or clamps as required.
c) Check for a hose touching other engine parts and adjust or reroute the hose to prevent further contact.
d) Check for an inoperative bypass valve and replace if necessary.
e) Check for an inoperative check valve and replace if necessary.
f) Check for loose pump or pulley mounting fasteners and tighten as necessary.
g) Check for a restricted or bent pump outlet fitting. Inspect the fitting and remove any casting flash blocking the air passageway. Replace bent fittings.
h) Check for air dumping through the bypass valve (only at idle). On many vehicles, the system has been designed to dump air at idle to prevent overheating the catalytic converter. This condition is normal. Determine that the noise persists at higher speeds before proceeding.
i) Check for air dumping through the bypass valve (the decel and idle dump). On many vehicles, the air is dumped into the air cleaner or the remote silencer. Make sure that the hoses are connected properly and are not cracked.

Checking the passive (Pulse Air) system

If the reed or check valve fails, you'll normally hear excessive exhaust system noise from under the hood and notice hardening of the rubber hose from the valve to the air cleaner.

If exhaust noise is excessive, check the air supply tube-to-exhaust manifold joint and the valve and air cleaner hose connections for leaks. If the manifold joint is leaking, retighten the tube fitting. If the hose connections are leaking, install new hose clamps (if the hose hasn't hardened). If the hose has hardened, replace it with a new one as well.

To determine if the valve has failed, disconnect the hose from the inlet. With the engine idling (transmission in Neutral), hold a strip of paper in front of the inlet - the paper should be sucked against the opening of the valve if it's working properly. If a steady stream of exhaust gas is escaping from the inlet (which will blow the paper away from the valve), the valve is defective and should be replaced with a new one. **Warning:** *Don't use your hand to feel for the exhaust pulses - the exhaust gas is very hot!*

Component replacement

To replace the air bypass valve, air supply control valve, check valve, combination air bypass/air control valve or the silencer, label and disconnect the hoses leading to them, replace the faulty component and reattach the hoses to the proper ports. Make sure the hoses are in good condition. If not, replace them with new ones.

To replace the air supply pump, first loosen the appropriate engine drivebelts, then remove the faulty pump from the mounting bracket. Label all wires and hoses as they're removed to facilitate installation of the new unit.

If you're replacing either of the check valves on a Pulse Air System (Thermactor II), be sure to use a back-up wrench.

After the new pump is installed, adjust the drivebelts to the specified tension.

Servicing air pumps

Many GM systems include air pumps that have a filter element that must be replaced periodically. Check your owner's manual for the mileage intervals. First remove the air pump drivebelt and the pulley. Use a pair of needle-nose pliers to remove the filter element **(see illustration)**. Use a factory filter replacement to avoid any problems with size and exact fit.

4.5 On many GM vehicles, the filter can be pulled out of the air pump with needle-nose pliers

5 Heated air intake (Thermac and EFE) systems

What it does

Although coming under different names and using different techniques, these systems produce the same result: improving engine efficiency and reducing hydrocarbons during the initial warm-up period. Two different methods are used to achieve this goal: Thermostatic air intake (Thermac) and Early Fuel Evaporation (EFE). Thermac warms the air as it enters the air cleaner while EFE heats the air/fuel mixture in the intake manifold. Virtually all later models use some form of Thermac and/or EFE system.

How it works

Thermac

The Thermostatic air intake system improves driveability, reduces emissions and prevents carburetor icing in cold weather by directing hot air from around the exhaust manifold to the air cleaner intake. The Thermac system is made up of the air cleaner housing, a temperature sensor, a vacuum-operated damper door mechanism in the air cleaner snorkel, a flexible tube connected to the exhaust manifold and associated vacuum hoses.

When the engine is cold, the temperature sensor in the air cleaner is closed and full vacuum reaches the vacuum motor which holds the damper door shut so only air heated by the exhaust manifold can enter the snorkel. As the engine warms up, the temperature sensor opens, bleeding off the vacuum motor vacuum and allowing its internal spring to push the door down. This closes off the heated air and allows only cold outside air to enter the snorkel. The vacuum motor spring and vacuum balance one another so the air entering the air cleaner is always at optimum temperature for the best fuel vaporization.

EFE

Two types of EFE are used to heat the vaporized fuel in the intake manifold for improved driveability and emissions during the warm-up period after the engine is first started. One type routes exhaust heat from the exhaust manifold to warm the intake manifold, while the other electrically heats the fuel/air mixture as it enters the manifold.

The exhaust-type EFE uses a valve in the exhaust manifold to recirculate hot exhaust gases which are then used to pre-heat the carburetor and choke for better driveability and emissions. When the engine is cold, the valve is shut,

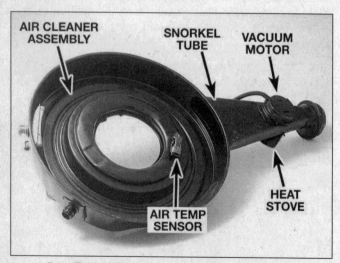

5.1a Typical Thermac system component layout

AIR CLEANER ASSEMBLY — SNORKEL TUBE — VACUUM MOTOR — AIR TEMP SENSOR — HEAT STOVE

5.1b A typical electric EFE, installed between the carburetor and the intake manifold (arrows indicate the heating grids)

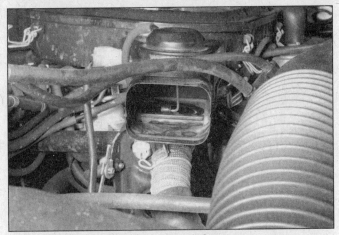

5.2 With the engine at operating temperature, the damper door in the air cleaner snorkel should be open

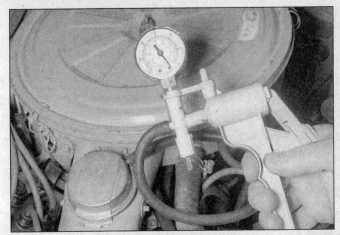

5.3 Use a vacuum pump to check that the vacuum motor will close the damper door and hold it closed

forcing hot exhaust gases to heat the intake manifold until the engine warms up and the valve opens.

The exhaust-type EFE system consists of a heat riser valve in the exhaust manifold, a thermostatic actuator and heat shroud or duct which directs heat to the intake manifold and carburetor. On some models the actuator is simply a counterweighted heat riser with a thermostatic coil spring that contracts when cold, closing the valve and relaxes and opens it when hot. On others the actuator is operated by engine vacuum. On this type, when the engine is cold, the vacuum actuator on the valve is held closed by vacuum from a thermostatic switch in a coolant passage. As the coolant heats up, the switch opens, cutting off the vacuum and the actuator opens the valve.

The electrical-type EFE system is quite simple. It consists of an electrical heating element between the carburetor or fuel injection throttle body which heats and vaporizes the air/fuel mixture as it is drawn into the intake manifold **(see illustration)**. The system is made up of the electrical grid which is activated by a thermostatic switch screwed into a coolant passage or by the computer.

Checking and component replacement

Note: *Symptoms of problems with the heated air intake system(s) include:*

When cold: Poor idle, uneven acceleration, hesitation on acceleration, generally poor performance.

When hot: Overheating, hard starting, poor idle, stalling and detonation

Thermac

With the engine cold, make sure the damper door in the snorkel is in the up (heat on) position. Then, start the engine and allow it to warm up. The door should slowly open, indicating that it is operating properly **(see illustration)**. If there is a problem, check the system components, as described below.

Damper door and vacuum motor

Check the door for binding and make sure it moves freely on the hinge pin. Use spray cleaner to remove any foreign matter and penetrating oil to lubricate it. Disconnect the vacuum hose and connect a vacuum pump to the motor **(see illustration)**. The door should be in the up (heat on) position with the vacuum applied and must hold vacuum.

Replacing the motor is a simple matter of removing the screws or rivets and detaching it from the air cleaner housing **(see illustration)**. On some later Japanese vehicles the motor "screws" into place and can be rotated counterclockwise and lifted out. Replacement motors are available at auto parts stores and dealers.

Temperature sensor

Detach the hoses and use a vacuum pump to make sure the sensor holds vacuum when it's cold and passes vacuum when the engine is hot. Most sensors are held in the air cleaner by clips, so, when replacing, all you have to do is pry up on the tabs of the clip with a screwdriver to detach the valve from the air cleaner. Dealers and auto parts stores carry these valves.

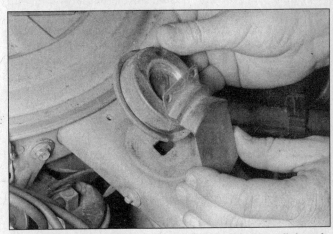

5.4 After removing the screws or rivets, detach the link and lift the vacuum motor out of the air cleaner housing

Hot air duct

Check the duct to make sure it is properly connected and free of tears **(see illustration)**. Replacement ducting hose is available at auto parts stores. If your duct is missing, you can make a new one with the proper length ducting, using large-diameter radiator hose clamps to fasten it in place. Missing plastic or metal ducts must be replaced with the same type (available from a dealer), not ducting hose.

Vacuum hoses

Trace the hoses from the temperature sensor to the manifold and the vacuum motors to make sure they are secure and undamaged. Auto parts stores usually carry vacuum hose in various sizes, so bring the old hose to the store and make sure replacement has the same inside diameter and length.

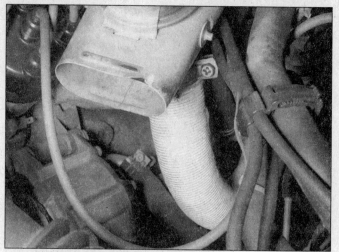

5.5 Inspect the hot air duct hose for damage and leaks

EFE

Exhaust type

Thermostatic spring-actuated

The heat riser is located in the exhaust pipe and is open to the elements, so corrosion can not only keep it from operating freely but can even freeze it in position. If the riser pivot bushings are worn the riser will make a knocking noise when the engine is started. With the engine cold, try moving the counterweight. The valve should move easily with no binding. Start the engine and make sure the valve moves to the closed position and then slowly opens as the engine warms up. A stuck or binding heat riser can often be loosened by soaking the valve in solvent or penetrating oil. Tapping lightly with a hammer can help loosen a stuck valve.

If the heat riser is frozen or the bushings are worn, you'll have to unbolt the exhaust pipe and install a new unit (available from a dealer or auto parts store).

Vacuum-actuated

Unplug the vacuum hose from the actuator and with the engine cold, start the engine. Put you finger over the end of the hose and determine that vacuum is felt. If there is no vacuum, the hose is plugged or the thermostatic switch is no good. If the hose is in good shape, unscrew the switch and replace it with a new one (available at a dealer or auto parts store). It may be necessary to drain the coolant to a level below the switch to avoid a mess as it runs out during the replacement.

To check the vacuum motor itself, connect a vacuum pump and apply about ten inches of vacuum, which should operate the valve. If the motor holds vacuum but doesn't operate the valve, the valve could be frozen. The motor can be unbolted and detached from its mount. To replace a frozen heat valve, you'll have to unbolt the exhaust pipe and detach the valve. Both the valve and actuator are available at a dealer or auto parts store.

Electrical type

Element

With the engine cold, unplug the EFE heating element electrical connector and check it with an ohmmeter. Check the connector on the unit to make sure there is around three ohms resistance. Also check for voltage at the wiring-harness-side of the connector with the ignition on and the engine cold. There should be voltage. Replacing the heating element will require removal of the carburetor or fuel-injection throttle-body unit.

Temperature switch

With the engine cold, unplug the EFE temperature switch and connect a test light to the terminals of the connector. With the ignition switch on and the engine off, the test light should glow. Replace the switch by draining the coolant to below the switch level and unscrewing it with a wrench. Before installing the new switch, apply gasket sealant to the threads (but not to the end of the sensor).

6 Carburetor control systems

This Section deals with the carburetor control systems that are installed onto carbureted engines to help control deceleration, acceleration, backfiring and emissions requirements. The carburetor controls installed on various carburetors will vary, but the purpose for each system is essentially similar. Here are some common carburetor control systems along with a brief explanation and some easy checks and adjustments.

Dashpot

The dashpot system installed on early carbureted engines slows the closing of the throttle on deceleration. This allows the carburetor to switch from the main fuel jets to the idle system, thereby preventing stalling due to an excessively rich air/fuel mixture. Also, the amount of HC (hydrocarbons) emissions is reduced. The air/fuel mixture richens when the intake manifold vacuum suddenly rises when the throttle is closed. The high vacuum will draw fuel into the carburetor from the float bowl without any dilution of air from the air horn (venturi).

The dashpot is made up of a small chamber with a spring-loaded diaphragm and a plunger. The dashpot plunger is in contact with the throttle lever during the last stages of deceleration. When the lever contacts the plunger on deceleration, the lever exerts force on the plunger and air or hydraulic fluid (depending on the type of dashpot) slowly leaks out of the diaphragm through a small hole. This allows the throttle plate to close slowly.

Some dashpot components are adjustable while others are not **(see illustration)**. Consult a factory service manual or other automotive repair manual for the exact procedure. Keep in mind that dashpots are often combined with other throttle devices into the same component.

Throttle positioner
What it is and how it works

Throttle positioners are used to control the engine's idle speed under various conditions. Some designs are vacuum actuated and others are electric solenoids. On vacuum-actuated positioners (which usually look the same as dashpots, except there is one or more vacuum hose(s) connected to it), some use vacuum to turn the positioner on while others use vacuum to turn it off. Be aware of this when checking vacuum conditions.

One basic type throttle positioner functions to prevent dieseling (engine run-on). This type is called a throttle stop solenoid or an idle stop solenoid. When the engine is started, the solenoid is energized and the plunger extends out, pushing against the throttle linkage. This forces the throttle plate to open slightly to the curb idle position. When the ignition switch is turned off, the throttle position solenoid is de-energized and the plunger returns to the normal position. The throttle plate closes completely and the air/fuel supply is cut off, effectively preventing dieseling.

Some throttle positioners are used to increase the curb idle speed to compensate for extra loads on the engine. In this situation, the throttle positioner is referred to as an idle speed-up solenoid or a throttle kicker **(see illustration)**. This type is often used on air-conditioned vehicles. When the air conditioner is switched on, the relay energizes the solenoid, which extends its plunger farther onto the throttle plate, thereby raising the idle speed. This keeps the engine running at a higher rpm to control emissions levels.

Throttle positioners are also used to control idle speed when the automatic transmission is engaged. A relay in the Park/Neutral switch signals the solenoid to raise the idle speed when the transmission is in gear. This opens the throttle slightly to compensate for the increased load on the engine.

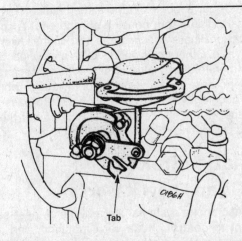

6.1 The dashpot on 1988 and later Hondas can be adjusted by bending this tab - other types of dashpots use screws for adjustment

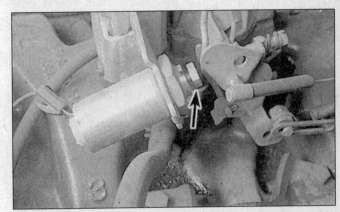

6.2 On some models, the idle speed screw is controlled by an electric solenoid - the adjustment is made at the end of the solenoid

Another type of system is sometimes used on vehicles equipped with power steering. When the steering wheel is turned while the vehicle is stationary and idling, the positioner solenoid raises the idle speed, compensating for the additional load the power steering pump is placing on the engine. This type of system has a switch located on the steering gear, power steering pump or power steering pressure hose. The switch completes the circuit to the solenoid when there's power steering fluid pressure at the switch.

Checking

Note: *A single throttle positioner may be used to operate the throttle under more than one condition (for example, when the air conditioning is switched on and when the automatic transmission is placed in gear). Be sure to check the positioner's function under all the conditions it is designed to operate.*

To check for proper positioner response, first locate the positioner on the carburetor, then start the engine and induce the appropriate load onto the engine and carefully watch the positioner as it is forced to activate. Depending on the type of system, this can be done by either switching the air conditioning system ON, turning the engine OFF (anti-dieseling solenoid), placing the transmission in Drive (wheels blocked, parking brake set and an assistant holding down the brake pedal) or turning the steering wheel from side to side. If the positioner does not actuate to increase the engine speed, first check the vacuum or electrical connections. Make sure the wires or hoses are in good shape. Then check the positioner plunger to make sure it moves freely and is not "frozen." If it is, replace the positioner. Next, apply battery voltage (electrical type) or vacuum to the positioner and see if it operates. If it does not, replace it. If it does operate, the problem is in the circuit or switches.

ISC (Idle Speed Control) motor

What it is and how it works

The ISC motor is a more advanced version of a throttle positioner (see above). The motor is under direct control of the computer, which has the desired idle speed programmed into its memory. The computer compares the actual idle speed from the engine (taken from the distributor or crankshaft position sensor ignition impulses) to the desired rpm reference in memory. When the two do not match, the ISC plunger is moved in or out. This automatically adjusts the throttle to hold an idle speed independent of engine loads.

Many ISC motors have a throttle contact switch at the end of the plunger. The position of the switch determines whether or not the ISC should control idle speed. When the throttle lever is resting against the ISC plunger, the switch contacts are closed, at which time the computer moves the ISC motor to the programmed idle speed. When the throttle lever is not contacting the ISC plunger, the switch contacts are open and the ECM stops sending idle speed commands and the driver controls engine speed.

Checking

With the engine warmed to normal operating temperature, remove the air cleaner assembly and any other components that obscure your view of the ISC motor. Hook up a tachometer in accordance with the manufacturer's instructions and check the VECI label under the hood to determine what the correct idle rpm should be.

Have an assistant start the engine. Check that the engine rpm is correct. Have your assistant turn on the air conditioning (if equipped), headlights and any other electrical accessories. If the vehicle is equipped with power steering, have your assistant turn the steering wheel from side to side. Note the reading on the tachometer. The engine speed should remain stable at the correct idle speed. If the vehicle is equipped with an automatic transmission, block the wheels and have your assistant set the parking brake, place his/her foot firmly on the brake pedal and place the transmission in Drive. Again, the engine rpm should remain stable at the correct speed. **Warning:** Do *not stand directly in front of the vehicle during this test.*

If the ISC motor is not functioning as it should, first check the condition of the wiring and electrical connector(s). Make sure the connector is securely attached and there is no corrosion at the terminals. For further diagnosis of this system, refer to the factory service manual for your particular vehicle or take the vehicle to a dealer service department or other qualified shop.

Fuel deceleration valve

The fuel deceleration valve is designed to prevent backfire during deceleration. This device opens a separate air/fuel mixture passage in the carburetor to dilute the fuel charge with additional air. When the intake manifold vacuum rises, the valve moves up to allow a mixture of air and fuel from the carburetor to flow into the intake manifold. The valve provides enough mixture to maintain proper combustion and prevent unburned fuel from being released out the tailpipe.

Some deceleration valves are not attached directly to the carburetor but accomplish the same results. This type of valve has a diaphragm housing on one end. A control manifold vacuum line is attached to a port on the lower portion of the valve. Other ports on the valve are connected to the intake manifold and air cleaner. When deceleration causes an increase in manifold vacuum, the diaphragm opens the deceleration valve and allows air to pass from the air cleaner to the intake manifold, leaning out the fuel mixture and preventing exhaust system backfire.

Automatic choke
What it is and how it works

Automatic choke systems use a bi-metal, heat-sensitive element to control choke valve position, and most modern choke systems also have an electric heater to speed warming up the bi-metal element (this causes the choke to disengage more quickly, helping reduce emissions) **(see illustration)**. The bi-metal element operates a choke valve which closes the carburetor air horn and is synchronized with the throttle plate(s). When the engine is cold, the choke valve closes and the throttle plate opens (operated by the fast idle cam) sufficiently to provide a rich mixture and an increased idle speed for easy starting. Many automatic choke systems are equipped with a choke breaker diaphragm that opens the choke valve when the engine is accelerating and the engine is cold. This prevents the engine from bogging from insufficient airflow.

Checking

The choke only operates when the engine is cold, so this check should be performed before the engine has been started for the day. Open the hood and remove the air cleaner cover and filter from the top of the carburetor. Locate the choke plate (the flat plate attached by small screws to a pivot shaft) in the carburetor throat.

Operate the throttle linkage and make sure the plate closes completely. Start the engine and watch the plate - when the engine starts, the choke plate should open slightly. Allow the engine to continue running at idle speed. As the engine warms up to operating temperature, the plate should slowly open. After several minutes, the choke plate should be fully open to the vertical position.

Note that the engine speed corresponds to the plate opening angle. With the plate closed, the engine should run at a fast idle speed. As the plate opens, the engine speed will decrease. The fast idle speed is controlled by the fast idle cam, and, even though the choke plate is open completely, the idle speed will remain high until the throttle plate is opened, releasing the fast idle cam. Check the drop in idle speed as the choke plate opens by occasionally tapping the accelerator.

If the choke doesn't work as described, shut off the engine and check the shaft and linkage for deposits which could cause binding. Use a spray-on choke cleaning solvent to remove the deposits as you operate the linkage. This should loosen up the linkage and the shaft and allow the choke to work properly. If the choke still fails to function correctly, the choke bimetal assembly is malfunctioning or in need of adjustment.

Some chokes use warm coolant to change the position of the butterfly valve. In this case, check for the proper water circulation to the choke heating element.

HIC (Hot Idle Compensator) valve

On some vehicles, when the engine is excessively hot, a hot idle compensator opens an air passage to lean the fuel/air mixture. This increases the idle speed, which in turn cools the engine and prevents excess fuel vaporization and consequently the release of unburned hydrocarbons. The compensator is controlled by a bimetallic strip which bends when it senses high temperatures, thereby opening the air passage.

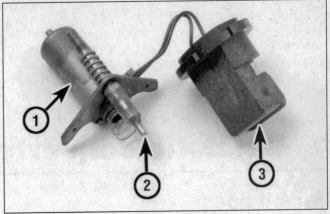

6.3 A typical Rochester carburetor mixture control solenoid assembly consists of:

1   The mixture control solenoid
2   The adjustment screw
3   The electrical connector

Mixture control solenoid

In the late 1970's, the feedback carburetor was introduced to reduce emissions on carbureted vehicles. This system incorporates a computer which controls certain solenoids and valves on the carburetor. The main solenoid controlled by computer is the mixture control solenoid **(see illustration)**. It is an electronically controlled metering rod that varies the amount of fuel that is allowed to pass into the main fuel jets of the carburetor. Some solenoids are mounted vertically and others are mounted horizontally. The computer is programmed to turn the solenoid ON and OFF (cycle) ten times per second. These solenoids are generally referred to as duty-cycle solenoids. Each cycle lasts about 100 milliseconds. The amount of fuel metered into the main fuel jet or passage is directly determined by how many milliseconds the solenoid is ON during each cycle. The solenoid can be ON almost 100% of the time or OFF nearly 100% of the time.

Use only a specialized meter to calculate the frequency of the solenoid to determine the duty-cycle for your vehicle. Consult a factory service manual for the checking procedure and correct duty-cycle measurements for your particular vehicle.

Fuel cut-off solenoid

Fuel cut-off solenoids are mounted onto the carburetor to instantly shut off the fuel to the main jet as the ignition is switched OFF. This prevents engine run-on and unnecessary vibration and backfire.

To check the operation of the fuel cut-off solenoid, simply turn the ignition key to ON and check for battery voltage at the solenoid connector. If the voltage is present, the solenoid should make a slight "clicking" noise as the plunger is energized. When the ignition is turned OFF the solenoid should click again, as the plunger extends into the carburetor.

7 Catalytic converter

What it does

The catalytic converter is a unique device because it promotes a reaction which changes the exhaust gases flowing through it without being affected itself. This catalytic reaction reduces the level of three major pollutants: Hydrocarbon (HC), Carbon Monoxide (CO) and Oxides of Nitrogen (NOx). By removing these major pollutants, the catalytic converter system allows the other fuel and emissions systems to be fine-tuned for optimum operation and driveability. These are controlled on later models by the computer and a network of engine sensors. This is called a "feedback" or "closed loop" system.

Catalytic converters are mounted in the exhaust system between the exhaust manifold and the muffler. Because they generate a lot of heat, they are surrounded by heat shields.

The catalytic elements in the converter are palladium, platinum and rhodium. By coating ceramic pellets in the bed of the converter or a ceramic honeycomb, a large surface area is provided for the gases to react on as they pass through the converter

There are two basic types of converters: oxidation and reduction. On later models, they are combined into one unit called a three-way converter. An oxidation converter uses platinum and palladium to oxidize (add oxygen to) hydrocarbons and carbon monoxide, converting them to water vapor. Since oxidization converters have little effect on NOx, a reduction converter containing rhodium and platinum is used to convert (reduce) the oxygen in the NOx into nitrogen and carbon dioxide.

One stage of a typical three-way converter contains a reduction-oxidation catalyst using rhodium and platinum which controls NOx, HC and CO emissions. The second stage has only a platinum catalyst for controlling the remaining HC and CO emission. On some models air is pumped directly into a chamber between the two stages (see illustration).

How it works

As the gases flow through the converter, they start to burn rapidly at temperatures reaching 1600-degrees F. The extra oxygen needed to support such high temperatures is provided by the air injection system which pumps air into the exhaust system or the converter itself, or by a lean air/fuel ratio. Three-way catalysts use air switching valves to direct air to the manifold during the high-emissions warm-up mode to help burn the HC and CO. It then shifts the air injection to the chamber in the middle of the converter when NOx production begins (normal operating temperature is reached).

Checking

Note: *About the only common noticeable catalytic converter problem is a plugged converter. This will cause a noticeable drop in power and, if severe enough, stalling or hard starting because of the extreme exhaust back-pressure. Melting of the catalyst pellets or disintegration of the ceramic honeycomb matrix is due to overheating caused by a rich mixture or a misfiring cylinder.*

Catalytic converter

Testing the catalytic system requires special equipment, but there are a couple of simple ways to check for a clogged converter. Tap the converter with a rubber mallet and listen for rattling which indicates that the catalysts have flaked off or the ceramic matrix is broken, meaning that replacement is in order (does not apply to ceramic bead-type converters).

Use a vacuum gauge to check for vacuum drop caused by a plugged converter. Connect the gauge to a direct intake manifold vacuum source and run the engine up to a speed around 3000 rpm and hold it there. If the exhaust system is blocked, the gauge will drop considerably at this speed. For example, if your gauge reads 18 inches of vacuum and you rev the engine up, the reading should be about 15 inches. If the gauge reading drops, there is a blockage.

Catalytic system

Every time the vehicle is raised, you can easily check the converter and components for damage. Check the heat shields to make sure they are all in place and securely mounted. Inspect the converter connections to the exhaust pipes for damage or missing bolts. Trace the air injection system hoses and pipes from the converter, making sure they aren't disconnected or leaking.

About replacement catalytic converters

The Environmental Protection Agency (EPA) closely regulates replacement catalytic converters, so be sure to familiarize yourself with their requirements before starting work. Not following the EPA guidelines is considered "tampering" with the emissions system and is punishable by a hefty fine. The EPA does realize that factory replacement catalytic converters are expensive so they have approved the installation of more reasonably priced aftermarket units under certain conditions.

The EPA says basically that you must use only a factory replacement converter on any vehicle which is still under the federally mandated emissions warranty (in which case the manufacturer would generally replace it at no charge anyway). You can use an approved aftermarket converter on any vehicles which are out of warranty and have damaged or non-functioning units.

Aftermarket converters and installation kits are available at auto parts stores. Also, most auto exhaust shops now install these aftermarket converters. Originally there were only a few "universal" units, but now the full range of aftermarket catalytic converters covers virtually every make and model. Be sure to check with the installer or auto parts store to make sure you are getting the right converter or kit for your car and that everything is in compliance with EPA regulations to avoid trouble later. The auto parts store should have all the necessary information along with advice on the hardware and pipes you'll need to do the job. Remember also that these replacement units come with a mandated lifetime guarantee.

Replacement

Raise the vehicle and support it securely on jackstands. The vehicle must be cold before starting work (let it set for several hours because converters can hold their heat for some time). Before beginning, check to make sure all the parts required for installation, as well as replacement clamps, bolts and nuts are with the converter. Removal of the existing hardware usually destroys it, so plan ahead. If your converter has air hoses, it's also a good idea to get new ones while you're at it. On the vehicle, squirt penetrat-

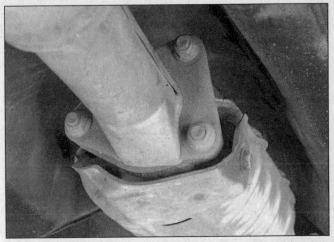

7.1 Most catalytic converters are installed using flanges like this

ing oil on the bolts or nuts which will have to be removed and let it soak in.

Most converters are attached to the exhaust pipes with clamps and flanges **(see illustration)**. Remove these clamps (not always a simple matter, so a nut splitter may be necessary). Some converters are welded in place. On these you'll have to cut the pipes next to the welds with a pipe cutter or hacksaw. Detach the air hose and lower the converter.

Install the new one in reverse order of the previous steps, clamping the new air hoses in place. Assemble everything loosely, making sure that all the hardware and gaskets are in place. All slip fittings must insert at least two inches over each other with the clamp over the center of the overlap. It's a good idea to apply anti-seize compound to each joint, to prepare for the day when you might have to disassemble the exhaust system. Make sure everything is lined up properly before tightening the bolts, clamps and hangers.

After installation, be sure to dispose of the old converter properly. Most wrecking yards will probably pay you for it because there is an ongoing program to reclaim the rhodium, platinum and palladium. Lastly, be sure to fix whatever condition caused the converter to go bad in the first place, so you won't have to repeat the job later.

8 Engine management systems

Note: *Some of the procedures in this Section require you to operate the vehicle after disconnecting a portion of the engine management system (such as a sensor or a vacuum line). This may set trouble codes in the computer. Be sure to clear any trouble codes (see Chapter 2) before returning the vehicle to normal service.*

This Section deals with the engine management systems used on modern, computer-controlled vehicles to meet new low-emission regulations. The system's computer, information sensors and output actuators interact with each other to collect, store and send data. Basically, the information sensors collect data (such as the intake air mass and/or temperature, coolant temperature, throttle position, exhaust gas oxygen content, etc.) and transmit this data, in the form of varying electrical signals, to the computer. The computer compares this data with its "map," which tells what these data should be under the engine's current operating conditions. If the data does not match the map, the computer sends signals to output actuators (fuel injectors or carburetor mixture control solenoid, Electronic Air Control Valve (EACV), Idle Speed Control (ISC) motor, etc.) which correct the engine's operation to match the map.

When the engine is warming up (and sensor input is not precise) or there is a malfunction in the system, the system operates in an "open loop" mode. In this mode, the computer does not rely on the sensors for input and sets the fuel/air mixture rich so the engine can continue operation until the engine warms up or repairs are made. **Note:** *The engine's thermostat rating and proper operation are critical to the operation of a computer-controlled vehicle. If the thermostat is rated at too low a temperature, is removed or stuck open, the computer may stay in "open loop" operation and emissions and fuel economy will suffer.*

The automotive computer

Automotive computers come in all sizes and shapes and are generally located under the dashboard, around the fender wells or under the front seat. The Environmental Protection Agency (EPA) and the Federal government require all automobile manufacturers to warranty their emissions systems for 5 years or 50,000 miles. This broad emissions warranty coverage will allow most computer malfunctions to be repaired by the dealership at their cost. Keep this in mind when diagnosing and/or repairing any emissions systems problems.

Computers have delicate internal circuitry which is easily damaged when subjected to excessive voltage, static electricity or magnetism. When diagnosing any electrical problems in a circuit connected to the computer, remember that most computers operate at a relatively low voltage (about 5 volts).

Observe the following precautions whenever working on or around the computer and engine management system circuits:

1) Do not damage the wiring or any electrical connectors in such a way as to cause it to ground or touch another source of voltage.

2) Do not use any electrical testing equipment (such as an ohmmeter) that is powered by a six-or-more-volt battery. The excessive voltage might cause an electrical component in the computer to burn or short. Use only a ten megaohm impedence multimeter when working on engine management circuits.

3) Do not remove or troubleshoot the computer without the proper tools and information, because any mistakes can void your warranty and/or damage components.

4) All spark plug wires should be at least one inch away from any sensor circuit or control wires. An unexpected problem in computer circuits is magnetic fields that send false signals to the computer, frequently resulting in hard-to-identify performance problems. Although there have been cases of high-power lines or transformers interfering with the computer, the most common cause of this problem in the sensor circuits is the position of the spark plug wires (too close to the computer wiring).

5) Use special care when handling or working near the computer. Remember that static electricity can cause computer damage by creating a very large surge in voltage (see *Static electricity and electronic components* below).

Static electricity and electronic components

Caution: *Static electricity can damage or destroy the computer and other electronic components. Read the following information carefully.*

Static electricity can cause two types of damage. The first and most obvious is complete failure of the device. The other type of damage is much more subtle and harder to detect as an electrical component failure. In this situation the integrated circuit is degraded and can become weakened over a period of time. It may perform erratically or appear as another component's intermittent failure.

The best way to prevent static electricity damage is to drain the charge from your body by grounding your body to the frame of body of the vehicle and then working strictly on a static-free area A static-control wrist strap properly worn and grounded to the frame or body of the vehicle will drain the charges from your body thereby preventing them from discharging into the electronic components. Consult your dealer parts department for a list of the static protection kits available.

Remember, it is often not possible to feel a static discharge until the charge level reaches 3,000 volts! It is very possible to be damaging the electrical components without even knowing it!

Information sensors

The information sensors are a series of highly specialized switches and temperature-sensitive electrical devices that transform physical properties of the engine such as temperature (air, coolant and fuel), air mass (air volume and density), air pressure and engine speed into electrical signals that can be translated into workable parameters for the computer.

Each sensor is designed specifically to detect data from one particular area of the engine; for example, the Mass Airflow Sensor is positioned inside the air intake system and it measures the volume and density of the in coming air to help the computer calculate how much fuel is needed to maintain the correct air/fuel mixture.

Diagnosing problems with the information sensors can easily overlap other management systems because of the interrelationships of the components. For instance, if a fuel-injected engine is experiencing a vacuum leak, the computer will often release a diagnostic code that refers to the oxygen sensor and/or its circuit. The first thought would be "Well, I'd better change my oxygen sensor." Actually, the intake leak is forcing more air into the combustion chamber than is required and the fuel/air mixture has become lean. The oxygen sensor relays the information to the computer which cannot compensate for the increased amount of oxygen and, as a result, the computer will store a fault code for the oxygen sensor.

The testing information in the following sections is generalized and applies to most fuel injection and feedback carburetor components. In order to solidify your diagnosis, it may be necessary to consult a factory service manual for the exact specifications for your vehicle.

MAP (Manifold Absolute Pressure) sensor

What it is and how it works

The MAP sensor reports engine load to the computer which uses the information to adjust spark advance and fuel enrichment **(see illustration)**. The MAP sensor measures intake manifold pressure and vacuum on the absolute scale (from zero instead of from sea-level atmospheric pressure [14.7 psi] as most gauges and sensors do). The MAP sensor reads vacuum and pressure through a hose connected to the intake manifold. A pressure-sensitive ceramic or silicon element and electronic circuit in the sensor generates a voltage signal that changes in direct proportion to pressure.

Under low-load, high-vacuum conditions, the computer leans the fuel/air mixture and advances the spark timing for better fuel economy. Under high-load, low-vacuum conditions, the computer richens the fuel/air mixture and retards

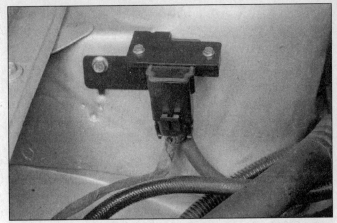

8.1 Here's a typical MAP sensor - this one, on a Plymouth Sundance, is located on the firewall, near the shock tower

timing to prevent detonation. The MAP sensor serves as the electronic equivalent of both a vacuum advance on a distributor and a power valve in the carburetor.

Checking

Anything that hinders accurate sensor input can upset both the fuel mixture and ignition timing. This includes the MAP sensor itself as well as shorts or opens in the sensor wiring circuit and/or vacuum leaks in the intake manifold or vacuum hose. Some of the most typical driveability symptoms associated with problems in the MAP sensor circuit include:

1) Detonation and misfire due to increased spark advance and a lean fuel mixture.
2) Loss of power and/or fuel economy and sometimes even black smoke due to retarded ignition timing and a very rich fuel mixture.
3) Poor fuel economy.
4) Hard starts and/or stalling.

Note: *A vacuum leak in the hose to the MAP sensor causes the MAP sensor to indicate a higher than normal pressure (less vacuum) in the manifold, which makes the computer think the engine is under much more load than it really is. As a result, the ignition timing is retarded and the fuel mixture is richened.*

When the MAP sensor trouble code is detected, be sure to first check for vacuum leaks in the hoses or electrical connectors or wiring damage in the MAP sensor circuit. Kinks in the line, blockage or splits can occur and deter the sensor's ability to respond accurately to the changes in the manifold pressure. Check for anything that is obvious and easily repaired before actually replacing the sensor itself.

A MAP sensor will typically produce a voltage signal that will drop with decreasing manifold pressure (rising vacuum). Test specifications will vary according to the manufacturer and engine type. A typical MAP sensor will read 4.6 to 4.8 volts with 0 in-Hg vacuum applied to it **(see illustration)**. Raise it to 5 in-Hg vacuum and the reading should drop to about 3.75 volts. Raise it up again to 20 in-Hg and the reading should drop to about 1.1 volts.

MAF (Mass Air Flow) sensor

What it is and how it works

The MAF sensor is positioned in the fresh air intake (see illustration), and it measures the amount of air entering the engine. Mass airflow sensors come in two basic varieties; hot wire and hot film. Both types work on the same principle, though they are designed differently. They measure the volume and density of the air entering the engine so the computer can calculate how much fuel is needed to maintain the correct fuel/air mixture.

MAF sensors have no moving parts. Contrary to the vane air flow sensors (see below) that use a spring-loaded flap, MAF sensors use an electrical current to measure airflow. There are two types of sensing elements; platinum wire (hot wire) or nickel foil grid (hot film). Each one is heated electrically to keep the temperature higher than the intake air temperature. With hot-film MAF sensors, the film is heated 170-degrees F warmer than the incoming air temperature. On hot-wire MAF sensors, the wire is heated to 210-degrees F above the incoming air temperature. As air flows past the element it cools the element and thereby increases the amount of current necessary to heat it up again. Because the necessary current varies directly with the temperature and the density of the air entering the intake, the amount of current is directly proportional to the air mass entering the engine. This information is fed into the computer and the fuel mixture is directly controlled according to the conditions.

Checking

The most effective method for testing the MAF sensor is measuring the sensor's output or its effect on the injector pulse width. On Bosch or Ford hot-wire systems, the voltage output can be read directly with a voltmeter by probing the appropriate sensor terminals (see illustrations). Refer to the your factory service manual for the correct terminal designations and specifications. If the voltage readings are not within range or the voltage fails to INCREASE when the throttle is OPENED with the engine running, the sensor is faulty and must be replaced with a new part. A dirty wire or a contaminated wire (a direct result of a faulty self-cleaning circuit) will deliver a slow response of the changes in airflow to the computer. Also, keep in mind that the self-cleaning circuit is controlled by relays. So, check the relays first if the MAF sensor appears to be sluggish or not responsive. Proper diagnosis of the MAF sensor is very important because this part is usually available only from a dealership parts department and the cost can be somewhat expensive. Be sure to check the diagnostic codes, if available, to make sure they indicate a problem with the MAF sensor rather than the MAF sensor circuit. If the wiring checks out and all other obvious areas are checked carefully, replace the sensor.

Another way to check MAF sensor output is to see what effect it has on injector pulse width (if this specification is available). Using a multimeter or oscilloscope that reads milliseconds, connect the positive probe directly to any injector signal wire and the negative probe to a ground terminal (see illustration). Remember that one injector terminal is connected to the supply voltage (battery voltage) and the other is connected to the computer (signal wire) which varies the amount of time the injector is grounded. **Note:** *Typically, if by chance you connect to the wrong side of the injector connector, one wire will give you a steady reading (battery voltage) while the signal wire will fluctuate slightly.* Look at the pulse width at idle or while cranking the engine. The injector pulse width will vary with different conditions. If the MAF sensor is not producing a signal, the pulse width will typically be FOUR times longer than the correct width. This will indicate an excessively rich fuel/ air mixture.

VAF (Vane Air Flow) sensor

What it is and how it works

VAF sensors are positioned in the air intake stream ahead of the throttle, and they monitor the volume of air entering the engine by means of a spring-loaded flap. The flap is pushed open by the air entering the system and a potentiometer (variable resistor) attached to the flap will vary the voltage signal to the computer according to the volume of air entering the engine (angle of the flap). The greater the airflow, the further the flap is forced open.

VAF sensors are used most commonly on Bosch L-Jetronic fuel injection systems, Nippondenso multi-port fuel injection systems and certain Ford multi-port fuel injection systems (Thunderbird, Mustang and Probe).

Checking

Diagnosing VAF sensors is quite different from diagnosing MAF or MAP sensors. Vane airflow sensors are vulnerable to dirt and grease. Unfiltered air that gets by a dirty or torn air filter will build up on the flap hinge or shaft, causing the flap to bind or hesitate as it swings. Remove the air intake boot and gently push open the flap with your finger; it should open and close smoothly. If necessary, spray a small amount of carburetor cleaner on the hinge and try to loosen the flap so it moves freely.

Disconnect the electrical connector to the VAF sensor. Install an ohmmeter to the electrical connector on the VAF sensor; the resistance should vary evenly as the flap opens and closes. If the resistance changes erratically or skips and jumps, you will have to replace the VAF with a new unit. **Note:** *Be sure to use an ANALOG ohmmeter for this check, since a digital meter will not usually register the rapid resistance changes that occur during this test.*

Another common problem to watch out for with VAF sensors is a bent or damaged flap caused by backfiring in the intake manifold. Some VAF sensors incorporate a "backfire" valve in the sensor body that prevents damage to the flap by venting any explosion. If the "backfire" valve leaks, the valve will cause the sensor to read low, consequently causing the engine to run on a rich fuel/air mixture.

The VAF sensor is manufactured as a sealed unit, preset at the factory with nothing that can be serviced except the idle mixture screw. Do not attempt to disassemble the unit if it is still under warranty, because tampering with the unit will void the warranty. Here again, be sure the diagno-

8.2 The MAP sensor voltage (measured at the signal wire) will decrease as vacuum is applied to the sensor

8.3 Here's a typical air flow sensor (this one's from a Nissan Maxima) - to remove it, remove the bolts (arrows)

8.4 The signal voltage on a typical Bosch MAF sensor will read 0.60 to 0.80 volts at idle and . . .

sis of the VAF sensor is complete and correct before buying a new unit because most often they are available only at a dealership parts department (and are expensive).

Air temperature sensor

What it is and how it works

The air temperature sensor is also known a Manifold Air Temperature (MAT) sensor, an Air Charge Temperature (ACT) sensor, a Vane Air Temperature (VAT) sensor, a Charge Temperature Sensor (CTS), an Air Temperature Sensor (ATS) and a Manifold Charging Temperature (MCT) sensor. The sensor is located in the intake manifold or air intake plenum **(see illustration)** and detects the temperature of the incoming air. The sensor usually consists of a temperature sensitive thermistor which changes the value of its voltage signal as the temperature changes. The computer uses the sensor signal to richen or lean the fuel/air mixture, and, on some applications, to delay the EGR valve opening until the manifold temperature reaches normal operating range.

Checking

The easiest way to check an air temperature sensor is to remove it from the manifold, then hook up an ohmmeter to its terminals and check the resistance when the sensor is cold. Then warm up the tip of the sensor with a blow drier (never a propane torch!) and watch for a decrease in resistance. No change in resistance indicates the sensor is defective. When reinstalling the sensor, be sure to use sealant on the threads so you don't end up with a vacuum leak.

On most GM vehicles equipped with the MAT sensor, a Code 23 or 25 will indicate a fault in the sensor (see Chapter 2). Be aware that problems with the EGR system might be caused by a defective MAT sensor.

TPS (Throttle Position Sensor)

What it is and how it works

The TPS or Throttle Position Sensor is usually mounted externally on the throttle body or carburetor. Some are inside the throttle body or carburetor. The TPS is attached directly to the throttle shaft and varies simultaneously with the angle of the throttle. Its job is to inform the computer about the rate of throttle opening and relative throttle position. A separate Wide Open Throttle (WOT) switch may be used to signal the computer when the throttle is wide open. The TPS consists of a variable resistor that changes resistance as the throttle changes its opening. By signaling the computer when the throttle opens, the computer can richen the fuel mixture to maintain the proper air/fuel ratio. The initial setting of the TPS sensor is very important because the voltage signal the computer receives tells the computer the exact position of the throttle at idle.

Checking

Throttle position sensors typically have their own types of driveability symptoms that can be distinguished from other information sensors. The most common symptom of a faulty or misadjusted sensor is hesitation or stumble during acceleration. The same symptom of a bad accelerator pump in a carbureted engine.

There are basically two voltage checks you can perform to test the Throttle Position Sensor. **Note:** *It is best to have the correct wiring diagram for the vehicle when performing the following checks.*

The first test is for the presence of voltage at the TPS sensor supply wire with the ignition key ON. The throttle position sensor cannot deliver the correct signal without the proper supply voltage. You can determine the function of each individual wire (ground, supply, signal wire) by probing each one with a voltmeter and checking the different voltages. The voltage that remains constant when the throttle is opened and closed will be the supply voltage. If there's no voltage at any of the wires, there's probably an open or short in the wiring harness to the sensor.

The second check is for the proper voltage change that occurs as the throttle opens and closes. As the throttle goes from closed-to-wide open, the voltage at the signal wire should typically increase smoothly from 1 volt to 5 volts.

8.5 . . . when the engine's rpm are raised to 2,500 to 3,500, the voltage increases to approximately 1.50 to 2.20 volts

8.6 Checking a MAF sensor (this one's on a Ford) - this test requires a special multimeter that detects pulse width variations

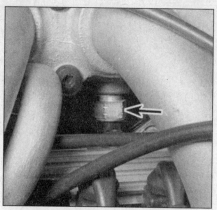

8.7 Here's a typical MAT sensor (this one's on a 1985 or later Corvette) - it's located in the underside of the air intake plenum

Note: *An alternate method for checking the range is the resistance test. Hook up an ohmmeter to the supply and signal wires. With the ignition key OFF slowly move the throttle through the complete range* **(see illustration)**. *Observe carefully for any unusual changes in the resistance (the change should be smooth) as it increases from low to high.*

Also, check your diagnostic codes for any differences in the circuit failures versus the actual sensor failure. Be sure you have checked all the obvious items before replacing the throttle position sensor.

Adjusting

TPS's seldom need adjustment. However, some TPS's must be adjusted when they are replaced. Since different makes and models of vehicles have different specifications and procedures for adjusting the TPS, we recommend you refer to a factory service manual for your specific vehicle to adjust the TPS. Also, dealer service departments or other qualified shops can usually adjust the TPS for you for a nominal fee. **Note:** *The adjustment information in the following paragraph may not be applicable to your vehicle. It is only intended to familiarize you with a typical procedure.*

Normally, you'll only need a voltmeter to adjust the TPS. Hook the meter up to the terminals specified in the manual and loosen the mounting screws. With the throttle in the specified position (usually against the throttle stop), rotate the sensor clockwise or counterclockwise until the specified voltage is obtained. Then retighten the mounting screws and check the voltage again.

Oxygen sensor
What it is and how it works

The oxygen sensor (also known as a Lambda or EGO sensor is located in the exhaust manifold (or in the exhaust pipe, near the exhaust manifold) and produces a voltage signal proportional to the content of oxygen in the exhaust **(see illustration)**. A higher oxygen content across the sensor tip will vary the oxygen differential, thereby lowering the sensor's output voltage. On the other hand, lower oxygen content will raise the output voltage. Typically, the voltage ranges from 0.10 volts (lean) to 0.90 volts (rich). The computer uses the sensor's input voltage to adjust the air/fuel mixture, leaning it out when the sensor detects a rich condition or enrichening it when it detects a lean condition. When

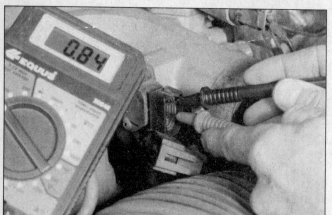

8.8 Slowly move the throttle and observe the resistance readings on the display - there should be a smooth transition as the resistance increases

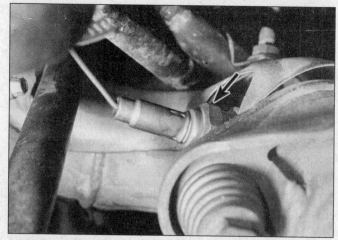

8.9 This oxygen sensor (arrow) is screwed into the exhaust manifold (GM 3.0L V6 engine shown)

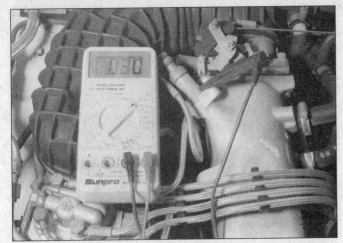

8.10 Very carefully observe the readings as the oxygen sensor cycles - note on paper the high and low values and try to come up with an average - also, if the VOM does not have a millivolt scale, just move the decimal point over; for example, 0.130 volt = 130 millivolts

the sensor reaches operating temperature (600-degrees F), it will produce variable voltage signal based on the difference between the amount of oxygen in the exhaust (internal) and the amount of oxygen in the air directly surrounding the sensor (external). The idea stochiometric fuel/air ratio (14.7:1) will produce about 0.45 volts

There are basically two types of oxygen sensors on the market. The most popular type uses a zirconia element in its tip. The latest type of oxygen sensor uses a titania element. Instead of producing its own voltage, the titania element resistance will alter voltage signal that is supplied by the computer itself. Although the titania element works differently than the zirconia element, the results are basically identical. The biggest difference is that the titania element responds faster and allows the computer to maintain more uniform control over a wide range of exhaust temperatures.

Contamination can directly affect the engine performance and life span of the oxygen sensor. There are basically three types of contamination; carbon, lead and silicon. Carbon buildup due to a rich-running condition will cause inaccurate readings and increase the problem's symptoms. Diagnose the fuel injection system or carburetor feedback controls for correct fuel adjustments. Once the system is repaired, run the engine at high rpm without a load (parked in the driveway) to remove the carbon deposits. Avoid leaded gasoline as it causes contamination of the oxygen sensor. Also, avoid using old-style silicone gasket sealant (RTV) that releases volatile compounds into the crankcase which eventually wind up on the sensor tip. Always check to make sure the RTV sealant you are using is compatible with modern emission systems.

Before an oxygen sensor can function properly it must reach a minimum operating temperature of 600-degrees F. The warm-up period prior to this is called "open loop." In this mode, the computer detects a low coolant temperature (cold start) and wide open throttle (warm-up) condition.

Until the engine reaches operating temperature, the computer ignores the oxygen sensor signals. During this time span, the emission controls are not precise! Once the engine is warm, the system is said to be in "closed loop" (using the oxygen sensor's input). Some manufacturers have designed an electric heating element to help the sensor reach operating temperature sooner. A typical heated sensor will consist of a ground wire, a sensor output wire (to the computer) and a third wire that supplies battery voltage to the resistance heater inside the oxygen sensor. Be careful when testing the oxygen sensor circuit! Clearly identify the function of each wire or you might confuse the data and draw the wrong conclusions.

Checking

Sometimes an apparent oxygen sensor problem is not the sensor's fault. An air leak in the exhaust manifold or a fouled spark plug or other problem in the ignition system causes the oxygen sensor to give a false lean-running condition. The sensor reacts only to the content of oxygen in the exhaust, and it has no way of knowing where the extra oxygen came from.

When checking the oxygen sensor it is important to remember that a good sensor produces a fluctuating signal that responds quickly to the changes in the exhaust oxygen content. To check the sensor you will need a 10 megaohm digital voltmeter. Never use an ohmmeter to check the oxygen sensor and never jump or ground the terminals. This can damage the sensor.

Connect the meter to the oxygen sensor circuit. Select the mV (millivolt) scale. If the engine is equipped with a later style (heated oxygen sensor), be sure you are connected to the signal wire and not one of the heater or ground wires. Start the engine and let it idle. Typically, the meter will respond with a fluctuating millivolt reading when connected properly. Also, be sure the engine is in closed loop (warmed-up to operating temperature).

Watch very carefully as the voltage oscillates. The display will flash values ranging from 100 mV to 900 mV (0.100 to 0.900 V). The numbers will flash very quickly, so be observant. Record the high and low values over a period of one minute. With the engine operating properly, the oxygen sensor should average approximately 500 mV (0.500 V) **(see illustration)**.

To further test the oxygen sensor, remove a vacuum line and observe the readings as the engine stumbles from the excessively LEAN mixture. The voltage should LOWER to an approximate value of 200 mV (0.200 V). Install the vacuum line. Now, obtain some propane gas mixture (bottled) and connect it to a vacuum port on the intake manifold. Start the engine and open the propane valve (open the propane valve only partially and do so a little at a time to prevent over-richening the mixture). This will create a RICH mixture. Watch carefully as the readings INCREASE. **Warning:** *Propane gas is highly flammable. Be sure there are no leaks in your connections or an explosion could result.* If the oxygen sensor responds correctly to the makeshift lean and rich conditions, the sensor is working properly.

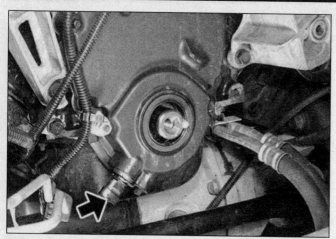

8.11a A typical GM crankshaft position sensor located in the timing cover

8.11b On Ford V6 engines, the pulse rings are directly behind the crankshaft pulley, easily detected by the sensor

EVP (EGR Valve Position) sensor

What it does and how it works

The EGR Valve Position (EVP) sensor monitors the position of the EGR valve and keeps the computer informed on the exact amount the valve is open or closed. From this data, the computer can calculate the optimum EGR flow for the lowest NOx emissions and the best driveability, then control the EGR valve to alter the EGR flow by means of the EGR solenoid.

The EVP sensor is a linear potentiometer that operates very much like a Throttle Position Sensor (TPS). Its electrical resistance changes in direct proportion to the movement of the EGR valve stem. When the EGR valve is closed, the EVP sensor registers maximum resistance. As the valve opens, resistance decreases until it finally reaches a minimum value when the EGR valve is fully open.

Checking

Typical symptoms of a malfunctioning EGR valve position sensor include hesitating during acceleration, rough idling and hard starting. Be sure to distinguish between an EGR valve problem and an EGR valve position sensor problem. Consult the section on EGR valves for additional information on testing the EGR valve itself.

Generally, the EGR valve position sensors should change resistance smoothly as the EGR valve is opened and closed. Be sure to check the appropriate factory service manual to determine which terminals of the sensor to hook the ohmmeter up to (there's often more than two). A typical Ford EVP sensor should have no more than 5,500 ohms resistance when the EGR valve is closed and no less than 100 ohms when the valve is fully open.

Crankshaft position sensor

What it is and how it works

A crankshaft position sensor works very similarly to an ignition pick-up coil or trigger wheel in an electronic distributor. The crankshaft position sensor provides an ignition timing

signal to the computer based on the position of the crankshaft. The difference between a crankshaft position sensor and a pick-up coil or trigger wheel is that the crankshaft position sensor reads the ignition timing signal directly off the crankshaft or harmonic balancer instead of from the distributor. This eliminates timing variations from backlash in the timing chain or distributor shaft. Crankshaft position sensors are necessary in most modern distributorless ignition (DIS) systems. Basically, the sensor reads the position of the crankshaft by detecting when pulse rings on the crankshaft or harmonic balancer pass by it **(see illustrations)**.

Checking

Most crankshaft position sensor problems can be traced to a fault in the wiring harness or connectors. These problems can cause a loss of the timing signal and consequently the engine will not start. When troubleshooting a crankshaft position sensor problem, it is advisable to follow the diagnostic flow chart in a factory service manual to isolate the faulty component. The problem could be in the ignition module, computer, wiring harness or crankshaft position sensor. Be aware of the interrelationship of these components.

If it is necessary to replace the sensor, be sure to install it correctly, paying attention to the alignment. Any rubbing or interference will cause driveability problems. Also, on variable reluctance type crankshaft position sensors, be sure to adjust the air gap properly. Consult a factory service manual for the correct specification.

VSS (Vehicle Speed Sensor)

What it is and how it works

Vehicle Speed Sensors (VSS) are used in modern vehicles for a number of different purposes. One purpose is to monitor the vehicle speed so the computer can determine the correct time for torque converter clutch (TCC) lock-up. The sensor may also provide input to the computer to control the function of various other emissions systems components based on vehicle speed. On some GM vehicles, the signal from the VSS is used by the computer to reset

8.12 Here's a typical knock sensor (this one's on a Corvette), mounted low on the side of the engine block

8.13 On many GM models, information from the knock sensor is sent to the Electronic Spark Control (ESC) module (arrow), which retards ignition timing if detonation is evident

the Idle Air Control valve as well as the canister purge valve. Another purpose is to assist with the power steering. Here, the sensor input is used by the electronic controller to vary the amount of power assist according to the vehicle speed. The lower the speed, the greater the assist for easier maneuverability for parking. The higher the speed, the less the assist for better road feel. Another purpose is to change the position of electronically adjustable shock absorbers used in ride control systems. The ride control systems in Mazda 626's and Ford Probes automatically switch the shocks to a "firm" setting above 50 mph in the AUTO mode and "extra firm" in the SPORT mode. Also, vehicle speed sensors replace the mechanical speedometer cable in some modern vehicles.

Checking

The driveability symptoms of a faulty vehicle speed sensor depend on what control functions require an accurate speed input. For example, on some GM vehicles, the idle quality may be affected by a faulty sensor. Other symptoms include hard steering with increased speed, premature torque converter lock-up or fluctuating or inaccurate speedometer readings.

Different vehicles require different testing techniques. It is best to consult a factory service manual for the specific test procedures for your particular vehicle. Also, it is rare, but sometimes the output shaft on the transmission has broken or missing teeth that affect the accuracy of the sensor's reading.

Knock sensor

What it is and how it works

The knock sensor (sometimes called an Electronic Spark Control [ESC] sensor) is an auxiliary sensor that is used to detect the onset of detonation **(see illustrations)**. Although the knock sensor influences ignition timing, it doesn't have direct impact on the fuel and emission systems. It affects ignition timing only.

The sensor, which is usually mounted on the intake manifold or engine block, generates a voltage signal when the engine vibrations are between 6 to 8 Hz. The location of the sensor is very critical because it must be positioned so it can detect any vibrations from the most detonation-prone cylinders. On some engines, it is necessary to install two knock sensors.

When the knock sensor detects a pinging or knocking vibration, it signals the computer to momentarily retard ignition timing. The computer then retards the timing a fixed number of degrees until the detonation stops.

This system is vital on turbocharged vehicles to achieve maximum performance. When the knock control system is working properly, the maximum timing advance for all driving conditions is achieved.

Checking

The most obvious symptom of knock sensor failure will be an audible pinging or knocking, especially during acceleration under a light load. Light detonation usually does not cause harm, but heavy detonation over a period of time will cause engine damage. Knock sensors sometimes are fooled by other sounds such as rod knocks or worn timing chains. Reduced fuel economy and poor performance result from the constantly retarded timing.

Another thing to keep in mind is that most engine detonation has other causes than the knock sensor. Some causes include:

1) Defective EGR valve
2) Too much compression due to accumulated carbon in the cylinders
3) Over-advanced ignition timing
4) Lean fuel/air mixture; Possible vacuum leak
5) Overheated engine
6) Low-octane fuel

To check the knock sensor, use a wrench to rap on the intake manifold (not too hard or you may damage the manifold!) near the sensor while the engine is idling. Never strike the sensor directly Observe the timing mark with a timing light. The vibration from the wrench will produce enough of a shock to cause the knock sensor to signal the

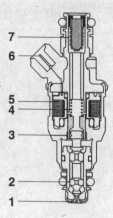

8.14a Cutaway of a typical fuel injector

1	Pintle	5	Solenoid winding
2	Needle	6	Electrical terminals
3	Armature	7	Fuel strainer
4	Spring		

8.14b Removing a fuel injector from a typical throttle-body-type fuel injection system (GM throttle body shown)

computer to back-off the timing. The timing should retard momentarily. If nothing happens, check the wiring, electrical connector or computer for any obvious shorts or problems. If the wiring and connectors are OK, the sensor is probably faulty.

The knock sensor is a sealed unit. If it is defective, replace it with a new part.

Output actuators

The output actuators receive commands from the computer and actuate the correct engine response after all the data and parameters have been analyzed by the computer. Output devices can be divided into three categories: solenoids, electric motors and controller modules.

Solenoids include the EGR solenoid, Canister Purge (CANP); solenoid, carburetor feedback solenoid (FBC), Electronic Air Control Valve (EACV), Torque Converter Clutch (TCC) solenoid and fuel injectors.

Electric motors include the Idle Speed Control motor (ISC), the fuel pump and cooling fan.

Controller modules are used to control more than one device. Modules can control air conditioner and cooling fan response as well as ignition functions.

The following discusses operation and diagnosis of the most common types of output actuators.

Fuel injectors

What they are and how they work

Fuel injectors are electro-mechanical devices which both meter and atomize fuel delivered to the engine. The injectors on multi-point fuel injection systems are usually mounted in the lower intake manifold and positioned so that their tips are directing fuel in front of each engine intake valve. On vehicles equipped with Throttle Body Injection (TBI), the injector(s) are mounted in the throttle body (the carburetor-like device on the intake manifold) **(see illustrations)**.

The injector bodies consist of a solenoid-actuated pintle and needle valve assembly. An electrical signal from the computer activates the solenoid, causing the pintle to move inward off the seat and allow fuel to inject into the engine.

Fuel flow to the engine is controlled by how long the solenoid is energized, since the injector flow orifice is fixed and the fuel pressure drop across the injector tip is constant. This duration can be measured electronically and is referred to as the injector pulse width.

Checking

On multi-point fuel injectors, check to make sure the wiring and electrical connectors to each fuel injector is/are in good shape and securely connected. With the engine running, listen to each injector through a mechanic's stethoscope (a long screwdriver can also be used - place the tip of the screwdriver against each injector and place the handle against your ear). **Warning:** *Be careful of rotating engine components when performing this check.* If you can hear a rapid clicking noise, the injector is functioning, although it could still be clogged or leaking. Many auto repair shops can clean the injectors for a reasonable charge. Also, fuel injector cleaners that can be added to the fuel tank are available at auto parts stores and are often very effective at cleaning injectors. Further diagnosis of multi-point injectors should be left to a dealer service department or other qualified auto repair shop.

On throttle body injectors, check to make sure the wiring and electrical connectors are secure and in good shape. With the engine running, remove the air cleaner or air intake duct to expose the top of the throttle body. Look at the spray pattern coming from the injector(s). The pattern should be even, conical in shape and reaching all the way to the throttle bore walls. Also, the injectors should not be dripping, both with the engine running and with it shut off. If the spray pattern is not as described, have the injector(s) cleaned by an auto repair shop or try some fuel injector cleaner in the fuel tank (available at auto parts stores). If cleaning does not correct the injector problem, it may need to be replaced (refer to the *Haynes Automotive Repair Manual* for your particular vehicle or the vehicle's factory service manual).

8.15 Hook up a vacuum gauge to the EGR-valve side of the solenoid - with the engine running at about 2,000 rpm, the gauge should register at least ten in-Hg of vacuum

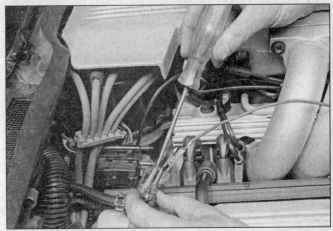

8.16 Connect a test light across the EGR solenoid wire harness terminals with the ignition switch ON (engine off) - the light should come on

EGR valve solenoid

What it is and how it works

On computer-controlled vehicles, the action of the EGR valve is usually controlled by commanding the EGR control solenoid(s). Refer to the information earlier in this Chapter on EGR valve position sensors for additional information concerning these systems. The EGR valve solenoid is computer controlled and located in the vacuum line between the EGR valve and vacuum source. It opens and closes electrically to maintain finer control of EGR flow than is possible with ported-vacuum-type systems. The computer uses information from the coolant temperature, throttle position and manifold pressure sensors to regulate the EGR valve solenoid.

During cold operation and at idle, the solenoid circuit is grounded by the computer to block vacuum to the EGR valve. When the solenoid circuit is not grounded by the computer, vacuum is allowed to the EGR valve.

Checking

Note: *For further information and checking procedures for the EGR system, see Chapter 1 and Section 1 of this Chapter.*

First, inspect all vacuum hoses, wires and electrical connectors associated with the EGR solenoid and system. Make sure nothing is damaged, loose or disconnected.

Locate the vacuum line that runs from the vacuum source to the EGR solenoid. Disconnect it at the solenoid and hook up a vacuum gauge to the hose. Start the engine, bring it to normal operating temperature and observe the vacuum reading. There should be at least ten in-Hg of vacuum. If not, repair the hose to the vacuum source. Disconnect the gauge and re-connect the hose.

If there is at least ten in-Hg vacuum to the EGR solenoid, locate the vacuum hose running from the EGR solenoid to the EGR valve. Disconnect and plug the hose at the solenoid and hook up a vacuum gauge to the solenoid. Open the EGR solenoid by starting the engine and raising the speed to about 2,000 rpm. With the solenoid open, the vacuum gauge should read at least ten in-Hg **(see illustration)**. If there is no vacuum, either the solenoid valve is defective or there is a problem in the wiring circuit or computer.

To check the wiring circuit, disconnect the electrical connector from the EGR solenoid. With the ignition on and the engine off, connect a test light across the two terminals of the connector **(see illustration)**. The test light should come on. If it does not, there is a problem in the wiring or computer. If the light does come on, but there is no vacuum from the EGR solenoid to the EGR valve, the solenoid is probably defective. Check the solenoid's resistance. Normally, it should not be less than about 20 ohms.

ISC (Idle Speed Control) motor

See the heading in Section 6, *Carburetor controls* for information on the ISC motor.

EACV (Electronic Air Control Valve)

What it is and how it works

The EACV (sometimes called an Idle Air Control [IAC] valve) changes the amount of air bypassed (not flowing through the throttle valve) into the intake manifold in response to the changes in the electrical signals from the computer. EACV's are usually located on the throttle body, although some are mounted remotely. After the engine starts, the EACV opens, allowing air to bypass the throttle and thus increase idle speed. While the coolant temperature is low, the EACV remains open to obtain the proper fast idle speed. As the engine warms up, the amount of bypassed air is controlled in relation to the coolant temperature. After the engine reaches normal operating temperature, the EACV is opened, as necessary, to maintain the correct idle speed.

Checking

To check the EACV valve circuit, connect the positive probe of a voltmeter to the signal wire in the EACV connector and the negative probe to the ground (see illustration). Check the voltage as the engine starts to warm up from cold to warm conditions. Most EACV valves will indicate an increase in voltage as the system warms and the valve slowly cuts off the additional air. Consult a factory service manual for the correct voltage specifications for your vehicle. If the voltage is correct, but the EACV valve is not opening or closing to provide the correct airflow, replace the valve.

TCC (Torque Converter Clutch) solenoid

What it is and how it works

Lock-up torque converters are installed on newer vehicles to help eliminate torque converter slippage and thus reduce power loss and poor fuel economy. The torque converter is equipped with a clutch that is activated by a solenoid valve. The computer determines the best time to lock up the clutch device based on data it receives from various sensors and switches.

When the vehicle speed sensor indicates speed above a certain range and the coolant temperature sensor is warm, the Throttle Position Sensor (TPS) determines the position of the throttle (acceleration or deceleration) and the transmission sensor relays the particular gear the transmission is operating in to the computer for a complete analysis of operating parameters. If all parameters are within a certain range, the computer sends an electrical signal to the clutch, telling it to lock up. Needless to say, diagnosing a problem in this system can become complicated.

Checking

One symptom of TCC failure is a clutch that will not disengage, causing the engine to stall when slowing to a stop. Another symptom is an increase in engine rpm at cruising speed, resulting in decreased fuel economy (this

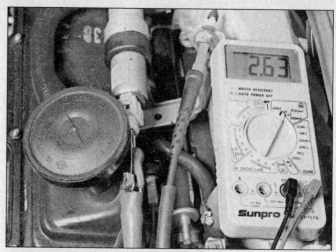

8.17 Observe the voltage reading at the EACV connector

usually means the converter is not locking up). If the converter is not locking up, the driver might not notice any differences unless he/she checks fuel consumption and the increase in tachometer readings. Without the TCC operating, the engine will turn an additional 300 to 500 rpm at cruising speed to maintain the same speed. Also, when the converter is not locking up, there is a chance the transmission will overheat and become damaged due to the higher operating temperatures.

Before diagnosing the TCC system as defective, make some preliminary checks. Check the transmission fluid level, linkage adjustment and the condition of the vacuum lines. After you've checked that all the basics are in order, check for any trouble codes (see Chapter 2). Further diagnosis should be referred to a dealer service department or other qualified repair shop.

4 Vacuum diagrams and VECI labels

General Information

The illustrations in this Chapter are intended to help you further your understanding of emissions control systems by studying the way components are connected on various types of vehicles. They do not attempt to cover all vehicles, but rather are a representative sampling.

To better understand your vehicle, you need to study the Vehicle Emission Control Information (VECI) label located under the hood (for more information on VECI labels, see Chapter 1). The VECI label contains tune-up specifications and vital information regarding the emission control devices and vacuum hose routing.

If your vehicle does not have a VECI label, it's possible that it never came with one or that it's missing. Sometimes when body panels are replaced with used ones, the VECI labels get replaced along with them, and often this results in the wrong VECI label being displayed under the hood. Check with the dealer parts department if your VECI label is missing or you think you have the wrong one. The dealer parts department can get the right one for you.

One more thing you could do if the VECI label is missing is take a photo or make a drawing of the vacuum hoses and connections before any work is started. Reassembly will then be simpler.

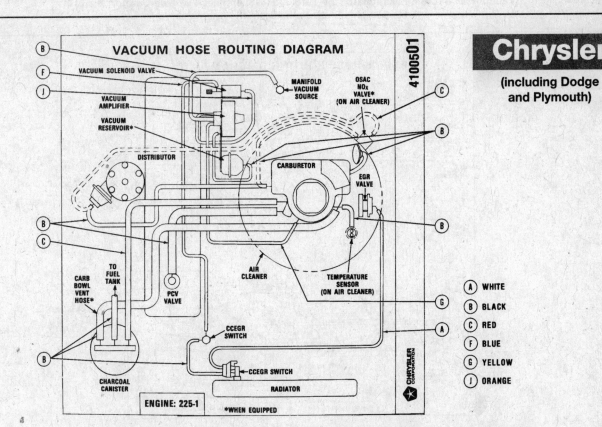

Vacuum hose routing diagram for the 1978 225 slant six-cylinder engine with 1 BBL carburetor
(Federal and Canada, manual and automatic transmission)

Chrysler

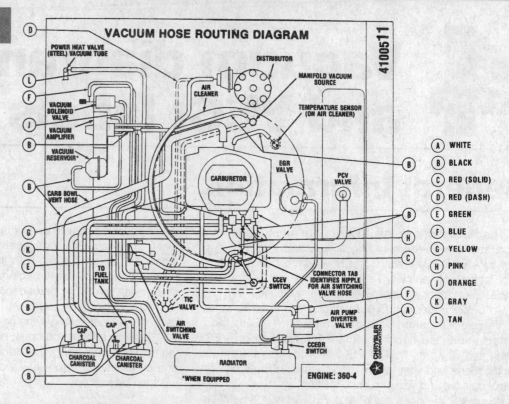

Vacuum hose routing diagram for the 1978 360 (V-8) engine, 4 BBL carburetor, B and C
(Federal high altitude with automatic transmission)

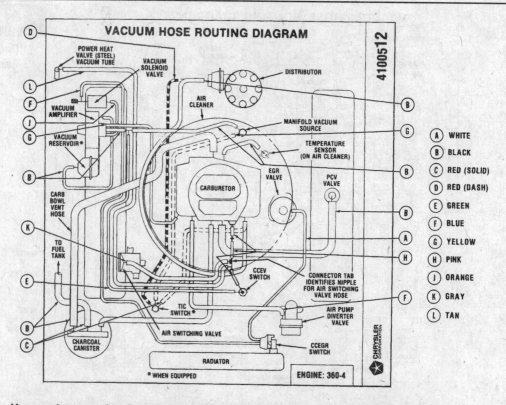

Vacuum hose routing diagram for the 1978 360 (V-8) engine, 2 and 4 BBL carburetor
(Federal high altitude and California F and M bodies with automatic transmission)

Chrysler

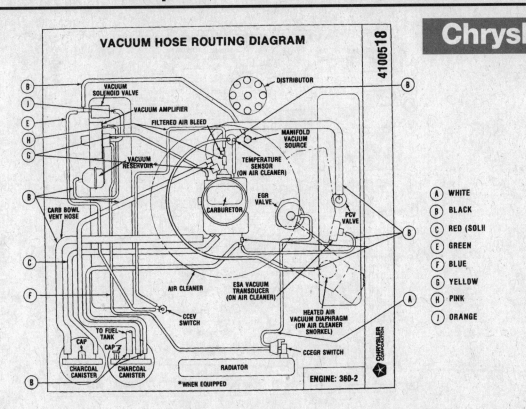

Vacuum hose routing diagram for the 1978 360 (V-8) engine, 2 BBL carburetor (Federal with ELB and catalyst, C body, automatic transmission)

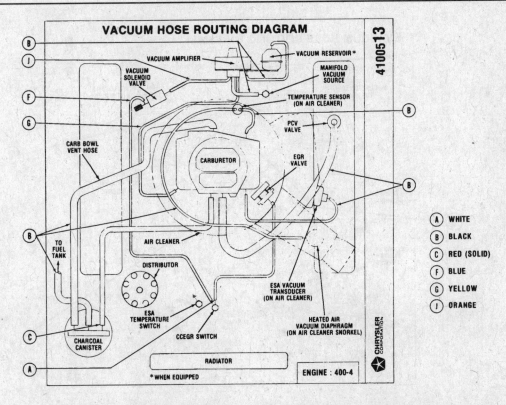

Vacuum hose routing diagram for the 1978 400 (V-8) engine, 4 BBL carburetor (Federal with ELB and catalyst, all except C body with automatic transmission)

The Haynes Emissions Control Manual

Chrysler

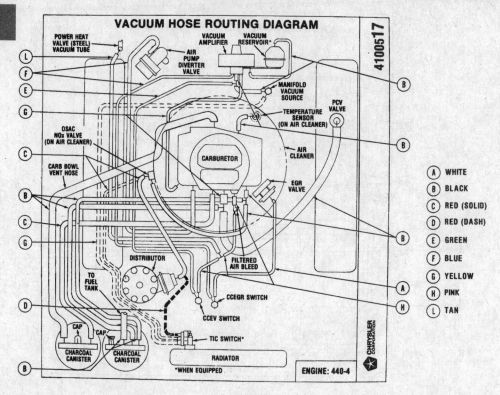

Vacuum hose routing diagram for the 1978 440 (V-8) engine, 4 BBL carburetor (California with catalyst and air pump and automatic transmission)

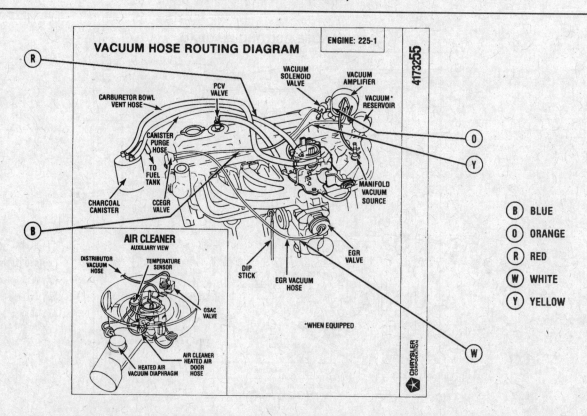

Vacuum hose routing diagram for the 1979 225 slant six-cylinder engine, 1 BBL carburetor (Federal and Canada)

Chrysler

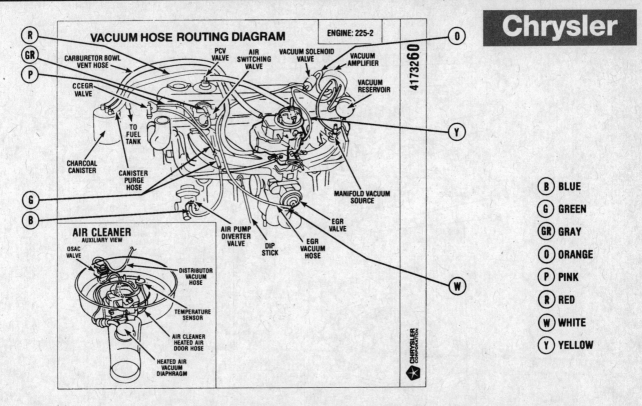

VACUUM HOSE ROUTING DIAGRAM

ENGINE: 225-2

4173260

R — CARBURETOR BOWL VENT HOSE
GR
P
CC EGR VALVE
TO FUEL TANK
CHARCOAL CANISTER
CANISTER PURGE HOSE
PCV VALVE
AIR SWITCHING VALVE
VACUUM SOLENOID VALVE
VACUUM AMPLIFIER
VACUUM RESERVOIR
O
Y
MANIFOLD VACUUM SOURCE
EGR VALVE
EGR VACUUM HOSE
DIP STICK
AIR PUMP DIVERTER VALVE
G
B
W

AIR CLEANER
AUXILIARY VIEW

OSAC VALVE
DISTRIBUTOR VACUUM HOSE
TEMPERATURE SENSOR
AIR CLEANER HEATED AIR DOOR HOSE
HEATED AIR VACUUM DIAPHRAGM

- **B** BLUE
- **G** GREEN
- **GR** GRAY
- **O** ORANGE
- **P** PINK
- **R** RED
- **W** WHITE
- **Y** YELLOW

CHRYSLER CORPORATION

Vacuum hose routing diagram for the 1979 225 slant six-cylinder engine with the #4000 2 BBL carburetor (Federal with automatic transmission)

VACUUM HOSE ROUTING DIAGRAM

ENGINE: 318-2

4173261

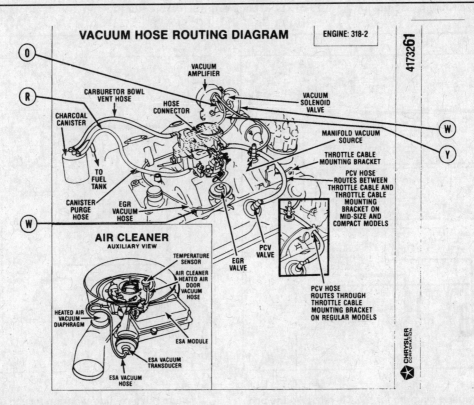

O
R
CHARCOAL CANISTER
CARBURETOR BOWL VENT HOSE
HOSE CONNECTOR
VACUUM AMPLIFIER
VACUUM SOLENOID VALVE
W
Y
MANIFOLD VACUUM SOURCE
THROTTLE CABLE MOUNTING BRACKET
PCV HOSE ROUTES BETWEEN THROTTLE CABLE AND THROTTLE CABLE MOUNTING BRACKET ON MID-SIZE AND COMPACT MODELS
TO FUEL TANK
CANISTER PURGE HOSE
EGR VACUUM HOSE
W
PCV VALVE
EGR VALVE
PCV HOSE ROUTES THROUGH THROTTLE CABLE MOUNTING BRACKET ON REGULAR MODELS

AIR CLEANER
AUXILIARY VIEW

TEMPERATURE SENSOR
AIR CLEANER HEATED AIR DOOR VACUUM HOSE
HEATED AIR VACUUM DIAPHRAGM
ESA MODULE
ESA VACUUM TRANSDUCER
ESA VACUUM HOSE

CHRYSLER CORPORATION

Vacuum hose routing diagram for the 1979 318 (V-8) engine, 2 BBL carburetor (Federal and Canada with automatic transmission)

Chrysler

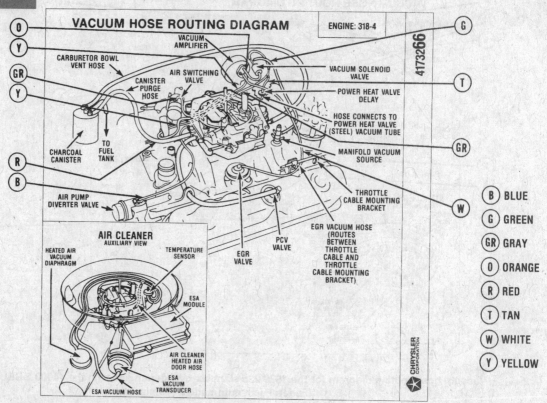

VACUUM HOSE ROUTING DIAGRAM   ENGINE: 318-4

4173266

- O
- Y
- GR
- Y
- R
- B

VACUUM AMPLIFIER

CARBURETOR BOWL VENT HOSE

AIR SWITCHING VALVE

CANISTER PURGE HOSE

CHARCOAL CANISTER

TO FUEL TANK

AIR PUMP DIVERTER VALVE

VACUUM SOLENOID VALVE

POWER HEAT VALVE DELAY

HOSE CONNECTS TO POWER HEAT VALVE (STEEL) VACUUM TUBE

MANIFOLD VACUUM SOURCE

THROTTLE CABLE MOUNTING BRACKET

EGR VACUUM HOSE (ROUTES BETWEEN THROTTLE CABLE AND THROTTLE CABLE MOUNTING BRACKET)

- G
- T
- GR
- W

AIR CLEANER AUXILIARY VIEW

HEATED AIR VACUUM DIAPHRAGM

TEMPERATURE SENSOR

ESA MODULE

AIR CLEANER HEATED AIR DOOR HOSE

ESA VACUUM HOSE

ESA VACUUM TRANSDUCER

EGR VALVE

PCV VALVE

- B BLUE
- G GREEN
- GR GRAY
- O ORANGE
- R RED
- T TAN
- W WHITE
- Y YELLOW

CHRYSLER CORPORATION

Vacuum hose routing diagram for the 1979 318 (V-8) engine, 4 BBL carburetor (California with automatic transmission)

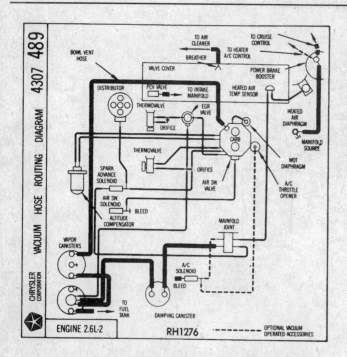

Vacuum hose routing diagram for the Chrysler, Dodge and Plymouth Mini Van with the 2.6L engine, 2 BBL carburetor (for California)

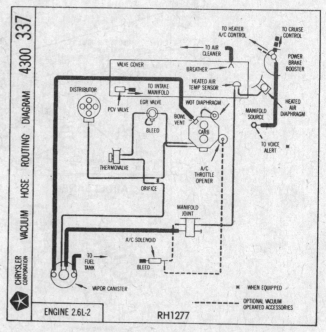

Vacuum hose routing diagram for the Chrysler, Dodge and Plymouth Mini Van equipped with the 2.6L engine (for Canada)

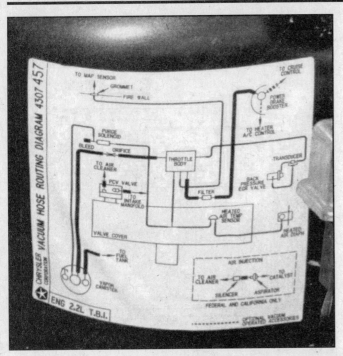

Vacuum hose routing diagram for the Chrysler Laser and Dodge Charger/Daytona equipped with the 2.2L engine with TBI (for California)

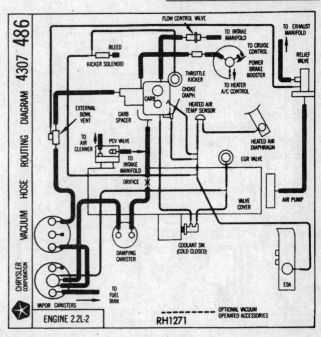

Typical vacuum hose routing diagram for the 2.2L engine, 2 BBL carburetor (Canada)

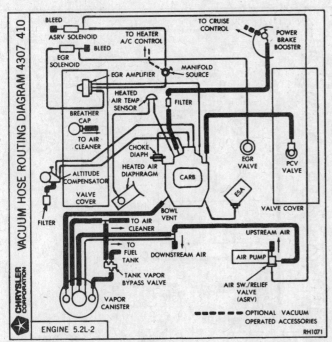

Vacuum hose routing diagram for the 1984 Dodge Diplomat with the 5.2L (318 V-8) engine, 2 BBL carburetor (Federal or California)

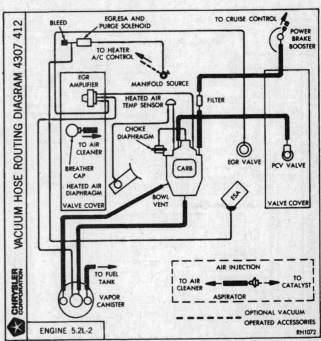

Vacuum hose routing diagram for the 1984 Plymouth Grand Fury with the 5.2L (318 V-8) engine, 2 BBL carburetor (Canada)

The Haynes Emissions Control Manual

Chrysler

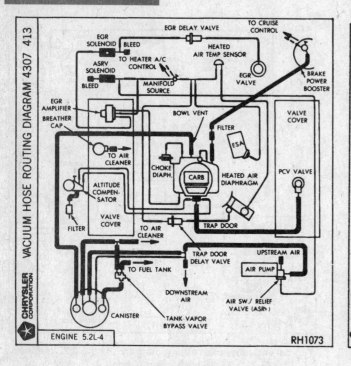

Vacuum hose routing diagram for the 1984 Chrysler Newport with the 5.2L (318 V-8) engine, 4 BBL carburetor (Federal and Canada)

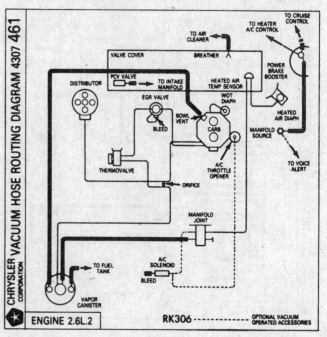

Vacuum hose routing diagram for the 1985 K and E cars with the 2.6L engine, 2 BBL carburetor (California and Canada)

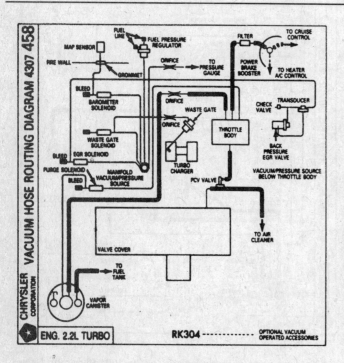

Vacuum hose routing diagram for the 1985 2.2L engine with TBI and turbo

Vacuum hose routing diagram for the 1985 2.6L engine with 2 BBL carburetor (Canada)

Chrysler

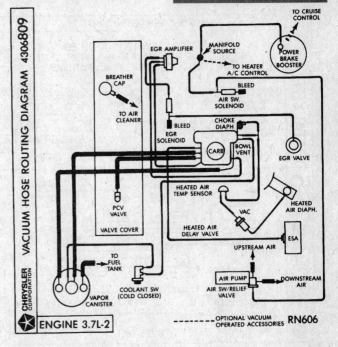

Vacuum hose routing diagram for the 1986 5.2L (318 V-8) engine, 2 BBL carburetor (Federal and Canada)

Vacuum hose routing diagram for the 1986 225 slant six-cylinder engine, 2 BBL carburetor, ESA with catalyst (Federal)

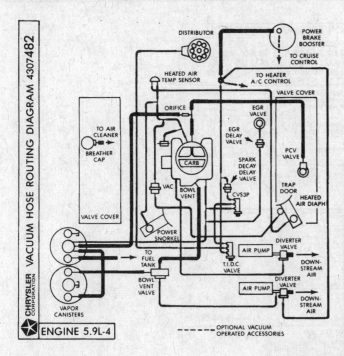

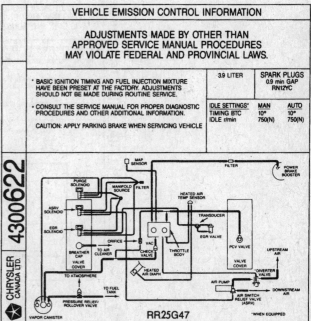

Vacuum hose routing diagram for the 1986 5.9L (360 V-8) engine, 4 BBL carburetor (California with air conditioning)

Vacuum hose routing diagram for the 1988 3.9L (V-6) engine with TBI (Canada)

The Haynes Emissions Control Manual

Chrysler

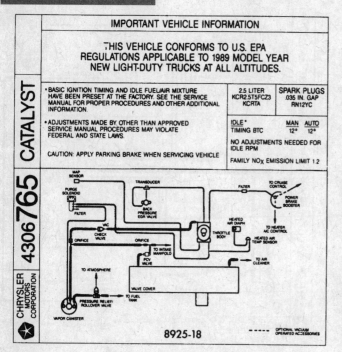

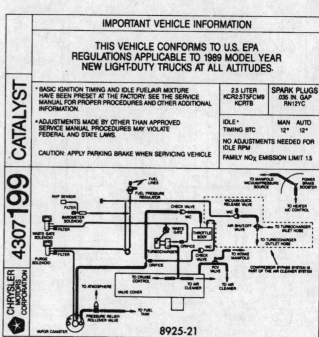

Vacuum hose routing diagram for the 1989 2.5L engine with TBI (California, Canada and Federal high altitude)

Vacuum hose routing diagram for the 1989 2.5L engine with TBI and turbo (California, Canada and Federal)

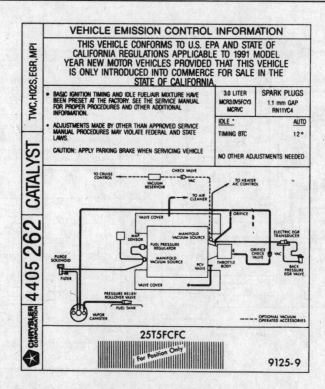

Vacuum hose routing diagram for the 1991 3.0L (V-6) engine with TBI and anti-lock brakes (California)

Honda

Typical vacuum hose routing diagram for a carbureted Honda Accord. Note that Honda vacuum hose routing often changes significantly from year to year

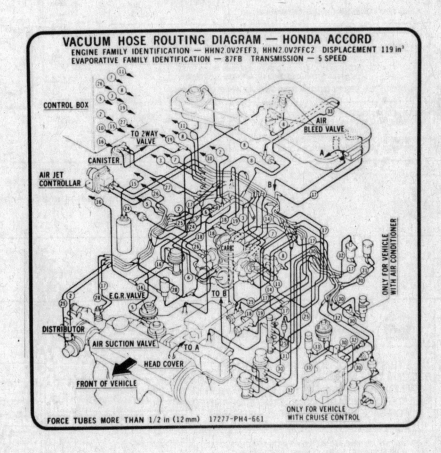

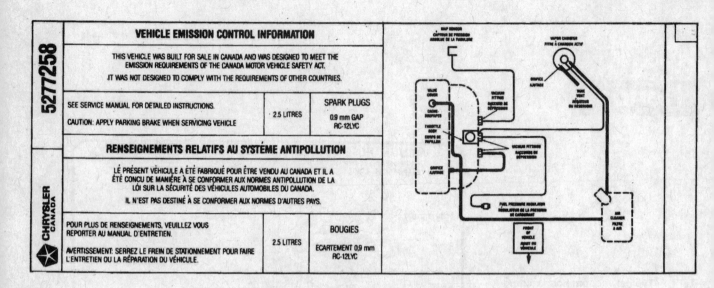

Typical VECI label for a 1990 Jeep with the 2.5L engine

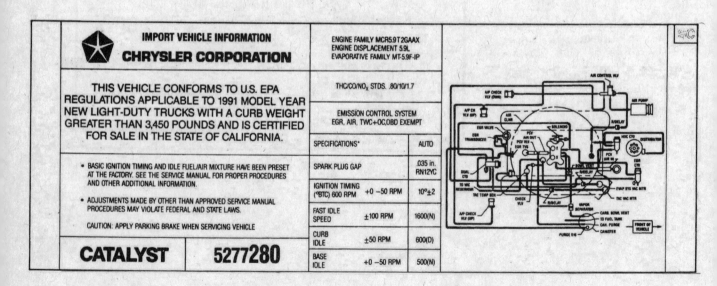

Typical VECI label for a 1991 Jeep Grand Wagoneer with the 5.9L (360) V8 engine

Mitsubishi

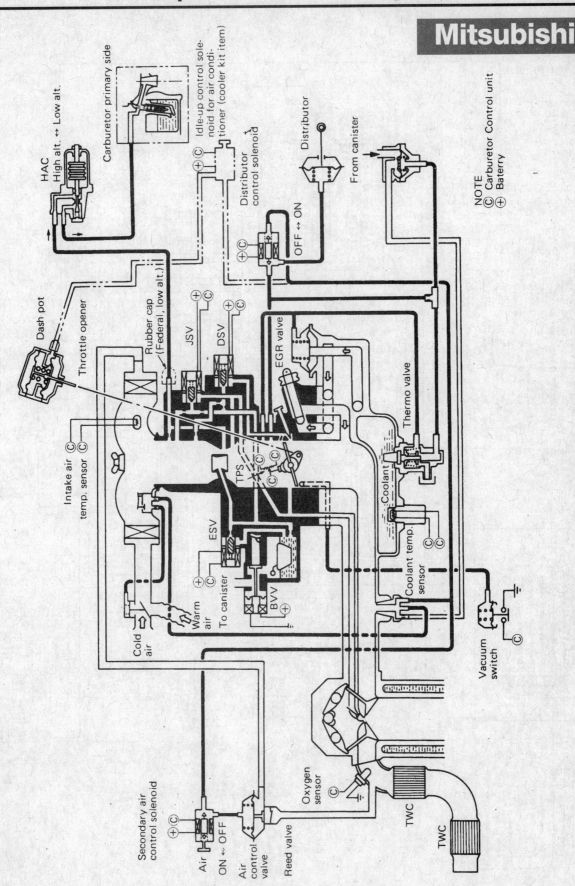

Vacuum hose routing diagram for the 1986 Mitsubishi Montero

The Haynes Emissions Control Manual

Mitsubishi

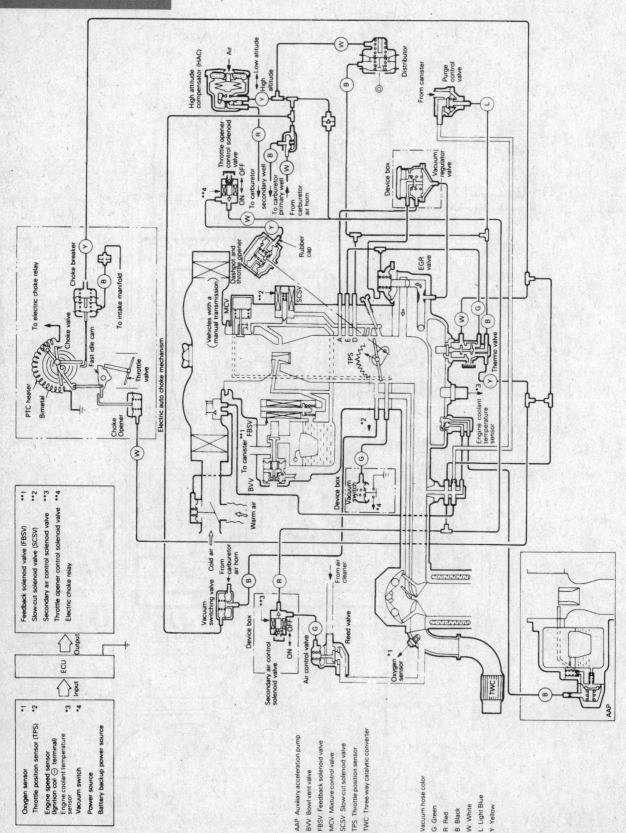

Vacuum hose routing diagram for the 1988 Mitsubishi Montero (high altitude, Federal)

AAP: Auxiliary acceleration pump
BVV: Bowl vent valve
FBSV: Feedback solenoid valve
MCV: Mixture control valve
SCSV: Slow-cut solenoid valve
TPS: Throttle position sensor
TWC: Three-way catalytic converter

Vacuum hose color
G: Green
R: Red
B: Black
W: White
L: Light blue
Y: Yellow

Mitsubishi

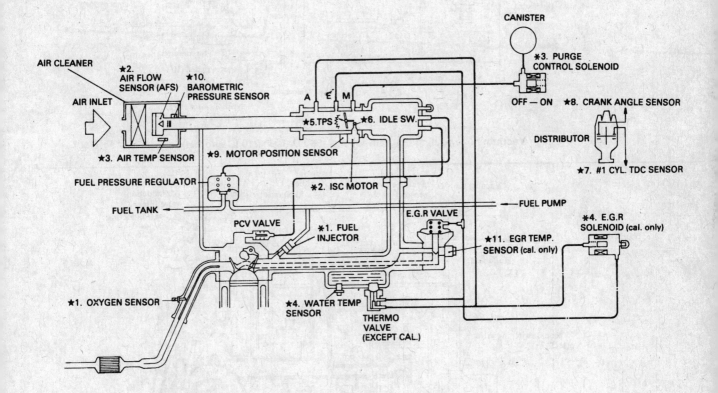

CANISTER

*3. PURGE CONTROL SOLENOID

OFF — ON

*8. CRANK ANGLE SENSOR

DISTRIBUTOR

*7. #1 CYL. TDC SENSOR

AIR CLEANER

*2. AIR FLOW SENSOR (AFS)

*10. BAROMETRIC PRESSURE SENSOR

AIR INLET

A E M

*5. TPS   *6. IDLE SW.

*3. AIR TEMP SENSOR

*9. MOTOR POSITION SENSOR

FUEL PRESSURE REGULATOR

*2. ISC MOTOR

FUEL TANK

FUEL PUMP

E.G.R VALVE

*4. E.G.R SOLENOID (cal. only)

PCV VALVE

*1. FUEL INJECTOR

*11. EGR TEMP. SENSOR (cal. only)

*1. OXYGEN SENSOR

*4. WATER TEMP SENSOR

THERMO VALVE (EXCEPT CAL.)

Vacuum hose routing diagram for the 1990 Mitsubishi Precis

The Haynes Emissions Control Manual

Nissan/Datsun

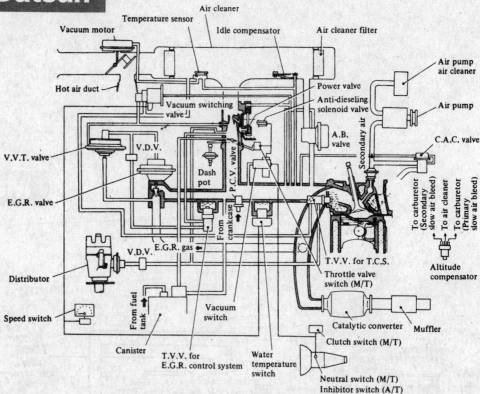

Vacuum hose routing diagram for the 1980 Datsun 210 (California)

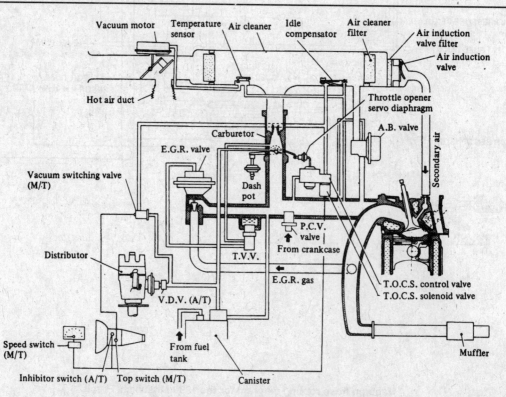

Vacuum hose routing diagram for the 1980 Datsun 210 (Canada)

Nissan/Datsun

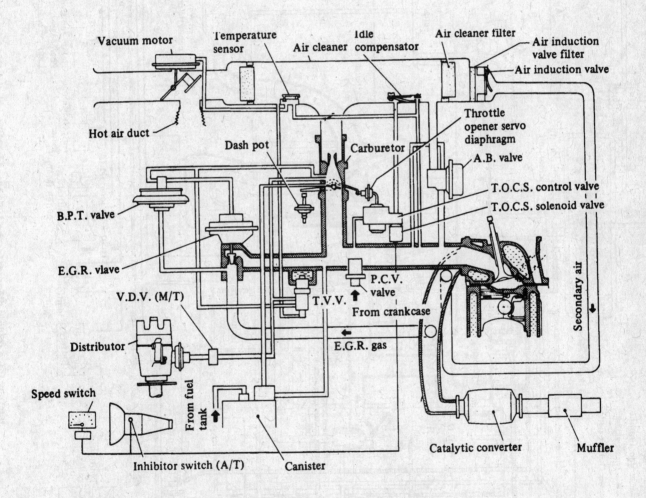

Vacuum hose routing diagram for the 1980 Datsun 210 (Federal)

Nissan/Datsun

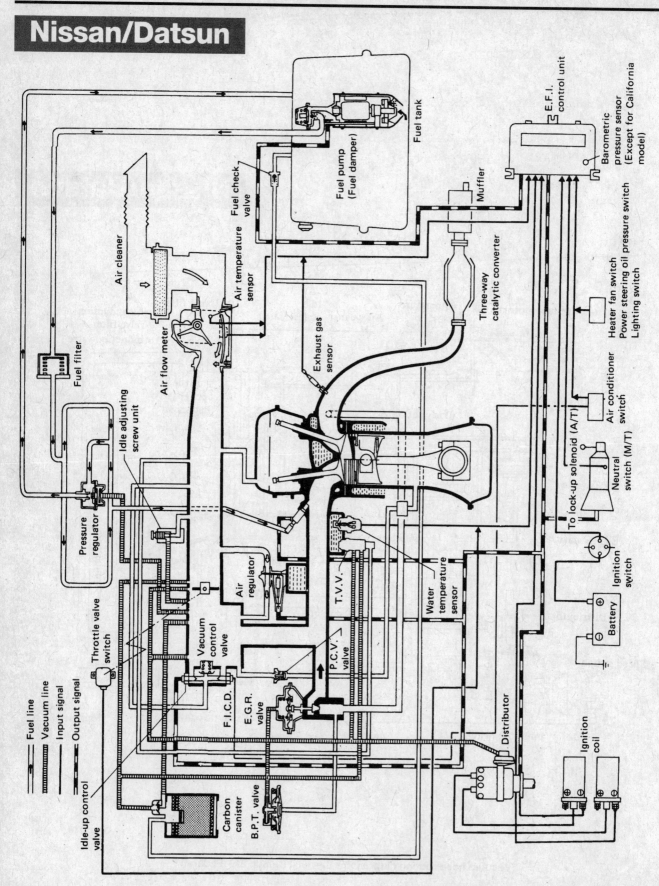

Vacuum hose routing diagram for the 1984 Nissan 200SX with the CA20E engine and EFI

Nissan/Datsun

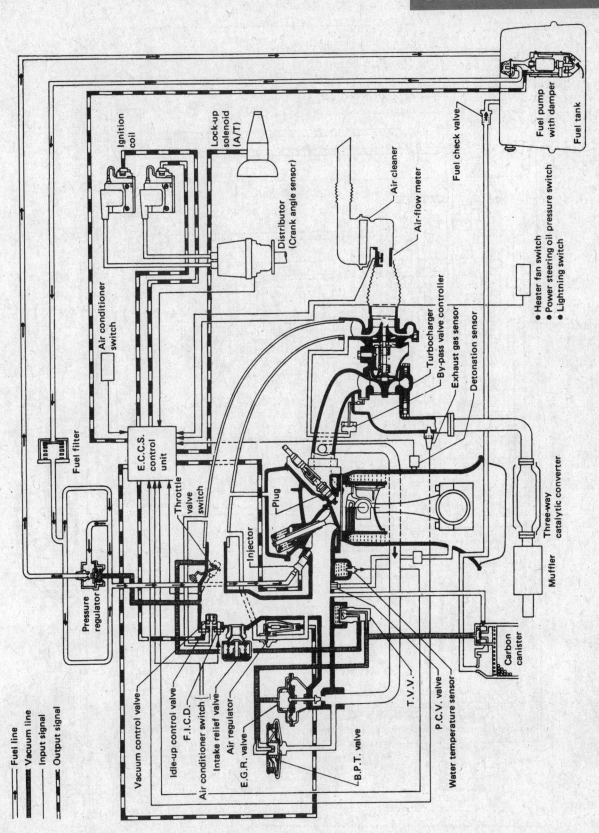

Vacuum hose routing diagram for the 1984 Nissan 200SX with the CA18ET engine

- Heater fan switch
- Power steering oil pressure switch
- Lightning switch

Ignition coil

Lock-up solenoid (A/T)

Air cleaner

Air-flow meter

Distributor (Crank angle sensor)

Fuel pump with damper

Fuel tank

Fuel check valve

Air conditioner switch

Turbocharger

By-pass valve controller

Exhaust gas sensor

Detonation sensor

Three-way catalytic converter

Muffler

Fuel filter

E.C.C.S. control unit

Throttle valve switch

Plug

Injector

Carbon canister

Pressure regulator

Vacuum control valve

Idle-up control valve

F.I.C.D.

Air conditioner switch

Intake relief valve

Air regulator

E.G.R. valve

B.P.T. valve

Water temperature sensor

P.C.V. valve

T.V.V.

Fuel line
Vacuum line
Input signal
Output signal

Nissan/Datsun

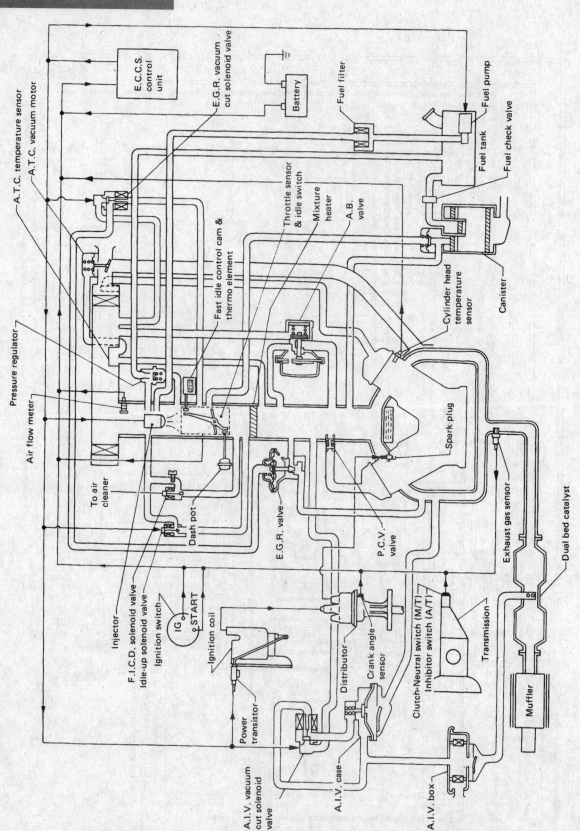

Vacuum hose routing diagram for the 1986 Nissan truck

Nissan/Datsun

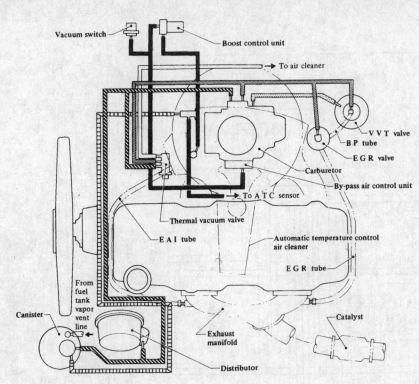

Vacuum switch

Boost control unit

To air cleaner

V V T valve

B P tube

E G R valve

Carburetor

By-pass air control unit

To A T C sensor

Thermal vacuum valve

E A I tube

Automatic temperature control air cleaner

E G R tube

From fuel tank vapor vent line

Canister

Exhaust manifold

Catalyst

Distributor

Typical vacuum hose routing diagram for the 1981 through 1985 Nissan pick-ups and Pathfinders with four-cylinder engines (Federal and Canada shown, California similar)

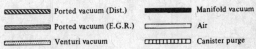

Ported vacuum (Dist.)	Manifold vacuum
Ported vacuum (E.G.R.)	Air
Venturi vacuum	Canister purge

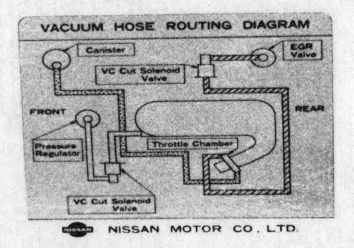

Vacuum hose routing diagram for the 1984 Nissan 300ZX

Nissan/Datsun

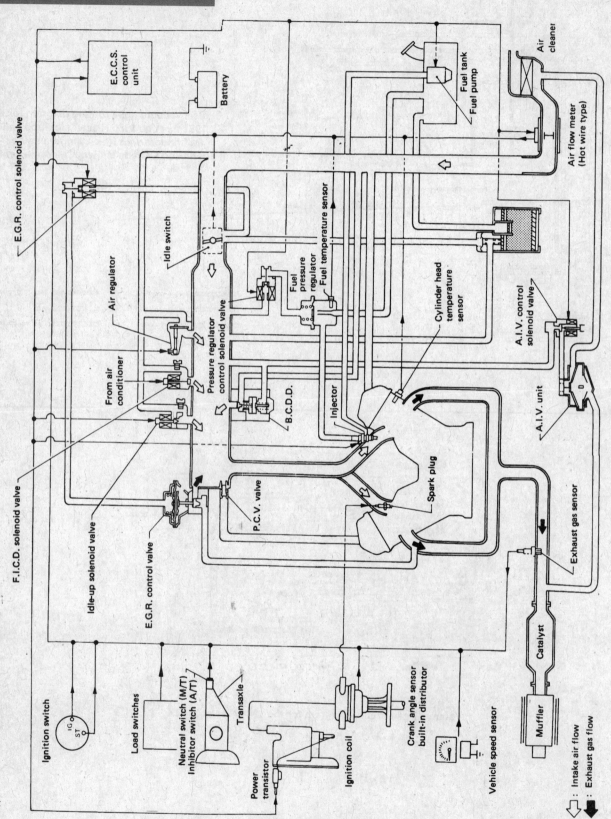

Vacuum hose routing diagram for the 1988 Nissan Maxima

Nissan/Datsun

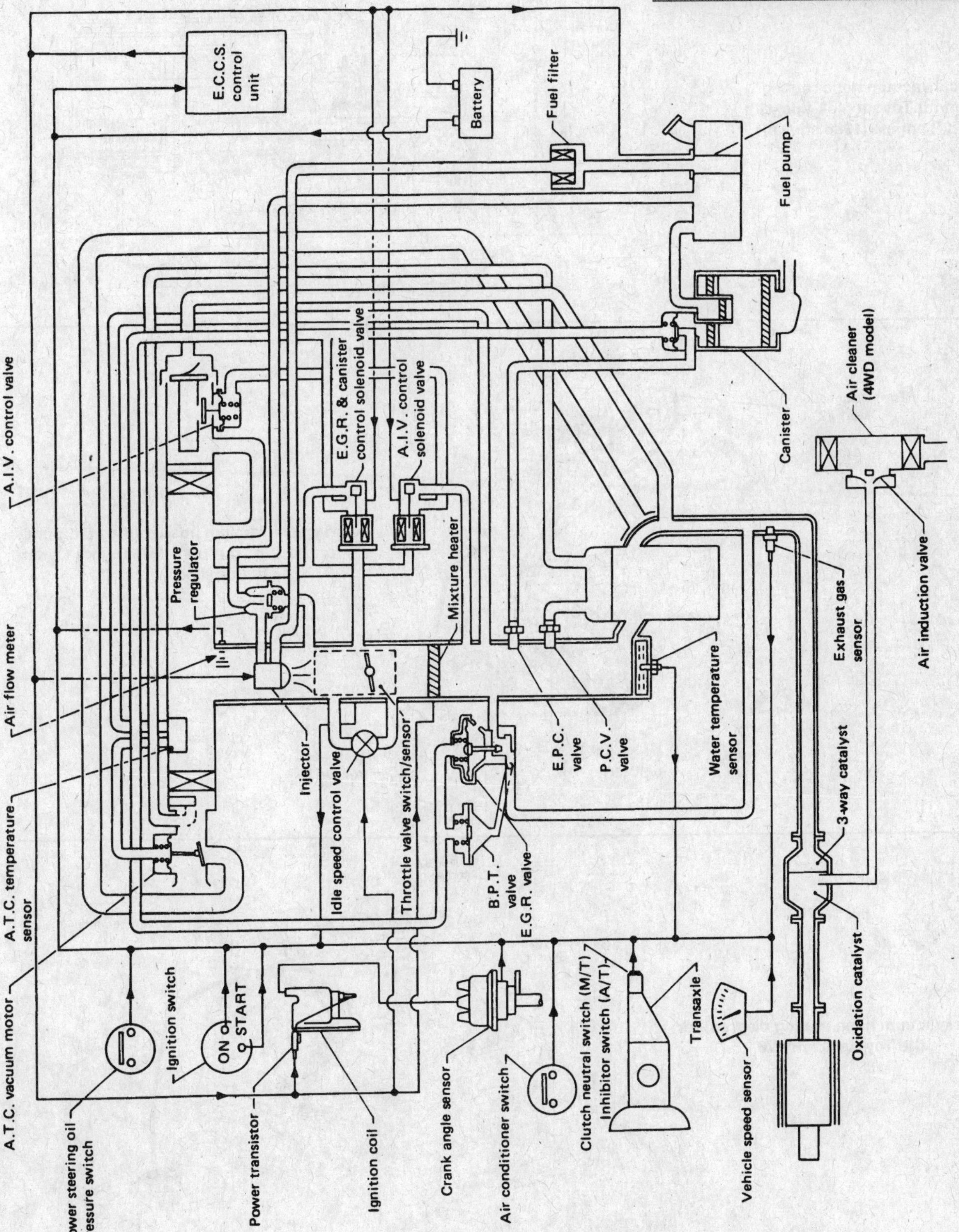

Vacuum hose routing diagram for the 1988 Nissan Sentra

E.C.C.S. control unit

Battery

Fuel filter

Fuel pump

Air cleaner (4WD model)

A.I.V. control valve

E.G.R. & canister control solenoid valve

A.I.V. control solenoid valve

Mixture heater

Canister

Pressure regulator

Air flow meter

Exhaust gas sensor

Air induction valve

A.T.C. temperature sensor

Injector

Idle speed control valve

Throttle valve switch/sensor

E.P.C. valve

P.C.V. valve

Water temperature sensor

3-way catalyst

A.T.C. vacuum motor

Power steering oil pressure switch

Ignition switch

ON START

Power transistor

Ignition coil

Crank angle sensor

Air conditioner switch

B.P.T. valve

E.G.R. valve

Clutch neutral switch (M/T) Inhibitor switch (A/T)

Transaxle

Vehicle speed sensor

Oxidation catalyst

The Haynes Emissions Control Manual

Toyota

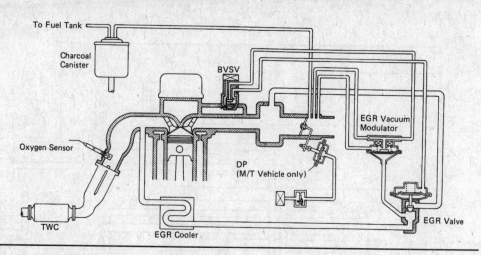

Typical vacuum hose routing diagram for Toyota pick-ups with the 22R engine (1986 shown)

To Fuel Tank
Charcoal Canister
BVSV
EGR Vacuum Modulator
Oxygen Sensor
DP (M/T Vehicle only)
TWC
EGR Cooler
EGR Valve

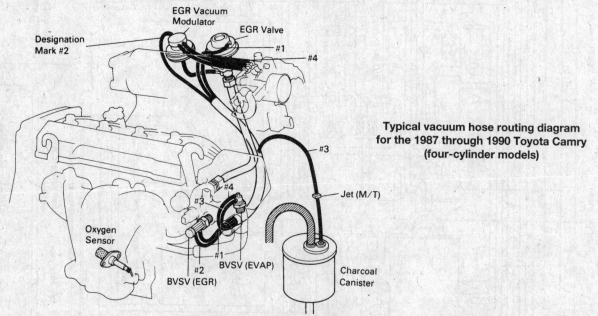

EGR Vacuum Modulator
EGR Valve
Designation Mark #2
#1
#4
#3
#4
#3
#1
#2
Jet (M/T)
Oxygen Sensor
BVSV (EVAP)
BVSV (EGR)
Charcoal Canister

Typical vacuum hose routing diagram for the 1987 through 1990 Toyota Camry (four-cylinder models)

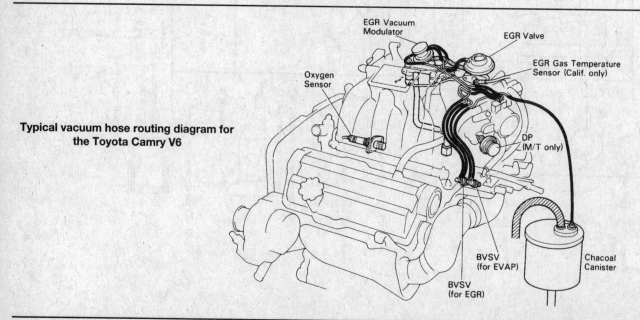

Typical vacuum hose routing diagram for the Toyota Camry V6

EGR Vacuum Modulator
EGR Valve
Oxygen Sensor
EGR Gas Temperature Sensor (Calif. only)
DP (M/T only)
BVSV (for EVAP)
BVSV (for EGR)
Chacoal Canister

 **Glossary**

A

AAS - Air Aspirator System or Aspirator Air System.

AAV - Anti-Afterburn Valve.

AB - Air Bleed.

ABPV or **ABV** - Air Bypass Valve.

A/C - Air Conditioner or Air Conditioning.

ACCC - A/C Compressor Clutch.

ACCS - A/C Clutch Cycling Switch.

ACL BI-Met - Air Cleaner Bimetal sensor.

ACL DV - Air Cleaner Duct and Valve Vacuum motor.

ACT - Air Charge Temperature sensor.

ACV - Air Control Valve.

Actuator - A device that delivers motion in response to an electrical signal; actuators alter the operation of the engine in response to commands from the engine management system computer. Examples are fuel injectors, Electronic Air Control Valves (EACV) and carburetor feedback solenoids.

AFC - AirFlow Controlled (usually refers to a type of fuel injector).

AFS - AirFlow Sensor.

AI - Air Injection. See "Air Injection System."

AICV - Air Injection Check Valve.

AIR - Air Injection Reactor system; typically the pump-operated air injection system used on GM vehicles. Also see "Air Injection System."

Air Aspirator System (AAS) - A passive air injection system that uses a one-way valve instead of an air pump to introduce extra air into the exhaust stream.

Air Bypass Valve (ABPV or ABV) - A backfire-suppressor valve used in air injection systems (also called an anti-backfire, diverter or gulp valve). During high engine vacuum conditions such as deceleration, it vents pressurized air from the air pump to the atmosphere in order to prevent backfiring. At other times, it sends air to the exhaust manifold; on vehicles with a three-way catalyst, it sends air to the oxidation catalyst only when the engine warms up.

Air Charge Temperature (ACT) sensor - A thermistor sensor that inputs the temperature of the incoming air stream in the air filter or intake manifold to the computer. It can be located in the intake manifold (EFI systems) or the air cleaner. On carbureted vehicles, if the air is cold, it signals the choke to let off slowly. It then alters engine speed after choke is off and, below a certain temperature, dumps air from the air injection system to the atmosphere for catalyst protection.

AIR-CHV - Air Check Valve.

Air Cleaner Bi-Metal (ACL BI-MET) sensor - A component of a thermostatic air cleaner system. It senses the temperature of incoming fresh air and bleeds off vacuum when the air is warm. When the air is cold, the sensor directs vacuum to the air cleaner vacuum motor.

Air Cleaner Duct and Valve (ACL DV) vacuum motor - A component of thermostatic air cleaner systems. It opens and closes the air duct valve to provide heated or unheated air to the engine in accordance with the temperature of the incoming air.

Air Conditioner Clutch Compressor (ACCC) signal - The input to the computer regarding the status of the A/C clutch (engaged or disengaged).

Air Control Valve (ACV) - A vacuum-controlled diverter valve (or a combination bypass/diverter valve) in an air injection system that diverts air pump air to either the upstream (exhaust manifold) or downstream (oxidation catalyst) air injection points as necessary.

AIR-DV - Air Diverter Valve. See "Diverter valve."

Air Guard (AG) - An American Motors air injection system that uses an air pump to supply air into the exhaust manifold to reduce HC and CO emissions.

Air Injection Reactor system - See "AIR" and "Air Injection System."

Air Injection System (AIS) - Any system that injects air into the exhaust stream to promote more complete oxidation of unburned exhaust gases.

AIR-IVV - Air Idle Vacuum Valve.

Air Management System (AMS) - Used to control the injected air to the exhaust manifold and catalytic converter. This improves the pollutant conversion efficiency in the converter.

Air Pump - A device which produces a slightly pressurized flow of air to the exhaust manifold and/or the catalytic converter. Also known as a Thermactor air supply pump.

Air Switching Valve (ASV) - A valve in an air injection system that senses intake manifold vacuum and, during heavy loads, dumps part of the air pump output to the air cleaner to reduce air injection system pressure.

AIS - Air Injection System.

AIS - Automatic Idle Speed motor.

AIV - Air Injection Valve.

ALCL - Assembly Line Communications Link.

ALDL - Assembly Line Diagnostic Link.

Altitude Compensation system - A barometric switch and solenoid used to provide better driveability over 4,000 ft. above sea level.

Ambient Temperature - The temperature of the air surrounding an object.

AMGV - Air Management Valve.

AMS - Air Management System.

ANTBV - Anti-Backfire valve.

Anti-Backfire Valve (ANTI-BFV) - See "Air Bypass Valve."

APDV - Air Pump Diverter Valve. See "Diverter valve."

AS - Airflow Sensor.

ASRV - Air Switching Relief Valve.

ASS - Air Switching Solenoid.

Assembly Line Communications Link (ALCL) or Assembly Line Diagnostic Link (ALDL) - On GM vehicles, the point where connector terminals are bridged to output trouble codes.

ASV - Air Switching Valve.

Atmospheric pressure - The weight of the air at sea level, which is about 14.7 pounds per square inch; decreases as the altitude increases.

ATS - Air Temperature Sensor.

Automotive emissions - Gaseous and particulate compounds (hydrocarbons, oxides of nitrogen and carbon monoxide) that are emitted from a vehicle's crankcase, exhaust, carburetor (or fuel injection system) and fuel tank.

Auxiliary Acceleration Pump (AAP) - A pump that increases driveability during cold engine operation by providing an extra amount of fuel to the acceleration nozzle to supplement the main acceleration pump.

B

Backfire Suppressor Valve - A device used in conjunction with earlier design air injection systems. Its primary function is to lean out the excessively rich fuel mixture which follows closing of the throttle after acceleration. It allows extra air into the induction system whenever the intake manifold vacuum decreases.

Backpressure Variable Transducer (BVT) - A system combining a ported EGR valve and a backpressure variable transducer to control emissions of NOx.

Barometric pressure - Atmospheric pressure.

BARO sensor - A barometric pressure sensor (see below).

Barometric and Manifold Absolute Pressure (BMAP) sensor - A housing containing both BP and MAP sensors.

Barometric Pressure (BP) sensor - Sends a variable frequency signal to the computer regarding the atmospheric pressure, allowing adjustment of the spark advance, EGR flow and air/fuel ratio as a function of altitude.

Base Idle - The idle speed determined by the throttle lever setting on the carburetor or throttle body while the Idle Speed Control (ISC) motor is fully retracted and disconnected.

BCDD - Boost-Controlled Deceleration Device.

BDC - Bottom Dead Center.

BHS - Bi-Metal Heat Sensor.

Bimetal Heat Sensor (BHS) - A strip (usually coiled) consisting of two metals with different expansion characteristics. Bimetal strips are used in thermostatically controlled devices because they move or bend toward the metal that expands least when heat is applied.

BMAP - Barometric and Manifold Absolute Pressure sensor.

Boost-Controlled Deceleration Device (BCDD) - A valve that, during deceleration, is triggered into action by high intake manifold vacuum. The BCDD valve allows an additional source of air and fuel to enter the intake manifold during deceleration to obtain a more burnable mixture.

Bowl Vent (BV) port - The port in the carburetor which vents fumes and excess pressure from the float bowl to maintain atmospheric pressure.

BP - Barometric Pressure sensor.

BPA - By-Pass Air solenoid.

BPEGR - Backpressure EGR.

BPS - Barometric Pressure Sensor.

Break-Out Box (BOB) - A service tool that tees-in between the computer and the multi-pin harness connector. Once connected in series with the computer and the harness, this test device permits measurements of computer inputs and outputs.

BV - Bowl Vent port.

BVT - Backpressure Variable Transducer.

Bypass Air (BPA) solenoid - Used to control the idle speed on some fuel-injected vehicles.

Bypass Valve (BPV) - A valve that opens under certain conditions to permit a flow of liquid or gas by some alternate to its normal route.

C

C-3 - Computer Command Control system (GM vehicles).

C-4 - Computer Controlled Catalytic Converter system (GM vehicles).

CAM - Choke Air Modulator switch.

Canister - A container in an evaporative emission control system; contains charcoal to trap vapors from the fuel system.

Canister Purge Shut-off Valve (CPSOV) - A vacuum-operated valve that shuts off canister purge when the air injection diverter valve dumps air downstream.

Canister purge solenoid - An electrical solenoid that opens the canister purge valve between the fuel vapor canister line and the intake manifold when energized.

Canister purge valve - Valve used to regulate the flow of vapors from the evaporative canister to the engine.

CANP - Canister Purge solenoid.

Carbon dioxide (CO$_2$) - A colorless gas that is a major constituent of automotive exhaust.

Carbon monoxide (CO) - A colorless, odorless and very poisonous gas that is a major product of incomplete combustion, especially at engine idle. As little as 0.3 percent by volume can be lethal within 30 minutes.

CAT - Catalytic Converter.

Catalyst - A compound or substance which can speed up or slow down the reaction of other substances without being consumed itself. In an automotive catalytic converter, special metals (i.e., platinum, palladium) are used to promote more complete combustion of unburned HC and CO.

Catalytic converter - A muffler-like device in the exhaust system that promotes a chemical reaction which converts certain air pollutants in the exhaust gases into harmless substances.

CAV - Coasting Air Valve.

CBVV - Carburetor Bowl Vent Valve.

CC - Catalytic Converter.

CCC - Computer Command Control; Converter Clutch Control solenoid.

CCEGR - Coolant Controlled Exhaust Gas Recirculation

CCEVS - Coolant Controlled Engine Vacuum Switch.

CCIE - Coolant Controlled Idle Enrichment.

CCO - Converter Clutch Override.

CCT - Computer Controlled Timing.

CCV - Closed Crankcase Ventilation system.

CEC - Combined Emission Control system; Computerized Emission Control system.

Central Fuel Injection (CFI) - A computer-controlled fuel metering system which sprays atomized fuel into a throttle body mounted on the intake manifold.

CES - Clutch Engine Switch.

"Check Engine" light - A light on the instrument panel that lets the driver know of any detectable engine management system malfunctions. Also used as an emissions maintenance reminder light on some vehicles. Often, when this light is on, a trouble code is stored in the computer (see Chapter 2).

Check Valve (CV) - A one-way valve which allows a liquid or gas to flow in one direction only.

Choke Thermal Vacuum Switch (CTVS) - A switch used on some GM vehicles to deny vacuum to either the front or the auxiliary choke vacuum breaks. Its purpose is to slow the opening of the choke and to provide better driveability when the engine is cold.

CIS - Continuous Injection System.

CKV - Check Valve.

CLC - Converter Lock-up Clutch.

Closed Crankcase Ventilation (CCV) system - Vents crankcase pressure and vapors back into the engine where they are burned during combustion rather than being vented to the atmosphere (See "PCV system").

Closed loop mode - Once the engine has reached "warm-up" temperature, the engine management computer collects the precise data from all the sensors (coolant temperature sensor, throttle position sensor, oxygen sensor etc.) to determine the most efficient air/fuel mixture for combustion.

CO - Carbon Monoxide.

CO$_2$ - Carbon Dioxide.

COC - Conventional Oxidation Catalyst.

Cold Weather Modulator (CWM) - A vacuum modulator located in the air cleaner on some models. The modulator prevents the air cleaner duct door from opening to non-heated intake air when outside air is below 55-degrees F. Similar to a Temperature Vacuum Switch.

Computer - A device that takes information, processes it, makes decisions and outputs those decisions.

Computer Command Control (C-3) system - An earlier engine management system used on General Motors vehicles.

Computer Controlled Catalytic Converter (C-4) system - A later engine management system used on General Motors vehicles.

Computer Controlled Timing (CCT) - A system that feeds input from various engine sensors into a computer. The computer then matches spark timing exactly to engine requirements throughout its full range of operations.

Continuous Injection System (CIS) - A mechanical fuel injection system designed and manufactured by Bosch, used on many German vehicles. In a CIS system, the fuel injectors are always open (i.e. they emit a continuous spray of fuel into the intake ports). The amount of fuel sprayed is determined by the fuel pressure in the system, which in turn is determined by the position of the throttle.

Conventional Oxidation Catalyst (COC) - A catalyst which acts on the two major pollutants, HC and CO.

Coolant Controlled Exhaust Gas Recirculation (CCEGR) - A system that prevents exhaust gas recirculation until engine coolant temperature reaches a specific value.

Coolant Temperature Override (CTO) switch - A switch that prevents vacuum from reaching a component until coolant temperature reaches a certain value.

Coolant Temperature sensor - tells the computer the temperature of the engine coolant. This sensor helps the computer control fuel metering and spark timing.

CP - Crankshaft Position sensor.

CPRV - Canister Purge Regulator Valve. See "Canister purge valve."

CPS - Canister Purge Solenoid.

CPV - Canister Purge Valve.

Crankcase Breather - A port or tube that vents fumes from the crankcase. An inlet breather allows fresh air into the crankcase.

CRV - Coasting Richener Valve.

CSOV - Canister purge Shut Off Valve.

CSSA - Cold Start Spark Advance system.

CSSH - Cold Start Spark Hold system.

CTAV - Cold Temperature Activated Vacuum.

CTO - Coolant Temperature Override switch.

CTS - Coolant Temperature Sensor; Coolant Temperature Switch.

CTVS - Choke Thermal Vacuum Switch.

Curb idle - Normal idle rpm; computer controlled on many modern vehicles.

CV - Check Valve.

CWM - Cold Weather Modulator.

D

Dash-Pot (DP) - A diaphragm that controls the rate at which the throttle closes.

DBC - Dual-Bed Catalytic Converter.

DEFI - Digital Electronic Fuel Injection.

Delay Vacuum Bypass (DVB) system - An optional system used by Ford that bypasses the spark delay valve during cold operation to improve driveability.

Delay valve - Vacuum restriction used to retard or delay the application of a vacuum signal. Also referred to as a Vacuum Delay Valve (VDV).

Detonation - An uncontrolled explosion (after the spark occurs at the spark plug) which spontaneously combusts the remaining air/fuel mixture, resulting in a "pinging" noise.

DFS - Deceleration Fuel Shut-off.

Dieseling - The tendency of an engine to continue running after the ignition is turned off.

Digital Volt-Ohm Multimeter (DVOM) - A digital electronic meter that displays voltage and resistance.

DIS - Distributorless Ignition System.

Diverter Valve - Used in air injection systems to channel airflow to either the exhaust manifold or oxidation catalyst under different operating conditions.

DLV - Delay Valve.

DP - Dashpot.

DRB II - Diagnostic Readout Box II. See "Break-Out Box."

DS - Detonation Sensor. See "Knock sensor."

DSAV - Deceleration Spark Advance system.

Dual Catalytic Converter - A Three-Way Catalyst (TWC). Also referred to as a dual-bed converter.

Duty cycle - The electronic measurement expressed in the percent of total time (On Time) the fuel injector is activated. This duration, or pulse width, is related directly to the amount of fuel injected into the combustion chamber.

DV - Delay Valve.

DVOM - Digital Volt-Ohmmeter.

DVTRV - Diverter Valve.

E

EACV - Electronic Air Control Valve. A valve used in fuel-injection systems, usually computer controlled, that controls the amount of air bypassing the throttle during idle. The more air that bypasses the throttle, the higher the idle speed.

Early Fuel Evaporation (EFE) system - A device that heats the air/fuel mixture entering the intake manifold when the engine is cold.

ECA - Electronic Control Assembly.

ECC - Electronic Controlled Carburetor.

ECM - Electronic Control Module.

ECS - Evaporation Control System.

ECT - Engine Coolant Temperature sensor.

ECU - Electronic Control Unit.

EDIS - Electronic Distributorless Ignition System.

EDM - Electronic Distributor Modulator.

EEC - Evaporative Emission Controls.

EEC/EEC-I/EEC-II/EEC-III/EEC-IV - Ford Electronic Engine Control systems.

EEGR - Electronic EGR valve.

EFC - Electronic Feedback Carburetor; Electronic Fuel Control.

EFE - Early Fuel Evaporation.

EFE TVS - EFE Thermal Vacuum Switch.

EFI - Electronic Fuel Injection.

EGO - Exhaust Gas Oxygen sensor.

EGR - Exhaust Gas Recirculation system.

EGR control solenoid (EGRC) - Energizes to allow manifold vacuum to the EGR valve.

EGR cooler assembly - Heat exchanger using engine coolant to reduce exhaust gas temperature.

EGR-EPV - EGR External Pressure Valve.

EGR-EVR - EGR Electronic Vacuum Regulator.

EGR-FDLV - EGR Forward Delay Valve.

EGR-RSR - EGR Reservoir.

EGR-S/O - EGR Shut-Off

EGR-TVS - EGR Thermal Vacuum Switch.

EGRV - EGR Vent solenoid.

EGR vacuum - A vacuum source above the closed throttle plate; used for control of ported EGR valves. Vacuum is zero at closed throttle.

EGR valve - A valve used to introduce exhaust gases into the intake air stream. There are several types (see "Integral Backpressure Transducer EGR valve," "Ported EGR valve," Electronic EGR valve" and "Valve and Transducer Assembly").

EGR Valve Position (EVP) sensor - A potentiometric sensor used in electronically controlled EGR systems. Sensor wiper position is proportional to EGR valve pintle position, which allows electronic control assembly to determine actual EGR flow at any point in time.

EGR-VCV - EGR Vacuum Control Valve.

EGR Vent (EGRV) solenoid - Electrical solenoid that normally vents EGRC vacuum line. When EGRV is energized, EGRC can open the EGR valve.

EGR venturi vacuum amplifier - A device that uses a relatively weak venturi vacuum to control a manifold vacuum signal to operate the EGR valve. Contains a check valve and relief valve that open whenever the venturi vacuum signal is equal to or greater than manifold vacuum.

EGR-VSOL - EGR Vacuum Solenoid.

EGR-VVA - EGR Venturi Vacuum Amplifier.

EHCV - Exhaust Heat Control Valve.

EIS - Electronic Ignition System.

ELB - Electronic Lean Burn.

Electronic Control Assembly (ECA) - A Ford vehicle computer consisting of a calibration assembly containing the computer memory, its control program and processor assembly (the computer hardware).

Electronic Control Module (ECM) - A GM term and also a generic term referring to the computer. The ECM is the brain of the engine control systems receiving information from various sensors in the engine compartment. The ECM calculates what is required for proper engine operation and controls the different actuators to achieve it.

Electronic EGR valve - EGR valve used in engine management systems in which the EGR flow is controlled by the computer (usually by means of an EGR valve position sensor attached to the EGR valve). Operating vacuum is supplied by EGR solenoid valve(s).

Electronic Engine Control (EEC) system - Ford's computerized engine control systems. There are four versions: EEC-I controls engine timing. EEC-II controls engine timing and fuel (on engines with an FBC system). EEC-III-FBC is a refined version of EEC-II. EEC-III-CFI controls engine timing and fuel (on engines with an EFI system). EEC-IV is a refined version of the EEC-III system.

Electronic Fuel Injection (EFI) - A computer controlled fuel system that distributes fuel through an injector located in each intake port of the engine.

Electronic Spark Timing (EST) system - This replaces the vacuum or centrifugal mechanisms in the distributor and uses the computer to advance or retard the spark timing.

Enable - A microcomputer decision that results in an engine management system being activated and permitted to operate.

Energized - Having the electrical current or electrical source turned on.

Engine Coolant Temperature (ECT) sensor - The thermistor sensor that provides coolant temperature information to the computer. Used to alter spark advance and EGR flow during warm-up or an overheating condition.

EPC - Electronic Pressure Control.

EPR-SOL - Exhaust Pressure Regulator Solenoid.

EPR-VLV - Exhaust Pressure Regulator Valve.

ERS - Engine Rpm Sensor.

ESC - Electronic Spark Control system.

ESS - Engine Speed Sensor.

ESSM - Engine Speed Switch Module.

EST - Electronic Spark Timing system.

ETC - Electronic Throttle Control.

EVAP - Evaporative emission control system.

Evaporation Control System (ECS) - A system used to prevent the escape of gasoline vapors to the atmosphere from the fuel tank and carburetor.

Evaporative Emission Control (EVAP or EEC) system - Emission control system that prevents fuel vapors from entering the atmosphere, primarily from the fuel tank and the carburetor.

Evaporative emissions - Hydrocarbon emissions formed by the evaporation of gasoline or other automotive fuels.

Evaporative Emission Shed System (EESS) - A Ford evaporative emission control system introduced in 1978.

EVCR - Emission Vacuum Control Regulator.

EVP - EGR Valve Position sensor.

EVR - EGR Vacuum Regulator.

Exhaust Back Pressure Transducer Valve (BPV or BPS) - A device used to sense exhaust pressure changes and control vacuum to the EGR valve in response to these changes.

Exhaust emissions - The tail pipe products of incomplete combustion of gasoline or other fuels.

Exhaust Gas Check (EGC) valve - A device that allows air injection system air to enter the exhaust manifold, but prevents a reverse flow in the event of improper operation of other components.

Exhaust Gas Oxygen (EGO) sensor - A device that changes its output voltage as the exhaust gas oxygen content changes when compared to the oxygen content of the atmosphere. This constantly changing voltage signal is sent to the processor for analysis and adjustment to the air/fuel ratio.

Exhaust Gas Recirculation (EGR) system - A system used to control oxides of nitrogen. The exhaust gases are recirculated, lowering the engine combustion temperatures, thereby reducing engine pollutants.

Exhaust Heat Control Valve (HCV) - A valve which routes hot exhaust gases to the intake manifold heat riser during cold engine operation. Valve can be thermostatically controlled, vacuum operated or computer controlled.

F

FAP - Forced Air Pre-heat system.

FBC - Feedback Carburetor system.

FBCA - Feedback Carburetor Actuator.

FCS - Feedback Carburetor Solenoid, Feedback Control System, Fuel Control Solenoid or Fuel Control System.

FCV - Fuel Cut-off Valve.

Feedback Carburetor Actuator - A computer-controlled stepper motor that varies the carburetor air/fuel mixture.

Feedback Control System (FCS) - A computer-controlled fuel system employing a stepper motor or a dithering solenoid that controls air-fuel mixture by bleeding precise amounts of air (determined by the computer) into the main and idle systems of the carburetor.

FI - Fuel Injection.

Fuel tank vapor valve - A valve mounted in the top of the fuel tank. Vents excess vapor and pressure from the fuel tank into the evaporative emission control system.

Fuel Vapor Recovery (FVR) system - A valve responsible for venting excess fuel vapor and pressure from the fuel system to the EEC system.

Fuel-vacuum separator - Used to filter waxy hydrocarbons from the carburetor ported vacuum to protect the vacuum delay and distributor vacuum controls.

FVEC - Fuel Vapor Emission Control.

FVR - Fuel Vapor Recovery system.

G

GND - Ground.

GRND - Ground.

Ground (GND or GRND) - The negatively charged side of a circuit. A ground can be a wire, the negative side of the battery or even the vehicle chassis.

Ground circuit - The return side of an electric circuit.

H

HAC - High altitude compensator.

HAEC - High Altitude Emission Control system.

HAI - Heated Air Inlet system.

HC - Hydrocarbon.

HCV - Heat control valve.

Heat riser valve - See "Exhaust Heat Control Valve (HCV)".

Heated Air Inlet (HAI) system - A system that operates during cold weather and cold start. Brings warm, filtered air into the engine to control the volume of air entering the engine, vaporize the fuel better and reduce HC and CO emissions.

Heated Exhaust Gas Oxygen (HEGO) sensor - An EGO sensor with a heating element.

HEGO - Heated EGO sensor.

HEI - High Energy Ignition.

Hg - The chemical abbreviation for Mercury. Inches of Mercury (In-Hg) is the unit of measurement used for when measuring vacuum.

High Energy Ignition (HEI) - An electronic ignition system used by General Motors (GM).

HSC - High Swirl Combustion chamber.

Hydrocarbons (HC) - Any compound that is made up of Hydrogen (H) and Carbon (C) molecules. Gasoline, diesel fuel, and lubricating oils are made up of hydrocarbons.

Hydrogen (H) - Highly flammable elemental gas.

Hydrogen Sulfide (H_2S) - A flammable poisonous gas that has an odor suggestive of rotten eggs.

I

IAC - Idle Air Control.

IAS - Inlet Air Solenoid valve.

IAT - Intake Air Temperature.

IBP - Integral Back Pressure.

ICM - Ignition Control Module.

Idle Speed Control (ISC) - Maintains the idle speed of the engine at a minimum level. There are currently two types of computer controlled idle speed control: DC motor ISC and air bypass ISC.

Idle Tracking Switch (ITS) - Used on CFI vehicles to inform the EEC if the throttle is in contact with the DC motor.

Idle Vacuum Valve (IVV) - This device may be used in conjunction with other vacuum controls to dump air injection system air during extended periods of idle, to protect the catalyst.

IGN - Ignition.

IMVC - Intake Manifold Vacuum Control.

Infrared Analyzer - An instrument used to measure unburned hydrocarbons (HC) and carbon monoxide (CO) discharged from a vehicle exhaust pipe.

INJ - Injector.

Injector - An electronic fuel-injection solenoid. When energized, it allows fuel to flow into the throttle body (throttle body injection) or the intake port (port injection systems). On vehicles with Bosch CIS (continuous injection system), the injector is always open (i.e. it's not an electronically operated solenoid).

INJ GND - Injector Ground.

Integral Backpressure Transducer EGR valve - This type of EGR valve combines inputs of exhaust backpressure and EGR ported vacuum into one unit. It requires both inputs to operate on vacuum alone. There are two common designs - poppet and tapered pintle.

ISS - Idle Stop Solenoid.

ITC - Ignition Timing Control system.

ITS - Idle Tracking Switch.

IVV - Idle Vacuum Valve.

J

JAS - Jet Air Stream.

JCAV - Jet-Controlled Air Valve.

JVS - Jet Valve System.

K

KAM - Keep Alive Memory.

Keep Alive Memory (KAM) - A series of vehicle battery powered memory locations in the computer which allows it to store input failures identified during normal operation for use in later diagnostic routines. KAM even adopts some calibration parameters to compensate for changes in the vehicle system.

KNK - Knock Sensor.

Knock - A general term used to describe various noises occurring in an engine; can be used to describe noises made by loose or worn mechanical parts, preignition, detonation, etc.

Knock Sensor (KNK or KS) - A piezoelectric accelerometer designed to resonate at approximately the same frequency as the engine knock frequency and provide this information to the computer. The computer retards ignition timing when knock is detected.

KS - Knock Sensor.

L

Lead (Tetraethyl lead) - An extremely toxic additive used in leaded gasoline to increase octane and provide valve wear protection.

Lead oxides and lead halogenates - Compounds formed when leaded gasoline is burned in an engine. Present in the exhaust and as engine deposits.

M

MAF - Mass Air Flow sensor.

MAFTS - Manifold Air/Fuel Temperature Sensor.

MAJC - Main Air Jet Control.

Malfunction Indicator Light (MIL) - An electric circuit between the computer and the "CHECK ENGINE" or "SERVICE ENGINE SOON" light on the dash panel of computer-equipped vehicles.

Manifold Absolute Pressure (MAP) sensor - A pressure-sensitive disk capacitor used to measure air pressure inside the intake manifold. The MAP sensor sends a signal to the computer which uses this information to determine load conditions so it can adjust spark timing and fuel mixture.

Manifold Charge Temperature (MCT) sensor - Same as the Air Charge Temperature (ACT) sensor.

Manifold Control Valve (MCV) - A thermostatically operated valve in the exhaust manifold for varying heat to the intake manifold with respect to the engine temperature. Exhaust Heat Control Valve.

Manifold Vacuum - The vacuum that occurs below the throttle plate of a carburetor or throttle body; present throughout the intake manifold. Generated by the pumping action of the pistons. Manifold vacuum is high at idle and lowers as the throttle plates open.

MAP - Manifold Absolute Pressure sensor.

Mass Air Flow (MAF) sensor - A device that measures the mass (volume) of intake air entering the engine.

MAT - Manifold Absolute Temperature sensor.

MCS - Mixture Control System.

MCU - Microprocessor Control Unit.

MEC - Motronic Engine Control.

MCT - Manifold Charge Temperature sensor.

MCU - Microprocessor Control Unit.

MECS - Mazda Equipped Control System.

MFI - Mechanical Fuel Injection, or Multi-port Fuel Injection.

MHCV - Manifold Heat Control Valve. See "Exhaust Heat Control Valve (HCV)".

Microcomputer - A device that takes information, processes it, makes decisions and outputs those decisions.

Microprocessor - An integrated circuit within a microcomputer that controls information flow within the microcomputer. Also called the Central Processing Unit (CPU).

Microprocessor Control Unit (MCU) - An integral part of an electronically controlled feedback carburetor using a TWC catalyst. Various sensors monitor conditions. MCU is widely used on Ford vehicles for the control of air-fuel ratios.

MIL - Malfunction Indicator Light.

Mixture control solenoid - A solenoid used in feedback carburetor systems. The computer controls the solenoid to provide the optimum air/fuel ratio for the current operating conditions.

Modulator - A device that controls or regulates the intensity of a vacuum, electrical, or pressure signal.

Monolithic Substrate - The ceramic honeycomb structure as a base to be coated with a metallic catalyst material for use in the catalytic converter.

MTA - Managed Thermactor Air.

N

Neutral Drive Switch (NDS) - A sensor that provides information on transmission status to the computer.

Nitrogen (N) - An element gas which is inert. Seventy-eight percent of the air is nitrogen.

Nitrogen dioxide (NO$_2$) - The main ingredient in the brownish haze we have become accustomed to seeing hanging over our cities.

Nitrogen oxides (NOx) - A compound formed during the engine's combustion process when oxygen in the air combines with nitrogen in the air to form the nitrogen oxides which are agents in photochemical smog.

NO$_2$ - Nitrogen Dioxide.

NOx - Oxides of Nitrogen.

O

O - Oxygen.

O$_3$ - Ozone.

OC - Oxidation Catalyst.

Ohmmeter - An instrument that measures resistance of a conductor in units called ohms.

Oil Thermal Vacuum Switch (OTVS) - A switch used by some GM vehicles to shut off vacuum to the early evaporation (EFE) valve when oil temperature reaches 150 degrees Fahrenheit.

Open circuit - An electrical circuit whose path has been interrupted or broken - either accidentally (a broken wire) or intentionally (a switch turned off).

Open loop mode - Mode in which the computer operates without feedback from the oxygen sensor while the engine is in the cold running condition.

Open system - Descriptive term for a crankcase emissions control system which vents to the atmosphere.

Orifice Spark Advance Control (OSAC) - A device used by Chrysler to apply vacuum advance over a period of time. By limiting the timing advance rate, NOx is reduced.

OS - Oxygen sensor.

OSAC - Orifice Spark Advance Control.

OTVS - Oil Thermal Vacuum Switch.

Output driver - A transistor in the output control area of the computer that is used to turn various actuators on and off.

Oxides of Nitrogen (NOx) - Usually a combination of colorless and odorless nitrogen oxide (NO) and toxic, pungent red-brown nitrogen dioxide (NO_2). Nitrogen oxides are a major constituent of smog.

OXS - Oxygen Sensor system.

Oxygen (O_2) - A colorless, odorless gas that makes up about 20 percent of our atmosphere and is necessary for combustion or burning to occur.

Oxygen Sensor (OXS) system - Tells the computer if there is an excess or absence of oxygen in the engine exhaust. The computer then keeps the air/fuel mixture at levels that produce the least emissions.

Ozone (O_3) - A form of oxygen with a pungent odor. Formed naturally in the upper atmosphere, its color gives the sky its bluish hue. Ozone forms a protective layer that screens out many of the sun's harmful ultraviolet rays before they reach the earth. It is also a major constituent of photochemical smog.

P

PA - Pulse Air.

PACV - Pulse Air Check Valve.

PAF - Pulse Air Feeder.

PAI - Pulse Air Injection.

Paraffins, olefins, aromatic hydrocarbons - Unburned hydrocarbons (HC) that are formed when gasoline and other hydrocarbon fuels are only partially combusted.

Particulate matter - Solids such as carbon and some liquids that are found in exhaust gases.

Parts Per Million (PPM) - A unit of measurement in emission analysis.

PAS - Pulse Air System.

PCOV - Purge Control Valve.

PCV - Positive Crankcase Ventilation system.

PCVS - PCV Solenoid.

PCVV - Positive Crankcase Ventilation Valve.

PECV - Power Enrichment Control Valve.

PFE - Pressure Feedback EGR sensor.

PFI - Port Fuel Injection.

Piezoelectric - Electric polarity due to pressure in quartz.

PIP - Profile Ignition Pickup.

Photochemical - The chemical action of radiant energy, or sunlight (photo) on air pollutants (chemicals), which creates smog.

Ported EGR Valve - Operated by a vacuum signal from the carburetor EGR port. The port signal actuates the valve diaphragm. As vacuum increases, spring pressure is overcome, opening the valve and allowing EGR flow. The amount of the flow is dependent on the position of the tapered pintle or poppet whose position reflects the strength of the vacuum signal.

Ported Vacuum Advance (PVA) - A port for a vacuum connection that is located above the idle position of the throttle plates. When the throttle plates are in the idle position, there is no vacuum at the port. When the throttle is opened, a vacuum is available to the vacuum advance unit.

Ported Vacuum Switch (PVS) - A temperature actuated switch that changes vacuum connections when the coolant temperature changes. (Originally used to switch spark port vacuum; now used for any vacuum switching function that requires coolant temperature sensing).

Positive Crankcase Ventilation (PCV) system - An emission control system that routes engine crankcase fumes into the intake manifold or air cleaner, where they are drawn into the cylinders and burned along with the air-fuel mixture.

Positive Crankcase Ventilation Valve (PCVV) - A one-way valve which controls the flow of vapors from the crankcase into the engine.

POT - Potentiometer.

PPM or ppm - see "Parts Per Million.

Preignition - The earlier-than-intended ignition of the air-fuel mixture in the combustion chamber. For example, the explosive mixture being fired in a cylinder by a flake of incandescent carbon before the electric spark occurs.

Processor - The onboard computer that receives data from a number of sensors and other electronic components. Based on input data information programmed into the computer's memory, the processor outputs signals to control various engine functions.

Profile Ignition Pickup (PIP) - A "Hall Effect" vane switch that furnishes crankshaft position data to the Ford EEC-IV processor.

Program - A set of detailed instructions that a computer follows when controlling a system.

PROM - Programmable Read Only Memory.

PSOV - Canister Purge Shut-Off Valve.

PSPS - Power Steering Pressure Switch.

PSV - Pulse Air Shut-off Valve.

PTC - Positive Temperature Coefficient choke heater.

Pulse Air system - An exhaust emission control system that utilizes exhaust pulses to pull air into the exhaust system through a reed-type check valve.

Pulse width - The electronic measurement in milliseconds of the duration of the signal that activates the fuel injector. The duration or pulse width is related directly to the amount of fuel injected into the combustion chamber.

Purge Control Valve (PURGE CV) - Used to control the release of fuel vapors from the charcoal canister into the engine.

PURGE CV - Purge Control Valve.

Purge solenoid - A device used to control the operation of the purge valve in an evaporative control emission system.

PVA - Ported Vacuum Advance.

PVCS - Ported Vacuum Control System.

PVFFC - Pressure/Vacuum Fuel Filler Cap.

PVS - Ported Vacuum Switch.

PWR GND - Power Ground.

R

RAM - Random Access Memory.

Random Access Memory - A type of memory which is used to store information temporarily.

RC - Rear Catalytic Converter.

RDV - Retard Delay Valve or Reverse Delay Valve.

Read - A microcomputer operation wherein information is retrieved from memory.

Read Only Memory - A type of memory used to store information permanently. Information can't be written to ROM, it can only be read.

Reed valve - A check-valve used on some air injection systems. Prevents a reverse flow of air from the exhaust manifold to the intake air cleaner.

Reference Voltage - A voltage provided by a voltage regulator to operate potentiometers and other sensors at a constant level.

Relay - A switching device, operated by a low current circuit, that controls the opening and closing of another circuit of higher current capacity.

Relief valve - A pressure limiting valve located in the air injection system. It functions to relieve part of the airflow if the pressure exceeds a calibrated value.

Resistance - The opposition offered by a substance or body to the passage of electric current through it.

Retard Delay Valve (RDV) - Vacuum restriction used to retard or delay the application of a vacuum signal.

ROM - Read Only Memory.

RVSV - Rollover/Vapor Separator Valve.

S

Sampling - The act of periodically collecting information from a sensor. The computer samples input from various sensors in the process of controlling a system.

SAS - Secondary Air Supply system. See "Air Injection System".

SBC - Single Bed Catalytic converter.

SCC - Spark Control Computer.

SCS - Spark Control System, or Speed Controlled Spark.

SCVAC - Speed Control Vacuum Control.

SDV - Spark Delay Valve.

SEC ACT - Secondary Actuator.

SEFI - Sequential Electronic Fuel Injection.

Sensor - A device that measures an operating condition and provides an input signal to a microcomputer.

Sequential Electronic Fuel Injection (SEFI) - A computer controlled fuel system that distributes fuel through an injector located in each intake port of the engine. Each injector is fired separately and has individual circuits.

Separator Assembly - Fuel Vacuum (SA-FV) - Fuel Vacuum Separator FVS.

SFI - Sequential Fuel Injection. See "Sequential Electronic Fuel Injection."

SHED - Sealed Housing Evaporative Determination system.

Shift Indicator Light (SIL) - A system that provides a visual indication to the driver when to shift to the next higher gear to obtain optimum fuel economy.

Signal - A voltage condition that transmits specific information in an electronic system.

SIL - Shift Indicator Light.

SIS - Solenoid Idle Stop.

Smog - The air pollution created when unburned hydrocarbons (HC) and oxides of nitrogen (NOx) combine in the presence of sunlight. These then react to form ozone, nitrogen dioxide and nitrogen nitrate.

SO₂ - Sulfur Oxides.

SOL - Solenoid.

Solenoid - A wire coil with a moveable core that changes position by means of electro-magnetism when current flows through the coil.

Solenoid Vent Valve (SVV) - Energized by ignition switch to control fuel vapor flow to the canister. When the ignition is off, the valve is open.

Solid State Ignition (SSI) system - A system used by Ford.

SOL V - EGR Solenoid Vacuum Valve Assembly.

Spacer entry EGR system - Exhaust gases are routed directly from the exhaust manifold through a stainless steel tube to the carburetor base.

Spark Delay Valve (SDV) - A valve in the vacuum advance hose that delays the vacuum to the vacuum advance unit during rapid acceleration from idle or from speeds below 15 mph, and cuts off spark advance immediately on deceleration. Has an internal sintered orifice to slow air in one direction, a check valve for free air flow in the opposite direction and a filter.

Spark knock - Same as preignition.

SPFI - Single-Point Fuel Injection.

S-Port - A special carburetor port for ported vacuum.

SSI - Solid State Ignition system.

Stoichiometric - Chemically correct. An air/fuel mixture is considered stoichiometric when it's neither too rich nor too lean; stoichiometric ratio is 14.7 parts of air for every part of fuel.

Sulfur Oxides (SO₂) - A major air pollutant, formed when gasoline with sulfur impurities is combusted.

SVCBV - Solenoid Valve Carburetor Bowl Vent.

SVV - Solenoid Vent Valve.

T

TAB - Thermactor Air Bypass solenoid (Ford Systems).

TAC - Thermostatic Air Cleaner system (Ford Systems).

TAD - Thermactor Air Diverter solenoid.

TAV - Temperature Activated Vacuum system.

TC - Throttle Closer.

TCAC - Thermostatic Controlled Air Cleaner system.

TCC - Transaxle Converter Clutch system.

TCS - Throttle Control System, or Transmission Controlled Spark system or Transmission Converter Switch.

TDP - Throttle closing Dashpot.

TDS - Time Delay Solenoid.

TEC - Thermactor Exhaust Control system.

Temperature Vacuum Switch (TVS) - Controls vacuum to the EGR valve and/or canister purge valve based on coolant or intake air temperature. Canister purge and EGR do not typically operate when the engine is cold.

TES - Thermal Electric Switch.

TFI, TFI-IV - Thick Film Integrated Ignition (Ford systems).

Thermactor - An air injection type of exhaust emission control system used on Ford vehicles.

Thermactor II - Another name for Ford's Pulse Air System.

Thermactor Air Bypass solenoid (TAB) - An electrical solenoid that switches engine manifold vacuum to bypass the atmosphere.

Thermactor Air Control solenoid vacuum valve assembly - Used on Thermactor air control systems; consists of two normally open solenoid valves with vents.

Thermactor Air Control valve - Combines a bypass (dump) valve with a diverter (upstream/downstream) valve; controls the flow of the Thermactor air in response to vacuum signals to its diaphragms.

Thermactor Air Diverter (TAD) solenoid - An electrical solenoid that switches engine manifold vacuum; when energized, switches Thermactor air from downstream (past the oxygen sensor) to upstream (before the oxygen sensor).

Thermactor Exhaust Control (TEC) system - An air injection type of exhaust emission control system used by Ford.

Thermal Ignition Control (TIC) - A device used by Chrysler that shifts the vacuum advance vacuum source from ported vacuum to manifold vacuum when coolant temperature exceed 225-degrees Fahrenheit.

Thermal Reactor (TR) - A specially designed exhaust manifold that uses heat and air to burn the unburned hydrocarbons in the exhaust gases to reduce pollution.

Thermal Vacuum Switch (TVS) - A temperature sensitive switch that shifts the source of the advance from ported to manifold vacuum when coolant temperature reaches approximately 225-degrees Fahrenheit.

Thermal Vent Valve (TVV) - A temperature-sensitive valve assembly located in the canister vent line. The TVV closes when the engine is cold and opens when it's hot to prevent fuel tank vapors from being vented through the carburetor fuel bowl when the fuel tank heats up before the engine compartment.

Thermistor - A resistor that changes its resistance with temperature.

Thick Film Integrated (TFI) - A Ford electronic ignition system.

Three-Way Catalyst (TWC) - A catalyst designed to simultaneously convert hydrocarbons, carbon monoxide and oxides of nitrogen into relatively inert substances.

Throttle Kicker - A type of throttle position solenoid specifically designed to speed-up the engine rpm by pushing on the throttle plate on the carburetor.

Throttle Position Sensor (TPS) - A potentiometric sensor that tells the computer the position (angle) of the throttle plate. The sensor wiper position is proportional to throttle position. The computer uses this information to control fuel flow.

TIC - Thermal Ignition Control.

TIV - Thermactor Idle Vacuum valve.

TK - Throttle Kicker vacuum solenoid valve.

TKA - Throttle Kicker Actuator.

TKS - Throttle Kicker Solenoid.

TO - Thermal Override.

TOC - Throttle Opener Control system.

TP - Throttle Position, or Throttle Position Sensor.

TPI - Tuned Port Injection. A fuel injection system used by General Motors that combines port fuel injection with tuned intake runners for higher engine torque.

TPS - Throttle Position Sensor.

TR - Thermal Reactor.

Transducer - A device that receives a signal from one system (such as exhaust backpressure) and transfers that signal to another system (such as a vacuum source.

TSD - Throttle Solenoid.

TSP - Throttle Solenoid Positioner.

TVS - Temperature Vacuum Switch or Thermal Vacuum Switch.

TVSV - Thermostatic Vacuum Switch Valve.

TVV - Thermal Vacuum Valve, or Thermal Vent Valve.

TWC - Three-Way Catalyst.

U

UBC - Underbody Catalyst.

Unburned or partially burned hydrocarbons (HC) - Organic compounds such as paraffins, olefins, aromatics, aldehydes, key-notes and carboxylic acids that contain hydrogen and carbon in varying amounts. Many hydrocarbons are considered carcinogenic. Unburned hydrocarbons, always when an internal combustion engine does not operate at 100-percent efficiency, are another main component of photochemical smog.

V

VAC - Vacuum Advance Control.

Vacuum - A pressure that is LESS than atmospheric pressure. Vacuum is used extensively for control purposes and is generally measured in inches of mercury (Hg.). There are three types of vacuum: manifold, ported and venturi. The strength of these vacuums depends on the throttle opening, engine speed and load.

Vacuum Check Valve (VCK-V) - A one-way valve used to retain a vacuum signal in a line after the vacuum source is gone.

Vacuum Control Valve (VCV) - A ported vacuum switch; controls vacuum to other emission devices during engine warm-up.

Vacuum Delay Valve (VDV) - A valve used by GM to bleed ported vacuum to the vacuum advance unit through a small orifice and control vacuum advance rate.

Vacuum Differential Valve (VDV) - A device used in Thermactor systems with a catalyst that senses intake manifold vacuum and triggers the bypass valve to dump injected air to the atmosphere during deceleration.

Vacuum Operated Exhaust Heat Control valve (VHC) - A vacuum operated heat riser valve used by Ford to cause the exhaust to flow through the intake manifold crossover passage for preheating of the air-fuel mixture.

Vacuum Gauge - An instrument used to measure the amount of intake vacuum.

Vacuum pump/gauge - A hand-operated pump used to apply vacuum to a device or system in order to test it; a gauge on the pump indicates the amount of vacuum applied and can be used to measure how long a device or system can hold vacuum.

Vacuum Reducer Valve (VRV) - A valve used by GM on some models to reduce the vacuum signal to the vacuum advance unit by one and one-half to three inches Hg when coolant temperature is greater than 220-degrees to reduce detonation.

Vacuum Regulator - A device that provides constant vacuum output from the manifold when the vehicle is at idle.

Vacuum Regulator Valve (VRV) two-port - This vacuum regulator provides a constant output signal when the input level is greater than a preset level. At a lower input vacuum, the output equals the input.

Vacuum Regulator Valve (VRV) three and four-port - This type of vacuum regulator valve is used to control the vacuum advance to the distributor.

Vacuum Reservoir (VRESER) - Stores excess vacuum to prevent rapid fluctuations and sudden drops in a vacuum signal, such as during acceleration.

Vacuum Restrictor (VREST) - Controls the flow rate and/or timing in actions to the different emission control components.

Vacuum Retard Delay Valve (VRDV) - Delays a decrease in vacuum at the distributor vacuum advance unit when the source vacuum decreases. Used to delay release of vacuum from a diaphragm - a "momentary" vacuum trap.

Vacuum Switching Valve (VSV) - An electrically controlled vacuum switching valve used to control emission control devices.

Vacuum Transmitting Valve (VTV) - A valve used to limit the rate of vacuum advance.

Vacuum Vent Valve (VVV) - Controls the induction of fresh air into a vacuum system to prevent chemical decay of the vacuum diaphragm that can occur on contact with fuel.

VAF - Vane Air Flow meter.

Valve and Transducer Assembly - This type of EGR valve consists of a modified ported EGR valve and a remote transducer. Works the same way as an Integral Backpressure Transducer EGR valve.

Vane Air-Flow (VAF) meter - A sensor with a movable vane connected to a potentiometer calibrated to measure the amount of air flowing to the engine.

Vane Air Temperature (VAT) sensor - Located inside the vane airflow meter housing; senses the temperature of the air flowing into the engine.

Vapor-recovery system - Another name for the evaporative emission control system.

Variable Reluctance Sensor (VR or VRS) - A non-contact transducer that converts mechanical motion into electrical control signals.

VAT - Vane Air Temperature sensor.

VAV - Vacuum Advance Valve.

VB - Vacuum Break.

VBV - Vacuum Bias valve.

VCKV - Vacuum Check Valve.

VCS - Vapor Control System, or Vacuum Control Switch.

VCV - Vacuum Control Valve.

VDV - Vacuum Delay Valve or Vacuum Differential Valve.

VECI - Vehicle Emission Control Information decal.

Vehicle Emission Control Information (VECI) decal - Critical specifications for servicing the emission systems.

Venturi Vacuum - A weak vacuum signal that originates at the venturi of the carburetor. As engine speed increases, the venturi signal increases.

Venturi Vacuum Amplifier (VVA) - Used with some EGR systems so that carburetor venturi vacuum can control EGR valve operation; venturi vacuum is desirable because it's proportional to the airflow through the carburetor.

VHC - Vacuum Operated exhaust Heat Control valve.

VIN - Vehicle Identification Number.

VMV - Vacuum Modulator Valve.

Volatile Organic Compounds - Unburned hydrocarbon (HC) portions of gasoline.

Volt-Ohm Meter (VOM) - Used to measure voltage and resistance.

VOM - Volt-Ohm Meter.

VOTM - Vacuum-Operated Throttle Modulator.

VP - Vacuum Pump.

VRDV - Vacuum Retard Delay Valve.

VRESER - Vacuum Reservoir.

VREST - Vacuum Restrictor.

VR or VRS - Variable Reluctance Sensor.

VR/S - Vacuum Regulator Solenoid.

V-RSR - Vacuum reservoir.

V-RST - Vacuum restrictor.

VRDV - Vacuum Retard Delay Valve.

VRES - Vacuum Reservoir.

VREST - Vacuum Restrictor.

VRV - Vacuum Reducer Valve, or Vacuum Regulator Valve.

VS - Vacuum Switch.

VSA - Vacuum Switch Assembly.

VSC - Vehicle Speed Control sensor.

VSS - Vehicle Speed Sensor, or Vacuum Switch Solenoid.

VSV - Vacuum Solenoid Valve, or Vacuum Switching Valve.

VTM - Vacuum Throttle Modulator.

VTP - Vacuum Throttle Positioner.

VTV - Vacuum Transmitting Valve.

VVA - Venturi Vacuum Amplifier.

VVC - Variable Voltage Choke.

VVV - Vacuum Vent Valve.

W

WAC - Wide-open throttle Air conditioner Cutoff.

WOT - Wide-Open Throttle.

WOTS - Wide-Open Throttle Switch.

WOTV - Wide Open Throttle Valve.

6 Computer trouble codes

Acura

  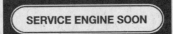

Code*	Probable cause	Code*	Probable cause
1	Oxygen sensor or circuit (Integra)	18	Ignition timing adjustment
1	Left or front oxygen sensor V6	19	Lock-up control solenoid valve
2	Left or rear oxygen sensor V6	20	Electric load
3	Manifold absolute pressure (MAP) sensor or circuit	21	Front VTEC solenoid valve (NSX)
4	Crank position sensor No. 1	21	Front spool solenoid valve (some models)
5	Manifold absolute pressure (MAP) sensor or circuit	22	Front VTEC pressure switch (NSX)
6	Coolant temperature sensor or circuit	22	Front valve timing oil pressure switch (some models)
7**	Throttle position sensor or circuit	23	Front knock sensor (some NSX, Vigor)
8	TDC sensor or circuit (Integra)	30	A/T FI signal A
9	Crank position sensor or circuit	31	A/T FI signal B
9	Camshaft position sensor	35	TC standby signal
10	Intake air temperature sensor or circuit	36	TC FC signal
12	EGR control system	41	Oxygen sensor heater (Integra)
13	Barometric pressure sensor or circuit	41	Front oxygen sensor heater
14	Idle air control system	42	Rear oxygen sensor heater (Legend, 3.0L)
15	Ignition output signal	43	Fuel supply system (4-cylinder models)
16	Fuel injector	43	Front fuel supply system (V6 models)
17**	Vehicle speed sensor or circuit	44	Rear fuel supply system (V6 models)

The Haynes Emissions Control Manual

Acura (continued)

Code*	Probable cause	Code*	Probable cause
45	Front fuel metering system	71	Misfire, cylinder no. 1
46	Rear fuel metering system	72	Misfire, cylinder no. 2
47	Fuel pump	73	Misfire, cylinder no. 3
50	Mass Air Flow sensor	74	Misfire, cylinder no. 4
51	Rear spool solenoid valve (Legend)	75	Misfire, cylinder no. 5 (V6 models)
51	Rear VTEC solenoid valve (other models)	76	Misfire, cylinder no. 6 (V6 models)
52	Rear valve timing oil pressure switch (Legend)	76	Random misfire (all except 6-cylinder engines)
52	Rear VTEC pressure switch (other models)	79	Spark plug voltage detection circuit
53	Rear knock sensor	80	Low EGR flow
54	Crank position sensor	86	Coolant temperature sensor out of range
59	No. 1 cylinder position	90	EVAP system leak
61	Upstream oxygen sensor, slow response	92	EVAP purge control solenoid
63	Downstream oxygen sensor, slow response		
65	Downstream oxygen sensor heater		
67	Low catalytic converter efficiency		
70	Transaxle		

* If codes other than these are indicated, repeat self-diagnosis. If code(s) reappear, substitute a known good ECM, and recheck codes.

** On Legend models, if S4 on the automatic transaxle indicator panel also blinks, automatic transaxle control unit may require diagnosis.

Audi

Code	Location or description of fault	Probable cause
1111	ECM	a) Defective ECM unit b) Faulty ECM circuit
1119	Transmission range sensor	a) Defective transmission range sensor b) Faulty transmission range sensor circuit
1213	Vehicle speed sensor	a) Defective speed sensor b) Faulty speed sensor circuit
1231	Vehicle speed sensor	a) Defective speed sensor b) Faulty speed sensor circuit
2111	RPM sensor	a) Defective RPM sensor b) Faulty RPM sensor circuit

Code	Location or description of fault	Probable cause
2112	Timing sensor	a) Defective timing sensor b) Faulty timing sensor circuit
2113	RPM sensor	No signal from Hall sender
2114	Hall reference	Camshaft timing out of phase
2121	Idle switch	a) Defective idle switch b) Faulty idle switch circuit
2122	Hall sender	a) Defective Hall sender b) Faulty Hall sender circuit
2123	Throttle position switch	a) Defective throttle position switch b) Faulty throttle position switch circuit
2132	Control unit	No signal from ignition to injection
2141	Knock control	Excessive detonation signal
2142	Knock control	a) No knock control sensor signal b) Defective knock control sensor c) Faulty knock control sensor circuit
2143	Knock control	Detonation from sensor no. 2, cylinder 4 or 5
2144	Knock control	a) Defective sensor no. 2 b) Faulty sensor no. 2 circuit
2212	Throttle valve	Sensor voltage out of range
2214	RPM signal	Idle speed too high
2214	RPM	Engine over-revved
2221	Vacuum control	No vacuum to control unit
2222	Pressure sensor	Defective control unit pressure sensor
2222	Manifold vacuum	a) Defective vacuum line b) Defective wastegate valve c) Defective turbocharger
2223	Altitude sensor	a) Defective altitude sensor b) Faulty altitude sensor circuit
2224	Manifold pressure	a) Turbo control unit b) Overboost
2224	Boost pressure	a) Air leak b) Defective wastegate valve c) Vacuum leak d) Defective pressure sensor
2231	Air mass sensor	a) Defective air mass sensor b) Faulty air mass sensor circuit
2231	Idle control	Idle speed outside control limits
2231	Idle stabilizer	a) Air leak b) Defective idle stabilizer valve c) Faulty idle stabilizer valve circuit

Code	Location or description of fault	Probable cause
2232	MAF sensor	a) No MAF sensor signal b) Defective MAF sensor c) Faulty MAF sensor circuit
2233	MAF sensor	High reference voltage
2233	Reference voltage	No reference signal to control units
2234	ECM	Low supply voltage
2234	System voltage	Out-of-range system voltage
2242	CO sensor	Low sensor voltage
2312	Engine coolant temperature	a) No engine coolant temperature sensor signal b) Defective engine coolant temperature sensor c) Faulty engine coolant temperature sensor circuit
2314	Signal wire	Short circuit to ground between TCM and ECM
2314	Transmission	Faulty engine-to-transmission circuit
2322	Intake air temperature	a) No intake air temperature sensor signal b) Defective intake air temperature sensor c) Faulty intake air temperature sensor circuit
2324	MAF sensor	a) Defective MAF sensor b) Faulty MAF sensor circuit
2331	Oxygen ratio	a) Defective ignition system b) Defective air/fuel system
2332	Oxygen sensor II	a) Short circuit b) Open circuit
2341	Oxygen sensor	System operating outside control limits
2342	Oxygen sensor	a) No oxygen sensor signal b) Defective oxygen sensor c) Faulty oxygen sensor circuit
2343	Fuel mixture	System running too lean
2344	Fuel mixture	System running too rich
2411	EGR system	System malfunction (California models only)
2413	Mixture control	System running too rich
2413	Fuel pressure	System pressure too low
3424	Fault lamp	System not operating
4312	EGR system	System malfunction (except for California models)
4332	Ignition circuit	a) Open or short to positive b) Open or short to ground

Code	Location or description of fault	Probable cause
4343	EVAP canister purge	a) Defective solenoid sensor circuit b) Faulty solenoid sensor circuit
4411	Fuel injector	a) Check injectors 1 and 5 b) Check circuit for injectors 1 and 5
4412	Fuel injector	a) Check injectors 2 and 7 b) Check circuit for injectors 2 and 7
4413	Fuel injector	a) Check injectors 3 and 6 b) Check circuit for injectors 3 and 6
4413	Fuel injector no. 3	a) Defective injector no. 3 b) Faulty injector no. 3 circuit
4414	Fuel injector	a) Check injectors 4 and 8 b) Check circuit for injectors 4 and 8
4421	Fuel injector no. 5	a) Defective injector no. 5 b) Faulty injector no. 5 circuit
4422	Fuel injector no. 6	a) Defective injector no. 6 b) Faulty injector no. 6 circuit
4423	Fuel injector no. 7	a) Defective injector no. 7 b) Faulty injector no. 7 circuit
4424	Fuel injector no. 8	Listen or feel for pulse at wide open throttle
4431	Idle stabilizer	a) Defective idle stabilizer b) Faulty idle stabilizer circuit
4433	Fuel pump	Listen to see if pump is running (5-cylinder models only)
4442	Wastegate	a) Defective frequency valve b) Faulty frequency valve circuit
4442	Boost pressure	Short circuit
4443	Canister purge	Listen to solenoid to see if it cycles on and off
4444	No faults	Stored memory is clear
0000	End diagnosis	No additional stored codes
16486	MAF sensor	a) Signal from MAF sensor too low b) Air leak c) Plugged air filter d) Faulty MAF sensor circuit
16487	MAF sensor	a) Signal from MAF sensor too high b) Wiring circuit shorted to positive
16500	Coolant temperature sensor	a) Faulty circuit b) Damp circuit
16501	Coolant temperature sensor	a) Short to ground in circuit b) Low signal

The Haynes Emissions Control Manual

Audi (continued)

Code	Location or description of fault	Probable cause
16502	Coolant temperature sensor	a) High signal b) Short to positive in circuit c) Broken wiring
16504	TP sensor	Faulty switch
16505	TP sensor	a) Air leak b) Moisture in wiring
16506	TP sensor	a) Low signal b) Broken wiring c) Short to ground
16507	TP sensor	a) High signal b) Broken wiring c) Short to ground
16514	Oxygen sensor	a) Corrosion in wiring or connectors b) Moisture in wiring or connectors
16516	Oxygen sensor	a) High voltage b) Short to positive c) Defective spark plug d) Faulty connector(s) e) Faulty ignition wire(s) f) Defective sensor
16518	Oxygen sensor	a) Broken wiring b) Defective sensor
16520	Oxygen sensor	Malfunction in bank no. 1, sensor no. 2
16521	Oxygen sensor	Low voltage in bank no. 1, sensor no. 2
16522	Oxygen sensor	High voltage in bank no. 1, sensor no. 2
16524	Oxygen sensor	No activity detected in bank no. 1, sensor no. 2
16534	Oxygen sensor	Moisture in connector
16536	Oxygen sensor	a) High voltage b) Short to positive c) Defective sensor d) Defective spark plug(s) e) Faulty wiring f) Faulty connector(s)
16537	Oxygen sensor	Slow response from bank no. 2, sensor 1
16538	Oxygen sensor	a) Broken wiring b) Defective sensor
16539	Oxygen sensor	Malfunction in bank no. 2, sensor no. 1
16540	Oxygen sensor	Malfunction in bank no. 2, sensor no. 2
16541	Oxygen sensor	Low voltage in bank no. 2, sensor no. 2

Code	Location or description of fault	Probable cause
16542	Oxygen sensor	High voltage in bank no. 2, sensor no. 2
16554	Fuel system	a) Air leak in manifold b) Fuel in engine oil c) False signal from MAF sensor d) Burning oil
16555	Fuel system	a) System too lean b) Air leak to MAF sensor c) Air leak in exhaust system upstream from oxygen sensor d) Low fuel pump quality e) Plugged fuel filter f) Defective fuel pressure regulator g) Sticking EVAP purge solenoid
16556	Fuel system	a) System too rich b) Defective fuel pressure regulator c) Injector(s) not closing
16557	Fuel system	a) Air leak in manifold b) Oil thinning caused by fuel contamination c) Defective MAF sensor d) Oil burning caused by worn or broken piston
16558	Fuel system	a) System too lean b) Air leak to MAF sensor c) Air leak in exhaust system upstream from heated oxygen sensor d) Defective fuel pump e) Plugged fuel filter f) Defective fuel pressure regulator g) Sticking EVAP purge regulator valve
16559	Fuel system	a) System too rich b) Defective pressure regulator c) Injector(s) not closing
16706	Engine speed sensor	a) Short to ground b) Defective engine speed sensor
16711	Knock sensor	a) Corrosion or moisture in connector b) Faulty wiring c) Short to ground d) Defective knock sensor
16716	Knock sensor	a) Corrosion or moisture in connector b) Faulty wiring c) Short to ground or positive d) Defective shielding sensor
16721	Crankcase sensor	a) Low signal b) Bad ground c) Faulty wiring d) Short to ground e) Defective sensor

The Haynes Emissions Control Manual

Audi (continued)

Code	Location or description of fault	Probable cause
16785	EGR	a) Low throughput b) Defective vacuum hose c) Sticking EGR valve
16786	'EGR	a) High throughput b) Sticking or leaking EGR valve
16804	Catalyst system	Bank no. 1 efficiency below threshold
16885	Speed sensor	a) Faulty wiring b) Defective sensor
16955	Cruise/brake switch	Circuit malfunction
16989	Control module	Defective module
17509	Oxygen sensor (bank no. 1)	a) Air leak to MAF sensor b) Air leak in exhaust system upstream from oxygen sensor c) Faulty wiring d) Sticking EVAP canister purge regulator valve e) Plugged fuel filter f) Defective fuel pressure regulator g) Low fuel supply h) Defective oxygen sensor
17514	Oxygen sensor (bank no. 2)	a) Air leak to MAF sensor b) Air leak in exhaust system upstream from oxygen sensor c) Faulty wiring d) Sticking EVAP canister purge regulator valve e) Plugged fuel filter f) Defective fuel pressure regulator g) Low fuel supply h) Defective oxygen sensor
17609	Injector no. 1	a) Short to ground b) Voltage supply problem c) Defective injector
17610	Injector no. 2	a) Short to ground b) Voltage supply problem c) Defective injector
17611	Injector no. 3	a) Short to ground b) Voltage supply problem c) Defective injector
17612	Injector no. 4	a) Short to ground b) Voltage supply problem c) Defective injector
17613	Injector no. 5	a) Short to ground b) Voltage supply problem c) Defective injector

Code	Location or description of fault	Probable cause
17614	Injector no. 6	a) Short to ground b) Voltage supply problem c) Defective injector
17621	Injector no. 1 control circuit	a) Short to positive b) Defective injector c) Injector input problem
17622	Injector no. 2 control circuit	a) Short to positive b) Defective injector c) Injector input problem
17623	Injector no. 3 control circuit	a) Short to positive b) Defective injector c) Injector input problem
17624	Injector no. 4 control circuit	a) Short to positive b) Defective injector c) Injector input problem
17625	Injector no. 5 control circuit	a) Short to positive b) Defective injector c) Injector input problem
17626	Injector no. 6 control circuit	a) Short to positive b) Defective injector c) Injector input problem
17733	Knock sensor (cylinder no. 1)	a) Faulty wiring b) Poor fuel quality (below 95 RON) c) Defective knock control module in ECM d) Damaged engine e) Loose subassembly
17734	Knock sensor (cylinder no. 2)	a) Faulty wiring b) Poor fuel quality (below 95 RON) c) Defective knock control module in ECM d) Damaged engine e) Loose subassembly
17735	Knock sensor (cylinder no. 3)	a) Faulty wiring b) Poor fuel quality (below 95 RON) c) Defective knock control module in ECM d) Damaged engine e) Loose subassembly
17736	Knock sensor (cylinder no. 4)	a) Faulty wiring b) Poor fuel quality (below 95 RON) c) Defective knock control module in ECM d) Damaged engine e) Loose subassembly
17737	Knock sensor (cylinder no. 5)	a) Faulty wiring b) Poor fuel quality (below 95 RON) c) Defective knock control module in ECM d) Damaged engine e) Loose subassembly

Audi (continued)

Code	Location or description of fault	Probable cause
17738	Knock sensor (cylinder no. 6)	a) Faulty wiring b) Poor fuel quality (below 95 RON) c) Defective knock control module in ECM d) Damaged engine e) Loose subassembly
17747	Crankshaft position/engine speed sensor	Connectors switched
17748	Crankcase/camshaft signal	V-belt off track
17749	Ignition amplifier no. 1 control circuit	a) Short to ground b) Defective ignition coil power output stage
17751	Ignition amplifier no. 2 control circuit	a) Short to ground b) Defective ignition coil power output stage
17753	Ignition amplifier no. 3 control circuit	a) Short to ground b) Defective ignition coil power output stage
17799	Camshaft position sensor	a) Short to ground b) Defective camshaft position sensor
17800	Camshaft position sensor	a) Incorrect voltage or ground supply b) Faulty wiring c) Short to positive d) Defective camshaft position sensor
17801	Ignition amplifier no. 1 control circuit	a) Short to ground b) Defective ignition coil power output stage
17802	Ignition amplifier no. 2 control circuit	a) Short to ground b) Defective ignition coil power output stage
17803	Ignition amplifier no. 3 control circuit	a) Short to ground b) Defective ignition coil power output stage
17808	EGR valve	a) Faulty wiring b) Defective EGR valve c) Incorrect voltage supply to EGR vacuum regulator solenoid valve
17810	EGR valve control circuit	a) Short to positive b) Defective vacuum regulator solenoid valve
17815	EGR temperature sensor	a) Short to ground b) Defective EGR temperature sensor
17816	EGR temperature sensor	a) Incorrect ground supply b) Defective EGR temperature sensor c) Short to positive
17817	EVAP canister purge regulator valve	a) Incorrect voltage supply b) Defective EVAP canister purge regulator valve c) Short to ground
17818	EVAP canister purge regulator valve	a) Defective valve b) Short to positive

Code	Location or description of fault	Probable cause
17819	Secondary air injection (bank no. 2)	a) Defective vacuum hose b) Defective combination valve c) Restricted flow
17822	Secondary air injection (bank no. 2)	a) Leaking combination valve b) Defective combination valve
17828	Secondary air injection control valve	a) Short to ground b) Defective control valve c) Incorrect voltage supply
17830	Secondary air injection control valve	Short to positive
17831	Secondary air injection (bank no. 1)	a) Defective vacuum hose b) Defective combination valve c) Restricted flow
17832	Secondary air injection (bank no. 2)	a) Leaking combination valve b) Defective combination valve
17842	Secondary air system pump relay	a) Short to positive b) Defective relay
17844	Secondary air system pump relay	a) Short to ground b) Incorrect voltage supply c) Defective relay
17908	Fuel pump relay circuit	a) Faulty wiring b) Defective pump relay
17912	Intake system	a) Air leak b) Defective air control valve c) Throttle body second stage not closing
17913	Throttle position switch	a) Floormat pressing on gas pedal b) Throttle misadjusted c) Sticking throttle d) Defective throttle position switch e) Faulty wiring
17914	Throttle position switch	a) Short to ground b) Moisture in connector c) Defective throttle position switch
17918	Throttle position switch	a) Short to positive b) Defective throttle position switch
17919	Intake manifold change-over valve	a) Faulty wiring b) Defective change-over valve
17920	Intake manifold change-over valve	Short to positive
17978	ECM	ECM not adapted
18008	Low voltage at supply terminal	a) Discharged battery b) Bad ground to ECM c) Current drain with ignition turned off
18020	ECM incorrectly coded	a) Manual transmission coded for automatic, or vice versa b) Not coded for Automatic Traction Control (ATC)

The Haynes Emissions Control Manual

BMW

   CHECK ENGINE LIGHT

1988 3-Series

Code	Probable cause
Code 1	Airflow meter or Mass Air Flow sensor
Code 2	Oxygen sensor
Code 3	Coolant temperature sensor
Code 4	TPS

1989 and later 3, 5 and 7-Series

Code	Probable cause
1000, 2000	End of diagnosis
1211, 2211	Electronic Control Unit (ECU)
1215, 2215	Mass Air Flow sensor
1216, 2216	Throttle Position Sensor
1221, 2221	Oxygen sensor
1222	Oxygen sensor control out of range
1222, 2222	Oxygen sensor regulation
1223, 2223	Coolant temperature sensor
1224, 2224	Intake air temperature sensor

Code	Probable cause
1231, 2231	Battery voltage out of range
1232, 2232	Idle switch
1233, 2233	Wide open throttle switch
1251, 2251	Fuel injectors (final stage 1)
1252, 2252	Fuel injectors (final stage 2)
1253	Cylinder no. 3 fuel injector
1254	Cylinder no. 4 fuel injector
1255	Cylinder no. 5 fuel injector
1256	Cylinder no. 6 fuel injector
1261, 2261	Fuel pump relay
1262	Idle speed controller or idle air control valve
1263, 2263	EVAP canister purge valve
1264, 2264	Oxygen sensor heating relay
1444, 2444	No faults in memory

Note: On 12-cylinder models, codes starting with 1 indicate problems on the right cylinder bank (cylinders 1 through 6). Codes starting with 2 indicate problems on the left cylinder bank (cylinders 7 through 12).

Chrysler, Dodge and Plymouth - domestic cars and light trucks

  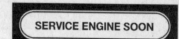 CHECK ENGINE LIGHT

Code	Probable cause
11	No distributor reference signal during engine cranking
12	Battery power to computer disconnected in last 50 to 100 cycles; memory standby power lost (1983 through 1990)

Code	Probable cause
13*	Manifold Absolute Pressure (MAP) sensor vacuum circuit - slow or no change in MAP sensor input and/or output
14*	Manifold Absolute Pressure (MAP) sensor electrical circuit - high or low voltage
15**	Vehicle speed/distance sensor circuit
16*	Loss of battery voltage (1983 through 1989)
16*	Knock sensor (1993 on)
17	Knock sensor circuit open or shorted during engine operation (1985 and 1986 turbo models)
17	Engine running too cold
21**	Oxygen sensor circuit - voltage in neutral zone or above normal range
22**	Coolant temperature sensor unit - high or low voltage
23	Throttle body air temperature sensor circuit - high or low voltage (1987 through 1990 TBI models)
23	Intake air temperature sensor circuit - high or low voltage (1991 through 1998)
24*	Throttle position sensor circuit - high or low voltage
25**	Idle speed control (ISC) or Idle air control (IAC) motor driver - circuit shorted
25**	Automatic idle speed (AIS) motor driver - circuit shorted
26*	Peak injector driver current not reached because of high resistance in circuit
27*	Injector driver not responding correctly to injector control signal
31**	Canister purge solenoid circuit open or shorted
32**	Exhaust Gas Recirculation (EGR) transducer solenoid - circuit open or shorted, or EGR system failed to respond to command (1987 through 1994)
32	Malfunction indicator lamp (MIL) circuit open or shorted (1983 through 1986)
33	Air conditioning clutch relay circuit open or shorted
34	Spare driver circuit open or shorted (1985 models)
34*	Open or shorted circuit at the EGR solenoid (1983 through 1985 models)
34	Speed control vacuum or vent solenoid circuit open or shorted
35	Cooling fan relay circuit open or shorted
35	Idle switch circuit open or shorted (1988 through 1994 RWD models)
36	Spare driver circuit open or shorted (1985 models)
36*	Turbocharger wastegate solenoid circuit open or shorted
36*	Air switching solenoid circuit open or shorted
37	Shift indicator lamp circuit open or shorted (1985 and 1986 models with manual transmission)
37	Part-throttle unlock solenoid driver circuit open or shorted (1988 through 1994 models with automatic transmission only)
37	Baro solenoid circuit open or shorted (turbo models)

Chrysler, Dodge and Plymouth (continued)

Code	Probable cause
41	Charging system excess or lack of field current
42	Automatic shutdown driver (ASD) relay circuit open or shorted
43	Ignition coil control circuit or spark interface circuit - output stage not responding to control command
44	Fault in computer (1983 and 1984 models)
44	Battery temperature signal out-of-range (1985 through 1987 and 1992 through 1994 3.3L and 3.8L)
44	No fused circuit voltage at computer connector during engine operation (1987 through 1989 models)
45	Overboost shut-off circuit on MAP sensor reading above overboost limit
45	Overdrive solenoid circuit open or shorted (1989 through 1994 RWD models)
46*	Charging system voltage too high
47*	Charging system voltage too low
51**	Oxygen sensor voltage indicates lean during engine operation
52**	Oxygen sensor voltage indicates rich during engine operation
52	Fault present in computer (1983 through 1986 models)
53	Module internal problem; SMEC/SBEC failure; internal engine controller fault condition detected
54	Problem with the distributor synchronization circuit - no sync pick-up signal detected during operation
55	End of code output
61*	BARO solenoid circuit open or shorted (1989 on turbo models)
62	Emissions maintenance reminder light mileage is not being updated (1989 on)
63	EEPROM write denied - controller failure (1989 on)
64	Speed control vent solenoid no. 1 circuit open or shorted (1990 2.2L turbo)
64	Flexible fuel (methanol) sensor indicates concentration sensor input more than the acceptable voltage
64	Flexible fuel (methanol) sensor indicates concentration sensor input less than the acceptable voltage
65	Manifold tuning valve solenoid circuit open or shorted
65	Power steering switch failure (1996 models)
66	No message from the transmission control module (TCM) to the powertrain control module (PCM)
66	No message from the body control module (BCM) to the powertrain control module (PCM)
71	5-volt PCM output low
72	Catalytic converter efficiency failure
77	Speed control power relay circuit
88	Start of test

* These codes light up Check Engine light
** These codes light up Check Engine light on vehicles with special California emission controls

Eagle Summit and Talon (1988 through 1998)

 CHECK   MIL  SERVICE ENGINE SOON   CHECK CHECK ENGINE LIGHT

Code*	Probable cause	Code*	Probable cause
11	Oxygen sensor	39	Oxygen sensor
12	Airflow sensor	41	Injector
13	Intake air temperature sensor	42	Fuel pump
14	Throttle position sensor	43	EGR
15	Idle speed motor or idle air control position sensor	44	Ignition coil power circuit
21	Coolant temperature sensor	52	Ignition coil (cylinders 2 and 5)
22	Crank angle sensor (crankshaft position sensor)	53	Ignition coil (cylinders 3 and 6)
23	Top dead center sensor (camshaft position sensor)	55	Idle air control valve
24	Vehicle speed sensor	59	Heated oxygen sensor (rear)
25	Barometric pressure sensor	61	ECM-transaxle interlink
31	Knock sensor (turbo models)	62	Warm-up valve position sensor
32	MAP sensor	71	Traction Control vacuum valve solenoid
36	Ignition timing adjustment signal		

Eagle Premier (1991 and 1992) and Vision (1993 through 1997)

 CHECK   MIL 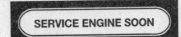 SERVICE ENGINE SOON   CHECK CHECK ENGINE LIGHT

Trouble codes

Note: *Not all trouble codes apply to all models.*

Code 11	No crank reference signal detected during engine cranking. Check the circuit between the crankshaft position sensor and the PCM.
Code 12	Problem with the battery connection. Direct battery input to controller disconnected within the last 50 ignition key-on cycles.
Code 13**	Indicates a problem with the MAP sensor pneumatic (vacuum) system.
Code 14**	MAP sensor voltage too low or too high.

The Haynes Emissions Control Manual

Code 15**	A problem with the vehicle distance/speed signal. No distance/speed sensor signal detected during road load conditions.
Code 16	Loss of battery voltage.
Code 17	Engine is cold too long. Engine coolant temperature remains below normal operating temperatures during operation (check the thermostat).
Code 21**	Problem with oxygen sensor signal circuit. Sensor voltage to computer not fluctuating.
Code 22**	Coolant sensor voltage too high or too low. Test coolant temperature sensor.
Code 23**	Indicates that the air temperature sensor input is below the minimum acceptable voltage or sensor input is above the maximum acceptable voltage.
Code 24**	Throttle position sensor voltage high or low. Test the throttle position sensor.
Code 25**	Idle Air Control (IAC) valve circuits. A shorted condition is detected in one or more of the IAC valve circuits.
Code 26	Peak injector current not reached (1991 and 1992 Premier models)
Code 26	injector circuit (1991 and 1992 Premier models)
Code 27	One of the injector control circuit output drivers does not respond properly to the control signal. Check the circuits.
Code 31**	Problem with the canister purge solenoid circuit.
Code 32**	An open or shorted condition detected in the EGR solenoid circuit. Possible air/fuel ratio imbalance not detected during diagnosis.
Code 33	Air conditioning clutch relay circuit. An open or shorted condition detected in the compressor clutch relay circuit.
Code 34	Open or shorted condition detected in the speed control vacuum or vent solenoid circuits.
Code 35	Open or shorted condition detected in the radiator fan low speed relay circuit.
Code 41**	Problem with the charging system. Occurs when battery voltage from the ASD relay is below 11.75-volts.
Code 42	Auto shutdown relay (ASD) control circuit indicates an open or shorted circuit condition.
Code 43**	Peak primary circuit current not achieved with the maximum dwell time.
Code 44	Battery temperature sensor volts malfunction. Problem with the battery temperature voltage circuit in the PCM.
Code 46**	Charging system voltage too high. Computer indicates that the battery voltage is not properly regulated.
Code 47**	Charging system voltage too low. Battery voltage sense input below target charging voltage during engine operation and no significant change in voltage detected during active test of alternator output.
Code 51*	Oxygen sensor signal input indicates lean fuel/air ratio condition during engine operation.
Code 52**	Oxygen sensor signal input indicates rich fuel/air ratio condition during engine operation.
Code 53	Internal PCM failure detected.
Code 54	No camshaft position sensor signal at PCM. Problem with the camshaft position sensor synchronization circuit.
Code 55	Completion of fault code display on CHECK ENGINE lamp. This is an end of message code.

Code 62	Unsuccessful attempt to update EMR mileage in the controller EEPROM.
Code 63	Controller failure. EEPROM write denied. Check the PCM.
Code 64**	The Flexible Fuel sensor voltage is low. Methanol concentration sensor input below the maximum acceptable voltage requirements.
Code 65	An open or shorted condition detected in the Manifold Tuning Valve (MTV) solenoid circuit.
Code 66	PCM is not receiving CCD Bus signals.
Code 77	Speed Control Power relay circuit is open or shorted.

** These codes light up the CHECK ENGINE light on the instrument panel during engine operation once the trouble code has been recorded.

Ford, Lincoln and Mercury

2-digit trouble codes

Code No.	Test condition*	Probable cause
10	R	Cylinder no. 1 low during cylinder balance test
11	O,R,C	System PASS
12	R	Cannot control rpm during high rpm test
13	R	Cannot control rpm during low rpm test
13	O	D.C. motor doesn't move (1987 through 1990 1.9L CFI and 2.3L CFI)
13	C	D.C. motor doesn't follow dashpot (1987 through 1990 1.9L CFI and 2.3L CFI)
14	C	PIP circuit failure
15	O	EEC Read Only Memory (ROM) failed, or Keep Alive Memory (KAM) in continuous
15	C	EEC Keep Alive Memory (KAM) failed (1990)
16	R	ISC rpm exceeds self-test range (1987 through 1989 1.9L and 2.5L)
16	R	Idle rpm too high with ISC retracted (1990 1.9L and 2.5L)
16	O	Ignition Diagnostic Module (IDM) signal not received (1990 and 1991 3.0L, 1991 4.0L truck)
16	R	Idle rpm too low to perform EGO test (2.3L OHC and 5.0L SFI) or HEGO test (5.0L car)
16	R	Air/fuel mixture not within self-test range
17	R	ISC rpm exceeds self-test range (1987 through 1989 1.9L and 2.5L)

*O = Key On, Engine Off; C = Continuous Memory; R = Engine Running

The Haynes Emissions Control Manual

Ford, Lincoln and Mercury (continued)

2-digit trouble codes (continued)

Code No.	Test condition*	Probable cause
17	R	Idle rpm too low with ISC retracted (1990 1.9L and 2.5L)
17	R	Air/fuel mixture not within self-test range (1985 3.0L and 5.0L CFI)
18	R,C	Loss of TACH input to ECA - SPOUT circuit grounded (1984 on)
18	C	SPOUT circuit open (1987 on)
19	O	Failure in EEC reference voltage circuit (1986 through 1989, except 1.9L, 2.3L, 3.0L MA and 3.8L SC)
19	R	RPM for EGR test too low (1988 through 1990 1.9L CFI)
19	R	Engine stumble during hard idle test set (1988 through 1990 1.9L PFI)
19	C	CID circuit failure - DIS (1989 through 1991 3.0L MA, 3.8L SC and 4.0L)
20	R	Cylinder no. 2 low during cylinder balance test
21	O,R	ECT out of range during self test
22	O,C,R	MAP/BP sensor out of range during self test (through 1991)
23	O,R	TP sensor out of range during self test
24	O,R	VAT sensor out of range during self test (1.6L PFI and 2.3L Turbo)
24	O,R	ACT sensor out of range during self test (except 1.6L PFI, 1.9L PFI and 2.3L Turbo)
25	R	Knock not sensed during dynamic response test
26	O,R	VAF sensor out of range during self test (1.6L PFI, 1.9L PFI and 2.3L Turbo, through 1990)
26	O,R	MAF/VAF sensor out of range during self test (1988 1.9L PFI, 2.3L Turbo and 5.0L PFI)
26	O,R	MAF sensor out of range during self test (1989 through 1991 2.3L PFI, 2.9L PFI, 3.0L SHO, 3.8L SC, 4.0L SEFI and 5.0L SEFI)
26	O,R	TOT sensor out of range during self test (1989 and later 5.8L, 7.3L diesel and 7.5L trucks with E4OD)
27	C	Insufficient input from vehicle speed sensor (1987 through 1989 2.3L Turbo)
27	R	Servo leaks down during integrated vehicle speed control test (1987 through 1990)
28	R	Servo leaks up during integrated vehicle speed control test (1987 through 1990)
28	O,R	Intake air temperature at VAF meter out of range during self test
28	C	Loss of (right) primary TACH (1989 and 1990 dual-plug DIS)
30	R	Cylinder no. 3 low during cylinder power balance test
31	O,C,R	EVP voltage out of range during self test (1983 through 1988, 1991 and 1992 2.3L OHC and 3.8L CFI)

*O = Key On, Engine Off; C = Continuous Memory; R = Engine Running

Code No.	Test condition*	Probable cause
31	O,C,R	PFE/EPT/EVP below minimum voltage (1987 through 1990 and 1993)
32	R	EGR not controlling (1983 through 1990 2.3L OHC and 3.8L CFI)
32	C,R	EGR valve not seated (1991 1.9L, 2.3L HSC and 3.0L SHO)
32	O,C,R	EGR/EVP closed voltage too low (1991 on)
33	C,R	EGV valve not seated (1983 through 1989 1.9L CFI, 2.3L OHC, 3.0L and 3.8L SFI)
33	C,R	EGR valve not opening, or opening not detected (1985 through 1990 PFE and Sonic)
33	R	EGR valve not returning to closed position (1990 2.3L OHC)
33	C,R	Insufficient EGR flow detected (191 on PFE and Sonic)
33	C	Throttle position noise (1993 7.3L diesel)
34	R	EVP voltage out of range during self test
34	O	Defective PFI/EPT sensor (1985 through 1989 1.9L CFI, 2.9L and 3.0L)
34	C,R	Exhaust pressure high, or defective PFE/EPT sensor (1985 through 1991)
34	O,C,R	EVP voltage above closed limit (1986 through 1990)
35	R	RPM too low to perform EGR test (1983, 1987 through 1990)
35	R	Exhaust pressure high, defective EPT sensor (1984)
35	O,C,R	PFE/EPT/EVP circuit above maximum voltage (1985 on)
36	R	Insufficient rpm increase during integrated vehicle speed control test (1987 through 1991)
37	R	Insufficient rpm decrease during integrated vehicle speed control test (1987 through 1991)
38	C	ITS circuit open (1987 through 1990 1.9L CFI, 2.3L CFI and 2.5L CFI)
39	C	Automatic transaxle lock-up circuit failed (1986 through 1990 3.0L cars)
40	R	Cylinder no. 4 low during cylinder balance test
41	C,R	EGO sensor indicates system lean (1983 through 1990)
41	C	No EGO sensor switching detected (1987 through 1990)
42	C,R	EGO sensor indicates system rich (1983 through 1990)
42	C	No EGO sensor switching detected (1987 through 1990)
43	C	EGO lean at wide open throttle (1987 through 1990 1.9L PFI and 2.3L Turbo)
44	R	Thermactor air system or secondary air injection system inoperative
45	R	Thermactor air upstream during self test (through 1992)
46	R	Thermactor air not bypassed during self-test
50	R	Cylinder no. 5 low during cylinder balance test
51	O,C	ECT sensor circuit open or ECT indicates -40 degrees F (through 1991)

*0 = Key On, Engine Off; C = Continuous Memory; R = Engine Running

2-digit trouble codes (continued)

Code No.	Test condition*	Probable cause
52	O	Power steering pressure switch open (1985 on)
53	O,C	TP sensor circuit open (1983) or above maximum voltage (1984 on)
54	OC	VAT sensor circuit open (1985 and 1986 1.6L PFI, 1.9L PFI and 2.3L turbo)
54	O,C	ACT sensor circuit open or ACT indicates -40 degrees F (1985 through 1991, except 1.6L PFI, 1.9L PFI and 2.3L turbo)
55	O,C,R	Key power circuit low (1985 through 1990 1.9L CFI, 2.3L CFI and 2.5L CFI)
56	O,C	MAF/VAF circuit above maximum voltage (1983 through 1990 1.6L PFI, 1.9L PFI, 2.3L turbo, 3.0L SHO, 3.8L SC and 5.0L PFI)
56	O,C	TOT sensor circuit open or -40 degrees F. indicated by TOT (1989 on with transmission oil temperature sensor)
57	C	NPS circuit failed open (1986 through 1990 3.0L car)
58	R	ITS stuck closed or circuit grounded (1987 through 1990 1.9L CFI, 2.3L CFI and 2.5L CFI)
58	O	ITS circuit open (1987 through 1990 1.9L CFI, 2.3L CFI and 2.5L CFI)
58	O,C	VAT sensor circuit open or -40 degrees F. indicated by VAT (1987 through 1990 1.9L CFI)
58	O	Crank fuel delay service pin in use or circuit grounded (1990 2.9L)
59	C	Automatic transaxle 4/3 circuit failed open (1986 through 1990 3.0L and 3.8L)
59	C	2/3 shift error (1991 on 7.3L diesel, 5.8L and 7.5L with E4OD)
59	C	AXOD 4/3 circuit failed closed
60	R	Cylinder no. 6 low during cylinder balance test
61	O,C,R	ECT sensor circuit grounded or below minimum voltage
62	O,R	Automatic transaxle 3/2 or 4/3 circuit grounded (1986 through 1990 3.0L)
62	C	Converter clutch error (1989 through 1991 5.8L, 7.3L diesel and 7.5L with E4OD)
63	O,C	TP sensor circuit below minimum voltage (through 1991)
63	O,C	Fuel injector pump lever circuit below minimum voltage (1989 through 1991 7.3L diesel with E4OD)
64	O,C	ACT sensor out of range during self test (1983 2.3L turbo and 2.8L)
64	O,C	VAT sensor grounded (1984 through 1986 1.6L PFI, 1.9L PFI and 2.3L turbo)
64	O,C	ACT sensor circuit grounded, or 254 degrees F indicated by ACT/VAT sensor (1984 through 1991, except 1.6L PFI, 1.9L PFI and 2.3L turbo)
65	C,R	Key power low (1984 and 1985 2.8L, 3.8L CFI and 5.0L CFI)

*O = Key On, Engine Off; C = Continuous Memory; R = Engine Running

Code No.	Test condition*	Probable cause
65	R	Overdrive cancel switch not changing status (1989 5.8L, 7.3L diesel and 7.5L with E4OD)
65	C	System did not go into closed loop (1988 through 1990 1.9L PFI and 2.3L turbo)
66	O,C	VAF sensor circuit input voltage below minimum (1983 through 1990 1.6L PFI, 1.9L PFI and 2.3L turbo)
66	C	MAF sensor circuit input voltage below minimum (1989 through 1991 3.0L SHO, 3.8L SC, 4.0L and 5.0L SEFI)
66	O,C	290 degrees F indicated by TOT sensor or circuit grounded (1989 and 1990 4.9L, 5.0L, 5.8L, 7.3L diesel and 7.5L with E4OD)
66	O,C	TOT sensor circuit below minimum voltage (1991 and later 7.3L diesel, 5.8L and 7.5L)
67	O	NDS circuit open with A/C on during self-test (1983 through 1991)
67	C	A/C clutch energized during self test (1983 2.3L turbo)
68	O	RPM not within self-test range (1983 through 1986)
69	C	Automatic transaxle 3/2 input circuit failed open (1986 through 1990 3.0L and 3.8L)
69	C	Automatic transaxle 3/2 input circuit failed closed (1988 and 1989 3.8L)
69	C	Automatic transaxle 3/4 shift error (1989 on 5.8L, 7.3L diesel and 7.5L with E4OD)
70	R	Cylinder no. 7 low during cylinder balance test
70	C	Data Communication Link (DCL) or ECA circuit failure (1989 and 1990 3.8L)
71	C	Software reinitialization detected (1987 through 1990 1.9L PFI and 2.3L turbo)
71	C	ITS circuit shorted to ground on pre-position (1987 through 1990 1.9L CFI and 2.3L CFI)
72	R	Insufficient MAF/MAP change during dynamic response test (1983 2.3L HSC and 2.8L; 1987 through 1990; 1993 on)
73	R	Insufficient TPS change during dynamic response test (1983 through 1991; 1993 on)
74	R	Brake on/off (BOO) switch circuit open or circuit failure (1985 on)
75	R	Brake on/off (BOO) switch circuit closed or ECA input open (1985 through 1991)
76	R	Insufficient VAF change during dynamic response test (1983 through 1990 1.6L PFI, 1.9L PFI and 2.3L turbo)
77	R	Operator error during dynamic response test or cylinder balance test (1983 through 1991)
77	R	Insufficient rpm change during self test, invalid cylinder balance test (caused by moved throttle), or CID sensor circuit failure (1992 on)
78	R	Power interrupt detected (1987 and 1988 2.3L CFI and 2.5L CFI)
79	O	A/C on during self test (1987 through 1990 2.3L PFI, 2.9L PFI, 3.0L SHO, 3.8L PFI, 4.0L PFI, 5.0L PFI and 5.0L SFI)
80	R	Cylinder no. 8 low during cylinder balance test
81	O	Air management no. 2 circuit failure (1984 through 1992)
81	O	Boost circuit failure (1987 and 1988 2.3L turbo)

*0 = Key On, Engine Off; C = Continuous Memory; R = Engine Running

Ford, Lincoln and Mercury (continued)

2-digit trouble codes (continued)

Code No.	Test condition*	Probable cause
81	O	Speed control vent circuit failure (1987 through 1991)
82	O	Speed control vent circuit failure (1987 through 1991)
82	O	Electro drive fan (EDF) circuit failure (1987 and 1988 2.3L turbo)
82	O	Supercharger bypass solenoid circuit failure (1989 and 1990 3.8L SC)
83	O	EGR control circuit failure (1984 through 1990)
83	O	High speed electro drive fan circuit failure (1986 through 1991 2.5L CFI and 3.0L)
84	O	EGR circuit, vent, shut-off or vacuum regulator failure (1984 on)
85	O,R	Canister purge circuit failure (1984 on)
87	O,C,R	Primary fuel pump or fuel pump relay circuit failure (1984 on)
87	O	Temperature compensated pump fault (1984 and 1985 2.8L)
88	O	Idle speed not within self test range (1983 through 1985 5.0L CFI)
88	O	Electric cooling fan circuit failure (1983 through 1986 3.0L V6)
88	O	Variable voltage choke circuit failure (1983 through 1986 2.8L)
88	O	Clutch converter override circuit failure (1987 and 1988 2.3L turbo)
89	O	Clutch converter override circuit failure (2.3L PFI , 2.8L and 5.0L CFI)
89	O	Exhaust heat crossover circuit failure (1984 through 1987 3.8L CFI and 5.0L CFI)
89	O	Lock-up solenoid circuit failure (1986 through 1990 3.0L, 3.8L and 4.0L)
90	R	Pass cylinder balance test
91	R	Air/fuel mixture not within self test range (1984 through 1986 3.8L CFI and 5.0L)
92	R	Air/fuel mixture not within self test range (1984 through 1986 3.8L CFI and 5.0L)
94	R	Air/fuel mixture not within self test range (1984 through 1986)
94	R	Thermactor air system inoperative (1985 on 3.8L CFI and 5.0L)
95	R	Air/fuel mixture not within self test range (1984 through 1986)
95	R	Thermactor air system inoperative (1985 3.8L CFI and 5.0L)
96	R	Air/fuel mixture not within self test range (1984 through 1986)
96	R	Thermactor air system inoperative (1985 3.8L CFI and 5.0L)
96	O,C	Fuel pump circuit open - battery to ECA (1988 on)
97	R	Air/fuel mixture not within self test range (1985 3.8L CFI)

*0 = Key On, Engine Off; C = Continuous Memory; R = Engine Running

Code No.	Test condition*	Probable cause
98	R	Air/fuel mixture not within self test range (1985 3.8L CFI)
98	R	Hard fault present (1986 through 1991 2.3L OHC, 2.9L, 3.0L, 4.9L, 5.0L and 7.5L)
98	O	Electronic pressure control (EPC) driver open in ECA (1989 on)
99	R	Idle not learned (1986 through 1990 1.9L CFI, 2.3L CFI and 2.5L CFI)
99	O,C	Electronic pressure control (EPC) circuit failure (1989 on)

3-digit trouble codes

Code No.	Test condition*	Probable cause
111	O,C,R	Pass
112	O,C,R	ACT/VAT sensor circuit grounded or 254 degrees F indicated by ACT/VAT sensor (1990)
112	O,C,R	ACT/IAT sensor circuit below minimum voltage (1991 on)
113	O,R	ACT/VAT sensor circuit open, or -40 degrees F indicated by ACT/VAT sensor (1990)
113	O,C,R	ACT/IAT sensor circuit above minimum voltage (1991 on)
114	O,R	ACT/VAT sensor out of range during self test (1990 through 1992)
114	O,R	IAT sensor out of range during self test (1993 on)
116	O,R	ECT sensor out of range during self test (1990 on)
117	O,C,R	ECT sensor circuit grounded or 254 degrees F indicated by ECT (1990)
117	O,C,R	ECT sensor circuit below minimum voltage or 254 degrees F indicated by ECT (1991 on)
118	O,C,R	ECT sensor circuit open or -40 degrees F indicated by ECT (1990)
118	O,C,R	ECT sensor above maximum voltage or -40 degrees F indicated by ECT (1991 on)
121	O,C,R	TP sensor voltage out of range during self test (1990)
121	O,C,R	Closed TP sensor voltage out of range during self test (1991 on)
121	O,C,R	TP sensor voltage not consistent with air meter input (1993 on)
122	O,C,R	TP sensor circuit below minimum voltage (1990 on)
123	O,C,R	TP sensor circuit above maximum voltage (1990 on)
124	O,C,R	TP sensor voltage higher than expected (1991 on)
125	O,C,R	TP sensor voltage lower than expected (1991 on)
126	O,C,R	MAP/BARO sensor voltage higher than expected (1990 on)
128	O,C,R	MAP/BARO sensor vacuum hose damaged or disconnected (1991 on)
129	O,C,R	Insufficient MAP/MAF sensor voltage change during dynamic response check

*0 = Key On, Engine Off; C = Continuous Memory; R = Engine Running

3-digit trouble codes

Code No.	Test condition*	Probable cause
136	R	HEGO sensor indicates lean condition, cylinder bank no. 2 (1991 on)
137	R	HEGO sensor indicates rich condition, cylinder bank no. 2 (1991 on)
139	C	No HEGO sensor switching detected, cylinder bank no. 2
144	C	No HEGO sensor switching detected, cylinder bank no. 1
157	R	MAF sensor below minimum voltage (1991 on)
158	R	MAF sensor above maximum voltage (1991 on)
159	R	MAF sensor out of range during self test (1991 on)
167	C,R	Insufficient TP sensor change during dynamic response check (1990 on)
171	C,R	HEGO sensor unable to switch, cylinder bank no. 1; fuel system at adaptive limit (1990 on)
172	O,R	HEGO sensor indicates lean condition, cylinder bank no. 1 (1990 on)
173	O,R	HEGO sensor indicates rich condition, cylinder bank no. 1 (1990 on)
174	C	HEGO sensor switching too slow, cylinder bank no. 1 (1990)
175	R	HEGO sensor unable to switch, cylinder bank no. 2; fuel system at adaptive limit (1990 on)
176	R	HEGO sensor indicates lean condition, cylinder bank no. 2 (1990 on)
177	R	HEGO sensor indicates rich condition, cylinder bank no. 2 (1990 on)
178	C	HEGO sensor switching too slowly
179	R	Adaptive fuel lean limit reached at part throttle, system rich, cylinder bank no. 1 (1990 on)
181	R	Adaptive fuel rich limit reached at part throttle, system lean, cylinder bank no. 1 (1990 on)
182	R	Adaptive fuel lean limit reached at idle, system rich, cylinder bank no. 1 (1990 through 1992)
183	R	Adaptive fuel rich limit reached at idle, system lean, cylinder bank no. 1 (1990 through 1992)
184	R	MAF higher than expected (1991 on)
185	R	MAF lower than expected (1991 on)
186	R	Injector pulse width higher than expected, with BP/BARO sensor (1991 on)
187	R	Injector pulse width lower than expected, with BP/BARO sensor (1991 on)
188	R	Adaptive fuel lean limit reached at part throttle, system rich, cylinder bank no. 2 (1991 on)
189	R	Adaptive fuel rich limit reached at part throttle, system lean, cylinder bank no. 2 (1991 on)
191	R	Adaptive fuel lean limit reached at idle, system rich, cylinder bank no. 2 (1991 on)
192	R	Adaptive fuel rich limit reached at idle, system lean, cylinder bank no. 2 (1991 on)

*0 = Key On, Engine Off; C = Continuous Memory; R = Engine Running

Code No.	Test condition*	Probable cause
193	O,C	Flexible fuel (FF) sensor circuit fault (1993 on)
211	C	PIP sensor circuit fault (1990 on)
212	C	Loss of TACH input to ECA, SPOUT circuit grounded (1990)
212	C	Loss of IDM input to ECA (1991 on)
213	R	SPOUT circuit open (1990 on)
214	R	Cylinder identification (CID) circuit fault (1991 on)
215	R	EEC processor/ECA detected coil no. 1 primary circuit fault (1991 on)
216	R	EEC processor/ECA detected coil no. 2 primary circuit fault (1991 on)
217	R	EEC processor/ECA detected coil no. 3 primary circuit fault (1991 on)
219	R	Spark timing defaulted to 10 degrees, SPOUT circuit open (1991 on)
221	R	Spark timing error (DIS/EDIS) (1991 on)
222	R	Loss of IDM signal, right side (dual plug DIS) (1991 on)
223	R	Loss of dual plug inhibit control (dual plug DIS) (1991 on)
224	R	EEC processor/ECA detected coil 1, 2, 3 or 4 primary circuit fault (dual plug DIS) (1991 on)
225	R	Knock not detected during dynamic response test (1991 on)
226	R	IDM signal not received (DIS/EDIS) (1991 on)
232	R	EEC processor/ECA detected coil 1, 2, 3 or 4 primary circuit fault (DIS/EDIS) (1991 on)
233	R	Spark angle pulse width error (EDIS) (1991 and 1992)
238	R	EEC processor/ECA detected coil 4 primary circuit fault (DIS/EDIS) (1991 on)
239	O,C,R	CPS signal received with engine off (1991 and 1992)
241	O,C,R	EDIS-to-ECA IDM pulse width transmission error (1991 on)
242	O,C,R	Operating in DIS failure mode (1991 and 1992)
243	O,C,R	Secondary circuit fault code 1, 2, 3 or 4 (DIS) (1991 and 1992)
244	R	CID circuit fault present during cylinder balance test (1993 on)
311	R	Thermactor air system inoperative (right side on dual EGR systems)
313	R	Thermactor air not bypassed during self-test (1990 on)
314	R	Thermactor air system inoperative (cylinder bank no. 2 with dual HEGO) (1990 on)
326	O,C,R	EGR (EPT) circuit voltage lower than expected (PFE) (1991 on)
327	O,C,R	EGR (EVP/EPT) circuit voltage below minimum voltage (Sonic PFE) (1990 on)
328	O,C,R	EGR (EVP) closed valve voltage below closed limit, or lower than expected (1990 on)
332	C,R	EGR valve opening not detected (1990 Sonic PFE)

*0 = Key On, Engine Off; C = Continuous Memory; R = Engine Running

3-digit trouble codes

Code No.	Test condition*	Probable cause
334	O,C,R	EVP voltage above closed limit (1990 Sonic), or EGR (EVP) closed valve voltage higher than expected (1991 on Sonic)
335	O	EGR (EPT) sensor voltage out of range during self test (1991 on)
336	R	Exhaust gas pressure high/EGR (EPT) circuit voltage higher than expected (1991 on)
337	O,C,R	EGR (EVP/EVT) circuit above maximum voltage (1990 on Sonic/PFE)
341	O,C,R	Octane adjust service pin in use (1991 on)
381	C	Frequent A/C clutch cycling (1993 on)
411	R	Unable to control rpm during low-rpm self test (1990 on)
412	R	Unable to control rpm during high-rpm self test (1990 on)
415	R	ISC system at minimum learning limit (1993 on)
416	R	IAC system at maximum learning limit (1993 on)
452	O,C,R	No input from VSS (1990 on)
453	O	Servo leaking down during self test (1993 on)
454	O	Servo leaking up during self test (1993 on)
455	R	Insufficient rpm increase during self-test (1993 on)
456	R	Insufficient rpm decrease during self-test (1993 on)
457	O	Speed control command switch(es) circuit not functioning during self test (1993 on)
458	O	Speed control command switch(es) stuck, or circuit grounded, during self-test (1993 on)
459	O	Speed control ground circuit open during self-test
511	O	Read Only Memory test failed; replace ECA
512	O,C,R	Keep alive memory (KAM) test failed
513	O,C,R	Internal voltage fault in ECA
519	O,C,R	PSPS circuit open (1991 on)
521	R	PSPS circuit does not change states during self-test (1991 on)
522	O	P/N switch indicates vehicle in gear with A/C on (1991 and 1992)
522	O	Vehicle not in Park or Neutral during self test (1993 on)
525	O,C,R	Indicates vehicle in gear (1991 and 1992)
528	O,C,R	Clutch switch circuit fault (1991 on)
529	O,C,R	DCL or ECA circuit fault (1991 on)
532	O	CCA circuit fault (1993 on)

*O = Key On, Engine Off; C = Continuous Memory; R = Engine Running

Code No.	Test condition*	Probable cause
533	O,C,R	DCL or EIC circuit fault (1993 on)
536	R	BOO switch circuit fault/not activated during KOER test (1990 on)
538	R	Operator error during dynamic response or cylinder balance test (1990)
538	R	Insufficient rpm change during KOER dynamic response test (1991 on)
538	R	Invalid cylinder balance test caused by CID sensor circuit fault (1991 on)
539	O	A/C or DEFROST on during KOEO test (1991 on)
542	O,C	Fuel pump circuit open, ECA to pump motor ground (1990 on)
543	O,C	Fuel pump circuit open, battery to ECA (1990 on)
551	O,C	IAC circuit fault in KOEO self test (1991 on)
552	O,C,R	Air management no. 1 circuit fault (1991 and 1992)
552	O	Secondary air injection bypass circuit fault (1993 on)
553	O,C,R	Air management no. 2 circuit fault (1990 through 1992)
553	O	Secondary air injection diverter circuit fault (1993 on)
554	O,C,R	Fuel pump pressure regulator control circuit fault (1993 on)
556	O,C	Primary fuel pump circuit fault (1990)
556	O,C	Fuel pump relay primary circuit fault (1991 on)
557	O,C	Low speed fuel pump primary circuit fault (1993 on)
558	O,C,R	EGR (EVR) circuit fault (1990 on)
559	O	A/C ON relay circuit fault (1993 on)
562	O,C,R	AEDF circuit fault (1991 and 1992)
563	O	HEDF circuit fault (1992)
563	O	High fan control circuit fault (1993 on)
564	O,C,R	EDF circuit fault (1991 and 1992)
564	O	Fan control circuit fault (1993 on)
565	O	Canister purge circuit fault (1990 on)
566	O	3/4 shift solenoid circuit fault (A4LD transmission) (1993 on)
567	O	Speed control vent circuit fault (1993 on)
568	O	Speed control vacuum circuit fault (1993 on)
569	O	Auxiliary canister purge circuit fault (1991 on)
571	O	EGRA solenoid circuit fault during KOEO test
572	O	EGRV solenoid circuit fault during KOEO test
578	O,C,R	A/C pressure sensor circuit shorted (VCRM) (1993 on)

0 = Key On, Engine Off; C = Continuous Memory; R = Engine Running

Ford, Lincoln and Mercury (continued)

3-digit trouble codes

Code No.	Test condition*	Probable cause
579	O,C,R	Insufficient A/C pressure change (VCRM) (1993 on)
581	O,C,R	Power to fan circuit over current (VCRM) (1993 on)
582	O,C,R	Fan circuit open (VCRM) (1993 on)
583	O,C,R	Power to fuel pump over current (VCRM) (1993 on)
584	O,C,R	VCRM power ground circuit open (VCRM, Pin 1) (1993 on)
585	O,C,R	Power to A/C clutch over current (VCRM) (1993 on)
586	O,C,R	A/C clutch circuit open (VCRM) (1993 on)
587	O,C,R	VCRM communication failure (1993 on)
617	O,C,R	1-2 shift error (1990 on)
618	C	2-3 shift error (1990 on)
619	C	3-4 shift error (1990 on)
621	O,C	Shift solenoid no. 1 circuit fault (1990 on)
622	O	Shift solenoid no. 2 circuit fault (1990 on)
623	O	Transmission control indicator light circuit fault
624	O,C,R	EPC circuit fault (1990 on)
625	O,C,R	EPC driver open in ECA (1990 on)
626	O,C,R	Coast clutch/converter clutch solenoid circuit fault (1990 on)
627	O,C,R	Converter clutch control solenoid circuit fault (1990 on)
628	O,C,R	Excessive converter clutch slippage (1990 on)
629	O,C	Converter clutch control circuit fault (1991 on)
631	O,C,R	Transmission control indicator lamp circuit fault during KOEO test
632	R	Overdrive cancel switch circuit does not change during KOEO test (1990 on)
633	O	4 X 4 switch closed during KOEO test (1990 on)
634	O,C,R	MLP sensor voltage higher or lower than expected (1990 on)
636	O,R	TOT sensor voltage higher or lower than expected (1990 on)
637	O,C,R	-40 degrees F indicated by TOT sensor, or sensor circuit above maximum voltage, or sensor circuit open (1990 on)
638	O,C,R	290 degrees F indicated by TOT sensor, or sensor circuit below minimum voltage, or sensor circuit shorted (1990 on)
639	O,C,R	Insufficient input from TSS (1991 on)

*0 = Key On, Engine Off; C = Continuous Memory; R = Engine Running

Code No.	Test condition*	Probable cause
641	O,C	Shift solenoid no. 3 circuit fault (1991 on)
643	O,C	Shift solenoid no. 4 circuit fault (1992 on)
645	C	Incorrect gear ratio obtained for first gear
646	C	Incorrect gear ratio obtained for second gear
647	C	Incorrect gear ratio obtained for third gear
648	C	Incorrect gear ratio obtained for fourth gear
649	O,C,R	EPC higher or lower than expected (1992 on)
651	O,C,R	EPC circuit fault (1992 on)
653	R	Transmission control switch did not change states during KOER test
652	O,C,R	Modulated lock-up solenoid circuit fault (1992)
652	O,C,R	Torque converter clutch solenoid circuit fault (1993 on)
654	O	MLP sensor not indicating PARK during KOEO test (1991 on)
656	O,C,R	Torque converter clutch control continuous slip error (1992 on)
657	C	Transmission over temperature condition occurred
659	C	High vehicle speed in PARK indicated
667	C	Transmission range sensor circuit voltage below minimum voltage
668	C	Transmission range circuit voltage above maximum voltage
675	C	Transmission range sensor circuit voltage out of range
998	O	Hard fault present - FMEM mode activated

Ford Imports

1994 and 1995 Aspire (1.3L)

Code No.	Test condition*	Probable cause
02	O, R	Crankshaft position sensor circuit
03	O, R	Camshaft position sensor circuit
04	O, R	Crankshaft position sensor circuit
06	O, R	Vehicle speed sensor circuit

*0 = Key On, Engine Off; C = Continuous Memory; R = Engine Running

Ford Imports (continued)

1994 and 1995 Aspire (1.3L) (continued)

Code No.	Test condition*	Probable cause
08	O, R	Mass airflow sensor circuit
09	O, R	Engine coolant temperature sensor circuit
10	O, R	Intake air temperature sensor circuit
12	O, R	Throttle position sensor circuit
15	O, R	Oxygen sensor circuit fault (voltage below 0.55 volt)
16	O, R	EGR valve position sensor circuit
17	O, R	Oxygen sensor defective (voltage doesn't change)
25	O, R	EVAP canister purge solenoid circuit
26	O, R	EGR control (EGRC) solenoid circuit
28	O, R	EGR vent (EGRV) solenoid circuit
29	O, R	Idle air control (IAC) solenoid circuit
34	O, R	Idle air control (IAC) solenoid circuit

1993 through 1995 Escort/Tracer (1.8L)

Code No.	Test condition*	Probable cause
01	C	Ignition diagnostic monitor circuit
02	C	Crankshaft position sensor circuit
03	C	Cylinder identification 1 circuit
08	C	Vane airflow sensor circuit
09	C	Engine coolant temperature sensor circuit
10	C	Intake air temperature sensor circuit
12	C	Throttle position sensor circuit
14	C	Barometric pressure sensor circuit
15	C	Oxygen sensor circuit
17	C	Oxygen sensor signal too rich or too lean
25	C	Fuel pressure regulator solenoid circuit
26	C	Canister purge solenoid circuit
34	C	Idle speed control valve circuit
41	C	Variable inertia charging system solenoid circuit

*O = Key On, Engine Off; C = Continuous Memory; R = Engine Running

1993 through 1995 Probe (2.5L V6)

Code No.	Test condition*	Probable cause
02	C	Crankshaft position sensor no. 2 circuit
03	C	Cylinder identification circuit
04	C	Crankshaft position sensor no. 1 circuit
05	C	Knock sensor circuit
08	C	Measuring-core vane airflow sensor circuit
09	C	Engine coolant temperature sensor circuit
10	C	Intake air temperature sensor circuit
12	C	Throttle position sensor circuit
14	C	Barometric pressure sensor circuit
15	C	Left oxygen sensor circuit
16	C	EGR valve position sensor circuit
17	C	Right oxygen sensor circuit
23	C	Feedback system fault (left oxygen sensor)
24	C	Feedback system fault (right oxygen sensor)
25	C	Fuel pressure regulator solenoid circuit
26	C	Canister purge solenoid circuit
28	C	EGR vacuum control circuit
29	C	EGR vent control solenoid circuit
34	C	Idle speed control valve circuit
41	C	Variable resonance induction system solenoid no 1 circuit
46	C	Variable resonance induction system solenoid no. 2 circuit
67	C	Cooling fan relay circuit
69	C	Engine coolant temperature fan circuit

1993 through 1995 Villager (3.0L V6)

Code No.	Test condition*	Probable cause
11	C	Crankshaft position sensor circuit
12	C	Mass airflow sensor circuit
13	C	Engine coolant temperature sensor circuit
14	C	Vehicle speed sensor circuit

*0 = Key On, Engine Off; C = Continuous Memory; R = Engine Running

Ford Imports (continued)

1993 through 1995 Villager (3.0L V6) (continued)

Code No.	Test condition*	Probable cause
21	C	Ignition signal circuit
31	C	PCM internal fault
32	C	EGR control solenoid circuit
33	C	Heated oxygen sensor circuit
34	C	Knock sensor circuit
35	C	EGR vent solenoid circuit
43	C	Throttle position sensor circuit
45	C	Fuel injector leak detected
51	C	Fuel injector signal fault detected
55		EEC system pass code

*0 = Key On, Engine Off; C = Continuous Memory; R = Engine Running.

General Motors
domestic cars and trucks (except Geo, Nova and Sprint)

  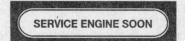

Code	Probable cause
12	No spark reference from ignition control module or distributor (Cadillac)
12	No TACH signal to ECM - system normal
13	Oxygen sensor (right sensor on 1990 and later models) malfunction or circuit fault (Cadillac)
13	Oxygen sensor circuit fault (driver's side on two-sensor systems)
14	ECT sensor indicates high temperature, or ECT sensor circuit shorted
15	ECT sensor indicates low temperature, or ECT sensor open
16	DIS circuit fault
16	Distributor ignition system or Opti-Spark ignition timing system, low resolution pulse
16	Missing 2X reference circuit

Code	Probable cause
16	Transmission speed error (models with 4L60-E transmission or 4.3L S and T vehicle with manual transmission)
16	System voltage out of range
17	Oxygen sensor (left sensor on 1990 and later models) malfunction or circuit fault (Cadillac)
17	Crank signal circuit shorted, or defective ECM
17	Camshaft position sensor (1993 and 1994 with SFI)
17	Spark reference signal fault (Buick and Oldsmobile)
18	Crank signal circuit open, or faulty ECM
18	Injector circuit(s) (engine VIN code P - 5.7L)
18	Cam and crank sensor sync error (1988 through 1993 models with DIS ignition)
19	Fuel pump circuit shorted
19	Crankshaft position sensor circuit (1988 through 1991)
19	Intermittent 7X reference circuit
20	Fuel pump circuit open
21	TPS circuit shorted (Cadillac)
21	TPS circuit open, or voltage out of range (probably high)
21	Grounded wide-open-throttle circuit
22	TPS circuit open (Cadillac)
22	Grounded wide-open-throttle circuit
23	Open or grounded M/C solenoid (feedback carburetors)
23	IAT or MAT sensor circuit out of range, or low temperature indicated (Buick and Oldsmobile)
23	EST or IC circuit fault (Cadillac DFI)
24	VSS defective or circuit faulty
25	MAT sensor defective, sensor circuit out of range (probably high) or circuit shorted
25	Modulated displacement failure (1981 Cadillac V8-6-4)
25	EST (Cadillac HT4100)
26	Quad driver circuit (dealer serviced)
26	Transaxle gear switch circuit
26	EVAP purge solenoid circuit (VIN P - 5.7L)
26	TPS circuit shorted

The Haynes Emissions Control Manual

Code	Probable cause
26	ECM failure (Buick and Oldsmobile)
26	Idle speed control (ISC) motor/throttle switch circuit shorted
27	TPS circuit open
27	2nd gear switch circuit fault (Buick and Oldsmobile)
27	EGR vacuum control solenoid circuit (VIN P - 5.7L)
27	Quad-driver circuit fault (VIN P - 5.7L)
27	Idle speed control (ISC) motor/throttle switch circuit open
28	3rd or 4th gear switch circuit fault (Cadillac)
28	Third gear switch circuit fault (Buick and Oldsmobile)
28	Quad-driver circuit fault (VIN P - 5.7L)
28	Transaxle pressure switch problem (Cadillac)
28	Transmission range pressure switch (V8)
29	Transaxle shift B solenoid problem (Cadillac)
29	Fourth gear switch circuit fault
29	Secondary AIR pump circuit (VIN P - 5.7L)
30	ISC circuit problem (Cadillac TBI)
30	RPM error (Cadillac MFI)
31	Wastegate circuit signal (turbo models)
31	PNP switch or circuit fault (Buick and Oldsmobile)
31	MAT sensor or circuit (Cadillac DFI)
31	EVAP canister purge solenoid circuit (carbureted models)
31	Camshaft sensor or circuit fault
31	EGR circuit (1988 through 1990 TBI)
31	MAP sensor circuit shorted (Cadillac)
32	BARO or altitude sensor or circuit (carbureted models)
32	EGR vacuum control system failure (Buick and Oldsmobile)
32	Digital EGR circuit (3.1L)
32	MAP sensor circuit open (Cadillac)

Code	Probable cause
33	Extended travel brake switch input circuit problem (Cadillac)
33	MAP sensor or circuit (low vacuum)
33	MAF sensor or circuit voltage out of range, probably high
33	MAP sensor signal voltage out of range (Cadillac)
34	MAF sensor or circuit fault (Buick and Oldsmobile)
34	MAP sensor out of range (Cadillac)
35	Ignition ground voltage out of range (Cadillac)
35	ISC or IAC valve or circuit
35	ISC throttle switch or circuit shorted (feedback carburetor)
35	BARO sensor or circuit shorted (Cadillac DFI)
36	EGR pintle valve position out of range (Cadillac)
36	BARO sensor or circuit open (Cadillac DFI)
36	MAF sensor burn-off circuit (1988 through 1990)
36	DIS (Quad-4)
36	Transaxle shift control (3.8L)
36	Closed throttle shift control (1991)
36	24X signal error circuit (1993 through 1995 with SFI)
36	DIS ignition circuit (Corvette and VIN P - 5.7L)
37	IAT or MAT sensor circuit shorted (Cadillac)
37	MAT sensor temperature high (1984 to 1986)
37	Brake switch stuck on (4L60-E transmission)
38	IAT or MAT sensor circuit open (Cadillac)
38	Brake light switch circuit (1988 and later Buick and Oldsmobile)
38	MAT sensor temperature low (1984 to 1986)
38	Brake switch stuck off (4L60-E transmission)
39	TCC engagement problem (Cadillac)
39	TCC signal error
39	Clutch input circuit fault
39	Knock sensor circuit shorted (4.3L engine with manual transmission, "S" and "T" truck models)

Code	Probable cause
40	Power steering pressure switch circuit open (Cadillac)
40	Power steering pressure switch circuit fault
41	No distributor signals to ECM, or faulty ignition module
41	Cam sensor circuit fault or ignition control reference pulse error
41	Cylinder select error
41	Quad-4 engine 1X reference pulse error
41	EST circuit open or shorted (Cadillac)
41	Opti-Spark EST circuit open or grounded (5.7L "F" and "Y" bodies)
42	Opti-Spark EST circuit grounded (5.7L "F" and "Y" bodies)
42	EST circuit fault (Buick and Oldsmobile)
42	Left oxygen sensor signal lean (1990 and later Cadillac)
43	ESC unit circuit fault (Buick and Oldsmobile)
43	TPS out of adjustment
43	Left oxygen sensor signal rich (1990 and later Cadillac)
43	Knock sensor signal error
44	Oxygen sensor no. 2 lean exhaust signal (Cadillac)
44	Oxygen sensor or circuit, lean exhaust detected (driver's side on two-sensor system)
45	Oxygen sensor no. 2 rich exhaust signal (Cadillac)
45	Oxygen sensor or circuit, rich exhaust detected (driver's side on two-sensor system)
46	Power steering pressure switch open (Buick and Oldsmobile)
46	Vehicle Anti-Theft System (VATS) or Personal Automotive Security System (PASS Key II)
46	Left bank-to-right bank fueling imbalance (Cadillac)
47	ECM - body control module (BCM) or IPC/PCM data fault (Cadillac)
47	A/C clutch and cruise circuit fault
47	PCM/BCM data circuit fault
48	Misfire detected (Buick and Oldsmobile)
48	EGR control system fault (Cadillac)
50	2nd gear pressure circuit fault (Cadillac)

Code	Probable cause
51	Faulty MEM-CAL, faulty EEPROM, ECM problem or calibration error
52	ECM memory reset indicator or PCM keep-alive memory reset (Cadillac)
52	Engine oil temperature sensor circuit, low temperature indicated
52	CALPAK missing or incorrect (Buick and Oldsmobile)
52	Over-voltage condition
52	EGR circuit fault
53	Spark reference signal interrupt from IC module (Cadillac)
53	System over-voltage (ECM over 17.7 volts)
53	EGR system (carbureted models)
53	Distributor signal interrupt (1983 and later Cadillac HT4100)
53	Alternator voltage out of range
53	Vehicle anti-theft (PASS-Key) circuit (5.0L TBI)
53	EGR fault (3.8L)
54	Mixture control solenoid circuit shorted (feedback carburetor system)
54	Fuel pump circuit, low voltage indicated (3.1L and 3.4L)
54	EGR fault (3.8L)
55	Closed throttle angle out of range or TPS incorrectly adjuster (Cadillac)
55	Grounded voltage reference, faulty oxygen sensor or fuel lean (feedback carburetor system)
55	ECM/PCM error, or not grounded (except 5.7L PFI systems, fuel lean monitor 5.7L - "F" and "Y" bodies)
55	ECM fault (Buick and Oldsmobile)
55	TPS out of range or out of adjustment (Cadillac)
55	Fuel lean monitor (Corvette and F-body VIN P - 5.7L)
55	EGR fault (3.8L)
56	Transaxle speed sensor input circuit fault (Cadillac)
56	Vacuum sensor circuit
56	Vacuum sensor circuit
56	Quad driver no. 2 circuit (3.8L)
56	Secondary air inlet valve actuator vacuum sensor circuit signal high (5.7L VIN J)
56	Anti-theft system (Cadillac)

General Motors - domestic (continued)

Code	Probable cause
57	Transaxle temperature sensor circuit shorted (Cadillac)
57	Boost control problem
58	Personal Automotive Security System (PASS) control fault (Cadillac)
58	Vehicle anti-theft system (PASS-Key) fuel enable circuit fault
58	Transmission code - TTS high temperature (sensor or signal wire grounded)
59	Transmission code - TTS low temperature (sensor or signal wire open)
60	Cruise control system - transaxle/transmission not in drive (Cadillac)
61	Oxygen sensor signal degraded or faulty
61	Cruise control system vent solenoid circuit fault (3.8L)
61	Secondary port throttle valve system fault (VIN J 5.7L)
61	A/C system performance (5.7L)
61	Transaxle gear switch signal
62	Transaxle gear switch signal circuit fault (3.1L V6 and Quad-4)
62	Engine oil temperature sensor, high temperature indicated (5.7L)
62	Cruise control system vacuum solenoid circuit fault (3.8L)
63	Cruise control system problem (difference between vehicle speed and set speed) (Cadillac)
63	EGR system fault (1990 and earlier Buick and Oldsmobile)
63	MAP sensor voltage out of range, probably high
63	Oxygen sensor circuit open, right side (5.7L)
63	Cruise control system problem (speed error)
64	Cruise control system, vehicle acceleration too high (Cadillac)
64	EGR system fault (1990 and earlier Buick and Oldsmobile)
64	MAP sensor voltage low
64	Oxygen sensor, lean exhaust indicated (right side on dual sensor models)
65	EGR system fault (1990 and earlier Buick and Oldsmobile)
65	Oxygen sensor, rich exhaust indicated (right side on dual sensor models)
65	Cruise servo position sensor circuit fault
65	Fuel injection circuit, low current (Quad-4)

Code	Probable cause
66	Cruise control system, engine rpm too high (Cadillac)
66	A/C pressure sensor circuit fault, probably low pressure
66	Engine power switch, voltage high or low, or PCM fault (VIN J 5.7L)
67	Cruise control system, SET/COAST or RESUME/ACCEL input shorted (Cadillac)
67	A/C pressure sensor circuit, sensor or A/C clutch circuit fault (Chevrolet)
67	Cruise switch circuit
68	Cruise Control Command (CCC) fault or servo position out of range (Cadillac)
68	A/C relay circuit (Chevrolet)
68	A/C compressor relay circuit shorted
68	Cruise system problem
69	Traction control active in cruise mode (Cadillac)
69	A/C clutch circuit fault, or head pressure too high (Chevrolet)
69	A/C head pressure switch circuit fault
69	Transmission code - torque converter stuck on (4L60-E)
70	TPS signal intermittent (Cadillac)
70	A/C refrigerant pressure sensor circuit, high pressure indicated (Chevrolet)
71	MAP sensor signal intermittent (Cadillac)
71	A/C evaporator temperature circuit, low temperature
72	Gear selector switch circuit (Chevrolet)
72	Transmission code - VSS signal loss (4L60-E)
73	ECT sensor signal intermittent (Cadillac)
73	A/C evaporator temperature sensor circuit, high temperature indicated
74	IAT sensor signal intermittent (Cadillac)
74	TCS circuit voltage low (1995 F-body VIN P)
75	Digital EGR no. 1 solenoid circuit fault
75	VSS signal intermittent (Cadillac)
75	EGR circuit (1995)
75	System voltage low (charging system problem)
75	Transmission system voltage low (1995 F-body VIN P)

General Motors - domestic (continued)

Code	Probable cause
76	Transaxle pressure control solenoid circuit malfunction (Cadillac)
76	Digital EGR no. 2 solenoid circuit fault
77	Digital EGR no. 3 solenoid circuit fault
79	Transmission fluid temperature high (4L60-E)
79	VSS circuit signal high
80	TPS idle learn not complete (Cadillac 4.6L)
80	Fuel system rich (Cadillac)
80	Transmission converter clutch slipping excessively (F-body 3.4L)
80	VSS circuit signal high
81	Cam-to-4X reference correlation problem (Cadillac)
81	Transmission code - QDM solenoid A (1st and 2nd gear) current error
81	Brake input circuit fault or torque converter clutch signal
82	Reference signal high (Cadillac)
82	Transmission code - QDM solenoid B (2nd and 3rd gear) current error
82	IC 3X signal error
83	Transmission code - QDM torque converter circuit fault (4L80-E)
83	24X reference signal high (Cadillac)
83	Reverse inhibit system (F-body, manual transmission, 5.7L)
85	Idle throttle angle high (Cadillac 4.6L)
85	Throttle body service required (Cadillac)
85	PROM error (1995 3.4L)
86	Undefined gear ratio (Cadillac)
86	Transmission code - low gear ratio (4L80-E)
86	Analog-to-digital ECM error
87	Transmission code - high gear ratio (4L80-E)
87	EEPROM error (1995 3.4L)
88	TCC not disengaging (Cadillac)
89	Long shift and maximum adapt (Cadillac)
90	TCC solenoid circuit (manual transmission)

Code	Probable cause
90	VCC brake switch input fault (Cadillac)
91	Skip shift lamp circuit (1995 F-body, VIN P)
91	P/N switch fault (Cadillac)
92	Heated windshield fault (Cadillac)
93	PCS circuit current error (1995 3.4L)
93	Traction control system PWM link failure (Cadillac)
94	Transaxle shift A solenoid problem (Cadillac)
95	Engine stall detected (Cadillac)
96	Transmission system voltage low (1995 F-body 3.4L)
96	Torque converter overstress (Cadillac)
97	VSS output circuit (1995 F-body VIN P)
97	P/N to Drive or Reverse at high throttle angle (Cadillac)
98	Invalid PCM program (1995 F-body 3.4L)
98	High rpm P/N to Drive or Reverse shift under idle speed control (Cadillac)
99	Power management, cruise control system
99	TACH output circuit (1995 F-body VIN P)
99	Invalid PCM program
99	Cruise control servo not applied in cruise (Cadillac)
102	Shorted brake booster vacuum sensor (Cadillac)
103	Open brake booster vacuum sensor (Cadillac)
105	Brake booster vacuum too low (Cadillac)
106	Stop lamp switch input circuit fault (Cadillac)
107	PCM/BCM data link problem (Cadillac)
108	PROM checksum mismatch (Cadillac)
109	PCM keep-alive memory reset (Cadillac)
110	Generator L-terminal circuit fault (Cadillac)
112	Total EEPROM failure (Cadillac)
117	Shift A or shift B circuit output open or shorted (Cadillac)
131	Knock sensor failure (Cadillac)
132	Knock sensor failure (Cadillac)

General Motors imports
Geo (Metro, Prizm, Storm, Tracker), Sprint, Nova and Spectrum

  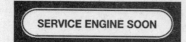

Geo (Metro, Prizm, Storm, Tracker), Sprint, Nova and Spectrum

Code	Circuit or system	Probable cause
Code 12	No distributor reference pulses to ECM	This code will flash whenever the diagnostic terminal is grounded with the ignition turned On and the engine not running. If additional trouble codes are stored in the ECM they will appear after this code has flashed three times. If this code appears while the engine is running, no reference pulses from the distributor are reaching the ECM.
Code 13	Oxygen sensor circuit	Check for a sticking or misadjusted throttle position sensor (TPS). Check the wiring and connectors from the oxygen sensor. Replace the oxygen sensor.*
Code 14	Coolant sensor - high or low temp	If the engine is experiencing cooling system problems the problem must be rectified before continuing. Check all wiring and connectors associated with the coolant temperature sensor. Replace the coolant temperature sensor.*
Code 21	Throttle position sensor - voltage high or low	Check for a sticking or misadjusted TPS plunger. Check all wiring and connections between the TPS and the ECM. Adjust or Replace the TPS.*
Code 23	Intake Air Temperature (IAT) sensor circuit voltage high or low	Check for continuity in the signal wire and the ground wire. Check the operation of the IAT sensor.
Code 24	Vehicle speed sensor	A fault in this circuit should be indicated only when the vehicle is in motion. Disregard Code 24 if it is set when the drive wheels are not turning. Check the connections at the ECM. Check the TPS setting.
Code 32	EGR (Exhaust Gas Recirculation)	EVRV shorted to ground on start-up, switch not closed after the ECM has commanded the EGR for a specified period of time or the EGR solenoid circuit is open for specified period of time. Replace the EGR valve.*
Code 33	MAP sensor voltage high or low	Check the vacuum hoses from the MAP sensor. Check the electrical connections at the ECM. Replace the MAP sensor.*
Code 42	Electronic Spark Timing circuit	Electronic Spark Timing (EST) bypass circuit or EST circuit is grounded or open. A malfunctioning HEI module can cause this code.
Code 44	O2 sensor indicates lean exhaust (heated type)	Check the ECM wiring connections. Check for vacuum leakage at the throttle body base gasket, vacuum hoses or the intake manifold gasket. Replace the oxygen sensor.*

Code	Circuit or system	Probable cause
Code 45	O2 sensor indicates rich exhaust	Possible rich or leaking injector, high fuel pressure or faulty TPS. Also, check the evaporative charcoal canister and its components for the presence of fuel. Replace the oxygen sensor.*
Code 51	ECM or EEPROM	Be sure that the ECM ground connections are tight. If they are, Replace the ECM.*

* Component replacement may not cure the problem in all cases. For this reason, you may want to seek professional advice before purchasing replacement parts.

Spectrum (non-turbo)

Code	Probable cause
12	No distributor reference pulses to ECM
13	Oxygen sensor or circuit
14	Coolant sensor or circuit (shorted)
15	Coolant sensor circuit (open)
16	Coolant sensor circuit (open)
21	Idle switch out of adjustment (or circuit open)
22	Fuel cut off relay or circuit (open)
23	Open or grounded Mixture Control (M/C) solenoid or circuit
25	Open or grounded vacuum switching valve or circuit
42	Fuel cut off relay or circuit
44	Oxygen sensor or circuit - lean exhaust indicated
45	Oxygen sensor or circuit - rich exhaust indicated
51	Faulty or improperly installed PROM
53	Shorted switching unit or faulty ECM
54	Mixture Control (M/C) solenoid or circuit shorted, or faulty ECM
55	Faulty ECM

Spectrum (turbo)

Code	Probable cause
12	No distributor reference pulses to ECM
13	Oxygen sensor or circuit
14	Coolant sensor or circuit (shorted)
15	Coolant sensor or circuit (open)
16	Coolant sensor or circuit (open)

Code	Probable cause
21	Throttle Position Sensor (TPS) voltage high
22	Throttle Position Sensor (TPS) voltage low
23	Intake Air Temperature (IAT), Manifold Air Temperature (MAT) sensor or circuit
24	Vehicle Speed Sensor or circuit
25	Air Switching Valve (ASV) or circuit
31	Wastegate control
33	Manifold Absolute Pressure (MAP) sensor voltage high
34	Manifold Absolute Pressure (MAP) sensor voltage low
42	Electronic Spark Timing (EST) circuit
43	Detonation (knock) sensor or circuit
45	Oxygen sensor - rich exhaust
51	Faulty PROM or ECM

Sprint (non-turbo)

Code	Probable cause
12	Diagnostic function working
13	Oxygen sensor or circuit
14	Coolant temperature sensor or circuit
21	Throttle position switches or circuit
23	Intake air temperature sensor or circuit
32	Barometric pressure sensor or circuit
51	Possible faulty ECM
52	Fuel cut solenoid or circuit
53	Secondary air sensor or circuit
54	Mixture control solenoid or circuit
55	Bowl vent solenoid or circuit

The Haynes Emissions Control Manual

1987 and 1988 Sprint Turbo, 1989 and later Metro, Tracker, Sunrunner, Storm, Sunfire

Code	Probable cause
12	Diagnostic function working
13	Oxygen sensor or circuit
14	Coolant temperature sensor or circuit (open)
15	Coolant temperature sensor or circuit (shorted)
21	Throttle position sensor or circuit (open)
22	Throttle position sensor or circuit (shorted)
23	Intake air temperature sensor or circuit (open)
24	Vehicle Speed Sensor (VSS) or circuit
25	Intake air temperature sensor or circuit (shorted)
31	High turbocharger pressure (1987 and 1988 models)
31	MAP or Barometric pressure sensor or circuit (1989 through 1995 models)
32	MAP or Barometric pressure sensor or circuit (1989 through 1995 models)
32	EGR system (1991 through 1993 models)
33	Air flow meter (turbo models)
33	Manifold Absolute Pressure (MAP) sensor (1990 through 1992 models)
41	Ignition signal problem
42	Crank angle sensor (except Storm, Sunfire)
42	Camshaft position sensor circuit (1994-1995)
42	Electronic Spark Timing (EST) (Storm, Sunfire)
44	ECM idle switch circuit open (1988 and 1989)
44	Idle switch circuit (1992 Tracker, Sunrunner
44	Oxygen sensor or circuit - lean exhaust
45	Oxygen sensor or circuit - rich exhaust
45	Idle switch circuit grounded (1992 Tracker, Sunrunner)

Code	Probable cause
46	Idle speed control motor
51	EGR system (except Storm, Sunfire)
51	ECM (Storm)
53	ECM ground circuit
On Steady	ECM fault

Prizm and Nova (with electronic fuel injection)

Code	Probable cause
Continuous Flashing	System normal
12	RPM signal
13	RPM signal
14	Ignition signal
16	PCM control circuit
21	Oxygen sensor or circuit
22	Coolant temperature sensor or circuit
24	Intake Air Temperature or Manifold Air Temperature sensor or circuit
25	Air/fuel ratio lean
26	Air/fuel ratio rich
27	Sub-oxygen sensor
31	Mass Air Flow (MAF) sensor or circuit
41	Throttle Position Sensor (TPS) or circuit
42	Vehicle Speed Sensor (VSS)
43	Starter signal
51	Air Conditioning Switch signal
52	Knock sensor circuit
53	ECM failure
71	EGR system

Honda

 CHECK MIL 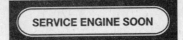 SERVICE ENGINE SOON CHECK | CHECK ENGINE LIGHT

1985 through 1987 models

	LED display	Symptom	Possible cause
1	(Dash warning light on)	Engine will not start	Check for a disconnected control unit ground connector. Also check for a loose connection at the ECU main relay resistor. Possible faulty ECU
2	(Dash warning light on)	Engine will not start	Check for a short circuit in the combination meter or warning light wire. Also check for a disconnected control unit ground wire. Possible faulty ECU
3	1	System does not operate	Faulty ECU
4	2	System does not operate	Faulty ECU
5	2 1	Fuel-fouled spark plugs, engine stalls, or hesitation	Check for a disconnected MAP sensor coupler or an open circuit in the MAP sensor wire. Also check for a faulty MAP sensor
6	4	System does not operate	Faulty ECU
7	4 1	Hesitation, fuel-fouled spark plugs or the engine stalls frequently	Check for disconnected MAP sensor vacuum hose
8	4 2	High idle speed during warm-up, continued high idle or hard starting at low temperature	Check for a disconnected coolant temperature sensor connector or an open circuit in the coolant temperature sensor wire. Also check for a faulty coolant temperature sensor
9	4 2 1	Poor engine response when opening the throttle rapidly, high idle speed or engine does not rev-up when cold	Check for a disconnected throttle angle sensor connector. Also check for an open circuit in the throttle angle sensor wire. Possible faulty throttle angle sensor
10	8	Engine does not rev-up, high idle speed or erratic idling	Check for a short or open circuit in the crank angle sensor wire. Spark plug wires interfering with the crank angle sensor wire. Also the crank angle sensor could be faulty
11	8 1	Same as above	Same as above
12	8 2	High idle speed or erratic idling when very cold	Check for a disconnected intake air temperature sensor or an open circuit in the intake air temperature sensor wire. Possible faulty intake air temperature sensor

The Haynes Emissions Control Manual

Honda (continued)

1985 through 1987 models (continued)

	LED display	Symptom	Possible cause
13	8 ● 2 ● 1 ●	Continued high idle speed	Check for a disconnected idle mixture adjuster sensor coupler or an open circuit in the idle mixture adjuster sensor wire. Possible faulty idle mixture adjuster sensor
14	8 ● 4 ●	System does not operate at all	Faulty ECU
15	8 ● 4 ● 1 ●	Poor acceleration at high altitude when cold	Check for a disconnected atmospheric pressure sensor coupler or an open circuit in the atmospheric pressure sensor wire. Possible faulty atmospheric pressure sensor
16	8 ● 4 ● 2 ●	System does not operate at all	Faulty ECU
17	8 ● 4 ● 2 ● 1 ●	Same as above	Same as above

1988 through 1995 models (except 1995 Accord V6)

Code	Probable cause
0	Faulty ECU
1	Left (front) oxygen sensor malfunction or circuit fault
2	Right (rear) oxygen sensor malfunction or circuit fault
3	MAP sensor or circuit electrical fault
4	Crank angle sensor malfunction or circuit fault
5	MAP sensor mechanical fault
6	Engine coolant temperature sensor malfunction or circuit fault
7	Throttle angle sensor malfunction or circuit fault
8	TDC sensor (crank/cylinder/TDC sensor) malfunction or circuit fault
9	Cylinder sensor (crank/cylinder sensor) malfunction or circuit fault
10	Intake air temperature sensor or circuit fault
11	Idle mixture adjuster sensor malfunction or circuit fault
12	EGR lift sensor malfunction or circuit fault
13	BARO or PA sensor malfunction or circuit fault
14	Electronic Air Control Valve (EACV) malfunction or circuit fault
15	No ignition output signal (possible faulty igniter)
16	Fuel injector circuit fault
17	Vehicle speed sensor malfunction or circuit fault
18	Ignition timing or adjuster sensor malfunction or circuit fault
19	Lock-up control solenoid valve (automatic transmission)
20	Electric load detector - possible open or grounded circuit in ECU wiring
21	VTEC spool solenoid valve malfunction or circuit fault
22	VTEC oil pressure switch malfunction or circuit fault
23	Left knock sensor malfunction or circuit fault
30	A/T control unit ECM fuel injection signal "A" (Accord and Prelude)
31	A/T control unit and ECM circuit signal "B" (Accord and Prelude)

Code	Probable cause
41	Left (front) heated oxygen sensor malfunction or circuit fault
42	Right (rear) heated oxygen sensor malfunction or circuit fault
43	Left (front) fuel supply system circuit fault (except D15Z1 engine)
44	Right (rear) fuel supply system circuit fault (except D15Z1 engine)
45	Left (front) air/fuel ratio out of range - rich or lean
46	Right (rear) air/fuel ratio out of range - rich or lean
48	Heated oxygen sensor circuit (D15Z1 engine)
48	Linear air/fuel sensor malfunction or circuit fault
50	Mass air flow sensor malfunction or circuit fault
53	Right knock sensor malfunction or circuit fault
54	Crank angle sensor no. 2 malfunction or circuit fault
59	Cylinder position sensor no. 2 malfunction or circuit fault

Code	Probable cause
61	Front oxygen sensor - slow response
63	Rear oxygen sensor circuit voltage out of range
65	Rear oxygen sensor circuit fault
67	Catalytic converter efficiency low
70	Automatic transaxle problem
71	Cylinder misfire
72	Cylinder misfire
73	Cylinder misfire
74	Cylinder misfire
75	Cylinder misfire
76	Cylinder misfire
80	Insufficient EGR flow
86	Engine coolant temperature sensor circuit
92	Evaporative emission purge flow problem

Hyundai

  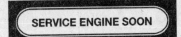

1988 Stellar

Code	Probable cause
1	Oxygen sensor or circuit
2	Ignition signal
3	Airflow sensor or circuit
4	Atmospheric pressure sensor or circuit
5	Throttle position sensor or circuit
6	Idle Speed Control (ISC) motor position sensor or circuit
7	Coolant temperature sensor or circuit
8	TDC sensor or circuit
9	Normal

Sonata, Excel (1990 on), Scoupe (1991 and 1992), Elantra

Code	Probable cause
1	Electronic Control Unit (ECU) (one long needle sweep)
9	ECU normal state
11	Oxygen sensor or circuit
12	Airflow sensor or circuit
13	Intake air temperature sensor or circuit
14	Throttle Position Sensor (TPS) or circuit
15	Motor position sensor or circuit
21	Coolant temperature sensor or circuit

Hyundai (continued)

Sonata, Excel (1990 on), Scoupe (1991 and 1992), Elantra (continued)

Code	Probable cause
22	Crank angle sensor or circuit
23	TDC sensor or circuit
24	Vehicle Speed Sensor or circuit
25	Barometric pressure sensor or circuit
41	Fuel injector or circuit
42	Fuel pump or circuit
43	EGR system
44	Ignition coil
59	Oxygen sensor

Scoupe (1993 through 1995) and Accent

Code	Probable cause
1122	ECM failure (ROM/RAM)
1169	ECM failure
1233	ECM failure (ROM)
1234	ECM failure (RAM)
2121	Turbo boost sensor control valve
3112	No. 1 fuel injector
3114	Idle Air Control (opening failure)
3116	No. 3 fuel injector
3117	Mass Airflow sensor
3121	Turbo boost sensor failure
3122	Idle Air Control (closing failure)
3128	Heated oxygen sensor

Code	Probable cause
3135	EVAP purge control solenoid valve
3137	Alternator output low
3145	Engine coolant temperature (ECT) sensor
3149	Air conditioning compressor
3152	Turbocharger overboost
3153	Throttle position switch (TPS)
3159	Vehicle speed sensor
3211	Knock sensor
3222	Phase sensor
3224	ECM failure (knock evaluation circuit)
3232	Crankshaft position sensor
3233	Same as code 3224
3234	No. 2 fuel injector
3235	No. 4 fuel injector
3241	ECM failure (injector or purge solenoid)
3242	ECM failure (IAC or air conditioning relay)
3243	ECM failure
4133	ECM failure
4151	Air/fuel control
4152	Air/fuel adaptive failure
4153	Air/fuel multiple adaptive failure
4154	Air/fuel additive adaptive failure
4155	ECM failure (A/C relay, IAC, PCV or injector)
4156	Same as code 3121
4444	Normal
3333	End of trouble codes

Infiniti

G20, J30 and Q45 models

Code	System Affected	Probable Cause
11 (1)	Crankshaft Position Sensor	(2) No crank signal
12	Mass Airflow Sensor Circuit	Open/shorted circuit
13	Engine Coolant Temp Sensor	Open/shorted circuit
14	Vehicle Speed Sensor (VSS)	No VSS signal
16 (1)	Traction Control System	Open/shorted circuit
21 (1)	Ignition signal circuit	(2) Open/shorted circuit
31	ECM	Signals not normal
32 (3)	EGR function	No EGR operation
33	Oxygen sensor (Left)	Open/shorted circuit - high oxygen sensor signal
34 (1)	Knock sensor	Open/shorted circuit
35 (3)	EGR temperature sensor	Open/shorted circuit
42	Fuel temperature sensor	Open/shorted circuit
43	Throttle Position Sensor	Open/shorted circuit
45 (3)	Injector leak	Leak at injectors
46 (1) (Q45 models with TCS)	Secondary Throttle Position Sensor	Open/shorted circuit
51	Injector circuit	Injector does not work
53	Oxygen sensor (right)	Open/shorted circuit - high for oxygen signal
54 (1)	Automatic transmission signal	Open signal - Transmission Control Unit
55 (1)	No malfunction	Normal condition

(1)   Trouble code will not activate Malfunction Indicator Light (MIL)
(2)   If codes 11 and 21 are present at the same time, check items causing a malfunction of the crankshaft position sensor circuit
(3)   California models

Isuzu

Note: *To determine which models a code applies to, refer to the parenthetical reference (A, B and/or C) following the probable cause, then cross-reference the letter(s) with their corresponding models at the end of this chart.*

Code	Probable cause
12	Idle switch not turned on (1982 through 1984 1.8L with feedback carburetor)
12	No TACH signal to ECM (A, B and C)
13	Idle switch not turned off (1982 through 1984 1.8L with feedback carburetor)
13	Oxygen sensor or circuit (A, B and C)
14	Wide open throttle switch not turned on (1982 through 1984 1.8L with feedback carburetor)
15	Wide open throttle switch not turned off (1982 through 1984 1.8L with feedback carburetor)
14	Engine coolant temperature (ECT) sensor shorted (A) or grounded (B) or out of range (C)
15	Engine coolant temperature (ECT) sensor - open circuit (A)
15	Engine coolant temperature (ECT) sensor - incorrect signal (B); open circuit on 1988 through 1994 2.6L
16	Engine coolant temperature (ECT) sensor - open circuit (B)
21	Output transistor is not turned on (1982 through 1984 1.8L with feedback carburetor)
21	Idle switch - open circuit; or Wide Open Throttle (WOT) switch - short circuit (A)
21	Throttle Valve Switch (TVS) system - idle contact and full contact made simultaneously (B)
21	Throttle position sensor (TPS) - voltage high (C)
21	Throttle position sensor (TPS) - out of range (D)
22	Output transistor not turned on (1982 through 1984 1.8L with feedback carburetor)
22	Fuel cut solenoid circuit open or grounded (A)
22	Starter - no signal input (B)
22	Throttle position sensor (TPS) signal - voltage low (C)
23	Abnormal oxygen sensor (1982 through 1984 1.8L with feedback carburetor)
23	Mixture control solenoid circuit failure (A)
23	Ignition power transistor circuit - output terminal grounded (B)
23	Intake Air Temperature (IAT) sensor voltage - high temperature indicated (C)
23	Intake Air Temperature (IAT) sensor - out of range (D)
24	Coolant temperature sensor malfunction (1982 through 1984 1.8L with feedback carburetor)
24	Vehicle speed sensor (VSS) circuit fault (A and C)

Code	Probable cause
24	Vehicle speed sensor (VSS) - no input signal (D)
24	Pressure regulator vacuum switching valve (1988 through 1994 2.3L)
25	Random Access Memory (RAM) (1982 through 1984 1.8L with feedback carburetor)
25	Air Injection Reactor(AIR) vacuum switch valve (VSV) circuit fault (1987 through 1989 1.5L; A and B)
25	Intake air temperature (IAT) - high temperature indicated (C)
26	Canister vacuum switching valve (VSV) system for canister purge - circuit open or grounded (A and B)
27	Vacuum switching valve (VSV) - constant high voltage to ECM (A)
27	Canister purge vacuum switching valve (VSV) - faulty transistor or bad ground circuit (B)
31	No ignition reference to ECM (A)
31	Wastegate control circuit fault - turbo models (C)
32	Exhaust Gas Recirculation (EGR) system failure (C)
33	Fuel injector circuit fault - output terminal open or grounded (B)
33	Manifold Absolute Pressure (MAP) sensor - voltage high (C)
33	Manifold Absolute Pressure (MAP) sensor - out of range (D)
34	Exhaust Gas Recirculation (EGR)/vacuum switching valve (VSV) - output terminal open or grounded (B)
34	Manifold Absolute Pressure (MAP) sensor - voltage low (C)
34	Exhaust Gas Recirculation (EGR) temperature sensor - electronic idle control circuit fault (A)
35	Ignition power transistor - open circuit (B)
41	Crank angle sensor (CAS) - no signal or faulty signal (B)
42	Electronic spark timing circuit fault (C)
42	Fuel cut-off relay malfunction or circuit fault (A)
43	Electronic spark control (ESC) - knock circuit fault (C)
43	Throttle valve switch - idle switch always closed (B)
44	Oxygen sensor - lean condition indicated (all models)
45	Oxygen sensor - rich condition indicated (all models)
51	Fuel cut-off solenoid circuit shorted, or faulty ECM (A)
51	Bad Programmable Read-Only Memory (PROM) or incorrect PROM installation (1985 through 1989 1.5L I-Mark; C)
51	Electronic Control Module (ECM) failure (B and D)
52	Electronic Control Module (ECM) failure (A and B)
52	CALPAK error - faulty, incorrectly installed or wrong CALPAK (C)
53	Faulty Electronic Control Module (ECM), or shorted air switching solenoid (ASS) or air injection system (A)
53	Vacuum switching valve (VSV) - grounded or faulty power transistor (B)
54	Fuel pump circuit - low voltage (C)

Isuzu (continued)

Code	Probable cause
54	Ignition power transistor - grounded or faulty power transistor (B)
54	Shorted mixture control solenoid, or faulty ECM (1987 through 1989 1.5L I-Mark; A)
55	Faulty Electronic Control Module (ECM) (A, B and C)
61	Air flow sensor (AFS) circuit fault - grounded, shorted or open HOW wire (B)
62	Air flow sensor (AFS) circuit fault - broken COLD wire (B)
63	Vehicle speed sensor (VSS) circuit - no signal input (B)
64	Fuel injector driver transistor circuit - grounded or faulty circuit (B)
65	Throttle valve switch always on (B)
66	Knock sensor failure - grounded or open circuit (B)
71	Throttle position sensor (TPS) - turbo control system signal abnormal (B)
72	Exhaust Gas Recirculation (EGR) vacuum switching valve (VSV) - faulty transistor or ground system (B)

A 1985 through 1989 1.5L engine (VIN 7) with feedback carburetor (FBC); 1983 1.8L truck engine with FBC; 1983 through 1986 2.0L engine (VIN A) with FBC; 1986 through 1994 2.3L engine (VIN L) with FBC

B 1985 through 1987 2.0L electronic fuel-injected (EFI) turbo engine (VIN F); 1983 through 1989 2.0L EFI engine (VIN A); 1988 and 1989 2.3L EFI (VIN L) engine; 1988 through 1994 2.6L EFI engine (VIN E)

C 1987 through 1989 1.5L electronic fuel-injected (EFI) turbo engine (VIN 9); 1989 1.6L EFI engine (VIN 5); 1991 and 1992 1.6L EFI turbo engine (VIN 4); 1989 through 1991 2.8L throttle body injection (TBI) engine (VIN R); 1991 through 1994 3.1L TBI engine (VIN Z)

D 1990 and 1991 1.6L electronic fuel-injected (EFI) engine (VIN 7); 1992 through 1994 1.8L EFI engine (VIN 8); 1991 through 1994 2.3L EFI engine (VIN 5, VIN 6); 1992 through 1994 3.2L EFI engine (VIN V, VIN W)

Jaguar

1988 and 1989 models

Code	System affected	Probable cause
1	Oxygen sensor	Open oxygen sensor circuit
2	Airflow sensor circuit	Not in operating range
3	Coolant temperature sensor	Not in operating range
4	Oxygen sensor	System indicates full rich
5	Throttle potentiometer/airflow sensor	Low throttle potentiometer signal with high airflow sensor signal

Code	System affected	Probable cause
6	Throttle potentiometer/airflow sensor	High throttle potentiometer signal with low airflow sensor signal
7	Throttle potentiometer	Idle fuel adjustment failure
8	Intake air temperature sensor	Open or shorted circuit in IAT sensor harness

All other models

Code	System affected	Probable cause
11	Idle potentiometer	Not in operating range
12	Airflow sensor	Not in operating range
13	PCME	No vacuum signal from pressure sensor, incorrect fuel pressure or PCME failure
14	Coolant temperature sensor	Not in operating range
16	Air temperature sensor	Not in operating range
17	Throttle potentiometer	Not in operating range
18	Throttle potentiometer/airflow sensor	Signal resistance low at wide open throttle
19	Throttle potentiometer/airflow sensor	Signal resistance high at idle
22	Heated oxygen sensor	Open or short circuit
22	Fuel pump circuit	Open or short circuit
23	Fuel supply	Rich exhaust indicated
23	Fuel supply (rich or lean)	Open or short in fuel supply circuit; restricted fuel line or injectors (5.3L)
24	Ignition amplifier circuit	Open or short circuit
26	Oxygen sensor circuit	Lean exhaust/vacuum leak
29	ECU	Self-check
33	Fuel injector circuit	Open or short circuit
34	Fuel injector circuit	Faulty injected indicated
34	Bank A (right) injectors	Open or short circuit; faulty or restricted fuel injectors (5.3L)
36	Bank B (left) injectors	Open or short circuit; faulty or restricted fuel injectors (5.3L)
37	EGR solenoid circuit	Short or open circuit
39	EGR circuit	Faulty system operation
44	Lambda (oxygen) sensor (right)	Circuit feedback out of control - rich or lean condition
45	Lambda (oxygen) sensor (left)	Circuit feedback out of control - rich or lean condition
46	Idle speed control valve (coil 1)	Open or short circuit
47	Idle speed control valve (coil 2)	Open or short circuit
48	Idle speed control valve	Not within specification
49	Fuel injection ballast resistor	Open circuit or faulty resistor (5.3L)

Jaguar (continued)

Code	System affected	Probable cause
66	Secondary air inception relay	Voltage out of range
68	Road speed sensor	Incorrect signal voltage
69	Neutral safety switch circuit	Engine cranks in drive (adjust or replace switch)
89	Purge control valve circuit	Open or short circuit

Jeep

  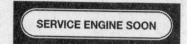

1984 through 1986 V6 models

Trouble Code	Circuit or system	Probable cause
12 (one flash, pause, two flashes)	No reference pulses to ECM	This code should flash whenever the test terminal is grounded with the ignition On and the engine not running. If additional trouble codes are stored (indicating a problem), they will appear after this code has flashed three times. With the engine running, the appearance of this code indicates that no references from the distributor are reaching the ECM. Carefully check the four terminal EST connector or the distributor.
13 (one flash, pause, three flashes)	Oxygen sensor circuit	Check for a sticking or misadjusted throttle position sensor. Check the wiring and connectors from the oxygen sensor. Replace oxygen sensor.*
14 (one flash, pause, four flashes)	Coolant sensor circuit (high temperature indicated)	If the engine is experiencing overheating problems the problem must be rectified before continuing. Check all wiring and connectors associated with the sensor. Replace the coolant sensor.*
15 (one flash, pause, five flashes)	Coolant sensor circuit (low temperature indicated)	See above.
21 (two flashes, pause, one flash)	TPS circuit (signal voltage high)	Check for sticking or misadjusted TPS. Check all wiring and connections at the TPS and at the ECM Adjust or replace TPS.*
23 (two flashes, pause, three flashes)	Mixture Control (M/C)	Check the electrical connections at the M/C solenoid. If solenoid circuit OK, clear the ECM memory and recheck for code(s) after driving the vehicle. Check wiring connections at the ECM. Check wiring from M/C solenoid.

Trouble Code	Circuit or system	Probable cause
34 (three flashes, pause, four flashes)	Manifold Absolute Pressure	Check the hose to the MAP sensor for a leak. Check the wiring from (MAP) sensor circuit the MAP sensor to the ECM. Check the connections at the ECM and the sensor. Replace the MAP sensor.*
41 (four flashes, pause, one flash)	No distributor signals	Check all wires and connections at the distributor. Check distributor pick-up coil connections.
42 (four flashes, pause, two flashes)	Bypass or EST problem	If the vehicle will start and run, check the wire leading to ECM terminal 12. An improper HEI module can also cause this trouble code.
44 (four flashes, pause, four flashes)	Lean exhaust	Check for a sticking M/C solenoid. Check ECM wiring connections. Check for vacuum leakage at carburetor base gasket, vacuum hoses or intake manifold gasket. Check for air leakage at air management system- to-exhaust ports and at decel valve. Replace oxygen sensor.*
44 and 45 at the same time	Oxygen sensor or circuit	Check the oxygen sensor circuit. Replace the oxygen sensor.*
45 (four flashes, pause, five flashes)	Rich exhaust	Check for a sticking M/C solenoid. Check wiring at M/C solenoid connector. Check the evaporative charcoal canister and its components for the presence of fuel. Replace oxygen sensor.*
51 (five flashes, pause, one flash)	PROM problem	Diagnosis should be performed by a dealer service department or other repair shop.
54 (five flashes, pause, four flashes)	Mixture control (M/C) solenoid	Check all M/C solenoid and ECM wires and connections. Replace the M/C solenoid.*
55 (five flashes, pause, five flashes)	Reference voltage problem	Check for a short to ground on the circuit to ECM. Possible faulty ECM or oxygen sensor.

Component replacement may not cure the problem in all cases. For this reason, you may want to seek professional advice before purchasing replacement parts.

1991 on
Trouble codes

Note: *Not all trouble codes apply to all models.*

Code 11	No distributor reference signal detected during engine cranking. Check the circuit between the distributor and the PCM.
Code 12	Problem with the battery connection. Direct battery input to controller disconnected within the last 50 ignition key-ons.
Code 13**	Indicates a problem with the MAP sensor pneumatic (vacuum) system.
Code 14**	MAP sensor voltage too low or too high.
Code 15**	A problem with the vehicle distance/speed signal. No distance/speed sensor signal detected during road load conditions.
Code 16	Loss of battery voltage.

The Haynes Emissions Control Manual

Jeep (continued)

1991 on

Code 17	Engine is cold too long. Engine coolant temperature remains below normal operating temperatures during operation (check the thermostat).
Code 21**	Problem with oxygen sensor signal circuit. Sensor voltage to computer not fluctuating.
Code 22**	Coolant sensor voltage too high or too low. Test coolant temperature sensor.
Code 23**	Indicates that the air temperature sensor input is below the minimum acceptable voltage or sensor input is above the maximum acceptable voltage.
Code 24**	Throttle position sensor voltage high or low. Test the throttle position sensor.
Code 25**	Idle Air Control (IAC) motor circuits. A shorted condition is detected in one or more of the IAC motor circuits.
Code 27	One of the injector control circuit output drivers does not respond properly to the control signal. Check the circuits.
Code 31**	Problem with the canister purge solenoid circuit.
Code 32**	An open or shorted condition detected in the EGR solenoid circuit. Possible air/fuel ratio imbalance not detected during diagnosis
Code 33	Air conditioner clutch relay circuit. An open or shorted condition detected in the air conditioning clutch relay circuit.
Code 34	Open or shorted condition detected in the speed control vacuum or vent solenoid circuits.
Code 37	Torque converter clutch solenoid circuit. An open or shorted condition detected in the torque converter part throttle unlock solenoid circuit (automatic transmissions models only).
Code 41**	Problem with the charging system. Occurs when battery voltage from the ASD relay is below 11.75-volts.
Code 42	Auto shutdown relay (ASD) control circuit indicates an open or shorted circuit condition.
Code 44	Battery temperature sensor volts malfunction. Problem with the battery temperature voltage circuit in the PCM
Code 45	Overdrive solenoid. Problem detected in the overdrive solenoid circuit.
Code 46**	Charging system voltage too high. Computer indicates that the battery voltage is not properly regulated.
Code 47**	Charging system voltage too low. Battery voltage sense input below target charging voltage during engine operation and no significant change in voltage detected during active test of alternator output.
Code 51*	Oxygen sensor signal input indicates lean fuel/air ratio condition during engine operation.
Code 52**	Oxygen sensor signal input indicates rich fuel/air ratio condition during engine operation.
Code 53	Internal PCM failure detected.
Code 54	No camshaft position sensor signal from distributor. Problem with the distributor synchronization circuit.
Code 55	Completion of fault code display on CHECK ENGINE lamp. This is an End of message code.
Code 62	Unsuccessful attempt to update EMR mileage in the controller EEPROM.
Code 63	Controller failure. EEPROM write denied. Check the PCM.

** *These codes light up the CHECK ENGINE light on the instrument panel during engine operation once the trouble code has been recorded*

Lexus

  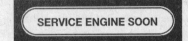

Code	Circuit or system	Trouble area
1	Normal	This code appears when the system is operating satisfactorily
12	RPM signal	The rpm NE, G1 or G2 signal to the ECU is missing for 2 or more seconds after the engine is cranked. Check the distributor and circuit, the igniter and circuit, the starter circuit, and the ECU
13	RPM signal	No NE signal to the ECU with an engine speed of more than 1000 rpm. Check the distributor circuit, the igniter and circuit, and the ECU
14	Ignition signal	Igniter IGF1 signal to ECU missing for eight successive ignitions. Check the igniter circuit, the igniter and the ECU
15	Ignition signal	Igniter IGF2 signal to ECU missing for eight consecutive ignitions. Check the igniter circuit, the igniter and the ECU
16	ECT control signal	Normal signal missing from ECT CPU (1990 through 1994 models)
16	A/T control signal	Normal signal missing between engine CPU and A/T CPU in the ECU (1995 models). Check the ECU
17	No. 1 cam position sensor	G1 signal to ECU missing. Check cam position sensor and circuit between sensor and ECU
18	No. 2 cam position sensor	G2 signal to ECU missing. Check cam position sensor and circuit between sensor and ECU
21*	Main oxygen sensor signal (left)	Signal voltage stays between 0.35 and 0.70 volts for 1 minute or more at 40 to 50 mph, with A/C on and ECT in 4th gear. Or sensor heater circuit open or shorted. Check sensor and circuit
22	Coolant temperature sensor	Open or short in the coolant temperature sensor, circuit or ECU
24	Intake air temperature sensor	Open or short in the intake air sensor circuit
25*	Air/fuel ratio lean malfunction	Air/fuel ratio feedback correction value or adaptive control value continues at the upper (lean) or lower (rich) limit for a certain period of time. Check the injector, injector circuit, oxygen sensor, sensor circuit, ECU, fuel line pressure (injector blockage or leakage), coolant temperature sensor or sensor circuit; air temperature sensor or sensor circuit; airflow meter; air intake system; ignition system. Look for an air leak.
26*	Air/fuel ratio rich malfunction	Air/fuel ratio is overly rich, or there's an open or short circuit in the oxygen sensor. Check the injector and circuit; coolant temperature sensor and circuit; air temperature sensor and circuit; airflow meter; oxygen sensor and circuit; cold start injector; and ECU
27*	Sub-oxygen sensor signal (left)	Open or shorted circuit in the sub-oxygen sensor or circuit. Check the sub-oxygen sensor and circuit, and the ECU

Lexus (continued)

Code	Circuit or system	Trouble area
28*	Main oxygen sensor signal (right)	Signal voltage stays between 0.35 and 0.70 volts for 1 minute or more at 40 to 50 mph, with A/C on and ECT in 4th gear. Or sensor heater circuit open or shorted. Check sensor and circuit
29*	Sub-oxygen sensor signal (right)	Open or shorted circuit in the sub-oxygen sensor or circuit. Check the sub-oxygen sensor and circuit, and the ECU
31	Airflow meter circuit signal to ECU	Airflow meter circuit signal to ECU missing for 2 seconds with engine speed over 300 rpm. Look for an open or short in the airflow meter circuit to the ECU
32	Airflow meter circuit	E2 circuit open or VC and VS shorted. Look for an open or short circuit in the airflow meter or circuit
35	HAC sensor circuit	Open or short for 0.5 seconds or more, or BARO sensor failure. Check the HAC sensor and circuit, or the BARO sensor and circuit
41	Throttle position sensor signal	Open or short in the throttle position sensor or circuit, or in the ECU
42	Vehicle speed sensor circuit	Engine speed over 2350 rpm but VSS indicates 0 mph. Check VSS and circuit
43	Starter signal	No starter signal to the ECU. Check the starter signal circuit, the ignition switch, the main relay switch and the ECU
47	Sub-throttle position sensor signal	Open or short for 0.5 seconds or more in the sub-throttle position sensor circuit (VTA2), or signal outputs exceed 1.45 volts with idle contacts on. Check the VTA2 circuit
51	Switch condition signal	A/C signal on when IDL contacts off, or shift in R, D, 2 or 1 range, during test mode. Check the A/C switch and circuit; A/C amplifier; neutral start switch (automatics); throttle position sensor; and ECU
52	No. 1 knock sensor signal	Knock sensor signal missing from ECU for 3 revolutions with engine speed between 1600 and 5200 rpm. Look for an open or short circuit in knock sensor circuit. Check the knock sensor and the ECU
53	Knock control signal	Problem with knock control system in ECU with engine speed between 650 and 5200 rpm. Check the ECU
55	No. 2 knock sensor signal	Knock sensor signal missing from ECU for 3 revolutions with engine speed between 1600 and 5200 rpm. Look for an open or short circuit in knock sensor circuit. Check the knock sensor and the ECU
71*	EGR gas temperature signal	EGR system gas temperature signal too low (below 149 degrees F for at least 90 seconds while under EGR control). Check the EGR valve, hoses, etc.; EGR gas temperature sensor or circuit; vacuum switching valve for the EGR circuit; ECU
78*	Fuel pump control signal	Open or short in the fuel pump control circuit

A single occurrence of this code will only be stored temporarily in computer memory, and the CHECK ENGINE light won't come on until the fault has been detected a second time during a separate ignition cycle.

Mazda

Code	Probable cause
1	Engine speed (1984 and 1985 2.0L)
1	Crank angle sensor (1984 through 1987 RX-7)
1	Ignition coil - trailing (1988 through 1991 RX-7)
1	No ignition pulse signal (1988 through 1994 1.6L, 1.8L, 2.0L, 2.2L, 2.5L, 2.6L and 3.0L)
2	Coolant thermosensor (1984 and 1985 2.0L)
2	Air flow meter (1984 through 1987 RX-7; 1986 and 1987 1.6L, 2.0L and 2.2L)
2	NE-2 signal - crankshaft (1992 and 1993 1.8L V6, 1994 2.0L and 1992 through 1994 3.0L)
3	Oxygen sensor (1984 and 1985 2.0L)
3	Coolant thermosensor (1984 through 1987 RX-7; 1986 and 1987 1.6L, 2.0L and 2.2L)
3	Crank position sensor - G1 signal/cam position sensor (2.2L turbo, 1988 through 1991 3.0L)
3	Crank angle sensor - G signal (1988 through 1991 RX-7)
4	Vacuum sensor (1984 and 1985 2.0L)
4	Intake air temperature sensor - in airflow meter (1984 through 1987 RX-7)
4	Intake air thermosensor (1986 and 1987 1.6L, 2.0L and 2.2L)
4	Crank position sensor (G2 signal) (2.2L turbo, 1988 through 1991 3.0L); distributor (NE1) signal (1992 through 1994 1.8L V6, 1994 2.0L, 1992 and 1993 3.0L)
5	EGR position sensor (1984 and 1985 2.0L)
5	Oxygen sensor (1984 through 1987 RX-7)
5	Feedback system (1986 and 1987 1.6L, 2.0L and 2.2L)
5	Left knock sensor, or control unit (1992 through 1994 3.0L)
5	Knock sensor (1993 RX-7)
6	Throttle sensor (1984 through 1987 RX-7)
6	Atmospheric pressure sensor (1986 and 1987 1.6L, 2.0L and 2.2L)
6	Speedometer sensor (1988 through 1994 1.6L, 1.8L, 2.0L, 2.2L, 2.5L, 2.6L and 3.0L)
6	Speedometer sensor (1993 RX-7)

Mazda (continued)

Code	Probable cause
7	Right knock sensor (1992 through 1994 3.0L)
7	Boost sensor/pressure sensor (1984 through 1987 RX-7 turbo)
8	EGR position sensor (1986 and 1987 1.6L, 2.0L and 2.2L)
8	Airflow meter (1988 through 1991 RX-7)
9	Atmospheric pressure sensor (1984 through 1987 RX-7)
9	Atmospheric pressure sensor (1986 and 1987 1.6L, 2.0L and 2.2L)
9	Coolant thermosensor (1988 through 1994 RX-7)
10	Intake air thermosensor - in airflow meter (1988 through 1991 RX-7)
10	Intake air thermosensor (1988 through 1994 1.6L, 1.8L, 2.0L, 2.2L and 2.5L)
11	Intake air thermosensor (1988 through 1993 RX-7)
11	Intake air thermosensor - dynamic chamber (1988 through 1994 2.6L and 3.0L)
12	Coil with igniter - trailing ((1984 through 1987 RX-7)
12	Throttle sensor - wide open throttle (1988 through 1994 RX-7)
13	Intake manifold pressure sensor (1988 through 1994 RX-7)
14	Atmospheric pressure sensor (1988 through 1994 2.6L and 1994 2.5L) (inside the ECU on these models)
14	Atmospheric pressure sensor (1988 through 1994 RX-7) (inside the ECU on 1993 models)
15	Intake air temperature sensor - in dynamic chamber (1984 through 1987 RX-7)
15	Oxygen sensor (1988 through 1994 1.6L, 1.8L, 2.0L, 2.2L, 2.5L, 2.6L, 3.0L and RX-7)
15	Left oxygen sensor (1992 through 1994 1.8L V6, 1994 2.5L and 1990 through 1994 3.0L)
16	EGR position sensor (1988 through 1994 1.6L, 1.8L, 2.0L, 2.2L, 2.5L, 2.6L and 3.0L)
16	EGR switch (1993 California RX-7)
17	Feedback system (1988 through 1994 1.6L, 1.8L, 2.0L, 2.2L, 2.5L, 2.6L, 3.0L and RX-7)
17	Left feedback system (1992 through 1994 1.8L V6, 1993 and 1994 2.5L and 1990 through 1994 3.0L)
18	Throttle sensor - narrow range (1988 through 1994 RX-7)
20	Metering oil pump position sensor (1988 through 1994 RX-7)
22	No. 1 cylinder sensor (1986 and 1987 2.2L turbo)
23	Right heated oxygen sensor (1992 through 1994 1.8L V6, 1994 2.5L and 1990 and 1991 3.0L)

Code	Probable cause
23	Fuel thermosensor (1993 RX-7)
24	Right feedback system (1992 through 1994 1.8L V6, 1993 and 1994 2.5L and 1990 through 1994 3.0L)
25	Solenoid valve - pressure regulator control (1988 through 1994 1.6L, 1.8L, 2.0L, 2.2L, 2.5L, 2.6L and 3.0L)
25	Solenoid valve - pressure regulator control (1993 RX-7)
26	Purge control solenoid valve no. 2 (1988 and 1989 3.0L)
26	Purge control solenoid valve (1988 through 1994 1.6L, 1.8L, 2.0L, 2.2L, 2.5L, 2.6L and 3.0L)
26	Metering oil pump stepping motor (1993 RX-7)
27	Purge control solenoid valve no. 1 (1988 and 1989 3.0L)
27	Purge control solenoid valve no. 2 (1989 1.6L)
27	Metering oil pump - step motor (1988 through 1991 RX-7)
27	Metering oil pump (1993 RX-7)
28	EGR solenoid valve (1993 RX-7)
28	Solenoid valve - EGR vacuum (1988 through 1994 1.6L, 1.8L, 2.0L, 2.2L, 2.5L, 2.6L and 3.0L)
29	Solenoid valve - EGR vent (1988 through 1994 1.6L, 1.8L, 2.0L, 2.2L, 2.5L, 2.6L and 3.0L)
30	Relay (or cold start injector, on 3.0L) (1988 through 1994 1.6L, 1.8L, 2.0L, 2.2L, 2.5L, 2.6L and 3.0L)
31	Solenoid valve - relief no. 1 (1988 through 1994 RX-7)
32	Solenoid valve - switching (1988 through 1994 RX-7)
33	Solenoid valve - port air bypass (1988 through 1994 RX-7)
34	Solenoid valve - bypass air control (1988 through 1991 RX-7)
34	Solenoid valve - idle speed control (1993 RX-7)
34	ISC valve (1988 through 1994 1.6L, 1.8L, 2.0L, 2.2L, 2.5L, 2.6L and 3.0L)
34	Idle air control valve (1993 and 1994 2.0L, 2.5L, 1.6L, 1.8L, 2.6L and 3.0L)
36	Oxygen sensor heater relay (1990 3.0L)
36	Right oxygen sensor heater (1992 through 1994 3.0L)
37	Left oxygen sensor heater (1992 through 1994 3.0L)
37	Metering oil pump (1988 through 1993 RX-7)
37	Coolant fan relay (1988 through 1994 1.6L, 1.8L, 2.0L, 2.2L, 2.5L, 2.6L and 3.0L)
38	Solenoid valve accelerated warm-up system (1988 through 1994)
39	Solenoid valve - relief 2 (1993 RX-7)

Mazda (continued)

Code	Probable cause
40	Solenoid (triple induction system) and oxygen sensor relay (1988 and 1989 3.0L)
40	Auxiliary port valve (1988 through 1991 RX-7)
40	Oxygen sensor heater relay (1991 3.0L)
40	Solenoid valve - purge control (1993 RX-7)
41	Solenoid valve - variable dynamic effect intake control (1988 through 1991 RX-7)
41	Solenoid valve - VRIS (1989 through 1994 3.0L MPV)
41	Solenoid valve VRIS 1 (1992 through 1994 1.8L V6 and 1993 2.5L)
41	Variable inertia charging system (VICS) (3.0L only)
42	Solenoid valve - turbo boost pressure regulator (1988 through 1991 RX-7)
42	Solenoid valve - turbo pre-control (1993 RX-7)
43	Solenoid valve - wastegate control (1993 RX-7)
44	Solenoid valve - turbo control (1993 RX-7)
45	Solenoid valve - charge control (1993 RX-7)
46	Solenoid valve - VRIS 2 (1992 through 1994 1.8L V6, and 1993 2.5L)
46	Solenoid valve - charge relief control (1993 RX-7)
50	Solenoid valve - double-throttle control (1993 RX-7)
51	Fuel pump relay (1988 through 1994 RX-7)
54	Air pump relay (1993 RX-7)
65	Air conditioning signal - PCMT (1992 through 1994 3.0L)
67	Coolant fan relay no. 1 (1993 2.5L)
67	Coolant fan relay no. 2 (1992 through 1994 1.8L V6)
68	Coolant fan relay no. 2 (no. 3 on automatics) (1993 2.5L)
69	Engine coolant temperature sensor - fan (1992 through 1994 1.8L V6; 1993 2.0L and 2.5L)
71	Injector - front secondary (1988 through 1994 RX-7)
73	Injector - rear secondary (1988 through 1994 RX-7)
76	Slip lock-up off signal (1993 RX-7)
77	Torque reduced signal (1993 RX-7)

Mercedes

  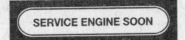

1990 through 1993 - 190E and 300 series (2.3L)

No.of Flashes	Probable cause
1	No System Malfunction
2	Throttle Valve Switch
3	Coolant Temperature Sensor
4	Airflow Sensor Position Indicator
5	Oxygen Sensor
6	Not Used
7	Td Signal
8	Altitude Correction Capsule
9	Electro-Hydraulic Actuator (EHA)
10	Throttle Valve Switch and/or Idle Speed Contact
11	Not Used
12	EGR Temperature Sensor

1991 and later - 300 series (2.8L and 3.2L)

No.of Flashes	Probable cause
1	No faults in system
2	Oxygen Sensor Inoperative
3	Lambda Control Inoperative
4	Air Injection inoperative
5	Exhaust Gas Recirculation (EGR) inoperative
6	Idle Speed Control Inoperative
7	Ignition System Failure
8	Coolant Temperature Sensor - Open Or Short Circuit
9	Intake Air Temperature Sensor - Open Or Short Circuit
10	Voltage At Air Mass Sensor Too High Or Low
11	TN (RPM) Signal Defective
12	Oxygen Sensor Heater Open Or Short Circuit
13	Camshaft Position Sensor Signal From - EZL/AKR Ignition Control Unit Defective
14	Intake Manifold Pressure At Start Too Low
15	Full Throttle Information Defective
16	Idle Speed Information Defective
17	Controller Area Network (CAN) Data Exchange - Malfunction Between Control Units
18	Adjustable Camshaft Timing Solenoid - Open Or Short Circuit
19	Fuel Injectors- Open Or Short Circuit, or Emission Control System Adaptation at Limit
20	Speed Signal Missing
21	Purge Switchover Valve - Open Or Short Circuit
22	Camshaft Position Sensor Signal Defective
23	Intake Manifold Pressure With Engine Running Too Low
24	Starter Ring Gear Segments Defective
25	Knock Sensors Defective
26	Upshift Delay Switch over Valve - Open Or Short Circuit
27	Coolant Temperature Sensor Deviation Between Sensor Circuit No. 1 and Sensor Circuit No. 2
28	Coolant Temperature Sensor (Coolant Temperature Change Monitor)

The Haynes Emissions Control Manual

Mercedes (continued)

1991 through 1993 - 190E and 300 series (2.6L and 3.0L)

No.of Flashes	Probable cause
1	No faults in system
2	Throttle Valve Switch (Full Throttle Contact)
3	Coolant Temperature Sensor
4	Airflow Sensor Potentiometer
5	Oxygen Sensor
6	Not assigned
7	TNA (Engine RPM) Signal
8	Altitude Pressure Signal From EZL Ignition Control Unit
9	Current To Electro-hydraulic Actuator
10	Throttle Valve switch (Idle Contact)
11	Air Injection System
12	Absolute Pressure Valves From EZL Ignition Control Unit
13	Intake Air Temperature Signal
14	Road Speed Signal At CIS-E Control Unit
15	Not assigned
16	Exhaust Gas Recirculation (EGR)
17	Oxygen Sensor Signal
18	Current To Idle Speed Air Valve
19	Not assigned
20	Not assigned
21	Not assigned
22	Oxygen Sensor Heating Current
23	Short Circuit To Positive In Regeneration Switch over Valve Circuit
24	Not assigned
25	Short Circuit To Positive in Start Valve Circuit
26	Short Circuit To Positive In Shift Point Retard Circuit
27	Data Exchange Fault Between CIS-E Control Unit and EZL Ignition Control Unit
28	Loose Contact In Coolant Temperature Sensor Circuit
29	Difference In Coolant Temperatures Between CIS-E Control Unit and EZL Ignition Control Unit
30	Not assigned
31	Loose Contact In Intake Air Temperature Sensor Circuit
32	Not assigned
33	Not assigned
34	Faulty Coolant Temperature Sensor Signal from EZL Ignition Control Unit

Mitsubishi

All 1984 through 1988 models (except 1988 Galant)*

Code	Probable cause
1	Exhaust gas sensor and/or ECU
2	Crankshaft angle sensor or ignition signal
3	Air flow sensor

Code	Probable cause
4	Atmospheric/Barometric pressure sensor
5	Throttle position sensor
6	Idle Speed Control (ISC) Motor Position Sensor (MPS)
7	Engine coolant temperature sensor
8	Top Dead Center (TDC) sensor or vehicle speed sensor
9	Top Dead Center (TDC) sensor

1988 Galant uses 1989 two-digit codes.

All 1989 through 1995 fuel-injected models (including 1988 Galant)

Code	Probable cause
1	Electronic Control Unit (ECU) (one long needle sweep)
9	Normal state (continuous short flashes)
11	Oxygen sensor or circuit
12	Air flow sensor or circuit
13	Intake air temperature sensor or circuit
14	Throttle Position Sensor (TPS) or circuit
15	Idle speed control (ISC) motor position sensor or circuit fault
21	Engine coolant temperature sensor or circuit
22	Crank angle sensor or circuit
23	No. 1 cylinder Top Dead Center (camshaft position) sensor or circuit
24	Vehicle Speed Sensor or circuit
25	Barometric pressure sensor or circuit
31	Detonation (knock) sensor
32	Manifold Absolute pressure (MAP) sensor faulty
36	Ignition timing adjustment signal fault
39	Front oxygen sensor (rear sensor on turbo models)
41	Fuel injector failure
42	Fuel pump or circuit
43	Exhaust Gas Recirculation (EGR) system (California models)
44	Ignition coil (except 3.0L DOHC V6)
44	Power transistor for coil (cylinders 1 and 4) (3.0L DOHC V6)

Mitsubishi (continued)

Code	Probable cause
52	Ignition coil (except 3.0L DOHC V6)
52	Power transistor for coil (cylinders 2 and 5) (DOHC V6)
53	Ignition coil (except 3.0L DOHC V6)
53	Power transistor for coil (cylinders 3 and 6) (3.0L DOHC V6)
55	Idle air control (IAC) valve position sensor fault
59	Heated oxygen sensor fault
61	ECM and transmission interlock
62	Induction control valve position sensor
69	Right rear oxygen sensor
71	Traction control vacuum valve solenoid fault
72	Traction control vent valve solenoid fault

Nissan/Datsun cars and trucks

  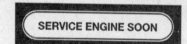

1984 and later

Code	Probable cause
11	Crank angle sensor/circuit (1988 to 1990); Camshaft position sensor (1991 to 1996)
12	Air flow meter/circuit open or shorted
13	Cylinder head temperature sensor (Maxima and 300ZX models); coolant temperature sensor circuit (all other models)
14	Vehicle speed sensor signal circuit is open (1988 on)
15	Mixture ratio is too lean despite feedback control; fuel injector clogged (1988)
21	Ignition signal in the primary circuit is not being entered to the ECU during cranking or running
22	Fuel pump circuit (Maxima and 1987 and later 300ZX models); idle speed control valve or circuit (all other models)
23	Idle switch (throttle valve switch) signal circuit is open
24	Park/Neutral switch malfunctioning (1984 through 1987)

Code	Probable cause
24	Fuel switch circuit or overdrive switch circuit
25	Idle speed control valve circuit is open or shorted
25	Auxiliary air control (AAC) valve circuit (1988 through 1991)
26	Turbo boost
28	Cooling fan
29	Fuel system rich
31	1984 through 1986 EFI models: Problem in air conditioning system; all other models: ECU control unit problem
32 (California)	1984 through 1986 EFI models: check starter system. All other models: EGR function
33	Oxygen sensor or circuit (300ZX left side) - all other models: EGR function
34	Detonation (knock) sensor
35 (California)	Exhaust gas temperature sensor
36	EGR transducer
37	Closed loop control/front oxygen sensor (Maxima)
41	Maxima and 1984 through 1987 300ZX models: fuel temp sensor circuit. All other models: air temperature sensor circuit
42	1988 and later 300ZX models: fuel temperature sensor circuit; all other models: throttle sensor circuit open or shorted
43 (1987 Sentra only)	The mixture ratio is too lean despite feedback control; fuel injector is clogged
43 (all others)	Throttle position sensor circuit is open or shorted
44	No trouble codes stored in ECU
45 (California)	Injector fuel leak
51 (California)	Fuel injector circuit open
53	Oxygen sensor (300ZX right side)
54	Short between automatic transmission control unit and ECU
55	Normal engine management system operation is indicated
63	Misfire detected - cylinder no. 6
64	Misfire detected - cylinder no. 5
65	Misfire detected - cylinder no. 4
66	Misfire detected - cylinder no. 3
67	Misfire detected - cylinder no. 2
68	Misfire detected - cylinder no. 1
71	Misfire detected (random)

Nissan/Datsun (continued)

Code	Probable cause
72	Catalytic converter malfunction (right side)
74	EVAP pressure sensor
75	EVAP leak
76	Fuel injection system
77	Rear oxygen sensor
81	Vacuum cut bypass valve
82	Crankshaft sensor
84	Automatic trans-to-fuel injection communication
85	VTC solenoid
87	EVAP canister purge control
91	Front oxygen sensor
95	Crankshaft sensor
98	Coolant temperature sensor
101	Camshaft sensor
103	Park/neutral switch
105	EGR and canister control valve
108	EVAP volume control

Porsche

  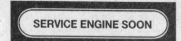

911 Carrera 4, 1989 928CS, 1989 through 1992 928GT, 1987 through 1992 928S4, 1987 through 1991 944S and 1986 through 1990 944 Turbo models

Code	System affected	Probable cause
1000		End of output
1111	ECM power supply	System voltage out of range (less than 10 volts)
1112 (2)	Throttle position (TP) switch	Idle switch contact grounded
1113	Throttle position (TP) switch	Full-load switch contact grounded
1114 (2)	Engine temperature sensor circuit	Open circuit

Code	System affected	Probable cause
1121 (2)	Mass airflow (MAF) sensor signal	Signal not plausible (3)
1122 (2)	Idle control circuit	Signal not plausible (3)
1123 (2)	Oxygen sensor	Air/fuel mixture too rich (928)
1123 (2)	Oxygen sensor	Signal out of range - control circuit fault (944S and 944 Turbo)
1124 (2)	Oxygen sensor	Air/fuel mixture too lean (928)
1124 (2)	Oxygen sensor	Control circuit fault (944S and 944 Turbo)
1125	Oxygen sensor	Open or short circuit or faulty sensor (928)
1125	Intake air temperature sensor	Open or short circuit (911 Carrera 4, 944S and 944 Turbo)
1131	Knock sensor no. 1	Signal not present (3) (944S and 944 Turbo)
1132	Knock sensor no. 2	Signal not present (3) (944S and 944 Turbo)
1133	Knock control regulation circuit	Knock computer faulty (944S and 944 Turbo)
1134	Camshaft position sensor	Open or short circuit (944S)
1134	Engine speed (rpm) sensor	Open or short circuit (944 Turbo)
1141 (2)	ECM	Faulty unit (944S and 944 Turbo)
1142	Fuel pump relay circuit	Open or short circuit (944S and 944 Turbo)
1143	Fuel tank vent solenoid	Open or short circuit (944S and 944 Turbo)
1145	MIL lamp	Open circuit
1151 (2)	Fuel injector no. 1	Open or short circuit (911 Carrera 4)
1152 (2)	Fuel injector no. 2	Open or short circuit (911 Carrera 4)
1153 (2)	Fuel injector no. 3	Open or short circuit (911 Carrera 4)
1154 (2)	Fuel injector no. 4	Open or short circuit (911 Carrera 4)
1155 (2)	Fuel injector no. 5	Open or short circuit (911 Carrera 4)
1156 (2)	Fuel injector no. 6	Open or short circuit (911 Carrera 4)
1311	Injectors	Open or short circuit (944 Turbo)
1321	Idle speed control	Open or short circuit (944 Turbo)
1322	EVAP canister purge (EVAP) valve	Open or short circuit (944 Turbo)
1334	A/C signal to ECM terminal 41	Open or short circuit (944 Turbo)
1335	A/C signal to ECM terminal 40	Open or short circuit (944 Turbo)
1500 (2)	System operating correctly	No fault codes stored in memory

The Haynes Emissions Control Manual

Porsche (continued)

1992 through 1995 968, 1995 911 Carrera, 911 with Tiptronic transmission

Code	Fault
11	ECM supply voltage (all models)
13	Supply voltage (911 with Tiptronic)
14	Engine coolant temperature (ECT) sensor (968, 1995 911 Carrera)
14	Supply voltage
15	Throttle potentiometer (1995 911 Carrera)
16	Throttle position (TP) sensor (968)
18	RPM signal (968 and 1995 911 Carrera)
19	Vehicle speed sensor (VSS) (968 and 1995 911 Carrera)
21	Mass air flow (MAF) sensor (968 and 1995 911 Carrera)
21	RPM signal (911 with Tiptronic)
22	Oxygen sensor signal (1995 911 Carrera)
22	Load signal (911 with Tiptronic)
23	Oxygen regulation/oxygen sensor (968 and 1995 911 Carrera)
24	Heated oxygen sensor (HO2S) (968 and 1995 911 Carrera)
24	Change of ignition timing (911 with Tiptronic)
25	Intake temperature sensor (1995 911 Carrera)
25	Throttle potentiometer (911 with Tiptronic)
26	Ignition timing change (968 and 1995 911 Carrera)
27	Idle air control (IAC) valve (968)
27	Opening winding of idle stabilizer (1995 911 Carrera)
28	Idle air control (IAC) valve (968)
28	Closing winding of idle stabilizer (1995 911 Carrera)
31	Knock sensor (KS) 1 (968 and 1995 911 Carrera)
31	Solenoid valve 1 (911 with Tiptronic)
32	Knock sensor (KS) 2 (968 and 1995 911 Carrera)
32	Solenoid valve 2 (911 with Tiptronic)
33	Engine control module (ECM) (968 and 1995 911 Carrera)
33	Torque converter clutch solenoid valve (911 with Tiptronic)
34	Hall signal (968 and 1995 911 Carrera)
34	Pressure regulator (911 with Tiptronic)
35	Camshaft position (968)
35	Selector lever switch (911 with Tiptronic)
36	Idle CO potentiometer (968 and 1995 911 Carrera)
36	Transmission speed sensor (911 with Tiptronic)
41	Engine control module (ECM) (968 and 1995 911 Carrera)
42	Fuel pump relay (968 and 1995 911 Carrera)
42	Control unit faulty (911 with Tiptronic)
43	Evaporative emission canister purge (EVAP) valve (968)
43	Tank ventilation relay (1995 911 Carrera)
43	Control unit faulty (911 with Tiptronic)
44	Air pump (1995 911 Carrera)
44	Control unit faulty (911 with Tiptronic)
45	Check Engine warning lamp (1995 911 Carrera)
45	Downshift protection (911 with Tiptronic)
46	Rev limiter (911 with Tiptronic)
51	Injector valve, cylinder no. 1 (968 and 1995 911 Carrera)
51	Manual program switch (911 with Tiptronic)
52	Injector valve, cylinder no. 2 (968)
52	Injector valve, cylinder no. 6 (1995 911 Carrera)
52	Up/down shift tip switch (911 with Tiptronic)
53	Injector valve, cylinder no. 3 (968)
53	Injector valve, cylinder no. 2 (1995 911 Carrera)
53	Kickdown switch (911 with Tiptronic)
54	Injector valve no. 4 (968 and 1995 911 Carrera)

Code	Fault
54	Transverse acceleration sensor (911 with Tiptronic)
55	Injector valve, cylinder no. 3 (1995 911 Carrera)
55	Speed signal 1 (ABS) (911 with Tiptronic)
56	Injector valve, cylinder no. 5 (1995 911 Carrera)
56	Combi-instrument input (911 with Tiptronic)
59	R-position switch (911 with Tiptronic)
60	Reverse light relay (911 with Tiptronic)
67	Ground and plug connections
69	Ground and plug connections

(1) *Except for codes 1000 and 1500, the second digit of all other codes can be a 2, indicating that the fault didn't exist during the last vehicle operation*

(2) *On 1991 and later models, these codes can also be displayed by* **check engine light**. *Other flashing codes are also possible but do not represent a warning regarding the check engine light*

(3) *Signal of a monitored component is not conforming with memory contents of DME control unit. The control unit recognizes that there is a faulty signal, but cannot always recognize the cause of the faulty signal*

  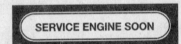 CHECK ENGINE LIGHT

Code	System affected	Probable cause
00000		No more fault codes or fault codes not detected
12111	Oxygen sensor adaptation fault	Air/fuel mixture during idling
12112	Oxygen sensor adaptation fault	Air/fuel mixture with engine running
12113	Idle air control (IAC) adaptation fault	Pulse ratio too low
12114	Idle air control (IAC) adaptation fault	Pulse ratio too high
12211	Incorrect battery voltage	Below 10 volts or above 16 volts
12212	Throttle position sensor	Faulty idle contacts (grounded when throttle is open)
12213	Throttle position sensor	Faulty full-throttle contacts (signal below 90 or above 160 degrees F)
12214	Coolant temperature sensor	Faulty signal (below -90 degrees or above 160 degree C)
12221	Mass Air Flow (MAF) sensor	Signal missing
12222	Idle Air Control (IAC) valve	Incorrect idle adjustment
12223	Air/fuel mixture	Too lean
12224	Air/fuel mixture	Too rich
12225	Heated oxygen sensor	Faulty sensor or preheater
12231	No ignition signal (engine switched off)	
12232	ECM	Memory voltage greater than one volt

Saab (continued)

Code	System affected	Probable cause
12233	EPROM	Incorrect EPROM (or ROM in 1992 and later models)
12241	Fuel injector	Injector malfunction (1992 and later models)
12242	Mass Air Flow (MAF) sensor	No filament burn-off (1992 and later models)
12243	Vehicle Speed Sensor (VSS)	Signal missing
12244	Transmission	No DRIVE signal to ECM (1992 and later automatics)
12245	Exhaust Gas Recirculation (EGR)	Faulty EGR operation
12251	Throttle Position (TP) sensor	Faulty sensor operation (1992 and later models)
12252	EVAP canister purge valve	Faulty valve operation (1992 and later models)
12253	Pre-ignition signal	Stays on more than 20 seconds (1992 and later models)
12254	Engine rpm signal	Signal missing (1992 and later models)

Saturn

  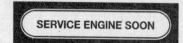

Code	Circuit or system	Probable cause
Code 11	Transaxle codes present	This indicates that there are trouble codes for the transaxle unit stored in the PCM. Read the codes after the engine code sequence on the SHIFT TO D2 light (1991 and 1992 models) or HOT light (1993 and later models).
Code 12	Diagnostic check only	Indicates the system is ready (ALDL grounded) and ready to flash the engine codes.
Code 13	Oxygen sensor circuit	Possible oxygen sensor ground loose; check the wiring and connectors from the oxygen sensor; replace the oxygen sensor.*
Code 14	Coolant sensor/high temperature	If the engine is experiencing cooling system problems, the problem must be rectified before continuing; check all the wiring and the connectors associated with the coolant temperature sensor; replace if necessary*.
Code 15	Coolant sensor/low temperature	See above, then check the wiring harness connector at the PCM for damage.
Code 17	PCM fault - Pull-up resistor	Faulty PCM resistor in PCM; replace PCM.
Code 19	6X signal fault (1992 to 1995 models)	PCM and/or ignition module may be defective; check all connections and grounds.

Code	Circuit or system	Probable cause
Code 21	Throttle position sensor voltage high	Check for a sticking or misadjusted TPS plunger; check all the wiring and connections between the TPS and the PCM; adjust or replace the TPS.*
Code 22	Throttle position sensor voltage low	Check the TPS adjustment; check the PCM connector; replace the TPS.*
Code 23	IAT circuit low	Intake air temperature sensor and/or circuit may be faulty; check sensor and replace if necessary.
Code 24	VSS circuit - no signal	A fault in this circuit should be indicated only when the vehicle is in motion. Disregard code 24 if it is set while the drive wheels are not turning (test situation) - check TPS and PCM.
Code 25	IAT circuit - temperature out of high range	Temperature range excessive causing a misreading by the PCM check IAT sensor.
Code 26 or code 27	Quad driver output fault	The PCM detects an improper voltage level on the circuit that is connected to the Quad Driver Module.
Code 32	EGR system fault	Vacuum switch shorted to ground on start-up, switch not closed after the PCM has commanded the EGR for a specified period of time or the EGR solenoid circuit is open for a specified amount of time; replace the EGR valve.*
Code 33	MAP circuit - voltage out of range high	Check the vacuum hoses from the MAP sensor - check the electrical connections at the PCM; replace the MAP sensor.
Code 34	MAP circuit - voltage out of range low	Signal voltage from MAP sensor too low - check MAP sensor circuit also TPS circuit.
Code 35	Idle air control (IAC) - rpm out of range	IAC motor possibly defective; idle control is high or low, possible PCM problem have the system diagnosed by a dealer service department.
Code 41	Ignition control circuit open or shorted	Possible defective ignition module. Also check circuit to PCM from ignition module.
Code 42	Bypass circuit - open or shorted	Bypass circuit from ignition module to PCM possibly open or shorted.
Codes 41 and 42	IC control circuit grounded/bypass open	Bypass circuit and/or ignition control circuit shorted causing no feedback pulses for the ignition cycle.
Code 43	Knock sensor circuit - open or shorted	Possible loose or defective knock sensor, also check knock sensor circuit.
Code 44	Oxygen sensor indicates lean exhaust	Check for vacuum leaks near the throttle body gasket, vacuum hoses or the intake manifold gasket. Also check for loose connections on PCM, oxygen sensor etc. Replace oxygen sensor if necessary.*
Code 45	Oxygen sensor indicates rich exhaust	Possibly rich or leaking injector, high fuel pressure or faulty TPS or MAP sensor; also, check the charcoal canister and its components for the presence of fuel; replace the oxygen sensor if necessary.*
Code 46	Power steering pressure circuit (1991 models only)	Possible defective power steering pressure switch, also check - open or shorted the circuit to the switch.

Saturn (continued)

Code	Circuit or system	Probable cause
Code 49	High idle indicates vacuum leak	Check all hoses to MAP sensor, PCV valve, brake booster, fuel pressure regulator, throttle body, intake manifold gasket and any other vacuum line.
Code 51	PCM memory error	Possible defective EEPROM, RAM or EPROM - have the vehicle diagnosed by a dealer service department or other qualified repair shop.
Code 53	System voltage error	Check charge voltage. If OK, have vehicle diagnosed by a dealer service department or other repair shop.
Code 55	A/D error	Defective PCM - have the vehicle diagnosed by a dealer service department or other qualified repair shop.
Code 58	Transmission fluid temperature too high	Sensor or signal wire grounded, radiator restricted
Code 59	Transmission fluid temperature too low	Sensor or signal wire open
Code 66 Or 67	A/C pressure sensor	Have the vehicle diagnosed by a dealer service department or other qualified repair shop
Code 81	ABS message fault	Defective ABS controller - have the vehicle diagnosed by a dealer service department or other qualified repair shop.
Code 82	PCM internal communication fault	Defective PCM - have the vehicle diagnosed by a dealer service department or other qualified repair shop.
Code 83	Low engine coolant	

Component replacement may not cure the problem in all cases. For this reason, you may want to seek professional advice before purchasing replacement parts.

Subaru

  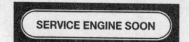

1983 carbureted models

Code	Probable cause
11, 12, 21, 22	Ignition pulse system
14, 24, 41, 42	Vacuum switches stay on or off
15, 51, 52	Solenoid valve stays on or off
23	Oxygen sensor or circuit
32	Coolant temperature sensor or circuit
33	Main system in feedback
34, 43	Choke power stays on or off
42	Clutch switch or circuit

1984 through 1988 carbureted models

Code	Probable cause
11	Ignition pulse system
22	Vehicle Speed Sensor (VSS) or circuit
23	Oxygen sensor or circuit
24	Coolant temperature sensor or circuit
25	Manifold vacuum sensor or circuit (coolant temperature sensor or circuit on 1984 models)
32	Duty solenoid valve or circuit

Code	Probable cause
33	Main system in feedback
34	Back up system
42	Clutch switch or circuit
52	Solenoid valve control system
53	Fuel pump or circuit
54	Choke control system
55	Upshift control
62	Exhaust Gas Recirculation (EGR) solenoid valve control
63	Canister solenoid valve or circuit
64	Vacuum line control valve or circuit
65	Float chamber vent control valve or circuit
71, 73, 74	Ignition pulse system

1983 through 1985 carbureted models

Code	Probable cause
14	Duty solenoid or circuit (fuel control)
15	Coasting Fuel Cut (CFC) system
16	Feedback system
17	Fuel pump and automatic choke
21	Coolant temperature sensor or circuit
22	VLC solenoid valve or circuit
23	Pressure sensor or circuit
24	Idle-up solenoid valve or circuit
25	Float chamber vent solenoid valve or circuit
32	Oxygen sensor or circuit
33	Vehicle speed sensor or circuit
34	EGR solenoid or circuit
35	Canister purge control solenoid or circuit
41	Feedback system (California models)

Code	Probable cause
46	Radiator fan control
52	Clutch switch
53	Altitude compensator switch
55	EGR sensor
56	EGR system
62	Idle-up system (lighting and defogger switch)
63	Idle-up system (fan motor switch)

1984 through 1986 fuel-injected models

Code	Probable cause
11	Ignition pulse
12	Starter switch off
13	Starter switch on
14	Airflow meter or circuit
15	Atmospheric pressure switch - fixed value
16	Crank angle sensor or circuit
17	Starter switch or circuit
21	Seized air flow meter flap
22	Pressure or vacuum switches - fixed value
23	Idle switch - fixed value
24	Wide open throttle switch - fixed value
25	Throttle sensor idle switch or circuit
31	Speed sensor or circuit
32	Oxygen sensor or circuit
33	Coolant sensor or circuit
34	Abnormal aspirated air thermosensor (in airflow meter)
35	Air flow meter or EGR solenoid switch or circuit
41	Atmosphere pressure sensor or circuit
42	Fuel injector - fixed value
43, 55	KDLH control system

The Haynes Emissions Control Manual

1984 through 1986
fuel-injected models (continued)

Code	Probable cause
46	Neutral or parking switch or circuit
47	Fuel injector
53	Fuel pump or circuit
57	Canister control system
58	Air control system
62	EGR control system
88	TBI control unit

1987 fuel-injected models

Code	Probable cause
11	Ignition pulse/crank angle sensor
12	Starter switch or circuit
13	Crank angle sensor or circuit
14	Injectors 1 and 2
15	Injectors 3 and 4
21	Coolant temperature sensor or circuit
22	Knock sensor or circuit
23	Air flow meter or circuit
24	Air control
31	Throttle sensor or circuit
32	Oxygen sensor or circuit
33	Vehicle Speed Sensor (VSS) or circuit
34	EGR solenoid valve stuck on or off
35	Purge control solenoid or circuit
41	Lean fuel mixture indicated
42	Idle switch or circuit
45	Kick-down relay or circuit
51	Neutral switch or circuit
61	Parking switch or circuit

1988 and later models with Single-Point Fuel Injection

Code	Probable cause
11	Crank angle sensor or circuit
12	Starter switch or circuit
13	Crank angle sensor or circuit
14	Fuel injector - abnormal output
21	Coolant temperature sensor or circuit
23	Air flow meter or circuit
24	Air control valve or circuit
31	Throttle sensor or circuit
32	Oxygen sensor or circuit
33	Vehicle Speed Sensor (VSS) or circuit
34	EGR solenoid or circuit
35	Purge control solenoid or circuit
42	Idle switch or circuit
45	Kick-down control relay or circuit
51	Neutral switch continuously in the on position
55	EGR temperature sensor or circuit
61	Parking switch or circuit

1988 and later models with Multi-Point Fuel Injection

Code	Probable cause
11	Crank angle sensor or circuit
12	Starter switch or circuit
13	Cam position sensor or circuit (TDC sensor on Justy)
14	Fuel injector no. 1 (Legacy, Impreza, Justy, SVX)
14	Fuel injector nos. 1 and 2 (XT, Loyale, GL, DL)
15	Fuel injector no. 2 (Legacy, Impreza, Justy, SVX)
15	Fuel injector nos. 3 and 4 (Loyale, GL, DL)
15	Fuel injector nos. 5 and 6 (XT6)

Code	Probable cause	Code	Probable cause
16	Fuel injector no. 3 (Legacy, Impreza, Justy, SVX)	36	Igniter circuit (Justy)
16	Fuel injector nos. 3 and 4 (XT)	37	Oxygen sensor (no. 2, left side, SVX)
17	Fuel injector no. 4 (Legacy, Impreza, SVX)	38	Engine torque control (SVX)
17	Fuel injector nos. 1 and 2 (XT6)	41	Air/fuel adaptive control
18	Fuel injector no. 5 (SVX)	42	Idle switch or circuit
19	Fuel injector no. 6 (SVX)	43	Throttle switch (Justy)
21	Coolant temperature sensor or circuit	44	Wastegate duty solenoid (turbo)
22	Knock sensor or circuit (right side on SVX)	45	Pressure sensor duty solenoid (turbo)
23	Airflow meter or circuit (exc. Justy)	45	Atmospheric pressure sensor or circuit (non-turbo)
23	Pressure sensor (Justy)	49	Airflow sensor
24	Air control valve or circuit (exc. Justy)	51	Neutral switch (MT); inhibitor switch (AT)
24	Idle Speed Control solenoid valve (Justy)	52	Parking brake switch (exc. Justy)
25	Fuel injector nos. 3 and 4 (XT6)	52	Clutch switch (Justy)
26	Air temperature sensor (Justy)	55	EGR temperature sensor
28	Knock sensor no. 2 (SVX, left side)	56	EGR system
29	Crank angle sensor (SVX, no. 2)	61	Parking brake switch (Loyale)
31	Throttle position sensor or circuit	61	Fuel tank pressure control solenoid valve (Impreza)
32	Oxygen sensor or circuit (no. 1, right side, on SVX)	62	Fuel temperature sensor (Impreza)
33	Vehicle Speed Sensor (VSS) or circuit	62	Electric load signal (Justy)
34	EGR solenoid valve	63	Fuel tank pressure sensor (Impreza)
35	Canister purge solenoid or circuit	63	Blower fan switch (Justy)
36	Air suction solenoid valve (Impreza)	65	Vacuum pressure sensor

Toyota

Camry (1983 through 1986 models), Corolla (1987 models), Pick-ups and 4-Runner (1984 through 1987 models)

Code	Probable cause		Probable cause
		3	Air Flow Meter Signal (1984 Trucks, 1983 through 1985 Camry)
1	Normal	3	No ignition signal from igniter
2	Air Flow Meter Signal	4	Coolant temperature sensor or circuit

Toyota (continued)

Code	Probable cause	Code	Probable cause
5	Oxygen sensor or circuit	11	Switch signal - air conditioning, TPS or Neutral start
6	No ignition signal (1984 trucks, 1983 through 1985 Camry)	11	ECU main relay (Cressida, Supra, Celica 3S-GE)
6	RPM signal (no signal to ECU)	12	Knock sensor or circuit (distributor or circuit on Cressida, Supra, Celica 3S-GE)
7	Throttle Position Sensor (TPS) or circuit	13	Knock sensor/CPU (ECU) faulty
8	Intake Air Temperature sensor or circuit	14	Turbocharger pressure (22R-TE/Turbo 22R models) - over-boost (abnormalities in air flow meter may also be detected)
9	Vehicle Speed Sensor (VSS) or circuit		
10	Starter signal	14	Ignitor (Cressida, Supra, Celica 3S-GE)

Camry (1987 through 1990 models), all other models (1988 through 1990)

Code	Probable cause
11	Momentary interruption in power supply to ECU
12	RPM signal/no NE or G Signal to ECU within several seconds after engine is cranked
13	RPM Signal/no signal to ECU when engine speed is above 1500 RPM
14	No ignition signal to ECU
21	Oxygen sensor circuit or oxygen sensor heater circuit failure
22	Coolant temperature sensor circuit
23/24	Intake air temperature circuit
25	Air fuel ratio - lean condition indicated
26	Air fuel ratio - rich condition indicated
27	Oxygen sensor circuit (open or shorted)
31	Air flow meter or circuit
31	1989 and 1990 Corolla - vacuum sensor signal
32	Air flow meter or circuit
41	Throttle position sensor or circuit
42	Vehicle Speed Sensor (VSS) or circuit
43	Starter signal/no start signal to ECU
51	Switch signal/Neutral start switch off or air conditioning on during diagnostic check
51	Switch signal - no IDL signal, NSW or air conditioning signal to ECU (1988 through 1990 Corolla, 1988-1/2 through 1990 Camry models)

Code	Probable cause
52	Knock sensor circuit
53	Knock sensor signal/faulty ECU
71	Exhaust Gas Recirculation (EGR) system malfunction

All models (1991 on)

Code	Circuit or system	Diagnosis	Probable cause
Code 1	Normal	This appears when none of the other codes are identified.	
Code 11	ECM	Interruption of power supply to ECM	
Code 12	RPM signal	No "Ne" signal to the ECM within several seconds after the engine is cranked. No "G" signal to the ECM two times in succession when engine speed is between 500 rpm and 4000 rpm.	Distributor circuit Distributor Igniter Igniter circuit Starter circuit ECM
Code 13	RPM signal	No "Ne" signal to the ECM engine speed is above 1500 rpm.	Distributor circuit Distributor Igniter Igniter circuit ECM
Code 14	Ignition signal	No "IGN" signal to the ECM 8 times in succession.	Igniter Igniter circuit ECM
Code 16	Transmission ECM	Fault in ECM signal.	Transmission ECM ECM
Code 21	Main oxygen sensor and heater	Problem in the main oxygen sensor circuit. Open or Short in the main oxygen heater circuit	Main oxygen sensor circuit ECM Main oxygen sensor heater sensor
Code 22	Coolant temperature sensor	Open or short in the coolant sensor circuit	Coolant temperature sensor circuit Coolant temperature sensor ECM
Code 23 or Code 24	Intake air temperature sensor	Open or short in the intake air sensor circuit.	Intake air temperature sensor Intake air temperature sensor circuit
Code 25	Air/fuel ratio lean malfunction	The air/fuel ratio feedback correction value or adaptive control value continues at the upper (lean) or lower (rich) limit for a certain period of time.	Injector circuit Oxygen sensor or circuit ECM Oxygen sensor Fuel line pressure (injector blockage or leakage) Air temperature sensor or circuit Air leak Air flow meter Air intake system Ignition system

Toyota (continued)

All models (1991 on) (continued)

Code	Circuit or system	Diagnosis	Probable cause
Code 26	Air/fuel ratio rich malfunction	The air/fuel ratio is overly rich. Open or short circuit in the oxygen sensor.	Injector or Injector circuit Coolant temperature sensor or circuit Air temperature sensor or circuit Airflow meter Oxygen sensor or circuit Cold start injector ECM
Code 27	Sub-oxygen sensor	Open or shorted circuit in the sub-oxygen sensor circuit.	Sub-oxygen sensor circuit ECM
Code 28	No. 2 Oxygen sensor signal or heater signal	Open or short in Oxygen sensor circuit or in sensor heater circuit	Oxygen sensor Oxygen signal or heater Sensor heater circuit
Code 31	Airflow meter	Open or short circuit in Vc to E2.	Airflow meter circuit
Code 31	MAP sensor, vacuum sensor signal	Open or short circuit in Vc to E2.	MAP sensor-to-ECM circuit
Code 31	Volume Air Flow (VAF) sensor or circuit (1995)	No VAF signal for 2 seconds after starting	VAF sensor or circuit
Code 32	Airflow meter	Open or short circuit in Vs to Vc or E2.	Airflow meter circuit/ECM
Code 34/35	Turbocharger	Pressure abnormal	Open or short circuit in turbocharger pressure or BARO sensor(s)
Code 35	High altitude compensation (HAC) sensor	Incorrect signal	Open or short in HAC sensor circuit
Code 36	Turbocharger (1992 through 1994)	Pressure sensor signal circuit	Open or short for at least 0.5 seconds in turbocharging pressure sensor
Code 41	Throttle position sensor	Open or short in the throttle position sensor circuit.	Throttle position sensor or circuit ECM
Code 42	Vehicle speed sensor	No "SPD" signal for 8 seconds when the engine speed is above 2000 rpm.	Vehicle speed sensor or circuit sensorECM
Code 43	Starter signal	No "STA" signal to the ECM until engine speed reaches 800 rpm with the vehicle not moving.	Starter signal circuit Ignition switch Main relay switch ECM
Code 47	TPS signal	Sub-throttle position sensor	Open or short circuit in sub-throttle position sensor

Code	Circuit or system	Diagnosis	Probable cause
Code 51	Switch condition signal	No IDL signal or no NSW signal or A/C signal to the ECM when the test connector E1 and TE1 are connected.	A/C switch or circuit A/C amplifier Neutral start switch (A/T) Throttle position sensor Throttle position sensor circuit
Code 52	Knock sensor signal	Open or short circuit in knock sensor circuit.	Knock sensor ECM
Code 53	Knock control signal	Problem with knock control system in ECM.	ECM
Code 55	Knock control signal	Open or short circuit in knock sensor circuit	Knock sensor ECM
Code 71	EGR	EGR gas temperature signal is too low.	EGR system (EGR valve, hoses, etc.) EGR gas temperature sensor or circuit . Vacuum switching valve for the EGR circuit ECM
Code 72	Fuel cut solenoid or circuit	Circuit open	Faulty solenoid or circuit
Code 78	Fuel pump	Open or short circuit in fuel pump control circuit.	Fuel pump electronic control unit (ECM) Fuel pump control circuit
Code 81	Transmission to ECM	Open in ECT1 circuit for at least 2-seconds.	ECM Transmission control module (TCM)
Code 83	Transmission to ECM	Open in ESA1 circuit for 1/2-second after the engine idles at least 1/2-second.	ECM Transmission control module (TCM)
Code 84	Transmission to ECM	Open in ESA1 circuit for 1/2-second after the engine idles at least 1/2-second.	ECM Transmission control module (TCM)
Code 85	Transmission to ECM	Open in ESA1 circuit for 1/2-second after the engine idles at least 1/2-second.	ECM Transmission control module (TCM)

Volkswagen

CHECK | MIL | SERVICE ENGINE SOON | CHECK | CHECK ENGINE LIGHT

Code	Location or description of fault	Probable cause
1111	Control unit	a) Defective control unit
1231	Speed sender	a) Open circuit b) Faulty sender
1232	Throttle actuator solenoid	a) Open or short circuit b) Faulty solenoid

The Haynes Emissions Control Manual

Volkswagen (continued)

Code	Location or description of fault	Probable cause
2111	Engine speed sensor	a) Open circuit b) Faulty sender
2112	Ignition reference sensor	a) Open circuit b) Faulty sensor
2113	Hall sender	a) No signal or faulty signal from Hall sender
2121	Idle switch	a) Open circuit or short to ground b) Switch faulty or misadjusted
2123	Full throttle switch	a) Open circuit b) Faulty switch
2141	Knock sensor	a) Engine knock b) Fuel of incorrect octane c) Incorrect ignition timing d) Damaged shield on knock sensor wiring
2142	Knock sensor	a) Open or short circuit in knock sensor wiring b) Faulty knock sensor c) Faulty control unit
2142 (Eurovan)	Transmission control module	a) Open circuit to control module b) Faulty module
2144	Knock sensor II	a) Open or short circuit in knock sensor wiring b) Faulty knock sensor c) Faulty control unit
2212	Throttle Position Sensor	a) Open or short circuit to ground or battery voltage b) Faulty sensor
2214	Maximum rpm exceeded	a) Engine rpm exceeded fuel injection cut-off point b) Interference on signal wire
2222 (Eurovan)	Manifold Absolute Pressure	a) No vacuum to ECM (check the hose) b) Faulty ECM
2231	Idle speed stabilizer system has exceeded adaptive range	a) Throttle valve basic adjustment incorrect b) Incorrect ignition timing c) Evaporative emission control system faulty d) Intake air leaks
2232	Air flow sensor Potentiometer	a) Open circuit or short to ground b) Potentiometer faulty
2234	System voltage out of range	a) Check battery b) Check charging system
2242	Throttle valve potentiometer	a) Open or short circuit b) Faulty potentiometer
2243	Fuel consumption signal	a) Short circuit to battery voltage in instrument panel
2312	Coolant temperature sensor	a) Faulty sensor b) Open circuit or short to ground

Chapter 6   Computer trouble codes

Code	Location or description of fault	Probable cause
2314	Transmission control signal	a) Short to ground in transmission control module circuit
2214	Full consumption signal	
2322	Intake air	a) Sensor faulty
2323	Airflow sensor signal is missing	a) Open circuit b) Faulty sensor
2324	Mass Airflow Sensor	a) Open or short circuit b) Faulty sensor
2341	Oxygen sensor control range exceeded	a) Idle mixture (%CO) incorrectly adjusted b) Faulty oxygen sensor wiring c) Leaking cold-start valve d) Evaporative emission control system faulty e) Intake air leaks
2342	Oxygen sensor system (faulty signal or exceeding adjustment range)	a) Open circuit b) Faulty oxygen sensor c) Incorrect idle speed d) Intake air leaks (leaking
2411	Exhaust Gas Recirculation (EGR) system (California cars only)	a) Intake air temperature sensor faulty b) Open circuit or short circuit to ground c) EGR system faulty or plugged
2412	Intake air temperature sensor	a) Open or short circuit b) Faulty sensor
2413	Fuel mixture out of limit	a) Fuel pressure too low or high b) Fuel injector(s) faulty c) Leak in intake or exhaust system d) Faulty EGR frequency valve
3434	Heated oxygen sensor relay	a) Open or short circuit b) Faulty relay
4312	EGR frequency valve	a) Open or short circuit b) Faulty valve
4332	ECM	a) Connectors at ECM loose b) Faulty ECM
4343	EVAP frequency valve	a) Open or short circuit b) Faulty valve
4411 (exc. Eurovan)	Injector no. 1	a) Open or short circuit b) Faulty injector
4411 (Eurovan)	Injector driver circuit	a) Open or short circuit b) Faulty injector
4412	Injector no. 2	a) Open or short circuit b) Faulty injector
4413	Injector no. 3	a) Open or short circuit b) Faulty injector
4414	Injector no. 4	a) Open or short circuit b) Faulty injector

The Haynes Emissions Control Manual

Volkswagen (continued)

Code	Location or description of fault	Probable cause
4421 (VR6)	Injector no. 5	a) Open or short circuit b) Faulty injector
4422 (VR6)	Injector no. 6	a) Open or short circuit b) Faulty injector
4431	Idle air control valve	a) Open circuit or short circuit to ground b) Control unit faulty c) Faulty IAC valve
4433	Fuel pump relay	a) Open or short circuit b) Faulty relay
4444	No faults stored in memory	
0000	End of code output sequence	

Volvo

  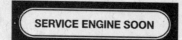

Code	Probable cause
1-1-1	No Faults
1-1-2	ECU fault
1-1-3	Fuel Injectors
1-1-3 (1994 on)	Heated oxygen sensor at maximum enrichment unit
1-1-5	Injector no. 1 – open or short circuit
1-2-1	Mass airflow signal missing or faulty (MAF) or air pressure sensor
1-2-2	Air temperature sensor signal missing or faulty
1-2-3	Coolant temperature sensor signal faulty or missing
1-2-5	Injector no. 2 open or short circuit
1-3-1	Ignition system RPM signal open or short circuit
1-3-2	Battery voltage out of range
1-3-3	Throttle switch signal (incorrect idle setting)
1-3-5	Injector no. 3 open or short circuit
1-4-2	ECU faulty
1-4-3	Knock sensor signal missing or sensor defective
1-4-4	Fuel system load signal (missing or defective)
1-4-5	Injector no. 4 open or short circuit

Code	Probable cause
1-5-3	Rear heated oxygen sensor signal open or short circuit
1-5-4	EGR system - leakage or excessive flow
1-5-5	Injector no. 5 open or short circuit
2-1-2	Oxygen Sensor Signal (front sensor on 1994 and later models) faulty or missing
2-1-3	Throttle switch signal (incorrect wide open setting)
2-1-4	Ignition rpm signal erratic
2-2-1	Lambda (oxygen sensor) running rich at part throttle
2-2-1	Heated oxygen sensor running rich at part throttle
2-2-2	Main relay signal missing or faulty
2-2-3	Idle valve signal missing or faulty
2-2-4	Coolant temperature sensor signal missing or faulty
2-2-5	A/C pressure sensor signal 3 sensor or circuit faulty
2-3-1	Lambda adjustment
2-3-1 (1994 on)	Heated oxygen sensor (mixture too lean under part throttle)
2-3-2	Lambda adjustment
2-3-2 (1994 on)	Adaptive heated oxygen sensor control lean or rich
2-3-3	Idle valve - closed, or intake air leak
2-3-4	Throttle switch signal missing
2-4-1	EGR malfunction
2-4-5	Idle Air Control valve - closing signal
3-1-1	Speedometer Signal
3-1-2	Knock/Fuel Enrichment signal missing
3-1-4	Camshaft position signal missing or defective
3-1-5	EVAP emission control system
3-2-1	Cold start valve - signal missing or circuit shorted
3-2-2	Airflow meter hot wire burn-off signal missing
3-2-4	Camshaft position signal erratic
3-2-5	ECU memory failure
3-3-5	TCM request for MIL (CHECK ENGINE light)
3-4-2	A/C blocking relay high current
4-1-1	Throttle switch signal faulty or missing
4-1-3	EGR temperature sensor signal incorrect or missing
4-1-4	Turbo boost regulation
4-1-6	Turbo boost reduction from TCM – faulty TCM circuit
4-2-1	Boost pressure sensor in control – faulty

Volvo (continued)

Code	Probable cause
4-2-3	Throttle position sensor signal faulty or missing
4-2-5	Temperature warning level no. 1
4-3-1	EGR temperature sensor faulty or missing
4-3-2	High temperature warning inside ECU
4-3-3	No rear knock sensor signal
4-3-5	Front heated oxygen sensor - slow response
4-3-6	Rear heated oxygen sensor compensation
4-4-3	Catalytic converter efficiency – faulty converter
4-4-4	Acceleration sensor signal – sensor or circuit faulty
4-5-1	Misfire, cylinder no. 1
4-5-2	Misfire, cylinder no. 2
4-5-3	Misfire, cylinder no. 3
4-5-4	Misfire, cylinder no. 4
4-5-5	Misfire, cylinder no. 5
5-1-1	Adaptive oxygen sensor control, provides leaner mixture at idle
5-1-2	Oxygen sensor at maximum lean running limit
5-1-3	High temperature warning inside ECU
5-1-4	Engine cooling fan - low speed signal faulty
5-2-1	Oxygen sensor preheating, front
5-2-2	Oxygen sensor preheating, rear
5-3-1	Power stage, group A – fuel injectors evap canister purge solenoid, circuit or ECU
5-3-2	Power stage; group B – fuel injectors, EVAP canister, purge solenoid circuit or ECU
5-3-3	Power stage; group C - fuel injectors, EVAP canister, purge solenoid circuit or ECU
5-3-4	Power stage; group D - fuel injectors, EVAP canister, purge solenoid circuit or ECU
5-3-5	TC wastegate control valve signal – open or short circuit
5-4-1	EVAP canister purge solenoid signal – faulty solenoid or open or circuit short
5-4-2	Misfire on more than one cylinder
5-4-3	Misfire on at least one cylinder
5-4-4	Misfire on more than one cylinder, catalytic converter damage
5-4-5	Misfire on at least one cylinder, catalytic converter damage
5-5-1	Misfire on cylinder no. 1, catalytic converter damage
5-5-2	Misfire on cylinder no. 2, catalytic converter damage
5-5-3	Misfire on cylinder no. 3, catalytic converter damage
5-5-4	Misfire on cylinder no. 4, catalytic converter damage
5-5-5	Misfire on cylinder no. 5, catalytic converter damage

OBD II Powertrain Diagnostic Trouble Codes

 CHECK   MIL   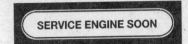 SERVICE ENGINE SOON   CHECK   CHECK ENGINE LIGHT

Note: *The following list of OBD II trouble codes is a generic list applicable to all models equipped with an OBD II system, although not all codes apply to all models.*

P0100	Mass air flow or volume air flow circuit malfunction
P0101	Mass air flow or volume air flow circuit, range or performance problem
P0102	Mass air flow or volume air flow circuit, low input
P0103	Mass air flow or volume air flow circuit, high input
P0104	Mass air flow or volume air flow circuit, intermittent
P0105	Manifold absolute pressure or barometric pressure circuit malfunction
P0106	Manifold absolute pressure or barometric pressure circuit, range or performance problem
P0107	Manifold absolute pressure or barometric pressure circuit, low input
P0108	Manifold absolute pressure or barometric pressure circuit, high input
P0109	Manifold absolute pressure or barometric pressure circuit, intermittent
P0110	Intake air temperature circuit malfunction
P0111	Intake air temperature circuit, range or performance problem
P0112	Intake air temperature circuit, low input
P0113	Intake air temperature circuit, high input
P0114	Intake air temperature circuit, intermittent
P0117	Engine coolant temperature circuit, low input
P0118	Engine coolant temperature circuit, high input
P0119	Engine coolant temperature circuit, intermittent
P0120	Throttle position or pedal position sensor/switch circuit malfunction
P0121	Throttle position or pedal position sensor/switch circuit, range or performance problem
P0122	Throttle position or pedal position sensor/switch circuit, low input
P0123	Throttle position or pedal position sensor/switch circuit, high input
P0124	Throttle position or pedal position sensor/switch circuit, intermittent
P0125	Insufficient coolant temperature for closed loop fuel control
P0126	Insufficient coolant temperature for stable operation
P0130	O2 sensor circuit malfunction (cylinder bank no. 1, sensor no. 1)
P0131	O2 sensor circuit, low voltage (cylinder bank no. 1, sensor no. 1)
P0132	O2 sensor circuit, high voltage (cylinder bank no. 1, sensor no. 1)
P0133	O2 sensor circuit, slow response (cylinder bank no. 1, sensor no. 1)
P0134	O2 sensor circuit - no activity detected (cylinder bank no. 1, sensor no. 1)
P0135	O2 sensor heater circuit malfunction (cylinder bank no. 1, sensor no. 1)
P0136	O2 sensor circuit malfunction (cylinder bank no. 1, sensor no. 2)

OBD II Powertrain Diagnostic Trouble Codes (continued)

P0137	O2 sensor circuit, low voltage (cylinder bank no. 1, sensor no. 2)
P0138	O2 sensor circuit, high voltage (cylinder bank no. 1, sensor no. 2)
P0139	O2 sensor circuit, slow response (cylinder bank no. 1, sensor no. 2)
P0140	O2 sensor circuit - no activity detected (cylinder bank no. 1, sensor no. 2)
P0141	O2 sensor heater circuit malfunction (cylinder bank no. 1, sensor no. 2)
P0142	O2 sensor circuit malfunction (cylinder bank no. 1, sensor no. 3)
P0143	O2 sensor circuit, low voltage (cylinder bank no. 1, sensor no. 3)
P0144	O2 sensor circuit, high voltage (cylinder bank no. 1, sensor no. 3)
P0145	O2 sensor circuit, slow response (cylinder bank no. 1, sensor no. 3)
P0146	O2 sensor circuit - no activity detected (cylinder bank no. 1, sensor no. 3)
P0147	O2 sensor heater circuit malfunction (cylinder bank no. 1, sensor 3)
P0150	O2 sensor circuit malfunction (cylinder bank no. 2, sensor no. 1
P0151	O2 sensor circuit, low voltage (cylinder bank no. 2, sensor no. 1)
P0152	O2 sensor circuit, high voltage (cylinder bank no. 2, sensor no. 1)
P0153	O2 sensor circuit, slow response (cylinder bank no. 2, sensor no. 1)
P0154	O2 sensor circuit - no activity detected (cylinder bank no. 2, sensor no. 1)
P0155	O2 sensor heater circuit malfunction (cylinder bank no. 2, sensor no. 1)
P0156	O2 sensor circuit malfunction (cylinder bank no. 2, sensor no. 2)
P0157	O2 sensor circuit, low voltage (cylinder bank no. 2, sensor no. 2)
P0158	O2 sensor circuit, high voltage (cylinder bank no. 2, sensor no. 2)
P0159	O2 sensor circuit, slow response (cylinder bank no. 2, sensor no. 2)
P0160	O2 sensor circuit - no activity detected (cylinder bank no. 2, sensor no. 2)
P0161	O2 sensor heater circuit malfunction (cylinder bank no. 2, sensor no. 2)
P0162	O2 sensor circuit malfunction (cylinder bank no. 2, sensor no. 3)
P0163	O2 sensor circuit, low voltage (cylinder bank no. 2, sensor no. 3)
P0164	O2 sensor circuit, high voltage (cylinder bank no. 2, sensor no. 3)
P0165	O2 sensor circuit, slow response (cylinder bank no. 2, sensor no. 3)
P0166	O2 sensor circuit - no activity detected (cylinder bank no. 2, sensor no. 3)
P0167	O2 sensor heater circuit malfunction (cylinder bank no. 2, sensor 3)
P0170	Fuel trim malfunction (cylinder bank no. 1)
P0171	System too lean (cylinder bank no. 1)
P0172	System too rich (cylinder bank no. 1)
P0173	Fuel trim malfunction (cylinder bank no. 2)
P0174	System too lean (cylinder bank no. 2)
P0175	System too rich (cylinder bank no. 2)
P0176	Fuel composition sensor circuit malfunction
P0177	Fuel composition sensor circuit, range or performance problem
P0178	Fuel composition sensor circuit, low input
P0179	Fuel composition sensor circuit, high input

P0180	Fuel temperature sensor A circuit malfunction
P0181	Fuel temperature sensor A circuit, range or performance problem
P0182	Fuel temperature sensor A circuit, low input
P0183	Fuel temperature sensor A circuit, high input
P0184	Fuel temperature sensor A circuit, intermittent
P0185	Fuel temperature sensor B circuit malfunction
P0186	Fuel temperature sensor B circuit, range or performance problem
P0187	Fuel temperature sensor B circuit, low input
P0188	Fuel temperature sensor B circuit, high input
P0189	Fuel temperature sensor B circuit, intermittent
P0190	Fuel rail pressure sensor circuit malfunction
P0191	Fuel rail pressure sensor circuit, range or performance problem
P0192	Fuel rail pressure sensor circuit, low input
P0193	Fuel rail pressure sensor circuit, high input
P0194	Fuel rail pressure sensor circuit, intermittent
P0195	Engine oil temperature sensor malfunction
P0196	Fuel rail pressure sensor circuit, range or performance problem
P0197	Fuel rail pressure sensor circuit, low input
P0198	Fuel rail pressure sensor circuit, high input
P0199	Fuel rail pressure sensor circuit, intermittent
P0200	Injector circuit malfunction
P0201	Injector circuit malfunction - cylinder no. 1
P0202	Injector circuit malfunction - cylinder no. 2
P0203	Injector circuit malfunction - cylinder no. 3
P0204	Injector circuit malfunction - cylinder no. 4
P0205	Injector circuit malfunction - cylinder no. 5
P0206	Injector circuit malfunction - cylinder no. 6
P0207	Injector circuit malfunction - cylinder no. 7
P0208	Injector circuit malfunction - cylinder no. 8
P0209	Injector circuit malfunction - cylinder no. 9
P0210	Injector circuit malfunction - cylinder no. 10
P0211	Injector circuit malfunction - cylinder no. 11
P0212	Injector circuit malfunction - cylinder no. 12
P0213	Cold start injector no. 1 malfunction
P0214	Cold start injector no. 2 malfunction
P0215	Engine shut-off solenoid malfunction
P0216	Injection timing control circuit malfunction
P0217	Engine overheating condition
P0218	Transmission overheating condition
P0219	Engine overspeed condition

The Haynes Emissions Control Manual

OBD II Powertrain Diagnostic Trouble Codes (continued)

P0220	Throttle position or pedal position sensor/switch B circuit malfunction
P0221	Throttle position or pedal position sensor/switch B, range or performance problem
P0222	Throttle position or pedal position sensor/switch B circuit, low input
P0223	Throttle position or pedal position sensor/switch B circuit, high input
P0224	Throttle position or pedal position sensor/switch B circuit, intermittent
P0225	Throttle position or pedal position sensor/switch C circuit malfunction
P0226	Throttle position or pedal position sensor/switch C, range or performance problem
P0227	Throttle position or pedal position sensor/switch C circuit, low input
P0228	Throttle position or pedal position sensor/switch C circuit, high input
P0229	Throttle position or pedal position sensor/switch C circuit, intermittent
P0230	Fuel pump primary circuit malfunction
P0231	Fuel pump secondary circuit, low
P0232	Fuel pump secondary circuit, high
P0233	Fuel pump secondary circuit, intermittent
P0234	Engine overboost condition
P0235	Turbocharger boost sensor A circuit malfunction
P0236	Turbocharger boost sensor A circuit, range or performance problem
P0237	Turbocharger boost sensor A circuit, low
P0238	Turbocharger boost sensor A circuit, high
P0239	Turbocharger boost sensor B circuit malfunction
P0240	Turbocharger boost sensor B circuit, range or performance problem
P0241	Turbocharger boost sensor B circuit, low
P0242	Turbocharger boost sensor B circuit, high
P0243	Turbocharger wastegate solenoid A malfunction
P0244	Turbocharger wastegate solenoid A, range or performance problem
P0245	Turbocharger wastegate solenoid A, low
P0246	Turbocharger wastegate solenoid A, high
P0247	Turbocharger wastegate solenoid B malfunction
P0248	Turbocharger wastegate solenoid B, range or performance problem
P0249	Turbocharger wastegate solenoid B, low
P0250	Turbocharger wastegate solenoid B, high
P0251	Injection pump fuel metering control A malfunction (cam/rotor/injector)
P0252	Injection pump fuel metering control A, range or performance problem (cam/rotor/injector)
P0253	Injection pump fuel metering control A, low (cam/rotor/injector)
P0254	Injection pump fuel metering control A, high (cam/rotor/injector)
P0255	Injection pump fuel metering control A, intermittent (cam/rotor/injector)
P0256	Injection pump fuel metering control B malfunction (cam/rotor/injector)
P0257	Injection pump fuel metering control B, range or performance problem (cam/rotor/injector)
P0258	Injection pump fuel metering control B, low (cam/rotor/injector)

P0259	Injection pump fuel metering control B, high (cam/rotor/injector)
P0260	Injection pump fuel metering control B, intermittent (cam/rotor/injector)
P0261	Cylinder no. 1 injector circuit, low
P0262	Cylinder no. 1 injector circuit, high
P0263	Cylinder no. 1 contribution/balance fault
P0264	Cylinder no. 2 injector circuit, low
P0265	Cylinder no. 2 injector circuit, high
P0266	Cylinder no. 2 contribution/balance fault
P0267	Cylinder no. 3 injector circuit, low
P0268	Cylinder no. 3 injector circuit, high
P0269	Cylinder no. 3 contribution/balance fault
P0270	Cylinder no. 4 injector circuit, low
P0271	Cylinder no. 4 injector circuit, high
P0272	Cylinder no. 4 contribution/balance fault
P0273	Cylinder no. 5 injector circuit, low
P0274	Cylinder no. 5 injector circuit, high
P0275	Cylinder no. 5 contribution/balance fault
P0276	Cylinder no. 6 injector circuit, low
P0277	Cylinder no. 6 injector circuit, high
P0278	Cylinder no. 6 contribution/balance fault
P0279	Cylinder no. 7 injector circuit, low
P0280	Cylinder no. 7 injector circuit, high
P0281	Cylinder no. 7 contribution/balance fault
P0282	Cylinder no. 8 injector circuit, low
P0283	Cylinder no. 8 injector circuit, high
P0284	Cylinder no. 8 contribution/balance fault
P0285	Cylinder no. 9 injector circuit, low
P0286	Cylinder no. 9 injector circuit, high
P0287	Cylinder no. 9 contribution/balance fault
P0288	Cylinder no. 10 injector circuit, low
P0289	Cylinder no. 10 injector circuit, high
P0290	Cylinder no. 10 contribution/balance fault
P0291	Cylinder no. 11 injector circuit, low
P0292	Cylinder no. 11 injector circuit, high
P0293	Cylinder no. 11 contribution/balance fault
P0294	Cylinder no. 12 injector circuit, low
P0295	Cylinder no. 12 injector circuit, high
P0296	Cylinder no. 12 contribution/balance fault
P0300	Random/multiple cylinder misfire detected
P0301	Cylinder no. 1misfire detected

OBD II Powertrain Diagnostic Trouble Codes (continued)

P0302	Cylinder no. 2 misfire detected
P0303	Cylinder no. 3 misfire detected
P0304	Cylinder no. 4 misfire detected
P0305	Cylinder no. 5 misfire detected
P0306	Cylinder no. 6 misfire detected
P0307	Cylinder no. 7 misfire detected
P0308	Cylinder no. 8 misfire detected
P0309	Cylinder no. 9 misfire detected
P0310	Cylinder no. 10 misfire detected
P0311	Cylinder no. 11 misfire detected
P0312	Cylinder no. 12 misfire detected
P0320	Ignition/distributor engine speed input circuit malfunction
P0321	Ignition/distributor engine speed input circuit, range or performance problem
P0322	Ignition/distributor engine speed input circuit, no signal
P0323	Ignition/distributor engine speed input circuit, intermittent
P0325	Knock sensor no. 1 circuit malfunction (cylinder bank no. 1 or single sensor)
P0326	Knock sensor no. 1 circuit, range or performance problem (cylinder bank no. 1 or single sensor)
P0327	Knock sensor no. 1 circuit, low input (cylinder bank no. 1 or single sensor)
P0328	Knock sensor no. 1 circuit, high input (cylinder bank no. 1 or single sensor)
P0329	Knock sensor no. 1 circuit, intermittent (cylinder bank no. 1 or single sensor)
P0330	Knock sensor no. 2 circuit malfunction (cylinder bank no. 2)
P0331	Knock sensor no. 2 circuit, range or performance problem (cylinder bank no. 2)
P0332	Knock sensor no. 2 circuit, low input (cylinder bank no. 2)
P0333	Knock sensor no. 2 circuit, high input (cylinder bank no. 2)
P0334	Knock sensor no. 2 circuit, intermittent (cylinder bank no. 2)
P0335	Crankshaft position sensor A circuit malfunction
P0336	Crankshaft position sensor A circuit, range or performance problem
P0337	Crankshaft position sensor A circuit, low input
P0338	Crankshaft position sensor A circuit, high input
P0339	Crankshaft position sensor A circuit, intermittent
P0340	Camshaft position sensor circuit malfunction
P0341	Camshaft position sensor circuit, range or performance problem
P0342	Camshaft position sensor circuit, low input
P0343	Camshaft position sensor circuit, high input
P0344	Camshaft position sensor circuit, intermittent
P0350	Ignition coil primary or secondary circuit malfunction
P0351	Ignition coil A primary or secondary circuit malfunction
P0352	Ignition coil B primary or secondary circuit malfunction

P0353	Ignition coil C primary or secondary circuit malfunction
P0354	Ignition coil D primary or secondary circuit malfunction
P0355	Ignition coil E primary or secondary circuit malfunction
P0356	Ignition coil F primary or secondary circuit malfunction
P0357	Ignition coil G primary or secondary circuit malfunction
P0358	Ignition coil H primary or secondary circuit malfunction
P0359	Ignition coil I primary or secondary circuit malfunction
P0360	Ignition coil J primary or secondary circuit malfunction
P0361	Ignition coil K primary or secondary circuit malfunction
P0362	Ignition coil L primary or secondary circuit malfunction
P0370	Timing reference high resolution signal A malfunction
P0371	Timing reference high resolution signal A, too many pulses
P0372	Timing reference high resolution signal A, too few pulses
P0373	Timing reference high resolution signal A, intermittent/erratic pulses
P0374	Timing reference high resolution signal A, no pulse
P0375	Timing reference high resolution signal B malfunction
P0376	Timing reference high resolution signal B, too many pulses
P0377	Timing reference high resolution signal B, too few pulses
P0378	Timing reference high resolution signal B, intermittent/erratic pulses
P0379	Timing reference high resolution signal B, no pulse
P0380	Glow plug/heater circuit A malfunction
P0381	Glow plug/heater indicator circuit malfunction
P0382	Glow plug/heater circuit B malfunction
P0385	Crankshaft position sensor B circuit malfunction
P0386	Crankshaft position sensor B circuit, range or performance problem
P0387	Crankshaft position sensor B circuit, low input
P0388	Crankshaft position sensor B circuit, high input
P0389	Crankshaft position sensor B circuit, intermittent
P0400	Exhaust gas recirculation flow malfunction
P0401	Exhaust gas recirculation, insufficient flow detected
P0402	Exhaust gas recirculation, excessive flow detected
P0403	Exhaust gas recirculation circuit malfunction
P0404	Exhaust gas recirculation circuit, range or performance problem
P0405	Exhaust gas recirculation sensor A circuit low
P0406	Exhaust gas recirculation sensor A circuit high
P0407	Exhaust gas recirculation sensor B circuit low
P0408	Exhaust gas recirculation sensor B circuit high
P0410	Secondary air injection system malfunction
P0411	Secondary air injection system, incorrect flow detected
P0412	Secondary air injection system switching valve A, circuit malfunction

P0413	Secondary air injection system switching valve A, open circuit
P0414	Secondary air injection system switching valve A, shorted circuit
P0415	Secondary air injection system switching valve B, circuit malfunction
P0416	Secondary air injection system switching valve B, open circuit
P0417	Secondary air injection system switching valve B, shorted circuit
P0418	Secondary air injection system, relay A circuit malfunction
P0419	Secondary air injection system, relay B circuit malfunction
P0420	Catalyst system efficiency below threshold (cylinder bank no. 1)
P0421	Warm-up catalyst efficiency below threshold (cylinder bank no. 1)
P0422	Main catalyst efficiency below threshold (cylinder bank no. 1)
P0423	Heated catalyst efficiency below threshold (cylinder bank no. 1)
P0424	Heated catalyst temperature below threshold (cylinder bank no. 1)
P0430	Catalyst system efficiency below threshold (cylinder bank no. 2)
P0431	Warm-up catalyst efficiency below threshold (cylinder bank no. 2)
P0432	Main catalyst efficiency below threshold (cylinder bank no. 2)
P0433	Heated catalyst efficiency below threshold (cylinder bank no. 2)
P0434	Heated catalyst temperature below threshold (cylinder bank no. 2)
P0440	Evaporative emission control system malfunction
P0441	Evaporative emission control system, incorrect purge flow
P0442	Evaporative emission control system, small leak detected
P0443	Evaporative emission control system, purge control valve circuit malfunction
P0444	Evaporative emission control system, open purge control valve circuit
P0445	Evaporative emission control system, short in purge control valve circuit
P0446	Evaporative emission control system, vent control circuit malfunction
P0447	Evaporative emission control system, open vent control circuit
P0448	Evaporative emission control system, shorted vent control circuit
P0449	Evaporative emission control system, vent valve/solenoid circuit malfunction
P0450	Evaporative emission control system, pressure sensor malfunction
P0451	Evaporative emission control system, pressure sensor range or performance problem
P0452	Evaporative emission control system, pressure sensor low input
P0453	Evaporative emission control system, pressure sensor high input
P0454	Evaporative emission control system, pressure sensor intermittent
P0460	Fuel level sensor circuit malfunction
P0461	Fuel level sensor circuit, range or performance problem
P0462	Fuel level sensor circuit, low input
P0463	Fuel level sensor circuit, high input
P0464	Fuel level sensor circuit, intermittent
P0465	Purge flow sensor circuit malfunction

P0466	Purge flow sensor circuit, range or performance problem
P0467	Purge flow sensor circuit, low input
P0468	Purge flow sensor circuit, high input
P0469	Purge flow sensor circuit, intermittent
P0470	Exhaust pressure sensor malfunction
P0471	Exhaust pressure sensor, range or performance problem
P0472	Exhaust pressure sensor, low
P0473	Exhaust pressure sensor, high
P0474	Exhaust pressure sensor, intermittent
P0475	Exhaust pressure control valve malfunction
P0476	Exhaust pressure control valve, range or performance problem
P0477	Exhaust pressure control valve, low
P0478	Exhaust pressure sensor, high
P0479	Exhaust pressure sensor, intermittent
P0480	Cooling fan no. 1, control circuit malfunction
P0481	Cooling fan no. 2, control circuit malfunction
P0482	Cooling fan no. 3, control circuit malfunction
P0483	Cooling fan rationality check malfunction
P0484	Cooling fan circuit, high current
P0485	Cooling fan power/ground circuit malfunction
P0500	Vehicle speed sensor malfunction
P0501	Vehicle speed sensor, range or performance problem
P0502	Vehicle speed sensor circuit, low input
P0503	Vehicle speed sensor circuit, intermittent, erratic or high input
P0505	Idle control system malfunction
P0506	Idle control system, rpm lower than expected
P0507	Idle control system, rpm higher than expected
P0510	Closed throttle position switch malfunction
P0520	Engine oil pressure sensor/switch circuit malfunction
P0521	Engine oil pressure sensor/switch circuit, range or performance problem
P0522	Engine oil pressure sensor/switch circuit, low voltage
P0523	Engine oil pressure sensor/switch circuit, high voltage
P0530	A/C refrigerant pressure sensor, circuit malfunction
P0531	A/C refrigerant pressure sensor, range or performance problem
P0532	A/C refrigerant pressure sensor, low input
P0533	A/C refrigerant pressure sensor, high input
P0534	A/C refrigerant charge loss
P0550	Power steering pressure sensor, circuit malfunction
P0551	Power steering pressure sensor circuit, range or performance problem
P0552	Power steering pressure sensor circuit, low input

OBD II Powertrain Diagnostic Trouble Codes (continued)

P0553	Power steering pressure sensor circuit, high input
P0554	Power steering pressure sensor circuit, intermittent input
P0560	System voltage malfunction
P0561	System voltage unstable
P0562	System voltage low
P0563	System voltage high
P0565	Cruise control on signal malfunction
P0566	Cruise control off signal malfunction
P0567	Cruise control resume signal malfunction
P0568	Cruise control set signal malfunction
P0569	Cruise control coast signal malfunction
P0570	Cruise control accel signal malfunction
P0571	Cruise control/brake switch A, circuit malfunction
P0572	Cruise control/brake switch A, circuit low
P0573	Cruise control/brake switch A, circuit high
P0600	Serial communication link malfunction
P0601	Internal control module, memory check sum error
P0602	Control module, programming error
P0603	Internal control module, keep alive memory (KAM) error
P0604	Internal control module, random access memory (RAM) error
P0605	Internal control module, read only memory (ROM) error
P0606	PCM processor fault
P0608	Control module VSS, output A malfunction
P0609	Control module VSS, output B malfunction
P0620	Generator control circuit malfunction
P0621	Generator lamp L, control circuit malfunction
P0622	Generator lamp F, control circuit malfunction
P0650	Malfunction indicator lamp (MIL), control circuit malfunction
P0654	Engine rpm output, circuit malfunction
P0655	Engine hot lamp output control, circuit malfunction
P0656	Fuel level output, circuit malfunction
P0700	Transmission control system malfunction
P0701	Transmission control system, range or performance problem
P0702	Transmission control system, electrical
P0703	Torque converter/brake switch B, circuit malfunction
P0704	Clutch switch input circuit malfunction
P0705	Transmission range sensor, circuit malfunction (PRNDL input)
P0706	Transmission range sensor circuit, range or performance problem

P0707	Transmission range sensor circuit, low input
P0708	Transmission range sensor circuit, high input
P0709	Transmission range sensor circuit, intermittent input
P0710	Transmission fluid temperature sensor, circuit malfunction
P0711	Transmission fluid temperature sensor circuit, range or performance problem
P0712	Transmission fluid temperature sensor circuit, low input
P0713	Transmission fluid temperature sensor circuit, high input
P0714	Transmission fluid temperature sensor circuit, intermittent input
P0715	Input/turbine speed sensor circuit malfunction
P0716	Input/turbine speed sensor circuit, range or performance problem
P0717	Input/turbine speed sensor circuit, no signal
P0718	Input/turbine speed sensor circuit, intermittent signal
P0719	Torque converter/brake switch B, circuit low
P0720	Output speed sensor malfunction
P0721	Output speed sensor circuit, range or performance problem
P0722	Output speed sensor circuit, no signal
P0723	Output speed sensor circuit, intermittent signal
P0724	Torque converter/brake switch B circuit, high
P0725	Engine speed input circuit malfunction
P0726	Engine speed input circuit, range or performance problem
P0727	Engine speed input circuit, no signal
P0728	Engine speed input circuit, intermittent signal
P0730	Incorrect gear ratio
P0731	Incorrect gear ratio, first gear
P0732	Incorrect gear ratio, second gear
P0733	Incorrect gear ratio, third gear
P0734	Incorrect gear ratio, fourth gear
P0735	Incorrect gear ratio, fifth gear
P0736	Incorrect gear ratio, reverse gear
P0740	Torque converter clutch, circuit malfunction
P0741	Torque converter clutch, circuit performance or stuck in off position
P0742	Torque converter clutch circuit, stuck in on position
P0743	Torque converter clutch circuit, electrical problem
P0744	Torque converter clutch circuit, intermittent
P0745	Pressure control solenoid malfunction
P0746	Pressure control solenoid, performance problem or stuck in off position
P0747	Pressure control solenoid, stuck in on position
P0748	Pressure control solenoid, electrical problem
P0749	Pressure control solenoid, intermittent operation
P0750	Shift solenoid A malfunction

The Haynes Emissions Control Manual

P0751	Shift solenoid A, performance problem or stuck in off position
P0752	Shift solenoid A, stuck in on position
P0753	Shift solenoid A, electrical problem
P0754	Shift solenoid A, intermittent operation
P0755	Shift solenoid B malfunction
P0756	Shift solenoid B, performance problem or stuck in off position
P0757	Shift solenoid B, stuck in on position
P0758	Shift solenoid B, electrical problem
P0759	Shift solenoid B, intermittent operation
P0760	Shift solenoid C malfunction
P0761	Shift solenoid C, performance problem or stuck in off position
P0762	Shift solenoid C, stuck in on position
P0763	Shift solenoid C, electrical problem
P0764	Shift solenoid C, intermittent operation
P0765	Shift solenoid D malfunction
P0766	Shift solenoid D, performance problem or stuck in off position
P0767	Shift solenoid D, stuck in on position
P0768	Shift solenoid D, electrical problem
P0769	Shift solenoid D, intermittent operation
P0770	Shift solenoid E malfunction
P0771	Shift solenoid E, performance problem or stuck in off position
P0772	Shift solenoid E, stuck in on position
P0773	Shift solenoid E, electrical problem
P0774	Shift solenoid E, intermittent operation
P0780	Shift malfunction
P0781	First-to-second shift malfunction
P0782	Second-to-third shift malfunction
P0783	Third-to-fourth shift malfunction
P0784	Fourth-to-fifth shift malfunction
P0785	Shift/timing solenoid malfunction
P0786	Shift/timing solenoid, range or performance problem
P0787	Shift/timing solenoid, low
P0788	Shift/timing solenoid, high
P0789	Shift/timing solenoid, intermittent
P0790	Normal/performance switch circuit malfunction
P0801	Reverse inhibit control circuit malfunction
P0803	First-to-fourth upshift (skip shift) solenoid control circuit malfunction
P0804	First-to-fourth upshift (skip shift) lamp control circuit malfunction

Index

Haynes Automotive Manuals

NOTE: If you do not see a listing for your vehicle, consult your local Haynes dealer for the latest product information.

ACURA
12020 Integra '86 thru '89 & Legend '86 thru '90
12021 Integra '90 thru '93 & Legend '91 thru '95
12050 Acura TL all models '99 thru '08

AMC
Jeep CJ - see JEEP (50020)
14020 Concord/Hornet/Gremlin/Spirit '70 thru '83
14025 (Renault) Alliance & Encore '83 thru '87

AUDI
15020 4000 all models '80 thru '87
15025 5000 all models '77 thru '83
15026 5000 all models '84 thru '88
15030 Audi A4 '02 thru '08

AUSTIN
Healey Sprite - see MG Midget (66015)

BMW
18020 3/5 Series '82 thru '92
18021 3 Series including Z3 models '92 thru '98
18022 3-Series '99 thru '05, including Z4 models
18025 320i all 4 cyl models '75 thru '83
18050 1500 thru 2002 except Turbo '59 thru '77

BUICK
19010 Buick Century '97 thru '05
19020 Century (front-wheel drive) - see GM (38005)
Buick, Oldsmobile & Pontiac Full-size (Front wheel drive) '85 thru '05
19025 Buick, Oldsmobile & Pontiac Full-size (Rear wheel drive) '70 thru '90
19030 Mid-size Regal & Century '74 thru '87
Regal - see GENERAL MOTORS (38010)
Skyhawk - see GM (38030)
Skylark - see GM (38020, 38025)
Somerset - see GENERAL MOTORS (38025)

CADILLAC
21030 Cadillac Rear Wheel Drive '70 thru '93
Cimarron, Eldorado & Seville - see GM (38015, 38030, 38031)

CHEVROLET
10305 Chevrolet Engine Overhaul Manual
24010 Astro & GMC Safari Mini-vans '85 thru '05
24015 Camaro V8 all models '70 thru '81
24016 Camaro all models '82 thru '92, Cavalier - see GM (38015), Celebrity - see GM (38005)
24017 Camaro & Firebird '93 thru '02
24020 Chevelle, Malibu, El Camino '69 thru '87
24024 Chevette & Pontiac T1000 '76 thru '87
Citation - see GENERAL MOTORS (38020)
24027 Colorado & GMC Canyon '04 thru '08
24032 Corsica/Beretta all models '87 thru '96
24040 Corvette all V8 models '68 thru '82
24041 Corvette all models '84 thru '96
24045 Full-size Sedans Caprice, Impala, Biscayne, Bel Air & Wagons '69 thru '90
24046 Impala SS & Caprice and Buick Roadmaster '91 thru '96
Lumina '90 thru '94 - see GM (38010)
24047 Impala & Monte Carlo all models '06 thru '08
24048 Lumina & Monte Carlo '95 thru '05
Lumina APV - see GM (38035)
24050 Luv Pick-up all 2WD & 4WD '72 thru '82
Malibu - see GM (38026)
24055 Monte Carlo all models '70 thru '88
Monte Carlo '95 thru '01 - see LUMINA
24059 Nova all V8 models '69 thru '79
24060 Nova/Geo Prizm '85 thru '92
24064 Pick-ups '67 thru '87 - Chevrolet & GMC, all V8 & in-line 6 cyl, 2WD & 4WD '67 thru '87; Suburbans, Blazers & Jimmys '67 thru '91
24065 Pick-ups '88 thru '98 - Chevrolet & GMC, all full-size models '88 thru '98; C/K Classic '99 & '00; Blazer & Jimmy '92 thru '94; Suburban '92 thru '99; Tahoe & Yukon '95 thru '99
24066 Pick-ups '99 thru '06 - Chevrolet Silverado & GMC Sierra '99 thru '06; Suburban/Tahoe/Yukon/Yukon XL/Avalanche '00 thru '06
24067 Chevrolet Silverado & GMC Sierra '07 thru '09
24070 S-10 & GMC S-15 Pick-ups '82 thru '93
24071 S-10, Sonoma & Jimmy '94 thru '04
24072 Chevrolet TrailBlazer, GMC Envoy & Oldsmobile Bravada '02 thru '09
24075 Sprint '85 thru '88, Geo Metro '89 thru '01
24080 Vans - Chevrolet & GMC '68 thru '96
24081 Chevrolet Express & GMC Savana Full-size Vans '96 thru '07

CHRYSLER
10310 Chrysler Engine Overhaul Manual
25015 Chrysler Cirrus, Dodge Stratus, Plymouth Breeze, '95 thru '00
25020 Full-size Front-Wheel Drive '88 thru '93
K-Cars - see DODGE Aries (30008)
Laser - see DODGE Daytona (30030)
25025 Chrysler LHS, Concorde & New Yorker, Dodge Intrepid, Eagle Vision, '93 thru '97
25026 Chrysler LHS, Concorde, 300M, Dodge Intrepid '98 thru '04
25027 Chrysler 300, Dodge Charger & Magnum '05 thru '09
25030 Chrysler/Plym. Mid-size '82 thru '95
Rear-wheel Drive - see DODGE (30050)
25035 PT Cruiser all models '01 thru '09
25040 Chrysler Sebring/Dodge Avenger '95 thru '05, Dodge Stratus '01 thru '05

DATSUN
28005 200SX all models '80 thru '83
28007 B-210 all models '73 thru '78
28009 210 all models '78 thru '82
28012 240Z, 260Z & 280Z Coupe '70 thru '78
28014 280ZX Coupe & 2+2 '79 thru '83
300ZX - see NISSAN (72010)
28018 510 & PL521 Pick-up '68 thru '73
28020 510 all models '78 thru '81
28022 620 Series Pick-up all models '73 thru '79
720 Series Pick-up - see NISSAN (72030)
28025 810/Maxima all gas models, '77 thru '84

DODGE
400 & 600 - see CHRYSLER (25030)
30008 Aries & Plymouth Reliant '81 thru '89
30010 Caravan & Ply. Voyager '84 thru '95
30011 Caravan & Ply. Voyager '96 thru '02

30012 Challenger/Plymouth Saporro '78 thru '83
Challenger '67-'76 - see DART (30025)
30013 Caravan, Chrysler Voyager, Town & Country '03 thru '07
30016 Colt/Plymouth Champ '78 thru '87
30020 Dakota Pick-ups all models '87 thru '96
30021 Durango '98 & '99, Dakota '97 thru '99
30022 Durango '00 thru '03, Dakota '00 thru '04
30023 Durango '04 thru '06, Dakota '05 and '06
30025 Dart, Challenger/Plymouth Barracuda & Valiant 6 cyl models '67 thru '76
30030 Daytona & Chrysler Laser '84 thru '89
Intrepid - see Chrysler (25025, 25026)
30034 Dodge & Plymouth Neon '95 thru '99
30035 Omni & Plymouth Horizon '78 thru '90
30036 Dodge and Plymouth Neon '00 thru '05
30040 Pick-ups all full-size models '74 thru '93
30041 Pick-ups all full-size models '94 thru '01
30042 Pick-ups full-size models '02 thru '08
30045 Ram 50/D50 Pick-ups & Raider and Plymouth Arrow Pick-ups '79 thru '93
30050 Dodge/Ply./Chrysler RWD '71 thru '89
30055 Shadow/Plymouth Sundance '87 thru '94
30060 Spirit & Plymouth Acclaim '89 thru '95
30065 Vans - Dodge & Plymouth '71 thru '03

EAGLE
Talon - see MITSUBISHI (68020, 68031)
Vision - see CHRYSLER (25025)

FIAT
34010 124 Sport Coupe & Spider '68 thru '78
34025 X1/9 all models '74 thru '80

FORD
10320 Ford Engine Overhaul Manual
10355 Ford Automatic Transmission Overhaul
36004 Aerostar Mini-vans '86 thru '97
36006 Aspire all models - see FORD Festiva (36030)
36008 Contour/Mercury Mystique '95 thru '00
36012 Courier Pick-up all models '72 thru '82
36016 Crown Victoria & Mercury Grand Marquis '88 thru '10
36016 Escort/Mercury Lynx '81 thru '90
36020 Escort/Mercury Tracer '91 thru '02
36022 Expedition - see FORD Pick-up (36059)
36024 Escape & Mazda Tribute '01 thru '07
36025 Explorer & Mazda Navajo '91 thru '01
36028 Explorer/Mercury Mountaineer '02 thru '10
36028 Fairmont & Mercury Zephyr '78 thru '83
36030 Festiva & Aspire '88 thru '97
36032 Fiesta all models '77 thru '80
36034 Focus all models '00 thru '07
36036 Ford & Mercury Full-size '75 thru '87
36044 Ford & Mercury Mid-size '75 thru '86
36048 Mustang V8 all models '64-1/2 thru '73
36049 Mustang II 4 cyl, V6 & V8 '74 thru '78
36050 Mustang & Mercury Capri '79 thru '86
36051 Mustang all models '94 thru '04
36052 Mustang '05 thru '07
36054 Pick-ups and Bronco '73 thru '79
36058 Pick-ups and Bronco '80 thru '96
36059 F-150 & Expedition '97 thru '09, F-250 '97 thru '99 & Lincoln Navigator '98 thru '09
36060 Super Duty Pick-up, Excursion '99 thru '10
36061 F-150 Pick-up '04 thru '09
36062 Pinto & Mercury Bobcat '75 thru '80
36066 Probe all models '89 thru '92
36070 Ranger/Bronco II gas models '83 thru '92
36071 Ford Ranger '93 thru '10 &
Mazda Pick-ups '94 thru '09
36074 Taurus & Mercury Sable '86 thru '95
36075 Taurus & Mercury Sable '96 thru '05
36078 Tempo & Mercury Topaz '84 thru '94
36082 Thunderbird/Mercury Cougar '83 thru '88
36086 Thunderbird/Mercury Cougar '89 thru '97
36090 Vans all V8 Econoline models '69 thru '91
36094 Vans full size '92 thru '05
36097 Windstar Mini-van '95 thru '07

GENERAL MOTORS
10360 GM Automatic Transmission Overhaul
38005 Buick Century, Chevrolet Celebrity, Olds Cutlass Ciera & Pontiac 6000 '82 thru '96
38010 Buick Regal, Chevrolet Lumina, Oldsmobile Cutlass Supreme & Pontiac Grand Prix front wheel drive '88 thru '07
38015 Buick Skyhawk, Cadillac Cimarron, Chevrolet Cavalier, Oldsmobile Firenza Pontiac J-2000 & Sunbird '82 thru '94
38016 Chevrolet Cavalier/Pontiac Sunfire '95 thru '05
38017 Chevrolet Cobalt & Pontiac G5 '05 thru '09
38020 Buick Skylark, Chevrolet Citation, Olds Omega, Pontiac Phoenix '80 thru '85
38025 Buick Skylark & Somerset, Olds Achieva, Calais & Pontiac Grand Am '85 thru '98
38026 Chevrolet Malibu, Olds Alero & Cutlass, Pontiac Grand Am '97 thru '03
38027 Chevrolet Malibu '04 thru '07
38030 Cadillac Eldorado & Oldsmobile Toronado '71 thru '85, Seville '80 thru '85, Buick Riviera '79 thru '85
38031 Cadillac Eldorado & Seville '86 thru '91, DeVille & Buick Riviera '86 thru '93, Fleetwood & Olds Toronado '86 thru '92
38032 DeVille '94 thru '05, Seville '92 thru '04, Cadillac DTS '06 thru '10
38035 Chevrolet Lumina APV, Oldsmobile Silhouette & Pontiac Trans Sport '90 thru '96
38036 Chevrolet Venture, Olds Silhouette, Pontiac Trans Sport & Montana '97 thru '05
General Motors Full-size Rear-wheel Drive - see BUICK (19025)
38040 Chevrolet Equinox '05 thru '09
Pontiac Torrent '06 thru '09

GEO
Metro - see CHEVROLET Sprint (24075)
Prizm - see CHEVROLET (24060) or TOYOTA (92036)
40030 Storm all models '90 thru '93
Tracker - see SUZUKI Samurai (90010)

GMC
Vans & Pick-ups - see CHEVROLET

HONDA
42010 Accord CVCC all models '76 thru '83
42011 Accord all models '84 thru '89
42012 Accord all models '90 thru '93
42013 Accord all models '94 thru '97
42014 Accord all models '98 thru '02

42015 Accord models '03 thru '07
42020 Civic 1200 all models '73 thru '79
42021 Civic 1300 & 1500 CVCC '80 thru '83
42022 Civic 1500 CVCC all models '75 thru '79
42023 Civic all models '84 thru '91
42024 Civic & del Sol '92 thru '95
42025 Civic '96 thru '00, CR-V '97 thru '01, Acura Integra '94 thru '00
Passport - see ISUZU Rodeo (47017)
42026 Civic '01 thru '10, CR-V '02 thru '09
42035 Odyssey models '99 thru '04
42037 Honda Pilot '03 thru '07, Acura MDX '01 thru '07
42040 Prelude CVCC all models '79 thru '89

HYUNDAI
43010 Elantra all models '96 thru '06
43015 Excel & Accent all models '86 thru '09
43050 Santa Fe all models '01 thru '06
43055 Sonata all models '99 thru '08

ISUZU
Hombre - see CHEVROLET S-10 (24071)
47017 Rodeo, Amigo & Honda Passport '89 thru '02
47020 Trooper '84 thru '91, Pick-up '81 thru '93

JAGUAR
49010 XJ6 all 6 cyl models '68 thru '86
49011 XJ6 all models '88 thru '94
49015 XJ12 & XJS all 12 cyl models '72 thru '85

JEEP
50010 Cherokee, Comanche & Wagoneer Limited all models '84 thru '01
50020 CJ all models '49 thru '86
50025 Grand Cherokee all models '93 thru '04
50026 Grand Cherokee '05 thru '09
50029 Grand Wagoneer & Pick-up '72 thru '91
50030 Wrangler all models '87 thru '08
50035 Liberty '02 thru '07

KIA
54070 Sephia '94 thru '01, Spectra '00 thru '09

LEXUS
ES 300 - see TOYOTA Camry (92007)

LINCOLN
Navigator - see FORD Pick-up (36059)
59010 Rear Wheel Drive all models '70 thru '10

MAZDA
61010 GLC (rear wheel drive) '77 thru '83
61011 GLC (front wheel drive) '81 thru '85
61015 323 & Protegé '90 thru '00
61016 MX-5 Miata '90 thru '09
61020 MPV all models '89 thru '94
Navajo - see FORD Explorer (36024)
61030 Pick-ups '72 thru '93
Pick-ups '94 on - see Ford (36071)
61035 RX-7 all models '79 thru '85
61036 RX-7 all models '86 thru '91
61040 626 (rear wheel drive) '79 thru '82
61041 626 & MX-6 (front wheel drive) '83 thru '92
61042 626 '93 thru '01, & MX-6/Ford Probe '93 thru '01

MERCEDES-BENZ
63012 123 Series Diesel '76 thru '85
63015 190 Series 4-cyl gas models, '84 thru '88
63020 230, 250 & 280 6 cyl sohc '68 thru '72
63025 280 123 Series gas models '77 thru '81
63030 350 & 450 all models '71 thru '80
63040 C-Class: C230/C240/C280/C320/C350 '01 thru '07

MERCURY
64200 Villager & Nissan Quest '93 thru '01
All other titles, see FORD listing.

MG
66010 MGB Roadster & GT Coupe '62 thru '80
66015 MG Midget & Austin Healey Sprite Roadster '58 thru '80

MITSUBISHI
68020 Cordia, Tredia, Galant, Precis & Mirage '83 thru '93
68030 Eclipse, Eagle Talon & Plymouth Laser '90 thru '94
68031 Eclipse '95 thru '05, Eagle Talon '95 thru '98
68035 Galant '94 thru '03
68040 Pick-up '83 thru '96, Montero '83 thru '93

NISSAN
72010 300ZX all models incl. Turbo '84 thru '89
72011 350Z & Infiniti G35 all models '03 thru '08
72015 Altima all models '93 thru '06
72020 Maxima all models '85 thru '92
72021 Maxima all models '93 thru '01
72030 Pick-ups '80 thru '97, Pathfinder '87 thru '95
72031 Frontier Pick-up, Xterra, Pathfinder '96 thru '04
72032 Frontier & Xterra '05 thru '08
72040 Pulsar all models '83 thru '86
72050 Sentra all models '82 thru '94
72051 Sentra & 200SX all models '95 thru '06
72060 Stanza all models '82 thru '90
72070 Titan pick-ups '04 thru '09, Armada '05 thru '10

OLDSMOBILE
73015 Cutlass '74 thru '88
For other OLDSMOBILE titles, see BUICK, CHEVROLET or GM listings.

PLYMOUTH
For PLYMOUTH titles, see DODGE.

PONTIAC
79008 Fiero all models '84 thru '88
79018 Firebird V8 models except Turbo '70 thru '81
79019 Firebird all models '82 thru '92
79025 G6 all models '05 thru '09
79040 Mid-size Rear-wheel Drive '70 thru '87
For other PONTIAC titles, see BUICK, CHEVROLET or GM listings.

PORSCHE
80020 911 Coupe & Targa models '65 thru '89
80025 914 all 4 cyl models '69 thru '76
80030 924 all models incl. Turbo '76 thru '82
80035 944 all models incl. Turbo '83 thru '89

RENAULT
Alliance, Encore - see AMC (14020)

SAAB
84010 900 including Turbo '79 thru '88

SATURN
87010 Saturn all S-series models '91 thru '02
87011 Saturn Ion '03 thru '07
87020 Saturn all L-series models '00 thru '04
87040 Saturn VUE '02 thru '07

SUBARU
89002 1100, 1300, 1400 & 1600 '71 thru '79
89003 1600 & 1800 2WD & 4WD '80 thru '94
89100 Legacy models '90 thru '99
89101 Legacy & Forester '00 thru '06

SUZUKI
90010 Samurai/Sidekick/Geo Tracker '86 thru '01

TOYOTA
92005 Camry all models '83 thru '91
92006 Camry all models '92 thru '96
92007 Camry/Avalon/Solara/Lexus ES 300 '97 thru '01
92008 Toyota Camry, Avalon and Solara & Lexus ES 300/330 all models '02 thru '06
92015 Celica Rear Wheel Drive '71 thru '85
92020 Celica Front Wheel Drive '86 thru '99
92025 Celica Supra all models '79 thru '92
92030 Corolla all models '75 thru '79
92032 Corolla rear wheel drive models '80 thru '87
92035 Corolla front wheel drive models '84 thru '92
92036 Corolla & Geo Prizm '93 thru '02
92037 Corolla models '03 thru '08
92040 Corolla Tercel all models '80 thru '82
92045 Corona all models '74 thru '82
92050 Cressida all models '78 thru '82
92055 Land Cruiser FJ40/43/45/55 '68 thru '82
92056 Land Cruiser FJ60/62/80/FZJ80 '80 thru '96
92060 Matrix & Pontiac Vibe '03 thru '08
92065 MR2 all models '85 thru '87
92070 Pick-up all models '69 thru '78
92075 Pick-up all models '79 thru '95
92076 Tacoma, 4Runner & T100 '93 thru '04
92077 Tacoma all models '05 thru '09
92078 Tundra '00 thru '06, Sequoia '01 thru '07
92079 4Runner all models '03 thru '09
92080 Previa all models '91 thru '95
92081 Prius '01 thru '08
92082 RAV4 all models '96 thru '05
92085 Tercel all models '87 thru '94
92090 Sienna all models '98 thru '09
92095 Highlander & Lexus RX-330 '99 thru '06

TRIUMPH
94007 Spitfire all models '62 thru '81
94010 TR7 all models '75 thru '81

VW
96008 Beetle & Karmann Ghia '54 thru '79
96009 New Beetle '98 thru '05
96016 Rabbit, Jetta, Scirocco, & Pick-up gas models '75 thru '92 & Convertible '80 thru '92
96017 Golf, GTI & Jetta '93 thru '98, Cabrio '95 thru '02
96018 Golf, GTI & Jetta '99 thru '05
96020 Rabbit, Jetta, Pick-up diesel '77 thru '84
96023 Passat '98 thru '05, Audi A4 '96 thru '01
96030 Transporter 1600 all models '68 thru '79
96035 Transporter 1700, 1800, 2000 '72 thru '79
96040 Type 3 1500 & 1600 '63 thru '73
96045 Vanagon air-cooled models '80 thru '83

VOLVO
97010 120, 130 Series & 1800 Sports '61 thru '73
97015 140 Series all models '66 thru '74
97020 240 Series all models '76 thru '93
97040 740 & 760 Series all models '82 thru '88

TECHBOOK MANUALS
10205 Automotive Computer Codes
10206 OBD-II & Electronic Engine Management
10210 Automotive Emissions Control Manual
10215 Fuel Injection Manual, 1978 thru 1985
10220 Fuel Injection Manual, 1986 thru 1999
10225 Holley Carburetor Manual
10230 Rochester Carburetor Manual
10240 Weber/Zenith/Stromberg/SU Carburetor
10305 Chevrolet Engine Overhaul Manual
10310 Chrysler Engine Overhaul Manual
10320 Ford Engine Overhaul Manual
10330 GM and Ford Diesel Engine Repair
10333 Engine Performance Manual
10340 Small Engine Repair Manual
10345 Suspension, Steering & Driveline
10355 Ford Automatic Transmission Overhaul
10360 GM Automatic Transmission Overhaul
10405 Automotive Body Repair & Painting
10410 Automotive Brake Manual
10415 Automotive Detailing Manual
10420 Automotive Electrical Manual
10425 Automotive Heating & Air Conditioning
10430 Automotive Reference Dictionary
10435 Automotive Tools Manual
10440 Used Car Buying Guide
10445 Welding Manual
10450 ATV Basics
10452 Scooters 50cc to 250cc

SPANISH MANUALS
98903 Reparación de Carrocería & Pintura
98904 Carburadores para los modelos Holley & Rochester
98905 Códigos Automotrices de la Computadora
98910 Frenos Automotriz
98913 Electricidad Automotriz
98915 Inyección de Combustible 1986 al 1999
99040 Chevrolet & GMC Camionetas '67 al '87
99041 Chevrolet & GMC Camionetas '88 al '98
99042 Chevrolet Camionetas Cerradas '68 al '95
99043 Chevrolet/GMC Camionetas '94 al '04
99055 Dodge Caravan/Ply. Voyager '84 al '95
99075 Ford Camionetas y Bronco '80 al '94
99077 Ford Camionetas Cerradas '69 al '91
99088 Ford Modelos de Tamaño Mediano '75 al '86
99091 Ford Taurus & Mercury Sable '86 al '95
99095 GM Modelos de Tamaño Grande '70 al '90
99100 GM Modelos de Tamaño Mediano '70 al '88
99106 Jeep Cherokee, Wagoneer & Comanche '84 al '00
99110 Nissan Camionetas '80 al '96
99118 Nissan Sentra '82 al '94
99125 Toyota Camionetas y 4-Runner '79 al '95

Over 100 Haynes motorcycle manuals also available